MW00813299

MODERN AMERICAN DRAMA ON SCREEN

From its beginnings, the American film industry has profited from bringing popular and acclaimed dramatic works to the screen. This is the first book to offer a comprehensive account, focusing on key texts, of how Hollywood has given a second and enduring life to such classics of the American theatre as *Long Day's Journey into Night*, *A Streetcar Named Desire*, and *Who's Afraid of Virginia Woolf?* Each chapter is written by a leading scholar and focuses on Broadway's most admired and popular productions. The book is ideally suited for classroom use and offers an otherwise unavailable introduction to a subject which is of great interest to students and scholars alike.

WILLIAM ROBERT BRAY is a professor of English at Middle Tennessee State University. He is the founding editor of the *Tennessee Williams Annual Review* and the founding director of the Tennessee Williams Scholars Conference. He is the author of *Tennessee Williams and His Contemporaries* (2007) and (with R. Barton Palmer) *Hollywood's Tennessee: The Williams Films and Postwar America* (2009).

R. BARTON PALMER is the Calhoun Lemon Professor of Literature at Clemson University, where he also directs the Film Studies program. He is the author, editor, or general editor of more than fifty volumes on various literary and cinematic subjects, and a leading figure in the field of adaptation studies. Among other publications in this area, Palmer is the editor of two previous volumes for Cambridge University Press: *Nineteenth-Century American Fiction on Screen* (2007) and *Twentieth-Century American Fiction on Screen* (2007).

MODERN AMERICAN
DRAMA ON SCREEN

EDITED BY

WILLIAM ROBERT BRAY AND R. BARTON PALMER

CAMBRIDGE
UNIVERSITY PRESS

CAMBRIDGE
UNIVERSITY PRESS

University Printing House, Cambridge CB2 8BS, United Kingdom

Published in the United States of America by Cambridge University Press, New York

Cambridge University Press is part of the University of Cambridge.

It furthers the University's mission by disseminating knowledge in the pursuit of education, learning and research at the highest international levels of excellence.

www.cambridge.org
Information on this title: www.cambridge.org/9781107000650

© Cambridge University Press 2013

First published 2013

Printing in the United Kingdom by TJ International Ltd. Padstow Cornwall

A catalogue record for this publication is available from the British Library

Library of Congress Cataloging-in-Publication data
Modern American drama in screen / edited by William Robert Bray and R. Barton Palmer.
pages   cm
Includes bibliographical references and index.
ISBN 978-1-107-00065-0 (Hardback)
1. American drama–Film adaptations.   2. Film adaptations–History and criticism.
3. Motion pictures and literature–United States.   I. Bray, William Robert, 1951– editor
of compilation.   II. Palmer, R. Barton, 1946– editor of compilation.
PS338.M67M63 2013
791.430973–dc23   2013003980

ISBN 978-1-107-00065-0 Hardback

Contents

Illustrations

Notes on contributors

CHRISTOPHER AMES is Vice President for Academic Affairs at Shepherd University. He is the author of *The Life of the Party: Festive Vision in Modern Fiction* and *Movies about the Movies: Hollywood Reflected*.

JOHN S. BAK is a professeur at the Université de Lorraine in France, where he teaches courses in literary journalism and American drama and theatre. His articles have appeared in such journals as *Theatre Journal, Mississippi Quarterly, Journal of American Drama and Theatre, American Drama, The Tennessee Williams Annual Review, South Atlantic Review,* and *Studies in Musical Theatre.* His edited books include *Post/modern Dracula: From Victorian Themes to Postmodern Praxis* (2006), *New Selected Essays: Where I Live* (2009), and (with Bill Reynolds) *Literary Journalism across the Globe: Journalistic Traditions and Transnational Influences* (2011). He is the author of the monographs *Ernest Hemingway, Tennessee Williams, and Queer Masculinities* (2009) and *Tennessee Williams: A Literary Life* (2013).

WILLIAM ROBERT BRAY is the founding editor of *The Tennessee Williams Annual Review* and founding director of the Tennessee Williams Scholars Conference, an annual event held in conjunction with the Tennessee Williams/New Orleans Literary Festival. He has written over two dozen articles on Williams and is the author of *Tennessee Williams and His Contemporaries* (2007) and co-author of *Hollywood's Tennessee: The Williams Films and Postwar America* (with R. Barton Palmer, 2009). Bray is a professor of English at Middle Tennessee State University.

MARY F. BREWER lectures in the English and Drama Department at Loughborough University. Her research focuses on theatre and identity and religion and literature in English and American writing from the late nineteenth century through the contemporary period. She is the author of *Race, Sex and Gender in Contemporary Women's Theatre* (1999) and *Staging Whiteness* (2005), and has edited a collection of essays on feminist theory, *Exclusions in Feminist Thought: Challenging the Boundaries of Womanhood* (2002), and on Harold Pinter's *The Dumb Waiter* (2009). She is currently co-editing, with Lynette Goddard and Deirdre Osborne, a volume of essays on Black British Theatre.

DAVID ELDRIDGE is a senior lecturer in American Studies at the University of Hull, UK, and the author of *American Culture in the 1930s* (2008) and *Hollywood's History Films* (2006).

MARTIN HALLIWELL is a professor of American Studies at the University of Leicester, UK. His published work spans American cultural and intellectual history, the history of medicine and psychology, modern and contemporary American literature, American film after 1945, and avant-garde and popular culture. He is the author of eight monographs, including *Transatlantic Modernism* (2006), *American Culture in the 1950s* (2007), and *Therapeutic Revolutions: Medicine, Psychiatry, and American Culture, 1945–1970* (2013), as well as the co-edited volume *American Thought and Culture in the 21st Century* (2008).

AMANDA ANN KLEIN is an assistant professor of Film Studies in the Department of English at East Carolina University. She is the author of *American Film Cycles: Reframing Genres, Screening Social Problems, and Defining Subcultures* (2011). Her work has been published in *Jump Cut*, *Quarterly Review of Film and Video*, and *Flow TV*. She blogs about film, television, and new media at: http://judgmentalobserver.com.

DAVID LAVERY is a professor of English at Middle Tennessee State University. He is the author / co-author / editor / co-editor of over twenty books, including *Joss Whedon: Conversations* and the forthcoming *Joss Whedon, a Creative Portrait: From* Buffy the Vampire Slayer *to* The Avengers, and has published books on the Space Age, *Lost* (2), *Twin Peaks*, *X-Files*, *The Sopranos* (a trilogy), *Buffy the Vampire Slayer*, Teleparody, *Seinfeld*, *Deadwood*, *My So-Called Life*, *Gilmore Girls*, *Heroes*, *Battlestar Galactica*, Cult TV, and *Supernatural*. A founding co-editor of the journals *Slayage*, *Critical Studies in Television*, and *Series/Season/Show* and co-founder of the Whedon Studies Association, he has lectured around the world on the subject of television.

BRENDA MURPHY is Board of Trustees Distinguished Professor of English at the University of Connecticut. Among her seventeen books on American drama and theatre are *Tennessee Williams and Elia Kazan:*

A Collaboration in the Theatre (1992), *Understanding David Mamet* (2011), *Congressional Theatre: Dramatizing McCarthyism on Stage, Film, and Television* (1999), and as editor, *Critical Insights: Tennessee Williams* (2011) and *Critical Insights: A Streetcar Named Desire* (2010). She is currently at work on *The Theatre of Tennessee Williams*, which will be published in 2014.

R. BARTON PALMER is the Calhoun Lemon Professor of Literature at Clemson University, where he also directs the Global Cultural Studies and Cinema and World Cultures undergraduate degree programs. Palmer is the author, editor, or general editor of more than fifty volumes on various literary and cinematic subjects. For Cambridge University Press he has edited two volumes on film adaptation: *Nineteenth-Century American Fiction on Screen* and *Twentieth-Century American Fiction on Screen*. He wrote *To Kill a Mockingbird: The Relationship between the Text and the Film* (2008) and (with Robert Bray) *Hollywood's Tennessee: The Williams Films and Postwar America* (2009). He serves on the editorial board of the journal *Adaptation*.

TISON PUGH is a professor of English at the University of Central Florida, where he teaches courses in medieval English literature, film, and southern literature. He is the author/editor of seven books; his latest is *Innocence, Heterosexuality, and the Queerness of Children's Literature* (2011).

LAURENCE RAW is a professor of English in the Department of Education, Baskent University, Ankara, Turkey. A member of the editorial boards of *Literature-Film Quarterly*, *Journal of Adaptation in Film and Performance*, and *Adaptation*, he is also chief editor of the *Journal of American Studies in Turkey*. Recent publications include *Character Actors in Horror and Science Fiction Films 1930–1960* (2012), *Translation, Adaptation, and Transformation* (2012), and an edited collection of *Merchant-Ivory Interviews* (2012).

NANCY MCGUIRE ROCHE is a lecturer in English at Vanderbilt University and a senior lecturer in Film Studies at the Watkins Film School in Nashville, Tennessee. She holds an M.F.A. in Creative Writing from Brown University and a Ph.D. in English from Middle Tennessee State University. She specializes in gender studies and currently teaches American Independent Cinema, Adaptations, and courses on both British and American films of the 1960s.

ANNETTE J. SADDIK is a professor of Theatre and English at the City University of New York and teaches at the CUNY Graduate Center Doctoral Program in Theatre. Her area of specialization is twentieth- and twenty-first-century drama and performance. She is the author of two books and one edited collection: *Contemporary American Drama* (2007), an exploration of the postmodern performance of American identity on the stage since World War II; *The Politics of Reputation: The Critical Reception of Tennessee Williams' Later Plays* (1999), which was the first full-length study of Williams's late (post-1961) plays; and *Tennessee Williams: The Traveling Companion and Other Plays* (2008), a collection of Williams's previously unpublished late plays. She has also published essays on various dramatists in journals, critical anthologies and encyclopedias of theatre history, and is working on a new book on Williams, *The Strange, The Crazed, The Queer: Tennessee Williams's Late Plays and the Theater of Excess.*

NEIL SINYARD is Emeritus Professor of Film Studies at the University of Hull, UK. He has published over twenty books, including works on directors such as Hitchcock, Wilder, Spielberg, and Woody Allen, and books on film comedy, silent movies, representations of childhood on film, film adaptation (*Filming Literature*), and Graham Greene. He is currently completing a book on the films of William Wyler.

JOHN D. SYKES, JR. is Mary and Harry Brown Professor of English and Religion at Wingate University. His articles have appeared in such journals as *Modern Theology, Renascence, Literature and Theology, Mississippi Quarterly*, and *Flannery O'Connor Review*. His most recent book is *Flannery O'Connor, Walker Percy, and the Aesthetic of Revelation* (2007).

Introduction

R. Barton Palmer and William Robert Bray

Robert Knopf is of course correct in observing that the cinema is the "youthful offspring" of an "ancient mother," the theatre; so it is hardly surprising that the two institutions, and the performance arts which are at their center, have enjoyed in the US and elsewhere a close and mutually supportive relationship since the birth of the new medium (and soon business) at the end of the nineteenth century.[1] In the early 1900s, the venues for programs of one- and two-reeler films were converted store-fronts popularly known as nickelodeons. But in about fifteen years, the American film business started decamping to purpose-built auditoria that looked and functioned much like theatres, which was the name they were given. Inside, except for the presence of a screen and projection booth hidden from view, these elaborate "picture palaces" perfectly resembled the playhouses densely clustered in entertainment districts such as New York's Times Square. These city-center first-run theatres came to feature spacious lobbies, stadium seating, curtained proscenium stages, encircling balconies, theatrical lighting, spacious rest rooms, and orchestra pits. The fully developed "photoplay" of the era, with its formal structure based on time-tested dramaturgical principles, closely resembled the stage productions that often served filmmakers more directly as source material.

Both theatre and film are performance media invested in the design and production (in the largest sense of that term) of live action, even if this action is transformed by photography into a different form of artistic material. Because of the elemental homology of the two arts, actors and other creative workers (such as directors and art designers) could easily work in both. Moreover, techniques and traditions, such as acting styles, could be readily shared. And the two institutions were not true competitors in the marketplace, though both were angling for their share of the entertainment dollar. Addressing distinct, but overlapping clienteles, the American theatre and cinema were disposed toward a symbiosis that made for constant, mutually profitable exchange, in part because film, utilizing photography and thus "capturing" performance (which could then be infinitely duplicated), could overcome the necessary existential and logistical difficulties of readily nationalizing theatre offerings and reaching the proverbial mass public. A filmed drama could be everywhere at once, with its "performances" not limited in time, but always capable of being revived. Screen versioning provided a stage production with a reach and influence unthinkable for the theatre, whose clientele was geographically limited and whose patrons, because of the continuing costs of live production, were customarily relatively well-off urbanites who could afford ticket prices that were much higher than the commercial cinema.

Plays, of course, present fewer of the problems involved in adapting literary fiction for the screen, and, already produced, come with a vision for their effective mounting that is readily available should the filmmakers desire to make use of it, as often happens. Of proven popularity, hit shows from Broadway have thus been routinely adapted for the screen in something resembling (and often derived from) their stage form. In fact, it has been unusual since the 1930s for a successful Broadway play to not be adapted as a film. With television providing yet another exhibition outlet for full-length features since the postwar era, the screen versioning of plays has only become even more common.

It is this tradition of adaptation that the present volume addresses. The essays collected here, however, focus neither on the Victorian stage, so influential on film production from 1900 through 1920 but today no longer much esteemed, nor on the well-established tradition of what we might call entertainment productions – the musicals, revues, and light comedy or dramas that have constituted an important sector of Broadway offerings since the closing decades of the nineteenth century. Instead, the concern here is with the self-consciously "modern" theatre that emerges, at first rather defiantly, as the artistic and institutional "other" of the Victorian commercial stage. For literary critics the term "modern" usually reflects some scheme of periodization (modern as opposed to medieval, for example). In this instance, however, modern refers to a specific development within American theatrical writing and production, and it carries with it strong associations of value, marking off an area of highbrow cultural production from more middlebrow or popular forms.

1915: the beginnings of a national theatre

Literary traditions do not customarily begin with a single event, but modern American drama assumed its characteristic theatricality, themes, and tendentiousness in 1915 with the foundation of the Provincetown

Players, which was, in the words of historian Brenda Murphy, "the most significant and most influential American theatre group of the early twentieth century ... the first with a serious artistic agenda."[2] With the formation and subsequent flourishing of this playwriting producing collective, the international modernism introduced to the American public two years earlier in the famed Armory Exposition assumed a public, even at times provocative form. By 1915, it became possible, so suggest critics Adele Heller and Lois Rudnick, to speak unhesitatingly of "the New Politics, the New Woman, the New Psychology, the New Art, and the New Theatre."[3] With chapters devoted to each of these aspects of radical change, their edited volume *1915: The Cultural Moment* makes a strong argument that during this year the previously inchoate movement to "build a vital national culture" took on an increasingly concrete form.[4]

The era's politically active and culturally progressive Bohemians were strongly attracted to the theatre, which was hardly surprising. For this was the literary form, with its potentially forceful performative presence in the public sphere, that had demonstrated, in the shape it assumed under the influence of European naturalism, an ability to anatomize and deconstruct traditional values, as well as the institutions, especially the family, in which they were expressed. The aim of the naturalists was to transform the traditions of the Victorian theatre, rejecting its promotion of the spectacular in all its forms as well as the complex, melodramatic plotting of the well-made play (with its dependence on suspense, surprises, recognition scenes, and reversals). During 1915, the leading lights of the New York antiestablishment founded a playwriting and producing collective to be located in the Massachusetts coastal town where they regularly vacationed. What emerged with their early productions was a distinctly American dramatic culture – if by that we mean both the writing of provocative drama based on the model of European dramatic naturalism – as well as their subsequent successful commercial mounting in an alternative venue not under the control of the established theatre business.

The Provincetown Players moved production to Greenwich Village in 1916 (converting a building at 139 MacDougal Street into a theatre), but then more or less disbanded in 1922. Soon afterward, key members were instrumental in founding the Experimental Theater, Inc., staging a number of productions at the Greenwich Village Theater, where they drew an ever-widening audience. A number of O'Neill plays saw their first production there, including *Desire under the Elms*, which, debuting in 1924, proved popular enough as the decade wore on to merit transference to a succession of uptown venues, where it ran for over 400 performances, testimony to the growing taste among theatregoers for something beyond the spectacular revues, light comedy, and insubstantial dramas that constituted the bulk of the theatrical fare then available in New York.

The Provincetown movement broadly conceived revolutionized the national stage, bringing the radically new into a dramatic culture still firmly rooted in the quite different aims of the entertainment industry and, even more importantly, in the melodramatic forms and values of the previous century, whose theatrical dominance was challenged, if not eliminated, by the naturalism pioneered by both Ibsen and Strindberg. As C. W. E. Bigsby appropriately puts it, "To compare Ibsen with any product of the nineteenth-century American theatre is to compare . . . two wholly disproportionate worlds."[5] By the middle of the twentieth century that gap had closed, Bigsby suggests, with the evolution of a "style placing the individual in a more direct relationship to a material world which was increasingly seen as a generator of action and character."[6] The modern American dramatic tradition is dominated by both realism and *engagement*, and this is the broader subject that the various essays in this volume all take up and trace in the work of that tradition's most notable playwrights. However, the contributors would certainly agree with William W. Demastes that this tendentious realism has never become "a structurally unambitious, homogeneous, tunnel-visioned form . . . denying creation of a more open, pluralistic theatre."[7] A central aspect of the modern national theatre is that, as Demastes goes on to say, "a nation of many faces, perspectives, and beliefs . . . has adopted a theatrical form likewise of many faces, perspectives, and beliefs."[8] That said, however, it would be distorting to deny the pervasive influence on the Provincetown group and their successors of continental naturalism, particularly as represented by what were often at the time scandalous, even outlaw productions. The emergence of modern American drama was thus dependent on the fortunate fact that this European theatrical experimentalism, though slow in crossing the Atlantic, did find there, as Bigsby says, "a group of people who combined a studied aesthetic eclecticism with a conviction that the drama could have a central role in cultural and social life."[9] Naturalism was the other to the *fin de siècle* aestheticism that also influenced the complex mix then emerging as cultural modernism.

A transformed stage

In the decades before it was successfully taken up by intellectuals and artists as an object of cultural transformation, the American stage had a rich history of theatrical production, perhaps best typified by the Horatio

Alger career of David Belasco, who, starting as a script boy in San Francisco, eventually moved to New York, where he became one of Broadway's most successful stage managers, producers, and – to use an appropriate show business term then in vogue – impresarios. He was very nearly an industry in himself, mounting more than 400 productions during a long career, including many based on his own play scripts or adapted for the stage by him from other sources. More than forty American films all together derive from Belasco sources, perhaps making him the most adapted American dramatist. Belasco, however, can claim to have exerted no effect as a playwright on the development of a distinctly national and, above all else, authentically modern American drama.[10]

And yet Belasco cannot be dismissed entirely, for in his own way he participated in the general movement away from nineteenth-century theatricality, with its unconcern for realism. As a production designer, if not a playwright, Belasco made a substantial contribution (if unintentionally) to the drive toward modernism given such irresistible impetus by the Provincetown movement. The American theatre that since the late 1940s has achieved considerable world renown depends absolutely on a form of realism that situates individuals in a "material world" that, in the expressionist fashion, both reflects and inspires who they are and what they do; the carefully dressed set achieves a "defining power" in Bigsby's appropriate formulation.[11] If for Aristotle the least important aspect of dramatic presentation is *opsis* or spectacle (literally what the eye can see), the modern American theatre is crucially dependent on stagecraft, on the careful mutual adjustment of mise en scène broadly considered (including costuming, music, and so forth) to character. For Belasco, painted canvas sets and flimsy backdrops were an abomination; he proclaimed that "everything must be real."[12] His reflex in the postwar theatre is the art designer whose talents are crucial to the production as an aesthetic experience. It is hardly an accident that the two most acclaimed and influential plays of the postwar Broadway stage, Tennessee Williams's *A Streetcar Named Desire* (1947) and Arthur Miller's *Death of a Salesman* (1949), were especially effective drama because of their distinct "look," designed in both instances by Jo Mielziner, who in an extraordinary career provided the stage settings of over 200 Broadway productions and established as an institutional norm the "selective realism" that involves the carefully evocative or symbolic use of realistic structures or objects. The kind of stagecraft that Mielziner developed (heavily influenced by European developments) and furthered has been crucial now for more than half a century in determining the total effect of modern American theatre, dependent on a complex marriage of script, acting technique, and spectacle.

Spectacle, in fact, is one area in which the cinema, not tied to a play-space, disposes of advantages and resources unknown to the stage. The chariot race in both film versions of *Ben-Hur* (1925, Fred Niblo; 1959, William Wyler) is a defining moment of engaging dramatic action in which pure physicality dominates. What is little appreciated, however, is that this part of the drama was also emphasized in the first adaptation of Lew Wallace's bestseller (1880), the 1889 Klaw and Erlanger stage production, in which elaborate stage machinery (including giant treadmills and a moving cyclorama backdrop) made possible the use of real chariots, drawn by real horses, which raced outward toward amazed, and perhaps initially frightened, theatregoers. While the ingenuity and resourcefulness of the theatrical producers must be applauded, the chariot race as "staged" displays its inadequacy to the chariot race as "enacted" and made available for viewing through the medium of film. The stage version of Thomas Dixon's popular novel *The Clansman* (both 1905) was a substantial popular hit in tours throughout the South and the Midwest and even enjoyed a brief run on Broadway. But it could no more than point at the larger events with which it was concerned – the Civil War and Reconstruction. It took D. W. Griffith's film version, released eventually as *The Birth of a Nation* in 1915, to provide the dramatic action spectacle on the scale necessary for Dixon's fiction to be brought to full performance life, with seemingly vast armies competing on a field of battle substituting for a few soldiers crowding the stage; and, as we must remember, it was the national distribution of the film as well as its well-designed spectacle that made it possible for Dixon's regrettable racial politics to reach the widest possible audience in a form that directly aroused emotions and incited passions. It is this highly profitable, widely popular, and much discussed film that demonstrated the incredible cultural power of the emerging medium to bring dramatic art to a mass public, in a deep sense fulfilling the mission that the theatre, from its beginnings in ancient Greece, in some sense has always set for itself. The adaptations discussed in this book all represent (mostly for better, if occasionally for worse) the cinema's commitment to a performance art that transcends geographical, temporal, and cultural boundaries even as it embodies the more narrowly theatrical, subsuming in part the aim of the Provincetown group to establish a national drama that mattered.

Many years ago, film theorist André Bazin observed that the fully developed modern cinema will "give back to the theater unstintingly what it took from her," a generosity dependent on the principle that "there are no plays that cannot be brought to the screen, whatever their style, provided one can visualize a reconversion of stage space in accordance with the data."[13] It is this reconversion of stage space that is always at the center of the cinematic adaptation of theatrical properties, and it makes possible a truly artistic approach that avoids the numerous pitfalls of "canned theatre." If the film business can extend the reach of Broadway, offering playwrights a mass audience for their work that is theoretically unlimited in time and space, then the film medium possesses the ability to deepen the sense in which dramatic presentation depends on the interaction of characters with a world we can recognize fully as our own. Conceived for a different audience, making use of resources both available and unavailable to the playwright or stage producer, and limited by institutions or traditions that have no purchase on the theatre, screen adaptations of plays make a very strong case for consideration on their own merits and not as necessarily inferior versions of the honored properties on which they are based.

Modern American drama has developed as a literary and performance tradition of great authors (and of these there are not many) rather than genres or cycles, and that is hardly surprising given its origins and the dominating presence of Eugene O'Neill. The fifteen essays that constitute this volume address the work of all the major figures who have attained a significant presence on film since the beginning of the sound era, but some of these (e.g. Williams, Miller, and O'Neill) are better known than others (Hellman, Kingsley, Edson). Absent here are chapters on playwrights who are important figures of modern American drama (such as Susan Glaspell and Elmer Rice) but whose work has not generated cinematically important or artistically interesting adaptations. Each chapter centers on what editors and authors decided was the most representative or otherwise significant play/film, with a view toward making it possible for this book to serve as the basis for a semester's examination of the subject.

Endnotes

1 Robert Knopf, ed., *Theater and Film: A Comparative Anthology* (New Haven, CT: Yale University Press, 2005), 1.
2 Brenda Murphy, *The Provincetown Players and the Culture of Modernity* (Cambridge University Press, 2005), xiii.
3 Adele Heller and Lois Rudnick, eds., *1915: The Cultural Moment* (New Brunswick, NJ: Rutgers University Press, 1991), 1.
4 Ibid., 2.
5 C. W. E. Bigsby, *A Critical Introduction to Twentieth-Century American Drama: Volume One 1900–1940* (Cambridge University Press, 1982), 3.

6 Ibid., 3.
7 William W. Demastes, *Realism and the American Dramatic Tradition* (Tuscaloosa: University of Alabama Press, 1996), ix.
8 Ibid., xiv.
9 Bigsby, *Critical Introduction*, vii.
10 André Bazin, "Theater and Cinema," in Knopf, 126, 131 (110–133).
11 Bigsby, *Critical Introduction*, 4.
12 Quoted in ibid., 3.
13 Bazin, "Theater and Cinema," 131.

CHAPTER I

Realism, censorship, and the social promise of Dead End

Amanda Ann Klein

When Sidney Kingsley's play *Dead End* premiered at the Belasco Theater on October 28, 1935, reviewers praised its realistic rendering of the disparity between rich and poor in 1930s New York City. A 1935 Brooks Atkinson review of the play in the *New York Times* proclaims, "What you have seen and heard in New York, wondering and apprehensive as you trudge along our begrimed seacoast, has found lodgment in this flaring anecdote of an average day,"[1] while a 1937 *Washington Post* review praised the play because it "conveyed no false note, struck no minor chord and left no remembrance in the consciousness of the spectator but one of complete fidelity to life."[2] Both reviews are representative of *Dead End*'s overall critical reception: the play was viewed as realistic, timely, and socially important. Critics and audiences were also impressed with *Dead End*'s detailed set, meticulously constructed by famed designer Norman Bel Geddes. Audiences were said to gasp audibly when the curtain first opened, revealing his elaborate rendering of a New York City block, flanked on one side by crumbling tenements and on the other by a new high-rise apartment building.[3] Although a mix of gritty realism and salty dialogue was the play's primary draw and the reason for its success, this realism created numerous problems for film producer Samuel Goldwyn as he attempted to adapt the play into a social problem picture for MGM studios. Because Hollywood films were subject to far stricter censorship codes than stage productions, the 1937 adaptation of *Dead End* had to omit some of the more scandalous scenes and lines of dialogue from Kingsley's original play. Furthermore, most films of the era – even social problem films – were constrained by the basic conventions of classical Hollywood cinema, which required strong, morally unambiguous heroes and conclusive endings. Despite the resulting changes to the original script, however, director William Wyler's 1937 adaptation of *Dead End* stands as one of the most politically radical social problem films of the 1930s, effectively translating Kingsley's unflinching stage realism into cinematic terms.

Figure 1.1 The same cast of young boys was used in both the play and the
film versions of *Dead End*. (frame enlargement)

Social problem films and the 1930s climate of concern

Social problem films are defined as any film "which combines social
analysis and dramatic conflict within a coherent narrative structure."[4]
Charles Mayland adds that the social problem film is "generally animated
by a humane concern for the victim(s) of or crusader(s) against the social
problem."[5] The social problem film's content must also be timely so that
the contemporary viewer recognizes it as something that is happening
"now," as opposed to the historical past. These issues must affect a
significant segment of the population so that audiences recognize this issue
as a problem; film studios, always motivated by profit, want to make films
that appeal to the belief systems of their audiences in order to fill more
theatre seats.[6] In fact, Peter Stead argues that one of the primary motivations behind Warner Brothers' much-lauded output of "socially conscious" films in the 1930s (*I Was a Fugitive from a Chain Gang* [1932,
Mervyn LeRoy], *Wild Boys of the Road* [1933, William A. Wellman], *Heroes*

for Sale [1933, William A. Wellman], etc.) is that the majority of their movie houses were located in "the populous East" (New Jersey, New York, and Pennsylvania), and "it could be claimed that the studio knew and needed to know more about industrial America than some of its rivals."[7] This desire to appeal to the audience's current belief system explains why social problem films rarely conclude with any form of radical social critique that might challenge the status quo. Audiences want to leave a social problem film feeling like the suffering they have just witnessed can be resolved without requiring their intervention. Indeed, with the prominent exception of *I Was a Fugitive from a Chain Gang*, social problem films of the 1930s generate concern for a pressing social problem but then assure the viewer that this problem is easily fixed. Complicated, systemic social problems like poverty, unemployment, drug and alcohol abuse, and racism are solved through the intervention of an exceptional individual (a kindly judge, sympathetic policeman, or courageous reformer) or through the elimination of a single super-villain.[8] No matter how radical the critique, audience outrage is ultimately soothed with the promise of an easy, private solution.

Social problem films periodically reach a peak of popularity, depending on the social, economic, and political conditions of the time. The 1930s cycle of social problem films appeared at a time when American audiences were increasingly concerned about the plight of urban youth. The Great Depression created a large population of orphaned or abandoned children, and the dearth of viable employment for these disenfranchised youth led to a steady and disconcerting increase in the rates of juvenile crime.[9] These films also emphasized the environmental causes of criminality and the possibility of reforming those whom society had assumed were incapable of reformation. This "environmental" approach to understanding crime first appeared in the 1920s, following the findings of the Chicago School of Sociology, which was considered to be "the dominant academic institution developing sociological inquiry in the United States in the 1920s."[10] These social scientists believed that the environment in which a person is raised has a profound impact on his/her behavior. Studies from the period, such as Clifford Shaw's influential book *Delinquency Areas* (1929) and Harvey Zorbaugh's *The Gold Coast and the Slum* (1929), investigated the links between urbanization and crime.[11] Hence, the social problem films of the 1930s were in tune with public sentiment.

Dead End, which links the mise en scène of poverty with juvenile delinquency and, ultimately, adult delinquency, was thus a timely addition to the growing body of work on the interlinked subjects of environment, juvenile delinquency, and the need for intervention. As one drama critic explained in a 1937 review, *Dead End* "proves a notable exception to the axiom that good theatre and good sociology cannot be combined without sacrificing one to the other."[12] The play quickly became a touchstone for social crusaders looking to reform urban neighborhoods and aid children in need. First Lady Eleanor Roosevelt reportedly went to see the play three times, and later the cast was asked to perform *Dead End* at the White House at the request of President Roosevelt.[13] In 1936 the cast performed the play's third act on the radio, as part of the "Mobilization for Human Needs." After their perform-ance, Walter W. Head, the president of the Boy Scouts of America, gave an address "urging the need of proper environment for children."[14] In other words, the play was viewed as entertainment but also as effective propaganda for generating support for social welfare programs. Indeed, the Boys' Clubs of America attributed a threefold increase in contribu-tions to the play's rhetoric of social reform. Finally, Senator Robert Wagner cited the play as support for the Wagner-Steagall Housing Act of 1937, which sought to tear down crumbling tenement buildings and replace them with new, cleaner, housing projects for low-income fam-ilies.[15] It says much about the play's social impact that it was able to inspire legislation that ultimately helped real families to live in decent homes.

Dead End's social impact and its realism

Dead End dramatizes the lives of New Yorkers who live along the East River, where degenerating tenements and an exclusive new apartment house meet. The play's conceit – that great wealth and great poverty exist side by side – was a reality familiar to New York residents of the time. For example, a *New York Times* article from 1935 corroborates the phenom-enon documented in the play: "Especially along the East River in the Fifties you have ... the incongruous spectacle of sleek, impersonal apart-ment buildings rising cheek by jowl with frowsy tenement buildings."[16] Against this troubling backdrop, Kingsley provides a loose plot structure: the notorious gangster Baby Face Martin returns to the dead end, his former neighborhood, in order to see his mother and an old flame, Francey. Martin's dramatic foil is his childhood friend, Gimpty, a crippled architect who briefly escaped the neighborhood in order to complete his degree. Gimpty has since returned, unable to make a living in such an unforgiving economic climate. The third plot focuses on Tommy, a

Figure 1.2 Dave (Joel McCrea), the film's version of Gimpty,
is able-bodied and macho. (frame enlargement)

juvenile delinquent supported by his devoted, hard-working sister, Drina, who spends his days goofing off and committing petty crimes with a group of destitute street urchins, the play's now-infamous "Dead End Kids."[17]

Dead End's success and social impact was largely due to the play's convincing portrait of urban suffering. In her canonical study of realism in art, Linda Nochlin argues that the aim of realism is "to give a truthful, objective and impartial representation of the real world, based on meticulous observation of contemporary life."[18] Kingsley famously walked the streets of lower Manhattan, eavesdropping on the conversations coming from its back alleys, while preparing to write *Dead End*. In a lengthy editorial, "It Often Pays to Take a Walk Along the East River: In Which Mr. Kingsley Reveals a Few of the Events Leading Up to the Writing of 'Dead End,'" written for the *New York Times* in 1935, Kingsley explains his approach to playwriting: "But just open your eyes to the things about you, and you will see that they have a palpable, inescapable significance."

Kingsley acknowledged that simply recording the details of the real world and then translating them for the stage might feel banal at times, but he felt that the most important ideas were to be found in the small, observational details of life: "These are hard real times, and, therefore, perhaps best expressed in hard real terms. Romanticism is a nostalgic evasion, mysticism a beclouded one. Go to reality! There's the answer! Literally hold up a mirror to the times." Kingsley felt that awareness was all that was needed to create engagement with and empathy for the suffering of others and the impetus to intervene. This awareness was generated through the techniques of realism.[19]

As in life, environment creates character, and so playwrights working in the realist tradition focus on establishing a believable setting for their characters. George Becker has argued: "The ultimate subject of a realistic work is a milieu."[20] Indeed, Kingsley devotes almost two full pages of screen directions to establishing the play's only location, the dead end of a New York City street. While the setting described by Kingsley establishes a real location, it also serves a secondary purpose – explaining the behavior of his characters. The Dead End Kids live in apartments with "*hideous, water-stained, peeling wallpaper*" and "*old-broken down furniture.*" Their parents are too busy, or too demoralized, to bother taking old mattresses or empty milk bottles to the curb, and so "*The fire escapes are cluttered with gutted mattresses and quilts, old clothes, bread boxes, milk bottles, a canary cage, an occasional potted plant struggling for life.*"[21] This destitution is thrown into further relief by Kingsley's description of the East River Terrace apartments, where New York's elite reside: "*The wall is of rich, heavy masonry, guarded at the top by a row of pikes. Beyond the pikes, shutting off the view of the squalid street below, is a thick edging of lush green shrubbery.*"[22] Kingsley's language implies a world that is clean and fresh in comparison with the dank, mildewing world of the nearby tenements. Words like "guarded" and "shutting off" demonstrate how the tenement residents are denied access to this refined world. They can see the "*gaily colored sun umbrellas*" beyond the wall and hear the "*clink of glasses and laughter filter through the shrubs,*" but they may not experience these pleasures for themselves.[23]

This separation between rich and poor is also highlighted through the characters' differing dialects, another key component of the play's mise en scène. Kingsley stages a scene early in the play in which the Dead End Kids have a conversation with a wealthy boy of the same age, Phillip Griswald, about swimming in the polluted East River:

PHILIP. I wouldn't swim here.
T.B. He's yelluh, dat's what! Dat's what! He's godda yelluh streak up 'is back a mile wide.
PHILIP. It's dirty here.
DIPPY (*shocked*). Doity!
T.B. (*very indignant*). Doity! He sez doity! He sez it's doity! I'll sock 'im!
ANGEL. Lil fairy!
SPIT. Wassamattuh? Yuh sca'd yuh git a lil doit on yuh?
PHILIP. Besides, I haven't got my suit.[24]

The Dead End Kids are well aware that the river water is "dirty" – the play opens with the boys enthusiastically jumping into the East River and then wiping its filth from their skin after they emerge – but, as Kingsley's copious stage directions indicate, dirt is a part of their everyday lives. When Philip rejects the East River based on its "dirtiness," he is not simply rejecting the water; he is rejecting the way the Dead End Kids live their lives. Thus the boys are indignant – not just at Philip's elitism, but at his ability to choose between the clean water of the East River Terrace's indoor pool and the dirty water of the East River.

This dialogue also highlights the gulf between the boys' socioeconomic status and educations. The Dead End Kids, raised in the city streets, speak with heavy New York accents, profanities, and slang. By contrast, Philip, who has a personal tutor, enunciates each word in a proper Mid-Atlantic accent and eschews the slang of his contemporaries.[25] The audience does not need to be told directly that Philip is a wealthy, educated, privileged child while the Dead End Kids are poor and abused; their accents, dialects, and diction convey this information. Therefore, it should not be surprising that the profane nature of Kingsley's dialogue was a recurring subject in the play's critical reception. Although the version of *Dead End* that debuted to critics had already been censored – Kingsley had to make several changes to his script before the New York City council would allow it to run – audiences still found it shocking and, occasionally, offensive.[26] For example, early in the play the boys have an extended conversation about whether or not it is possible to make a cigarette out of "hawse-balls" (i.e., horse manure), as Angel enthusiastically rolls one up.[27] Later, the boys "cockalize" a new gang initiate, a hazing ritual that entails pulling down the boy's pants, rubbing dirt all over his groin, and spitting directly on to his genitals.[28] These scenes, and their attendant language, would be shocking in any context, but they are made more so by the fact that the actors are young boys.

The Production Code, classical Hollywood cinema, and Samuel Goldwyn's *Dead End*

Concerns over the play's vulgar content, including its dialogue and its frank treatment of taboo subjects like premarital sex, prostitution, venereal diseases, and child abuse, delayed *Dead End*'s big-screen adaptation for two years. The recently established Production Code Administration (PCA), the industry based organization that regulated American film content from 1934 until it was dismantled and replaced with a ratings system in 1968, opposed the depiction of children engaged in criminal activities. However, since it was the play's frank, realistic depiction of urban youth that led to its critical and commercial success,[29] producer Samuel Goldwyn wisely fought to retain as much of *Dead End*'s controversial material as possible, most notably its frank depiction of juvenile delinquency, its ambiguous conclusion, and its sympathetic treatment of strikers. In fact, Goldwyn was able to work with PCA head Joseph Breen to avoid heavy censorship by appealing to the film's social importance.[30] Like so many Hollywood films depicting crime, corruption, and social critique, *Dead End*'s "rhetoric of civic responsibility" allowed it some leeway in its depiction of otherwise banned material.[31]

Nevertheless, several changes were made to the original play in order to comply with PCA standards. First, the play's depiction of Baby Face Martin's violent death at the end of Act 2 had to be modified. According to PCA regulations, when a character is shot, whether deserving or not, the character cannot be shown to suffer. The reasoning here was that the more a body is shown to suffer due to an act of violence, the more the viewer would perceive that act *as violent*.[32] Thus, films deploy what Stephen Prince has described as the "clutch-and-fall aesthetic": a character who is shot or stabbed sinks out of the frame, as if falling asleep.[33] In the play, a group of policemen, tipped off by Gimpty, attempt to arrest Martin. When the gangster shoots an officer, Kingsley describes their retaliation as an explosion of gunfire:

> *From behind the hopper and the tenement doorway guns explode . . .* MARTIN *groans, wheels, and falls, his face in the gutter, his fingers clawing the sidewalk. One of the* G MEN *goes to aid his wounded comrade. The other* G MAN *stands over* MARTIN*'s body, pumping bullet after bullet into him, literally nailing him to the ground.*[34]

In order to comply with PCA regulations, the screen version of this scene has Martin's body out of the frame when he is shot (so we do not see his reaction) and, more importantly, we do not hear him react to the bullets that enter his body at close range. There is no "groaning" and no "clawing" at the sidewalk.

The PCA was also concerned with the depiction of law enforcement and government officials. The first General Principle of the Production Code states: "the sympathy of the audience shall never be thrown to the side of crime, wrong-doing, evil or sin."[35] The original play contains a scene in which a medical examiner's intern kneels beside Baby Face Martin's dead body and remarks, "Phew! They certainly did a job on him! Nothing left to look at but chopped meat. God, they didn't leave enough of him for a good p.m.!"[36] This statement is subtly critical of the police, who continued to shoot Martin's body long after it was necessary to do so; their excessive gunfire was motivated by vengeance (Martin shot a fellow officer) rather than justice. The inclusion of the intern's line, paired with the earlier stage directions describing Martin's death ("*literally nailing him to the ground*"), is characteristic of Kingsley's larger project of depicting the reality of life in Depression-era New York City. No single character in the play is uniformly good or uniformly evil; even the police find it difficult to separate their jobs from their emotions. However, a Hollywood film could not depict representatives of the law in a morally ambiguous light, no matter how justifiable their reaction might have been. As a result, this scene with the intern is eliminated from the film – no character references the state of Martin's corpse, and it never appears within the frame.

This moment of social critique is not entirely lost in the film adaptation. Instead, it is translated into a different scene. In both the play and the film, Baby Face Martin returns to the dead end, after years on the run, to see his mother and his former flame, Francey (Claire Trevor). However, upon recognizing her son, Mrs. Martin (Marjorie Main) slaps him across the face and rejects his offers of "blood money." She even laments his birth: "I ought to be cut open here for givin' yuh life."[37] The film's version of this scene is almost identical; Martin's rejection, by his own mother, is a profound statement on his immorality as well as a rejection of the gangster lifestyle in general. But the film adds a single shot that alters this message: moments after Martin dies, we hear a woman's anguished screams coming from offscreen. The next image is a low-angled, medium shot of Mrs. Martin, who is leaning out of her window, howling with grief. The inclusion of a scene in which Baby Face Martin's mother publicly laments her son's death humanizes and generates sympathy for the murderous gangster. When Mrs. Martin mourns her son's death, the viewer wonders if Martin is simply another victim of the slums, rather than an unequivocal villain. Was his death necessary, the viewer wonders, or could he have been reformed?

Another change to the screen version of the play lies in its dialogue. As previously mentioned, much of the play's dialogue was considered too profane for film, and so Samuel Goldwyn asked screenwriter Lillian Hellman to tone it down.[38] Several articles about the film's production note, with amusement, that the Kids were displeased with these changes to the original script:

> The dialogue in Lillian Hellman's script is a good deal different from that of Mr. Kingsley. The six assistant directors [i.e., the Dead End Kids] didn't understand that you can say certain things on the stage that are not permitted on the screen. They wanted "to protect Mr. Kingsley's interest."[39]

Since the PCA prohibited religious or ethnic slurs, several lines that highlighted the casual xenophobia of New York City living had to be cut. In one scene Spit spots Milty, the new Jewish kid on the block, and calls out "Come heah, Ikey!"[40] while another character mentions the neighborhood's "Chink laundry."[41] Section V of the Production Code also stated: "Pointed profanity (this includes the words, God, Lord, Jesus, Christ – unless used reverently – Hell, S.O.B., damn, Gawd), or every other profane or vulgar expression however used, is forbidden."[42] Thus, in the film version of *Dead End*, Angel (Bobby Jordan) can no longer yell "Fongoola!"[43] an Italian-American slang term meaning "fuck you," at the River Terrace doorman, and Dippy (Huntz Hall) cannot taunt Philip (Charles Peck) with the refrain "Sissy, sissy, sucks his mama's titty!"[44]

The stage version of *Dead End* was able to get away with these profanities because stage productions were held to different censorship standards than the cinema. The supplement to the Production Code outlines these distinctions: "Everything possible in a *play* is not possible in a film: a. Because of the *larger audience of the film*, and its inconsequential mixed character. Psychologically, the larger the audience, the lower the moral mass resistance to suggestion."[45] What remains unstated here is that because the cinema was a more democratic form of entertainment than the theatre – both affordable and amenable to schedules of the working, urban poor – it drew in many illiterate, immigrant, and racially and ethnically diverse filmgoers (i.e., the "mixed character" euphemistically referenced in the Production Code). In this "space of heterosocial leisure" these audiences were viewed not just as vulnerable, but also as *dangerous*.[46] The Production Code continues:

[Cinema] appeals at once to *every class*, immature, developed, undeveloped, law abiding, criminal. Music has its grades for different classes; so has literature and drama. This art of the motion picture, combining as it does the two fundamental appeals of looking at a *picture* and *listening to a story*, at once reaches every class of society.[47]

The primarily white, middle-to-upper-class audiences in attendance at the Belasco Theater might find *Dead End*'s profanity shocking, but their class and education were believed to make them capable of withstanding the morally corrupting effects of what transpired on stage. However, the working-class filmgoers watching the big-screen version of *Dead End* needed to be "protected" from such profane images and sounds, since they were believed to be more susceptible to imitating them.

The biggest changes to the stage play were the revisions made to Gimpty's character. In a large, sprawling cast of characters, Gimpty is the closest thing *Dead End* has to a central protagonist; his story overlaps with those of every other character, and he appears in most of the scenes. As a child, Gimpty developed rickets, a disease caused primarily by malnutrition. Therefore, his twisted leg is a permanent, visual marker of his class status, a reminder of how a child's environment can dramatically alter the person s/he will become. Gimpty is frustrated and resentful about how his life has turned out – he is an unemployed architect – despite his hard work, and he attempts to do the right thing. Furthermore, although turning Baby Face Martin in to the police was ultimately the "right thing" to do, it is unclear whether Gimpty's decision to become a "squealer" is motivated by fear (Martin had threatened his life) or by a sense of responsibility to keep his neighborhood free of gangsters. Regardless of his motivation, in the context of the play, squealers are characterized as traitors and are often given "the mark of the squealer" (a cut from the corner of the mouth to one ear). Thus, Gimpty is a flawed and occasionally morally ambiguous character.

By contrast, Dave (Joel McCrea), the film's version of this character, is able-bodied and macho. While Gimpty can only hurl verbal abuse at Baby Face Martin, Dave physically confronts the gangster and demands that he leave the neighborhood, resulting in a gunfight between the two alpha males. Given the 1935 moratorium on gangster films, this confrontation between a representative of right (Dave) and wrong (Martin) is necessary to firmly establish the film's moral code.[48] Furthermore, this climactic action sequence, which is entirely absent from the play, turns Dave into a traditional Hollywood leading man. Later, when a cop on the scene informs Dave that he is entitled to a reward for shooting Martin, he

cynically replies, "They pay you for it, huh?" In other words, even though
Martin's demise was justified in the film, Dave feels uncomfortable with
receiving financial compensation for the death of his childhood friend.

The film also alters Gimpty's romantic storyline. In the play, Gimpty
has a flirtation with Kay, a former dead-end resident who has upped her lot
by becoming the mistress of a wealthy man living in the River Terrace
apartments. Kay has romantic feelings for Gimpty but is determined to
never live a life of poverty again. Even after Gimpty obtains the reward
money for turning in Martin, Kay tells him that it is simply not enough:
"I could go and live with you and be happy – (*And she means it*) – and then
when poverty comes . . . and we begin to torture each other, what would
happen? I'd leave you and go back to Jack."[49] Gimpty is left feeling
rejected and broken-hearted. However, in the film it is Kay (Wendy
Barrie) who suggests that she and Dave run away together with his reward
money. Dave is infatuated with Kay but finds her snobbery distasteful and
ends the relationship. Dave is empowered by his choice to end things with
Kay, making his implied love match with Drina (Sylvia Sidney) feel like
the fulfillment of his character's romantic destiny, rather than like "settling" (as it does in the play).

The changes made to Gimpty's character for the screen version of *Dead
End* were motivated less by censorship constraints than by the conventions
of classical Hollywood cinema. Classical Hollywood cinema refers to a
broad set of conventions – in terms of narrative, editing style, cinematography, and mise en scène – that characterized the majority of films
released in Hollywood from roughly 1917 to 1960. In particular, classical
Hollywood cinema employed narratives focusing on a single, goal-focused
hero, often a male, who drives the narrative forward.[50] As Laura Mulvey
famously described it, the role of the male hero is "the active one of
forwarding the story, making things happen. The man controls the film
fantasy and also emerges as the representative of power in a further sense:
as the bearer of the look of the spectator."[51] Thus, most classical
Hollywood films contain male heroes who command and direct the events
of the plot and have clear, unambiguous motivations for their actions.
Dave must take on Baby Face Martin himself, rather than turn to the
police. He must actively select his love interest by rejecting the advances of
the superficial but glamorous Kay in favor of the mousy but hard-working
Drina. Unlike Gimpty, the crippled, passive, lovesick dreamer, Dave is a
strong, active male hero who controls narrative events. As one critic put it
in his 1937 film review: "Movie audiences are believed to dislike characters
suffering physical impairments. Audiences are known to have a decided

feeling about squealers. That's why Gimpy [*sic*] becomes known as Dave, a healthy stalwart and a 24-carat hero."[52]

Dead End's radicalism

Despite the many changes made to the original play, *Dead End* remains surprising more for what it got away with than for what was eliminated. Leonard Leff and Jerold Simmons argue that MGM was able to include material that was normally banned due to Joseph Breen's advocacy. Though Breen was often quite strict with film content, he "wanted to be considered a man of discernment, a man well-read. The Pulitzer Prize conferred on Kingsley two years before predisposed Breen to back the play."[53] Gregory Black points out that the Catholic Church was sympathetic with the problems of poverty depicted in both the play and the film. The influential "Catholic Legion of Decency strongly recommended the film version to all Catholics. Breen was aware of such support for *Dead End*, cleaned up some of the details, but left the message intact."[54] Thus, although the PCA was strict about the depiction of criminality, especially as it pertained to youth, the movie unabashedly portrays the Dead End Kids as criminals: they ambush Philip Griswald, beat him, and steal his watch; they organize and engage in street fights; and they steal money and food from their parents and other adults in the community. Despite these antisocial behaviors, most of the boys (with the possible exception of Spit [Leo Gorcey], the squealer) remain sympathetic. We bear witness to their poverty – signified by their tattered clothing, their absent parents, and their constant hunger – and so their criminal acts seem less disturbing and more deserving of our sympathy.

Furthermore, the film portrays many adult characters as callous, cruel, and exploitative in their treatment of children. In one early scene, Angel recounts a graphic story of being beaten by his drunken father the previous evening. The story culminates in the young boy wielding a knife to defend himself and his father passing out on the floor. Angel's nonchalant telling of the story, and the other boys' blasé response – they interrupt the story at one point to heckle one of the wealthy tenants across the street – indicate that such behavior from parents is expected. Another one of the boys, Milty (Bernard Punsly), has to spend the day watching his younger siblings, presumably because both parents work full-time. When he is momentarily distracted, we see a sweet-faced old woman snatch a cookie out of his infant sibling's hand. In this harsh environment, even an elderly woman, usually a signifier of nurturing and kindness toward children, will steal food from a baby in order to survive.

It is also significant that the film makes few changes to an ancillary plotline about Drina's involvement with a labor union. In both the play and the film, Drina's decision to strike is depicted as appropriate and necessary. In the play a policeman accuses Drina of being a "Red," and she responds: "Because I want a few more bucks a week so's I can live decent. God knows I earn it!"[55] This scene appears in a revised version in the film. When Tommy complains about Drina's decision to strike and the gossip it is generating around the neighborhood, she explains, "The next time those busybodies ask you what I'm striking for you tell them it's for money that's coming to me for hard work." The Roosevelt administration was tolerant of union activity; President Roosevelt signed the National Labor Relations Act in 1935, which guaranteed the right of employees to organize, form unions, and collectively bargain. However, other than a handful of films like *Black Fury* (1935, Michael Curtiz) and *John Meade's Woman* (1937, Richard Wallace), the majority of Hollywood films released at this time avoided any sympathetic portrayal of strikers and their complaints so as to avoid contributing to an overall atmosphere of labor unrest in the United States.[56] Peter Stead explains:

> By 1935, then, it was generally accepted in left-wing circles that Hollywood had become a propaganda agency and whenever it dealt with social themes it did so in such a way as to reflect the values sometimes of Washington, nearly always of Wall Street, and more often than not the views of California business interests . . .[57]

However, *Dead End* clearly throws sympathy on the side of undercompensated workers like Drina, who is depicted as being hard-working, selfless, and moral. At one point in the film Drina even appears with a bruised face after getting into an altercation with a "dirty cop" on the picket line. This image of actress Sylvia Sidney – a small, delicate woman – with an injury (inflicted by a man in uniform) would surely incite outrage in viewers.

Perhaps the most surprising aspect of the film was its retention of Sidney Kingsley's bleak ending. After Tommy (Billy Halop) is arrested for assaulting an upper-class man, it is unclear whether he will be released or sent to reform school. In the context of the original play, as well as most 1930s social problem films, reform school is viewed as the gateway to a life in crime. As Gimpty explains in the play:

> I knew [Baby Face Martin] when we were kids . . . He was strong. He had courage. He was a born leader. He even had a sense of fair play. But living in the streets kept making him bad . . . Then he was sent to reform school.

Figure 1.3 Drina's (Sylvia Sidney) face is bruised by a "dirty cop"
while on the picket line. (frame enlargement)

> Well, they reformed him all right! They taught him the ropes. He came out
> tough and hard and mean, with all the tricks of the trade.[58]

At the end of the play, Tommy is taken into custody while Drina worries
over how she will pay for a lawyer. Gimpty offers to cover the costs with the
money he was awarded for turning Baby Face Martin in to the police; one
hoodlum's demise creates the possibility (but not the certainty) of another
hoodlum's salvation. The play therefore ends on a note of ambiguity: as
Drina and Gimpty head downtown after Tommy, T. B. (Gabriel Dell)
teaches the other boys a song he learned in reform school. He sings: "If I had
de wings of a angel. Ovuh dese prison walls I wud fly."[59] Unlike the mortal
Angel, who endures daily beatings, the celestial angel of the boys' song can
fly high above the bars of the reform school or the dirty brick walls of the
dead end. The boys end their evening singing about transcendence and
freedom, while Kingsley offers his audiences no such comfort.

The film concludes in a similar fashion to the play. Tommy is taken
downtown and Drina and Dave follow him, intent on hiring the best

lawyer (blood) money can buy. The remaining Dead End Kids watch them disappear around the corner and then turn around to find the East River Terrace doorman extinguishing their trashcan fire. To the doorman the fire is yet another instance of the boys' delinquency, as well as a real threat to the safety of the East River Terrace residents. To the boys, however, the fire is their kitchen; they cook what appears to be their only meal of the day, some stolen potatoes, in its flames. Instead of lamenting the destruction of their dinner, the boys marvel at the smoke that curls up from the extinguished fire into the night sky. A lost potato, much like Tommy's arrest, cannot be mourned for very long. Life goes on, and the boys walk away from the river, singing "If I had de wings of a angel." The camera follows them as they make their way through the narrow, shadowed alleys between the tenement buildings and then leaves them to crane upward. The film concludes with an aerial shot of the city that resembles the film's opening shot.

This ambiguous ending was problematic for censors in light of *Dead End*'s overall tone of desperation: "The mix of poverty and social discord would worry the [PCA] . . . for Hays and the corporate bosses believed that the cinema should solve all problems at the final reel."[60] Had *Dead End* been a light comedy, its ambiguity would have been more tolerable. But the film is filled with so many bleak stories that to leave viewers without a sense that things will improve for residents of the dead end – especially the young boys – was both radical and risky. This ambiguous ending was also an anomaly in the realm of social problem films. As previously mentioned, most social problem films of the 1930s function as safety valves for society's anxieties about the problems they face. These films encourage the viewer to feel outrage, anger, or sadness, and then placate those emotions with a satisfying, close-ended conclusion. At the end of the film it is unclear whether Tommy will be sent to reform school or back to the dead end. Of course, even if Tommy is set free, he will return to the same life of delinquency and poverty. Kingsley generates outrage and despair – for the viewers to reflect upon after they exit the theatre.

Conclusions

In his seminal 1953 article, "Some Ideas on the Cinema," Neorealist screenwriter Cesare Zavattini convincingly argues that the films that are able to provide the most radical critiques of society are those that end inconclusively, without solutions and without hope. He argues that when films end on a note of resolution the viewer feels a sense of relief, and the urgency created by the depiction of the social problem dissipates: "It is not the concern of an artist to propound solutions. It is enough, and quite a lot, I should say, to make an audience feel the need, the urgency, for them."[61] Sidney Kingsley felt a profound sense of urgency when he looked around New York City and saw children digging through the garbage for food. Indeed, Kingsley wrote *Dead End* based on the belief that people are disengaged from the problems surrounding them because they do not, or will not, *see them.* Realism, therefore, does not simply reproduce the world before our eyes. Realism makes visible what is otherwise invisible. What we turn our eyes away from in real life, realism places before us in the world of entertainment. This is a curious alchemy, to be sure – we ignore human suffering when it stands before us, only to acknowledge (and cry over) its fictional doppelgänger. Nevertheless, the stage and screen versions of *Dead End* were successful in creating urgency about several interrelated social problems: urban poverty, housing reform, and juvenile delinquency. The urgency generated by these popular texts led to tangible social reform, such as the Wagner-Steagall Housing Act. Although *Dead End*'s political critique was challenged by the PCA, the conventions of classical Hollywood cinema, and MGM's need to generate profits, the film remains an outlier in social problem films of the era, and had a tangible impact on the audiences who went to see it.

Endnotes

1 Brooks Atkinson, "This Week's Theatre Involves Three Adaptations of River Realism," *New York Times*, November 3, 1935.
2 Nelson B. Bell, "Vivid Realism Is Not Lost to Drama, as Witness 'Dead End': Norman Bel Geddes' Production of 'Dead End,'" *Washington Post*, February 21, 1937.
3 Ben Brantley, "When Poor Were Perky as if Life Were Swell." *New York Times*, July 15, 1997.
4 Peter Roffman and Jim Purdy, *The Hollywood Social Problem Film: Madness, Despair, and Politics from the Depression to the Fifties* (Bloomington: Indiana University Press, 1981), viii.
5 Charles Mayland, "The Social Problem Film," in *Handbook of American Film Genres*, ed. Wes D. Ghering (New York: Greenwood Press, 1988), 307.
6 Ibid., 306.
7 Peter Stead, *Film and the Working Class: The Feature Film in British and American Society* (London: Routledge, 1989), 54.
8 Roffman and Purdy, *The Hollywood Social Problem Film*, 92.
9 James Gilbert, *A Cycle of Outrage: America's Reaction to the Juvenile Delinquent in the 1950s* (New York: Oxford University Press, 1986), 127.
10 Richard Maltby, "Why Boys Go Wrong: Gangsters, Hoodlums, and the Natural History of Delinquent Careers," in *Mob Culture: Hidden Histories*

of the American Gangster Film, ed. Lee Grieveson, Esther Sonnet, and Peter Stanfield (New Brunswick: Rutgers University Press, 2005), 41.

11 Gilbert, *A Cycle of Outrage*, 30; Maltby, "Why Boys Go Wrong," 44. In his *New York Times* editorial, Sidney Kingsley cites the prevalence of these studies as an explanation for why he chooses to write realist plays: "All the latest scientific research points to environment's tremendous conditioning influence in the manufactory of the criminal element … A strabismic society makes virulent saprophytes out of potentially good citizens, then spends huge sums fighting them" (1935).

12 "What's Going On in the Arts: Dead End," *Christian Science Monitor*, September 25, 1937. Not every critic agreed with this assessment of the play's didactic nature. A 1935 review of the play in the *Washington Post* dismisses the play's message: "It is a thinnish plea for slums reform hewn to the specifications of the stage. A few sociological pronouncements are interposed here and there to give the whole, one supposes, significance" (Keefe).

13 Sharon Waxman. "Splashing in the Waters of an Onstage Slum," *New York Times*, August 31, 2005, E1.

14 "Mobilization Program by 'Dead End' Cast," *Washington Post*, November 8, 1936.

15 Jeffrey Turner, "On Boyhood and Public Swimming: Sidney Kingsley's *Dead End* and Representations of Underclass Street Kids in American Cultural Production," in *The American Child: A Cultural Studies Reader*, ed. Caroline F. Levander and Carol J. Singley (New Brunswick: Rutgers University Press, 2003), 216.

16 Atkinson, "This Week's Theatre."

17 Most of the boys who starred in the play reprised their roles in the film. The boys were so popular that they went on to star in six spin-offs of the original *Dead End* with Warner Brothers. This cycle of films then led to three more: Universal's "The Dead End Kids and Little Tough Guys" (1938–1943), Monogram Studios' "The East Side Kids" (1940–1945), and Monogram's later cycle "The Bowery Boys" (1946–1958).

18 Linda Nochlin, *Realism* (Harmondsworth: Penguin, 1971), 13.

19 Sidney Kingsley, "It Often Pays to Take a Walk Along the East River: In Which Mr. Kingsley Reveals a Few of the Events Leading Up to the Writing of 'Dead End,'" *New York Times*, November 10, 1935.

20 Quoted in Brenda Murphy, *American Realism and American Drama, 1880–1940* (Cambridge University Press, 1987), 26.

21 Sidney Kingsley, *Dead End* in *Sixteen Famous American Plays*, ed. Bennett Cerf and Van H. Cartmell (New York: Garden City Publishing, 1941), 453.

22 Ibid.

23 Ibid.

24 Ibid., 461.

25 A Mid-Atlantic accent is a blend of American and British accents. In Hollywood films of the 1930s and 1940s this accent was associated with the educated, upper classes.

26 "News of the Stage: 'The Body Beautiful' Tonight – Lyda Roberti out of the 'Scandals' – Casting and Booking Items," *New York Times*, October 31, 1935, 17; Edwin Schallert, "'Dead End'; Bitterly Realistic Stage Drama," *Los Angeles Times*, June 8, 1937, 11.

27 Kingsley, *Dead End*, 456.

28 Ibid., 463.

29 Leonard J. Leff and Jerold L. Simmons, *The Dame in the Kimono: Hollywood, Censorship, and the Production Code from the 1920s to the 1960s* (New York: Grove Weidenfeld, 1990), 67. The show was a huge success, running for 684 performances ("News of the Stage: 'Dead End' to Close Long Run Saturday Night," *New York Times*, June 10, 1937, 26).

30 For an extended look at the PCA's deliberations over *Dead End*'s content, see Leff and Simmons, *The Dame in the Kimono*.

31 Maltby, "Why Boys Go Wrong," 42.

32 Ibid., 155.

33 Stephen Prince, *Classical Film Violence: Designing and Regulating Brutality in Hollywood, 1930–1968* (New Brunswick: Rutgers University Press, 2003), 153–154.

34 Kingsley, *Dead End*, 508.

35 Quoted in Stephen Tropiano, *Obscene, Indecent, Immoral, and Offensive: 100+ Years of Censored, Banned, and Controversial Films* (New York: Limelight Editions, 2009), 272.

36 Kingsley, *Dead End*, 510.

37 Ibid., 493.

38 Gregory D. Black, *Hollywood Censored: Morality Codes, Catholics, and the Movies* (Cambridge University Press, 1994), 277.

39 "The Kid Stars in 'Dead End' Appointed Selves Directors!" *Washington Post*, October 5, 1937.

40 Kingsley, *Dead End*, 462.

41 Ibid., 484.

42 Quoted in Tropiano, *Obscene, Indecent, Immoral, and Offensive*, 474.

43 Kingsley, *Dead End*, 530.

44 Ibid., 460.

45 Quoted in Tropiano, *Obscene, Indecent, Immoral, and Offensive*, 280.

46 Lee Grieveson, "The Thaw-White Scandal, *The Unwritten Law*, and the Scandal of Cinema," in *Headline Hollywood: A Century of Film Scandal*, ed. Adrienne L. MacLean and David A. Cook (New Brunswick: Rutgers University Press, 2001), 41.

47 Quoted in Tropiano, *Obscene, Indecent, Immoral, and Offensive*, 279.

48 After 1935, Hollywood films could contain gangster characters, but their criminal activities had to be condemned and their deaths justified.

49 Kingsley, *Dead End*, 520.

50 For an extended analysis of the conventions of classical Hollywood cinema, see David Bordwell, Janet Staiger, and Kristin Thompson, *The Classical Hollywood Cinema: Film Style and Mode of Production to 1960* (London: Routledge, 1985).

51 Laura Mulvey, "Visual Pleasure and Narrative Cinema," in *Film Theory and Criticism: Introductory Readings*, 5th edn., ed. Leo Braudy and Marshall Cohen (New York: Oxford University Press, 1999), 838.

52 Hubbard Keavy, "Kingsley's Play is Modified for Screen Purposes: 'Dead End' is Given Rigid Revision for Uses in the Celluloids," *Washington Post*, May 16, 1937.

53 Leff and Simmons, *The Dame in the Kimono*, 70.

54 Black, *Hollywood Censored*, 280–281.

55 Kingsley, *Dead End*, 499.

56 Leff and Simmons, *The Dame in the Kimono*, 69.

57 Peter Stead, *Film and the Working Class: The Feature Film in British and American Society* (London: Routledge, 1989), 82.

58 Kingsley, *Dead End*, 528.

59 Ibid., 531.

60 Leff and Simmons, *The Dame in the Kimono*, 67.

61 Cesare Zavattini, "Some Ideas on the Cinema," in *Vittorio De Sica: Contemporary Perspectives*, ed. Howard Curle and Stephen Snyder (University of Toronto Press, 2000), 56.

CHAPTER 2

Filming Our Town *(1940) or the problem of "looking at everything hard enough"*

David Eldridge

EMILY:

Softly, more in wonder than in grief.

I can't bear it . . . I love you all, everything. I can't look at everything hard enough.

First staged on Broadway in 1938, Thornton Wilder's Pulitzer Prize-winning *Our Town* has been adapted for television on several occasions, befitting its status as one of America's most performed plays. Small-screen transfers in 1950 and 1977 starred Burgess Meredith and Hal Holbrook, respectively, as the Stage Manager. The acclaimed Lincoln Center revival was filmed for television in 1989, and in 2003 PBS showcased the Westport County Playhouse's production in its *Masterpiece Theatre's American Collection*, featuring Paul Newman. In 1955, NBC even produced *Our Town* as a musical, with Frank Sinatra crooning such songs as "Love and Marriage." Yet, in Hollywood, Wilder's play has been filmed only once, just two years after it premiered. Producer Sol Lesser brought the rights for $75,000 early in 1939, engaged Sam Wood to direct, and in 1940 released *Our Town* through United Artists.[1]

Regrettably, Lesser's movie has gone down in film history as the epitome of Hollywood's philistine insistence on "happy endings." In Wilder's play, young Emily Webb dies in childbirth, with the third act conjuring a mystical scene of Emily's spirit going back in time to observe her former life, before she takes her place among the dead. The film, however, presents this death-experience as if it were all a dream, and Emily simply awakens to live "happily ever after" with her husband George and their new baby. Film historians have dismissed this as the "most embarrassing example" of "the difficulty Hollywood had in dealing with death," while modern viewers typically decry the "magical resurrection" as a clichéd "*Wizard of Oz* technique" that turned "Wilder's message about death" into "a joke."[2] Watching the film for a study undertaken by

Goldman and Kantor, students were universally of the opinion that the revised conclusion took "the entire powerful effect away from the story."[3] Moreover, Lesser's adaptation appears to lack many of the innovative qualities for which the original stage production was celebrated. When *Our Town* opened in theatres, audiences entered to see a "perfectly bare stage" in half-light, with the curtain already up and the back of the building visible. The Stage Manager was already there, watching "the late arrivals in the audience" and bringing on a few tables and chairs to represent the homes of the Webb and the Gibbs families, around whom the play centers. Offered wryly by the Stage Manager as "some scenery for those who think they have to have scenery," these sparse items require the audience to imagine for themselves the town of Grover's Corners.[4] Similarly, the actors mimed most of their activities, whether preparing breakfast or mowing the lawn, with no props. The 2003 PBS adaptation, directed by James Naughton, preserved this theatricalist presentation, including the Stage Manager playing a variety of roles; but in 1940, Lesser and Wood instead went for cinematic realism, creating Grover's Corners in rich visual detail. Consequently, when looking for a "faithful" adaptation, most viewers and critics turn to one of the television versions. In Scott Kennedy's recent documentary *OT: Our Town*, for instance, it is the 1977 Holbrook production that is used to bring the text "alive" for the students of a Compton high school.[5] Kennedy states that he "barely remembered" Lesser's film, except to recall that he "did not like it" because of the "changes which were made."[6]

Blame for these changes has been attributed variously to Lesser's lack of understanding of the play; the reaction of preview audiences to screenings of alternate endings; censorship and the supposedly malign influence of the Production Code; or, as Goldman's students simply put it, "the Almighty Dollar."[7] All of which is rather odd, since scholars have known the truth behind the adaptation since 1941, when correspondence between Wilder and Lesser was published in *Theatre Arts*, and demonstrated, among other things, that Wilder himself had pushed for the new ending: "Emily should live. I've always thought so."[8] In fact, the letters revealed a remarkably collegial working relationship, with Wilder intimately involved: from writing the original treatment with Lesser, to sending detailed considerations throughout the adaptation process, commenting on any alterations that the filmmakers proposed and suggesting his own. Indeed, Wilder found the adaptation to be "deeply stirring."[9] Furthermore, the contemporary critical establishment agreed, extolling it as a "masterful job of superior filmmaking," a "greatly human . . . emotional treat," and a "quietly

persuasive, deeply perceptive, luminous bit of Americana."[10] *Our Town*
may not have been a box-office smash, but it received six Academy Award
nominations, including one for Best Picture, and discerning audiences were
impressed.[11] One British film fan even wrote of how "those of us who
started picturegoing after talkies came have heard others speak with reverence of films like *Potemkin* and *The Cabinet of Dr. Caligari*. Now we can tell
of *Our Town* with equal emotion."[12] Reviewers also asserted that "every bit
of the play's original charm and power have not only been retained but
sometimes augmented," and that all of its "strangeness, charm, supernatur-
alism, and sweetness have been transplanted intact."[13] Such plaudits sharply
challenge modern-day impressions, suggesting that *Our Town* is a film long
overdue for serious consideration. When it comes to a play and film so
concerned with our perception of the details of everyday life, have we been
guilty of not looking hard enough?

"I doubt whether there has ever been a movie as faithful to its original text"

The altered ending and the transference of the play's action from a
Brechtian "empty stage" to Hollywood's "real world" depiction of small-
town America has distracted from the fact that Lesser's *Our Town* is
otherwise remarkably faithful. For the most part, the film maintains the
narrative, structure, pace, and philosophy of Wilder's play. As on the stage,
it opens in a New Hampshire village in 1901, presenting a day in the life of
two neighboring households: Dr. and Mrs. Gibbs and their children,
George and Rebecca; and Editor and Mrs. Webb and their offspring,
Emily and Wally. Little happens of a dramatic nature, but what does
happen are the fundamental things that are common to most people
throughout history – sharing breakfast as a family, chatting with neighbors, going to school or church, growing up. It becomes particularly
evident that George and Emily are falling in love, and the second act
depicts their wedding day three years later, along with a reminiscence of
their courtship to show how "this plan to spend a lifetime together"
began.[14] Then, in 1913, Emily experiences a difficult childbirth. Whether
dying in the play or dreaming of death in the film's sequence, the situation
is the same, as she joins other members of the town, now deceased, while
they wait in an unspecified spiritual realm. Among them are Wally, Mrs.
Gibbs, and Simon Stimson, the church organist. Realizing that she can go
back in time to observe and experience her former life, Emily does so –
choosing to remember her twelfth birthday in the play, or her fourteenth

Figure 2.1a and 2.1b The Minister (Charles Trowbridge) and Emily (Martha Scott) contemplating the thoughts and fears "deep in people's minds" as the wedding of George and Emily approaches.

in the film. It proves, however, to be heartbreaking to witness even the basic routines of daily life, for the perspective of death renders them almost unbearably poignant.

At the textual level, barely a word in the screenplay is not drawn from Wilder's original. Of course, cuts were made. Most were small, such as lines showing that Dr. Gibbs and Editor Webb share similar enthusiasms for history. Others stemmed from the decision that Emily "should live." A scene between undertaker Joe Stoddard and Emily's cousin, Sam Craig, was cut since it made no sense for Sam to return to town for Emily's funeral if she had not actually died. Instead, much of the information originally conveyed in Joe and Sam's dialogue, such as the fact that Stimson had committed suicide, was delivered by the film's equivalent of the Stage Manager character, Mr. Morgan. Archival script materials, moreover, show that such deletions were determined by Lesser and Wilder in the "Plan for Screen Treatment" produced after they spent six days in a New York hotel working together on their initial ideas.[15] Wilder did not want to write the actual screenplay, insistent that Lesser should engage a "skilful craftsman," more "educated" in the "specialized field of cinema" than himself, and so much of the script work was done in conjunction with Frank Craven, who had played *Our Town*'s original Stage Manager.[16] Craven had earlier been a writer for Fox Studios, his credits including the Laurel and Hardy classic *Sons of the Desert* (1933), as well as an adaptation of his own play, *That's Gratitude* (1934); so he had both the experience Lesser needed and the full confidence of Wilder. With Craven, Lesser worked out four different ways of playing the "scene between Emily and the dead"; while Wilder himself contributed "explanatory comments" to detail precisely what he wanted to achieve when Emily, from the perspective of death, is "struck with the fact that human beings . . . move about in self-preoccupied matter-of-factness," rarely aware of the simple beauty of life's experiences.[17] Sending or receiving more than sixty letters and telegrams, Wilder not only watched over the scripts but also advised on issues such as the publicity and the musical score.

Lesser knew that the involvement of Wilder and Craven, as "two of the personalities most closely associated with the play," could be marketed as a measure of his respect for the original.[18] Casting actors who had created the roles on Broadway furthered this too: not only Craven as the Stage Manager/Mr. Morgan, but also Martha Scott as Emily, whose performance was commended by *Variety* as "superb in delicacy and emotional power required in the shadings of the role."[19] Doro Merande and Arthur Allen also made the transfer to screen, as the gossipy Mrs. Soames and scholarly Professor Willard respectively. Lesser banked on this bringing "considerable insurance" in terms of "metropolitan New York prestige," and evidently understood the cultural value that accrues to fidelity in adaptation.[20] In the *New York Times* in June 1940, for example, he promoted the collaboration with Wilder as a long overdue corrective to the notorious "havoc played by the movies with the works of contemporary authors"; and with the publication of the correspondence in *Theatre Arts Monthly*, Lesser presumably hoped to encourage other playwrights to sell the rights to their works to his fledgling "Principal Productions" company. He was certainly ready to pontificate on the "obligations of the motion picture industry toward the men who write for it," and insist that the original author was the "only" person "justified to decree" what changes could be made in the "transcription of his book on to the screen." This, Lesser proclaimed ostentatiously, was "something I have been preaching for a long time."[21]

Because the correspondence was milked for publicity value, it does need to be approached carefully, but it still remains of great value. However, when it is occasionally cited by literary scholars such as Donald Haberman or Nancy Bunge, attitudes are typically dismissive. Haberman asserts that they demonstrate Lesser's "lack of understanding" of the play, giving no credence to the filmmaker's assurance that he intended to "carry this script through to its finality in as faithful a translation of its original as possible."[22] Bunge misleadingly claims that Wilder's tone is one of "resignation" to the inevitability of Hollywood changing his play.[23] However, Wilder never held back from criticizing other adaptations of *Our Town*: he disliked the Sinatra musical version so much that he "exercised his contractual right" to ensure it was never broadcast again.[24] In contrast, regarding Lesser's adaptation, Wilder "doubted whether there has ever been a movie as faithful to its original text."[25]

"Enhancing the scope of the screen"

Of course, the film could have been much more avant-garde, in emulation of the stage production. As the *New Yorker* noted, "we might have been asked to visualize a New Hampshire town while our eyes looked actually upon the machinery that goes to make a movie ... with careful camera shots of cameras, with views of the sets and the lots, of the naked studio itself."[26] This imagery would have paralleled the theatre audience's experience of encountering a bare stage and having to imagine the homes of Grover's Corners or the rows of stores on Main Street simply from the

Stage Manager's brief references. However, contemporary critics were of the opinion that to have tried "filming the feature without sets or backgrounds" would have been an "error," and actually commended Lesser for having attempted "nothing so odd or experimental."[27] Instead, in the film, when Mr. Morgan introduces Grover's Corners, we see an effects shot of the whole town at dawn, nestled in a valley, as a train ("the 5:45 for Boston") is visible crossing the screen. When Joe Crowell delivers the newspapers, he does not mime the action but throws an actual newspaper toward the camera. When Howie Newsome brings the milk, his horse Bessie is on screen pulling the milk-cart that theatre audiences had been asked to picture for themselves. Yet for literary scholars who stress how the theatricalist staging of the play was integral to the effectiveness of Wilder's design, this realism presents a problem.

When developing the play, Wilder was himself expressly critical of the "realism of the detailed portraiture" prevalent in American drama.[28] In Wilder's analysis, loading the stage with props and scenery that sought to realistically reproduce the surface appearances of life deprived "the audience of its imaginative participation" and undercut the theatre's ability to "strain towards a general truth."[29] "Every concrete object on the stage," he claimed, "fixes and narrows the action to one moment in time and place," discouraging the audience from then seeing the wider application of a play's themes to their own experiences. In contrast, overt theatricalism would "release the events from the particular."[30] As Wilder wrote in the preface to the play, *Our Town* was never "offered as a picture of life in a New Hampshire village" for, as specific as all the dates, places, and characters are in the text, the empty staging ensures that they nevertheless remain abstractions.[31] The film, however, is full of the "concrete objects" that Wilder had argued against in the theatre, and reviews highlighted the opulent detail by which turn-of-the-century Grover's Corners was recreated, observing "as fine a collection of atrocious lamps and bric-a-brac, good heavy pots and dishes, rail fences and . . . a Main Street skyscraper of two stories (as of 1903) as you'd find in a museum."[32] This was indeed a problematic aspect of the adaptation, for Wilder's purpose in the play had been to "provoke the audience into participating."[33] The need to imagine objects that did not exist, including the very town itself, required each spectator to construct his or her own vision of how these things would have looked like. Pantomiming of simple acts, such as Editor Webb pushing an imaginary lawnmower, isolated a "specific realistic detail" that the audience could recognize, but which they had to instinctively relate to their own "daily living," in order to picture it.[34] This mode of presentation thus worked to transcend the immediate context of Grover's Corners and underpin the notion that such everyday experiences are "common to all people in all times and in all places."[35] Thereby the audience's own lives were then implicated in the play's principal message: that even the most commonplace moments and actions are worth savouring as aspects of life itself.

The original "Plan for Screen Treatment" sought to convey the universality of the human condition through simple events and suggested starting with a close-up of Morgan "working on a jigsaw puzzle" of the United States, assembled "save for the state of New Hampshire"; which he would complete by inserting "an impressionistic picture of a small town" as the last piece.[36] Implying that Grover's Corners should be seen as only one of "many small towns that make up the United States," Wilder saw the method as echoing the play's "constant allusion to larger dimensions of time and space," as when Rebecca tells George of a letter received by her friend, addressed to: "Jane Crofut; The Crofut Farm; Grover's Corners; Sutton County; New Hampshire; United States of America; Continent of North America; Western Hemisphere; the Earth; the Solar System; the Universe; the Mind of God."[37] As "a reminder that the most ordinary address in an average town has a clear relation to the cosmic order," the film retained Rebecca's reflective moment, but the proposed jigsaw sequence was eventually abandoned as too "mechanical."[38] The filmmakers then considered using an effects shot of a model town. Wilder approved, "if the picture can avoid Giant Man looking over Toy Village," and an element of this remains when Morgan introduces Grover's Corners as if viewing it from a hill above the town.[39] In the end, however, the opening credits were simply superimposed over footage of Frank Craven (in silhouette) strolling along a country path. Although not satisfied, Lesser accepted that the "open air" setting of these establishing shots at least achieved some "feeling of air, broadness and scope" that might approximate the "largeness of design" that Wilder's bare stage had originally conveyed.[40]

They sought to do more, as well, in utilizing the play's sequences of characters addressing the audience. The approach had been used occasionally in films before, notably by French filmmaker Sacha Guitry; but it was still novel enough in 1940 to be regarded by Bosley Crowther as an "exciting technique" that "enhances the scope of the screen tremendously."[41] Morgan asks Editor Webb and Professor Willard to explain something of the history of Grover's Corners, and whereas the play planted actors among the audience to ask questions of Editor Webb, sound-designer Thomas Moulton "projected" voiceovers on the film's soundtrack to create the effect of inquisitors in the cinema shouting out questions from their seats. Guy Kibbee, playing Webb, was directed to "look out into the audience as if trying to locate owner of voice."[42] Additional elements were developed specifically for the medium of film. Craven's offscreen voice interrupts a conversation between Mrs. Webb and Mrs. Gibbs, who react directly to this "voice-of-God" and look up at the camera; and he even directs the cinema projectionist, peering from the screen as if to the back of the picture-house and proclaiming, "Alright operator let's start." At one point Morgan even possesses the ability to move the camera. As a scene ends between Emily and her mother, the shadow of a hand reaches forward as if grabbing the lens; the hand pulls back and is revealed as Craven's, and the setting has switched from Mrs. Webb's parlor to Morgan's store. Wilder praised this "projecting hand" as "invigorating" – and it certainly impressed upon critics that Lesser was not simply using the camera as a "recording machine" that showed only the "reality" before it.[43] Repeatedly breaking the fourth wall, Lesser's *Our Town* drew attention to its own status as a film, attempting to replicate the play's insistence that what happens should be treated as an allegory.

However, the tendency of cinema to fix narrative situations to specific people and places was inescapable, and this underscored Wilder's thinking about the revised ending. Lesser worried that "purists" would be "outraged" at his permitting Emily to survive, but it was Wilder who reassured him.[44] "In a movie," he argued, "you see the people so *close to* that a different relationship is established" between audience and characters:

> In the theatre they are halfway abstractions in an allegory; in the movie they are very concrete. So, insofar as the play is a generalized allegory, she dies – we die – they die; insofar as it's a concrete happening, it's not important that she die.[45]

This assertion that "it's not important that she die" may seem unexpected, but even in the play the cause of Emily's death ("trouble bringing a baby into the world") is "mentioned only as a kind of representation of an ironic truth," and the prime importance of the death is in creating the situation by which she is brought to awareness that life is "too wonderful for anybody to realize."[46] It is the *perspective* of death which gives an ordinary morning in the Webb household its extraordinary poignancy, and the film is still able to maintain this perspective because, until the final moments, the audience is given to assume that Emily *is* dead. Tragedy already inheres in the failing of humanity to recognize the value of each single moment of life. To end the film with Emily's return to the grave, Wilder believed,

Figure 2.2 From the perspective of death, Emily returns to re-experience
her fourteenth birthday. (frame enlargement)

would prove "disproportionately cruel" to a cinema audience that had
"come to love" Emily as a "real" person. "Let her live," advised Wilder, for
"the idea will have been imparted anyway."[47]

"We don't have time to look at one another"

Such aspects of the correspondence are attention-grabbing; yet to fully
understand the film, one needs to acknowledge the extent to which the
letters and scripting materials demonstrate how, rather than allowing the
visual details of cinema to compromise Wilder's themes, the filmmakers
continually searched for "unconventional" methods of imparting the play's
philosophy through a different medium.[48] In this quest, the work of
celebrated production designer William Cameron Menzies was crucial.
Himself a scion of small-town New England, born in New Haven,
Connecticut in 1896, Menzies had set new standards of design in
Hollywood since winning the first ever Oscar for Best Art Direction in
1928. He reached perhaps the apogee of his artistry immediately before

working on *Our Town*, spending a year storyboarding David Selznick's *Gone with the Wind* (1939), with his the "final word" on every aspect of the epic's overall look.[49] Thus acclaimed for having "elevated the Hollywood film to an art form," Menzies and his associate Harry Horner realized over 1,200 sketches for scenes, costumes, lighting, and camera angles for *Our Town*, which director Sam Wood followed with care.[50]

His work can be seen, for example, in the wedding of George and Emily. Wilder was concerned that, "realistically done," it "won't be interesting enough." After all, he had never seen an onscreen wedding "that followed through normally. Either it was interrupted ... or it showed the bride hating the groom ... or some other irregularity."[51] In this case, however, they could not artificially introduce dramatic incidents to the scene since it was imperative to the play's universalism that the ceremony be entirely traditional and normal: "the wedding of an Emily Webb and a George Gibbs is scarcely the point, for the wedding is everybody's."[52] Film audiences, however, would potentially find the scene something of a "let down when it all runs through as expected."[53] Menzies's response was to inject "novelty" through unusual shots that present the congregation in only the bottom third of the screen, their heads just visible over the pews. The remaining space above them is empty, except for an atmospheric projection of light from a church window. This low horizon brings the wedding guests down to the level of the seated cinema audience, fostering the sense of "identification" that Wilder wanted. Menzies also enhanced the play's use of "thinking aloud passages," whereby characters gave voice to their thoughts and fears: the Minister musing about having "married two hundred couples in my day"; Mrs. Webb on the verge of tears because her daughter will be "going out of my house"; Emily wishing she could "stay for a while just as I am."[54] In the play, the actors "stepped out" of the action and directed these thoughts to the audience; but the film reproduces them as voiceovers, exposing the "confusion way down deep in people's minds" that goes on "even at a good wedding."[55] Menzies set the camera in close to the faces of these characters as they think. Although now a common device, these close-ups were then unusual enough to be regarded as innovative in providing an "internal revelation" that offered a different perspective to the film's otherwise "external glance" at life in Grover's Corners.[56] The tightness of the close-ups was also seen as capturing something of the play's "non-use of scenery" by "eliminating scene proportions."[57] Moreover, Menzies framed these close-ups suggestively. Preparing for the ceremony, the Minister is seen reflected in a wardrobe mirror, and part of the window behind him is also reflected to create the symbolic image of a cross beside him. Thus, while his thoughts about weddings rarely being interesting may seem slightly inappropriate, the visuals remind the viewer of this man's relationship to God and the eternal qualities of the institution he presides over. By contrast, when Emily is seen, the background is out of focus and ethereal, with the lighting designed so that her wedding veil appears luminous. This foreshadows the way she will be presented after death, still wearing this wedding dress.

The sequence surrounding Emily's death presented Menzies with the opportunity to create something particularly unusual. The half-world of Emily's delirium, "where the dead live again, the past is present, and where time has no meaning," lent itself to imagery more associated with German Expressionist cinema than the naturalism that otherwise dominated the film's design.[58] Light from the door cuts the scene at an odd angle, as a nurse enters in the very close foreground. Emily, desperately ill in bed, looks tiny as Dr. Gibbs kneels beside her; and the shadow he casts looms over the patient as an ominous spectre of death. The camera then pans across the bedroom wall, to hold on a number of photographs and tintype images of family and friends. Lesser and Wilder conceived of this approach at their first meeting, and indicated that one of the portraits should be identifiable as Mrs. Gibbs, and another as Emily's brother, Wally, who (as the audience is informed) had died sometime earlier from a burst appendix. This arrangement of photographs then blurs, dissolving into a matching formation of headstones in the cemetery. A panning shot of the folds and bumps in Emily's patchwork bedspread likewise blurs into the "rise and fall of the hills" surrounding Grover's Corners, as the audience sees a funeral procession crossing that countryside.[59]

Menzies then adopted an aspect from the stage production, "where deep emotion is expressed by the tragic demeanour of a huddled group of mourners under umbrellas."[60] The pathos and dignity conveyed simply by a cluster of black umbrellas was regarded as an "unforgettable" theatrical image, and the filmmakers preserved it, portraying the scene in long shot except for a brief cut to identify George and Doctor Gibbs bowed in grief.[61] Otherwise "the coffin and pallbearers are still unseen, and the grave itself is curtained by the surrounding forms."[62] However, Menzies expanded on this, as the wet umbrellas refract pinpoints of light. Using this halation to particular effect, light "then strikes the corners of several tombstones which are still wet from the recent rain."[63] As the scene fades into darkness, these pricks of light take on the appearance of stars in the night sky – a "vast expanse" which then dissolves to a remarkable image of the dead inhabitants of the cemetery, each marked by a fading star, standing still where their gravestones once were.[64]

The play had simply used chairs to represent the tombstones, but the film presents the graves in a similar formation to the photographs above Emily's bed. Those who then stand in the cemetery "appear posed as they were in photograph. They stare straight ahead with immobile faces, and unseeing eyes."[65] Among the dead are Wally, Mrs. Gibbs, Mrs. Soames, and Simon Stimson, enabling Emily to commune with their spirits. Yet whereas in the play the dialogue alone had to convey the sense that Emily was not ready to "let hold of the earth" and join the rest of the dead, the film reinforced this visually.[66] Emily appears in full-length shot, bathed in a pillar of white light and, unlike the motionless dead, she can move, turn, and raise her arms. As Wilder realized, in presenting Emily this way, "we are legitimately preparing for the fact that she is different" – and thus that she "may possibly and finally go back to life itself."[67]

When Emily does look back on her birthday, Morgan is not her "spiritual guide," in the way that the Stage Manager is in the play. Having made Morgan an identifiable inhabitant of Grover's Corners, Wilder agreed that his presence in the sequence would complicate "the impression that all the intervening material is a dream or hallucination."[68] Emily instead returns to the past on her own volition, and the cinematic technique of double-exposure, used often in Hollywood's representation of ghosts, enables her spirit to witness the same things as in the play. She still waxes lyrical over the white picket fence that she had loved but forgotten; watches her mother preparing breakfast and her father returning home, and wonders "why did they ever get old"; and sees George bringing her a present (changed from a postcard album in the play to a photograph album in the film, to underscore the role that photographs play in Emily's delirium). Most importantly, superimposition enabled Emily to witness her younger self and for both to appear on the screen at the same time. On the stage, Martha Scott had to perform as if Emily's character was split in two, both "seeing" the earlier day and "living" it as well – and Mrs. Webb can hear her when she speaks as the thirteen-year-old Emily. On film, however, Emily's attempts to communicate to her mother "the splendour of life which she now sees" are thwarted – enhancing Emily's agony as she is "struck with the fact that human beings do fairly well move about in self-preoccupied matter of factness."[69] Indeed, not only are the living unable to hear or see her, but the use of superimposition means that Emily's family can now move *through* her insubstantial form, utterly oblivious to her presence. This effect brings a new dimension to Emily's lament that life "goes so fast, we don't have time to look at one another."[70]

"To find a value above all price from the smallest events of our daily life"

For all that the dream sequence was regarded at the time of release as "perhaps one of the most unusual scenes ever filmed," the most over-looked aspects of the film's originality in adaptation are actually the most ordinary – a point which is, of course, entirely pertinent to Wilder's message.[71] Lesser encouraged his collaborators to find ways of "raising" everyday life to "a higher plane than it has sometimes occupied," and to this end less obtrusive techniques were employed.[72] Cross-cut editing, for example, enhanced the opening scenes of breakfast at the Webb and Gibbs households. On stage, basic representations of both homes were present simultaneously, with dialogue between the Gibbs family members echoed by conversations in the Webb kitchen. Both mothers were seen calling their children down for breakfast at exactly the same time. Through such means, their specific actions were rendered as generalizations – this is how *all* families are. Cross-cutting back and forth from Mrs. Webb to Mrs. Gibbs achieved the same effect, to the point where the viewer almost loses track of which family they are looking at. Of similar intent was the use of deliberate repetition, which, for Wilder, played a vital role in revealing the underlying "pattern of life."[73] Act 2 of the play begins with a recurrence of ordinary events very similar to the way in which they happened at the start of Act 1: simple things such as the two housewives donning their aprons to start the day; the newspapers being delivered; or Howie dispensing the milk. On screen, visual markers show that things have changed over the intervening two years. Howie now brings milk in bottles rather than pouring it from a big can, and a different Crowell brother (Si rather than Joe) delivers the newspaper. Yet the fundamental pattern of the morning has barely been altered, and Wood underscores this by mirroring the images. On both mornings, we see the mothers going about their business, by peering at them through their respective windows. The shot of Si making his round is presented in exactly the same way as Joe was originally seen, framed between two trees and tossing the rolled newspaper toward the camera. Even as the details change, the presentation emphasizes continuity and thus the habitual, enduring aspects of life.

Figure 2.3 The use of props and unusual perspectives create curiosity about "details of daily life." (frame enlargement)

Wilder's intention for audiences to contemplate the "countless 'unimportant' details of our daily life" and realize their significance and beauty, also found its own cinematic expression, as Menzies discovered ways of "introducing properties" intended to "visualize something deeper."[74] Many of the shots of life in Grover's Corners are rendered intriguing because of the way that specific objects dominate the foreground. In the Gibbs household a waterpump by the kitchen sink looms larger than Dr. Gibbs. We can barely see Wally eating his breakfast, for only the top of his head is visible over a book propped up on a sugarbowl, both of which are rendered huge by Menzies's trick of perspective and low horizon line. When we look through Mrs. Gibbs's window on the morning of the wedding, our view of her bustling about in the background is obscured by giant flowerpots and an oversized coffee grinder. An elaborate soda fountain bisects the screen when Emily and George enter Morgan's store; and even at the cemetery, Morgan is dwarfed by gravestones which dictate our line of vision. This framing does not simply indulge Menzies's love of unusual angles; it actually serves the text. The effect of obstructing our view is provocative. Action is clearly taking place *behind* the objects, partially visible in Bert Glennon's deep-focus photography, increasing the audience's desire to see it. Yet what is actually going on is entirely humdrum – Howie pouring milk into Mrs. Webb's jug, or Wally eating his cereal. It is only the compositions which make these "details of daily life" of special interest. Thus, the curiosity that Wilder achieved on stage by compelling actors to mime in the absence of props was achieved on screen by the very use of props.

When the effect worked, the spectator found himself "taking in, almost for the first time, everything that comes within the framework of the screen."[75] And everything that was portrayed – whether objects, events, or people – was rendered inherently significant simply by being included on screen. That routine occurrences, such as deliverymen making their rounds, choir practice, or neighbors stringing beans, actually become the subject-matter of a film (or a play) accords them the status of "art." Art takes the "materials of everyday life" and challenges our "habitual perceptions" by placing that material in new contexts and new patterns – "defamiliarizing ordinary reality."[76] In the balancing act achieved in *Our Town*, that which is trivial is paradoxically significant. The first breakfast morning scene is merely an average occurrence on an average day. Yet because the audience has never before observed a Gibbs family breakfast, this unpretentious scene acquires its own authority as a novel situation. Raised by Menzies to an aesthetic experience, it also gains a beauty that might then alter the viewer's perception of such ordinary events in their own lives. As Wilder sought to impress in Emily's final scenes, her perspective enables her to see "beauties unrealized, even while living. Unimportant things – ticking clocks, newly ironed dresses, going to bed and waking up – take on new significance and beauty."[77] By encouraging audiences to view Grover's Corners from that perspective *throughout* the film, Wilder's "attempt to find a value above all price from the smallest events of our daily life" was adapted successfully.[78]

Conclusion

Lesser regarded *Our Town* as the best film of his career. Wilder, as well as regarding it as exceptionally faithful, welcomed particularly the impact of the revised ending. Some critics of the play had interpreted Emily's cry "that the world and the relationships in the world are too dear for anybody to realize them" as a "really pessimistic" repudiation of life.[79] In the play's text, this "misunderstanding" was reinforced when Emily ultimately takes her place among the dead and Simon Stimson states harshly: "Now you know! That's what it was to be alive. To move about in a cloud of ignorance ... To be always at the mercy of one self-centered passion or another."[80] These severe words apparently often undercut the playwright's desire for audiences to appreciate how "it was worthwhile having been alive at all, even under those conditions."[81] Since Emily returned to life in the film, this scene no longer existed; and the movie concludes instead with Morgan delivering a line transposed from earlier in the play: "It's like what one of those Midwestern poets said, 'You gotta love life to have life, and you gotta have life to love life.'"[82] Although it can be dismissed as "less profound," the "happy ending" that so many have criticized was precisely what Wilder liked best about the adaptation, hoping "it might send the audience home with a better taste in their mouth."[83]

It would, however, be misleading to suggest that the movie is a neglected classic, the perfect example of adapting an unconventional play. The changed ending *does* lack the pathos of the original, wherein Emily cannot benefit from having come to see life more clearly, because "she cannot live her life again, and has no future life that she can change."[84] Technically, there is much to admire in Menzies's ability to "take the most ordinary thing in a picture and make it so cinematically fascinating," yet for every critic who found the final reel to be "astonishingly mystical," another found the effects "rather swamping."[85] Moreover, the cinematic equivalences to Wilder's theatrical techniques were lost on even some of the most appreciative reviewers, who regarded, for instance, the cross-cutting between the breakfast scenes as "choppy and stilted" rather than integral to the theme.[86] As *Life* magazine suggested, while at times the film was "beautifully and profoundly moving," there were other moments at which, "because of its arbitrary theatrical form, it fits the screen uneasily."[87]

Additionally, there was one effect of the movie's realistic mise en scène which could not be avoided: the promotion of nostalgia. The play is often regarded as "a memorial to the myth of the sweet past in rural America," but that was never Wilder's intention.[88] Throughout performances, he had been adamant that nostalgia and sentiment "had to be eliminated."[89] During the making of the film, he even supported a short-lived idea to relocate events to the 1920s, because it would at least "close out those horse-and-buggy pre-automobile days which may have been a part of the

much-discussed 'nostalgia' which people found in the play."[90] Emily's
sadness when revisiting her youth stems not from a yearning for the "good
old days," but instead from the recognition that few "human beings ever
realize life where they live it – every, every minute."[91] Wilder wanted
audiences to "learn to live more fully in the moment," not look back-
ward.[92] The theatre's empty stage requires spectators to imagine the
settings within their own mind's eye, so any nostalgic effect is determined
by what they themselves bring to the play. The screenplay, however, called
for Grover's Corners to be filled with shopfronts that change to "mark the
improvements that would have been made from 1904 and 1913," towns-
people "attired in keeping with the period," and "old fashioned" cash-
registers, hatracks, and photograph frames that "we know as the early part
of this century."[93] Wood did indeed shoot particular period objects to
defamiliarizing effect, and critics may have found it "spell-binding," but
there is no escaping the fact that the realistic scenery and properties do tie
Our Town to a particular time and place and nostalgically "transport one
back to yesterday."[94]

Sometime after the film's release, if not during its production,
Wilder apparently realized this. In 1938, developing his ideas for theatrical works like *Our Town*, which could "combine the particular and
universal truth," he had expressed even greater faith in the cinema's
potential.[95] "If in a play," he wrote, "you represent time and space
with great freedom, you'll inevitably achieve novelty of form, and
novelty of form renews that essential quality, vitality of subject matter.
The films have [already] established a tremendous new freedom of
treatment."[96] With flashbacks, cross-cutting, voiceovers, depth-of-field
techniques, and Gothic special effects, Lesser's production sought to
accentuate such "freedom of treatment." Yet by the 1950s, Wilder was
including filmmakers among modern culture's "tyrants of imagination."[97] Citing Laurence Olivier's 1948 film version of *Hamlet* as one
which "pre-empted the whole stage of individual imagination," he
contrasted the film's "photographically exact depiction of people, dress
and atmosphere" with Shakespeare's ability to conjure in the minds of
audiences, "the forlornness of the graveyard scene trembling in the
shadow of absolute nihilism" with just "a few glorious sentences."[98]
"The camera," Wilder concluded, "is the recorder of the specific, and
imaginative literature does not move in that way."[99] Sadly, for all of
his initial enthusiasm for the project, it was probably as much
Lesser's adaptation of *Our Town* as Olivier's *Hamlet* that made
him feel this way.

Endnotes

1 American Film Institute, *American Film Institute Catalogue: Feature Films, 1931–1940* (Berkeley: University of California Press, 1993), 1590.

2 Michael Anderegg, "Home Front America and the Denial of Death in MGM's *The Human Comedy*," *Cinema Journal* 34.1 (1994), 16; Internet Movie Database User Reviews for *Our Town*, www.imdb.com/title/tt0032881/usercomments.

3 Susan Goldman and Ronald Kantor, "The Limits of Poetic License," *Poetics*, 22.1–2 (1993), 141.

4 References to the text of the play draw on the edition presented in Thornton Wilder, *Collected Plays and Writings on Theater* (hereafter *CP*) (New York: The Library of America, 2007), 149.

5 *OT: Our Town* (2002, Scott Kennedy).

6 Email correspondence between author and Scott Kennedy, October 10, 2010.

7 Donald Haberman, *The Plays of Thornton Wilder: A Critical Study* (Middletown, CT: Wesleyan University Press, 1967), 78; Anthony Slide, "*Our Town*" in *Our Town* clipping file, Margaret Herrick Library, Beverly Hills, CA (AMPAS); www.imdb.com/title/tt0032881/usercomments; Goldman and Kantor, "The Limits of Poetic License," 142.

8 "*Our Town*: From Stage to Screen. A Correspondence Between Thornton Wilder and Sol Lesser" was published in *Theatre Arts* 24 (November 1940), 815–824. This selection of correspondence is reproduced in Wilder, *CP*, 663–681, and references to the letters will draw primarily from this text. However, in the Sol Lesser Papers held at the University of Southern California (USC), unedited copies of Wilder's letters and telegrams to Lesser are available and I will refer to that source when the content differs.

9 Thornton Wilder to Sol Lesser, July 11, 1940, "Thornton Wilder Letters," Sol Lesser Collection, Box 7, USC.

10 *Hollywood Reporter*, May 10, 1940; Welford Beaton, *Hollywood Spectator*, June 1, 1940, 5; Sheridan Ames, *Rob Wagner's Script*, June 15, 1940, 16.

11 *Our Town* received Academy Award nominations for Best Picture, Best Actress in a Leading Role, Best Art Direction, Best Sound Recording, and two for Best Score.

12 "Reader's Review," *Picturegoer*, January 23, 1941, 16.

13 *Philadelphia Record* n.d., *Our Town* clipping file, AMPAS; "Movie of the Week," *Life*, May 27, 1940, 53.

14 Wilder, *CP*, 182.

15 "*Our Town*: Plan for Screen Treatment," September 12, 1939, Thornton Wilder Papers, YCAL MSS108, Box 80, f.2089, Yale Collection of American Literature, Beinecke Rare Book and Manuscript Library.

16 Theodore Kuper, *Reminiscences of Sol Lesser* (Oral Research Office, Columbia University, 1971), 102.

17 "Versions A, B, C and D" of "Scene Between Emily and the Dead," dating from December 16, 1939, can be found in the Wilder Papers, YCAL MSS108,

Box 80, f.2089; "Explanatory Comment by Mr. Wilder," in "*Our Town*: Plan for Screen Treatment," September 12, 1939, 18.

18 "Wilder, Craven Collaborate," *Los Angeles Times*, June 13, 1940, 16.

19 *Variety*, May 10, 1940.

20 Lesser to Wilder, February 21, 1940, *CP*, 680.

21 Sol Lesser, "Paging Thornton Wilder," *New York Times*, June 9, 1940.

22 Haberman, *Plays*, 78; Lesser to Wilder, November 2, 1939, *CP*, 668.

23 Nancy Bunge, "The Social Realism of *Our Town*: A Study in Misunderstanding," in Martin J. Blank, ed., *Thornton Wilder: New Essays* (West Cornwall, CT: Locust Hill Press, 1999), 354.

24 Sammy Cahn, *I Should Care* (New York: Arbor House, 1974), 156.

25 Wilder to Lesser, October 7, 1939, *CP*, 664.

26 *New Yorker*, June 18, 1940.

27 Richard Griffith, "*Our Town* Praise Sung in New York," *Los Angeles Times*, June 24, 1940, 11; *New Yorker*, June 18, 1940.

28 Among examples of such works, he included Eugene O'Neill's *Desire under the Elms*. Mildred Kuner, *Thornton Wilder: The Bright and the Dark* (New York: Crowell, 1972), 125.

29 Rex Burbank, *Thornton Wilder* (Boston: Twayne, 1978), 86–87.

30 Quoted in Haberman, *Our Town: An American Play* (Boston, MA: Twayne, 1989), 19–20.

31 Wilder, "Preface to Three Plays," in *CP*, 686.

32 Otis Ferguson, *New Republic*, June 17, 1940.

33 Kuner, *Thornton Wilder*, 126.

34 Haberman, *Our Town*, 44.

35 Blank, *Thornton Wilder*, xi.

36 "*Our Town*: Plan for Screen Treatment," 1. Revised First Draft Screenplay, October 20, 1939, 1–2, Wilder Papers, YCAL MSS108, Box 80, f.2091.

37 Lesser to Wilder, January 5, 1940, *CP*, 673; Wilder to Lesser, October 7, 1939, *CP*, 664.

38 David Castronovo, "*Our Town* as Folk Art," in Thomas Siebold, ed., *Readings on* Our Town (San Diego, CA: Greenhaven Press, 2000), 144; Lesser to Wilder, January 5, 1940, *CP*, 673.

39 Wilder to Lesser, November 12, 1939, *CP*, 672.

40 Lesser to Wilder, January 17, 1940, *CP*, 677; Wilder to Lesser, January 15, 1940, *CP*, 676.

41 *New York Times*, June 14, 1940.

42 First Rough Draft Screenplay, September 23, 1939, 27, Wilder Papers, YCAL MSS108, Box 80, f.2090.

43 Wilder to Lesser, October 29, 1939, Lesser Collection, USC; *New York Times*, June 14, 1940

44 Lesser to Wilder, March 21, 1940, *CP*, 680.

45 Wilder to Lesser, Easter Night, 1940, *CP*, 681.

46 Haberman, *Our Town*, 86; *CP*, 207.

47 Wilder to Lesser, Easter Night, 1940, *CP*, 681.

48 Lesser to Wilder, January 5, 1940, *CP*, 673.

49 David Bordwell, "William Cameron Menzies," March 2010, www.davidbordwell. net/essays/menzies.php.

50 "Movie of the Week," *Life*, May 27, 1940.

51 Wilder to Lesser, October 9, 1939, *CP*, 665–666.

52 Haberman, *Plays*, 63.

53 Wilder to Lesser, October 9, 1939, *CP*, 666.

54 Ibid.; *CP*, 190–192.

55 Ibid., 189.

56 *New York Times*, June 14, 1940.

57 Lesser to Wilder, January 9, 1940, *CP*, 674.

58 Synopsis in *Our Town* file, Production Code Administration Files, AMPAS.

59 "Version A" of "Scene Between Emily and the Dead," December 16, 1939, Wilder Papers, YCAL MSS108, Box 80, f.2089.

60 *Variety*, January 26, 1938.

61 Haberman, *Our Town*, 9, quoting Stark Young of *New Republic*.

62 "Version A" of "Scene Between Emily and the Dead."

63 Lesser to Wilder, January 17, 1940, *CP*, 677–678.

64 Ibid.

65 Revised First Draft Screenplay, October 20, 1939, 112.

66 *CP*, 197.

67 Wilder to Lesser, December 31, 1939, Lesser Collection, USC.

68 Wilder to Lesser, Easter Night, 1940, Lesser Collection, USC.

69 Basil Wright, *The Spectator*, November 29, 1940, 579; Wilder, "Explanatory Comment."

70 *CP*, 207.

71 "A Guide to the Study of the Screen Version of *Our Town*," *Photoplay Studies* 6.13 (1940).

72 Ibid.

73 See Haberman, *Our Town*, 40.

74 Wilder, "Preface for *Our Town*," in *CP*, 657; Lesser to Wilder, January 5, 1940, *CP*, 673.

75 *New Statesman*, November 30, 1940.

76 See Kristin Thompson, *Breaking the Glass Armor: Neoformalist Film Analysis* (Princeton University Press, 1988), 10–11.

77 "Version A" of "Scene Between Emily and the Dead."

78 Wilder, "Preface to Three Plays," in *CP*, 686.

79 Wilder, "Explanatory Comment."

80 *CP*, 207–208.

81 Wilder, "Explanatory Comment."

82 *CP*, 175.

83 Goldman and Kantor, 138; Wilder to Lesser, Easter Night, 1940, Lesser Collection, USC.

84 Haberman, *Our Town*, 87.

85 Ted Haworth, quoted in Vincent Lo Brutto, *By Design: Interviews with Film Production Designers* (Westport, CT: Praeger, 1992), 21; *The Spectator*, November 29, 1940, 579; *New Statesman*, November 30, 1940.

86 Otis Ferguson, *New Republic*, June 17, 1940.

87 *Life*, May 27, 1940.

88 Harold Clurman, quoted in Bunge, "The Social Realism of *Our Town*," 353.

89 Haberman, *Our Town*, 98.

90 Wilder to Lesser, October 7, 1939, Lesser Collection, USC.

91 *CP*, 207.

92 Bunge, "The Social Realism of *Our Town*," 353.

93 "Version A" of "Scene Between Emily and the Dead," 103; First Rough Draft Screenplay, 33, 94.

94 Richard Sheridan Ames, *Rob Wagner's Script*, June 15, 1940, 16.

95 Burbank, *Thornton Wilder*, 85.

96 "Stage Aside: From Thornton Wilder, 1938," in Jackson Bryar, ed., *Conversations with Thornton Wilder* (Jackson: University Press of Mississippi, 1992), 19–20.

97 "Against the Tyrants of Imagination, 1956," in Bryar, *Conversations with Thornton Wilder*, 62.

98 Ibid.

99 "Accept Crisis and Enjoy It, Advises Famed Author," in Bryar, *Conversations with Thornton Wilder*, 84–85.

CHAPTER 3

Screening Death of a Salesman: *Arthur Miller's cinema and its discontents*

R. Barton Palmer

Reaching beyond the already converted?

Along with Eugene O'Neill and Tennessee Williams, Arthur Miller was one of the playwrights who in the immediate postwar era proved that the Broadway stage could rival in seriousness and aesthetic brilliance the modernist drama of Europe. In the midst of wrenching cultural change and economic hardship, the European theatre was then enjoying a remarkable renaissance, with the ever-increasing international prominence of such luminaries as Jean Genet, Samuel Beckett, and Bertolt Brecht (who had just returned to Germany after the onset of the Red Scare investigations in Hollywood). Commercially speaking, the New York stage, with its commitment to providing a range of offerings from light entertainment to provocative drama, had found itself in continual decline since the 1920s.[1] The theatre district had gradually moved further uptown as more venues south of Times Square were forced to close because of declining attendance and hostile economics. But this was a time when not the impresario (in the mold of, say, Flo Ziegfeld), but rather the playwright was king. Interestingly, the less profitable that the New York stage became and the more its infrastructure dwindled or crumbled, the more cultural prestige its talented authors came to enjoy. To judge from the successful productions of the period, American theatregoers as the 1950s began were increasingly receptive to serious drama, however much they might not have supported such demanding intellectual engagement as a steady diet.

This taste for aesthetic challenge found its center in the lionizing of authors who were interested in providing more than witty entertainment in the tradition, for example, of the hugely profitable but essentially commercial collaborations between producers and writers such as Vinton Freedley and Cole Porter, the mainstay professionals of an earlier Broadway. Eugene O'Neill (who would die in 1953) had earlier brought the penetrating realism of Chekhov and Strindberg to the American stage,

Figure 3.1 Benedek's film opens with a shot of Willy Loman (Fredric March) returning from a business trip, defined less by family or home and more by the job at which he is progressively failing. (frame enlargement)

but, ironically, the greatest popularity he came to enjoy was either at the end of his career or posthumously. What would become three of his most acclaimed plays saw their initial commercial productions after the end of the war, including, most importantly, *Long Day's Journey into Night* (written in 1941, but debuted on Broadway in 1956). *Long Day's Journey* would win the Pulitzer Prize the following year. Achieving an initial success in 1945 with *The Glass Menagerie*, Tennessee Williams established himself as a major figure with *A Streetcar Named Desire*, whose 1947 Broadway production was one of the cultural landmarks of the era, receiving the Pulitzer in 1948. Like Williams, after an initial success that promised even more (*All My Sons*, which also debuted on Broadway in 1947), Miller broke new ground the next year with his own masterpiece, *Death of a Salesman*, which won the 1949 Pulitzer as Miller's career seemed to follow the path laid out by Williams.[2] Both of these landmark plays, among the best that ever emerged from the national theatre, offered tragic visions of the American experience. In *Streetcar*, Blanche DuBois is undone by a sexual desire that can find no legitimate or permanent form of expression, driving her into madness, while in *Salesman* Willy Loman discovers that a life devoted to selling goods by selling himself has brought no financial security even as it has alienated him from the family he had been eager to support and see prosper. If in the end Blanche finds a kind of refuge in psychotic disconnection, Willy seeks redemption in a suicide that he hopes will bestow on his wife and sons the dubious benefits of a life insurance payout.

The two young talents had much in common, as Miller would suggest in his autobiography. Williams, he said, was the only contemporary writer who shared with him the belief that a theatre "that did not want to change the world" was not "worth my time."[3] Miller was inclined to the view that contemporary Broadway was not particularly welcoming of challenging and engaging art. Instead, for him it was "a temple rotted out with commercialized junk." "Only by accident" did a play worthy of the name manage to get produced, and then only "under some disguise of popular cultural coloration such as a movie star in a leading role."[4] And yet in practice Miller did not always embrace such self-limiting elitism. After all, the Broadway stage provided both Williams and him with main chances. The reason was simple. Miller admitted that there was in the era "a certain balance within the audience ... between the alienated and the conformist," and that these constituencies with different tastes actually benefitted Williams, who would otherwise have been "relieved of the pressure to extend himself beyond a supportive culture environment."[5]

Williams, then, was writing for a group that, as Miller puts it, represented "more or less, all of America."[6] His work, Miller opined, might have been "narrowed" and "reduced in intensity" had he not been pressured to please a broad section of the public.[7] Much the same must surely be said of Miller's own theatre since, as he says, an American avant-garde was obligated to avoid the imitation of Brecht and Shaw if interested in reaching beyond those "already converted to its ways."[8] However much he may have felt constricted by the need to adapt his more polymorphous vision (always heavily influenced by European developments) to traditional notions of dramatic realism, psychological depth, and agonistic structure, Williams obviously agreed. Of course, he never found such compromises easy early in his career. Tellingly, he would abandon artistic caution after becoming a "bankable" name who could easily obtain backing even for properties that were increasingly more modernist or experimental. Eschewing the accessibility and emotional engagement theatregoers continued to desire, Williams then forfeited the broad popularity he had once enjoyed, as Miller might have predicted.

For the youthful Williams, of course, reaching beyond the comfortably approving world of high bourgeois New York literati meant more than addressing the average theatregoer. More importantly, from the beginning he focused on selling his work to Hollywood, then as now the great provider of performance-based narrative for general audiences. Concerned, and rightly so, that adaptation might dilute or disfigure his vision, Williams also participated insofar as practical and possible in the transference of his works to the silver screen. No doubt, it was because of the playwright's fruitful and energized partnership with director Elia Kazan that *Streetcar* became a landmark film that was nominated for Best Picture award of 1951. Williams played a central role in securing Kazan's participation in the project, and the director's show-business savvy, not to mention his broad talent, proved vital to the film's success. Because of Williams's deep interest in and support of the production, *Streetcar* became a film that pushed its surprised but approving audience toward an engagement with complex characters and controversial themes (including and especially the then surprising energies of female sexuality). Such material had hitherto been only cautiously explored by Hollywood, if at all. If, as Miller suggested, *Streetcar* was "flashier," "sexier," and thus "commercially successful," the play manifested a "unique voice" that persuaded Miller he "could go more in that direction with confidence."[9]

Setting out the corpse of a believer

In an age when the domestic industry, journalistic critics, and the viewing public considered the "movies" to be entertainment, not art, the popularity achieved by *Streetcar* was an amazing feat. Despite *Streetcar*'s many critical accolades and obvious pre-soldness (of key importance to flop-averse studio executives), there had been initially comparatively little interest among American producers in purchasing the screen rights. To put it in the general vision of the national postwar scene described by Miller, the resistance came from "the inbuilt inertia of a society that always wants to deny change and the pain it necessarily involves." For filmmakers like Kazan and Williams, the push-back came from the Production Code Administration, an industry-sponsored watchdog office that had been set up in 1934 to enforce a prescriptive and proscriptive code that was essentially hostile to modernist concepts of drama and narrative. Only films with a PCA certificate of approval were generally acceptable to exhibitors. A further hurdle for films to scale, once they were released for exhibition, was the Legion of Decency, a Catholic lay organization whose chief function was to rate Hollywood releases as either acceptable or in varying degrees unacceptable for Catholic viewers.[10] Like the PCA, the Legion promoted a conservative, traditional view of film art. Not unexpectedly, *Streetcar* encountered considerable difficulties from both the PCA and the Legion. The project's progress through the various stages of PCA review was contentious and difficult. Legion reviewers were initially appalled by the film's "carnality," and only last-minute changes (made without the consent or knowledge of either Kazan or Williams) persuaded that influential organization to withdraw its judgment of "condemned."

In the final analysis, it was the indefatigable perseverance of Williams and Kazan that led to the making and then successful release of a screen version of the play that was in all essentials faithful to what Broadway theatregoers had been privileged to see.[11] If Williams wanted to "change the world" with his drama, with the Hollywood version of *Streetcar* he managed to do so. As PCA executive Geoffrey Shurlock admitted: "for the first time we were confronted with a picture that was obviously not family entertainment . . . *Streetcar* broke the barrier . . . Tennessee Williams was something new to movies . . . The stage got a shock from Tennessee Williams. We got twice the shock. Now we know that a good deal of what we decide in censoring movies is not morality but taste. It began with *Streetcar*."[12] The clear implication is that because of its evident artistry, the film Williams and Kazan produced could not be judged simply on moral terms. This decision strikingly anticipates, even as it likely affected, how American culture was then moving toward a redemptive theory that isolates art from legal censure and actionability, effectively bracketing off judgments based on the long-hallowed concept of "obscenity."

For Arthur Miller, the Broadway success of Williams's play was also a signally transformative event. With *Streetcar*, Miller thought, Williams had given his fellow playwrights "the license to speak at full throat," not worrying excessively about entrenched opinion or the cultural status quo.[13] To some degree, they could, in Miller's view, disregard the "hints and pretexts of the natural" in building up a drama around verbal interchange and monologue, revealing depths of character, as had Williams, through infiltrating it "with a kind of superconsciousness," going beyond his model to create a play in which different objects of consciousness produce different levels and time values of "the real."[14] But if Miller followed the path blazed by Williams in terms of the modification (never wholesale abandon) of conventional realism, he did not seek out Hollywood as the most convenient and effective venue for reaching a larger audience so that he might fulfill his avowed aim to address "the whole

American mix" by offering in dramatic form "a wholeness of experience that would not require specialists or a coterie to be understood."[15]

Instead, for Miller, "the heart of decadence was Hollywood," and just the fact that Lillian Hellman was comfortable in Tinsel Town and had been accepted by leading figures in the industry was reason enough to dismiss her as a serious playwright. His judgment was harsh: "it did seem unlikely that a genuine light-bearer could be spending so much of her life working for Sam Goldwyn and the other merchants."[16] Though eager for all his suitable properties to be adapted for the screen, Williams apparently was sufficiently uncomfortable with most (if not all) Hollywood types to escape a similar condemnation. For Miller, Williams was always a "genuine light-bearer," never surrendering his unquestioned talent to commercial filmmaking, as it might be argued that, just to take the most obvious example of the period, Clifford Odets had done. And so it was possible, for Williams had provided the demonstration, for a serious playwright to turn Hollywood to his own purpose – that is, if one of those purposes was to reach a broader audience than could the theatre, with its inescapable institutional and geographical limitations.[17]

Remarkably enough, of the two plays that astounded the American scene in successive years at the end of the 1940s, it was only *Streetcar* that would make a lasting impression on "the whole American mix," not just the high culture and literary establishments. This was because the inevitable screen version of *Salesman* failed to reach and please a mass audience with a relatively faithful rendering of Miller's provocative and moving vision of American experience. Williams shocked the moviegoing public by exploring the depth of carnality in human experience, excavating and anatomizing the ineluctable connection between sex and death, between the streetcar of desire that all must ride and the end of the line – the cemetery – to which all must come. What has come to be known as the "sexual revolution" would confirm that the playwright had lifted the curtain on shared cultural concerns and anxieties. Williams would thus emerge as a prophetic voice anticipating the more strident countercultural visions of life in and of the body that would dominate a later age, most strikingly and characteristically underwritten by the eroticized Marxism of Herbert Marcuse, whose *Eros and Civilization* (first published in 1955) offers a penetrating analysis of the repressive societal norms that shape Blanche's discontent and "transgressiveness." Sensing at the end of the 1940s that a newly energized age of American empire was dawning, Miller intended telling a truth just as shocking, and his insights would also in the course of the 1960s earn the respect of the New Left. *Salesman*, as

Miller wrote with all the scorn of a Mark Rudd or Todd Gitlin, would set the "corpse of a believer ... before the new captains and so smugly confident kings" of a renascent capitalism.[18]

The deep-seated dissatisfaction with "the establishment" that was to emerge a decade and a half later would prove Miller right in claiming that what the times needed was the provocative gesture provided by *Salesman*'s deconstruction of the American drive for success in a system that used up and discarded the little men who served it. He saw clearly that in the immediate aftermath of the war what he called the "burgeoning calamity" in the American economic system and its imperialistic foreign policy was "not even hinted at in the theatre and fiction of the age," even as "the movies were dancing the country into a happy time."[19] Issuing a timely warning, the political theatre that was *Salesman* filled a desperate void, or at least that was how the playwright saw it. Miller was inclined in his later years to universalize Willy, understanding him as motivated by a desire "to excel, to win out over anonymity and meaninglessness ... to count."[20] But for Miller, Willy's tragedy was also historically specific, deeply connected to the drive in postindustrial American capitalism toward those individual-crushing, impersonal economic relations that would, a bit later in the 1950s, be so tellingly anatomized and indicted by sociologist William H. Whyte in his *The Organization Man* and by novelist Sloan Wilson in *The Man in the Gray Flannel Suit.*[21]

Melting the connection between man and society

Miller, it turned out, would not follow Williams in using Hollywood to reach "beyond the already converted," even though he had an important vision to share. Every bit the equal of *Streetcar* as a dramatic masterpiece with the capacity to "change the world," *Salesman* found neither popular-ity nor critical acclaim when it was inevitably brought to the screen after its highly profitable Broadway run. (Even the high-minded Miller could not refuse the substantial payday that a Hollywood sale entailed.)[22] A greater success might have been expected from the film, at least judging from the talent that was assembled for the production. The project would be overseen by one of the industry's most talented and politically sophisti-cated producers, Stanley Kramer, who would go on to make such notable films of the era as *High Noon* (1952), *The Defiant Ones* (1958), *Inherit the Wind* (1960), and *Judgment at Nuremberg* (1961). Release from an import-ant studio – Columbia Pictures – would likely ensure that Kramer's work would be properly marketed and reach a broad public through national distribution. As had been the case with *Streetcar*, the cast from the award-winning Broadway production (with the exception of the role of the protagonist) would be called upon to repeat the magic of their ensemble performance. Lee J. Cobb, who had garnered rave reviews for his incarnation of Willy Loman, would be replaced by Hollywood old hand Fredric March, but the filmmakers had every reason to expect that March was up to the challenge and might even be more suited to embody the character because he had been Miller's first choice to play Willy in the stage production. A definite plus for Kramer was that this was a part March was very eager to assay because of his leftist politics and his admiration for the play's not so subtle indictment of capitalism, here portrayed not as an economic system but as painful, lived experience. This combination made dramatic and thematic sense, but was to prove a lightning rod when the film was released into an America obsessed by the possibility of communist subversion.

László Benedek, a relative newcomer, was engaged to direct, but this was to be more of a producer's project and would bear the imprint of the politically committed and artistically talented Kramer, one of Hollywood's most defiant but successful independents. Director and producer agreed that "shooting the play" was the way to proceed, and little change was made to the basic outlines of what Miller and Kazan had offered to Broadway theatregoers. A superficial view of Kramer's career might suggest that he had a particular artistic interest in Broadway properties; he would oversee seven screen versionings of stage plays during his years as a producer. But Kramer's partiality to dramatic material in fact had a different and much more prosaic source, as he recounts:

> To be honest, I chose to do a number of plays because it took some of the responsibility away from the people who, in my own arrogance, I didn't completely trust – writers, for example. Plays are a safe commodity, and that's why I chose to produce lots of them in their screen versions. I knew what they were, and the screenplays turned out to be, basically, just adaptations.[23]

Elia Kazan felt a deep artistic commitment to *Streetcar*, and he devoted considerable energies to making sure the screen version did justice to the success the property had achieved on Broadway and the well-earned acclaim both he and Williams came to enjoy as a result. For Kramer, however, *Salesman* was nothing more than a "safe commodity" in which he had a largely financial interest. Tellingly, Columbia's studio head, Harry Cohn, thought the property "a piece of junk" and was appalled that

Kramer had paid so much (Miller drove a hard bargain because of the play's exceptional pre-soldness).[24] It was not *Salesman*'s dramatic excellence but its political themes that suited Kramer's social realist interests. He was never deeply invested in a play which, as critic Philip C. Kolin has observed, after 742 performances of the original production had already "entered the canon of American theatre with glory."[25]

If anything, however, what Kramer in the end produced detracted from rather than enhanced the reputation of the stage version, despite some appreciative reviews, notably from the era's most important tastemaker, Bosley Crowther of the *New York Times*. Crowther was elated at the release of a screen version of a play for which he had so much admiration, enthusing that "a great many more million people, not only in this country but in the world, will have a chance to see this shattering drama at what is probably its artistic best."[26] As he saw it, the resources of the film medium made it possible for Kramer to improve on Kazan's stage production. Miller had employed, so Crowther argues, essentially cinematic syntax in a quite different medium – the stage – in order to suggest that merging of Willy's drifting multi-temporal consciousness with the less plastic, strictly linear succession of moments that mark his gradual descent into self-destructive despair. In the film version, in contrast, he suggests that "past and present are run together with perfect smoothness and striking clarity." Such evident aesthetic success was the result, so Crowther would have us think, of the property at last finding its most suitable medium, a result of filmmaking artistry that remains today an impressive accomplishment. Critic Donald Spoto recounts how the film's art designer, Rudolph Sternad, and its two editors, Harry Gerstad and William Lyon, deployed "juxtaposed sets, elongated perspectives, eerily apposite lighting effects, and subtle gradations in lens apertures" to meld, yet differentiate, Willy's memories and his present experience.[27]

Despite this technical brilliance, Miller was deeply dissatisfied. The screen version was compromised, as the playwright came to believe, by directorial choices that fundamentally and disastrously altered the cultural point that Miller had been most eager to make, which was that Willy was representative of the society in which his place became untenable. The filmmakers had "melted the tension between a man and his society" by transforming Willy into a misfit.[28] It was not the result that the playwright had expected, but he had done little if anything to prevent it. Williams worked closely with Elia Kazan, his handpicked director, and politicked personally with the PCA to make certain that the play was not fundamentally altered in its transference to the screen. Isolated on the sidelines as the production proceeded, Miller, in contrast, could only complain at a result he viewed with increasing alarm and disappointment. In selling the property to Kramer, with whom he had no previous relationship, Miller had not sought participation in the screenwriting process (Kazan had wisely engaged Williams to assist with rewriting). If screenwriter Stanley Roberts managed, as Miller bemoaned, "to chop off almost every climax of the play as though with a lawnmower," he could in a sense blame only himself. Needing Miller's support for the project, Kramer tried to mollify the playwright by arranging a meeting with Roberts in New York, but nothing would change as a result.[29]

Not surprisingly, Miller was hardly mistaken in his judgment of what Kramer, the actors, Roberts (a seasoned professional), and studio executives had done with his play. For the most part, viewers agreed, and the film did only mediocre business. Interestingly, the Hollywood establishment rewarded Kramer's efforts with significant recognition during the Academy Awards. Though the filmmakers could boast of no winners, March was nominated for Best Actor, Mildred Dunnock and Kevin McCarthy for their supporting roles, Franz Planer for his cinematography, and Alex North for his score. The film did even better during the 1952 Golden Globe awards, with March winning the Best Actor award, Benedek cited as Best Director, and McCarthy recognized as Best Newcomer. But the praise of industry insiders and the critical establishment soon rang hollow. Kramer's film quickly sank from sight and has subsequently made virtually no impact on American culture. In fact, it carries so little cachet that no VHS was ever produced, nor has Columbia Pictures planned a DVD release, even though the company is otherwise remarketing on DVD most of their important films from the period. Movies Unlimited has recently released a DVD based on a faulty print that, difficult to watch, hardly does justice to what Kramer produced. As if to add insult to injury, his film is only rarely shown on television. Most cinephiles and admirers of Miller's theatre are hardly aware of its existence.

This neglect seems quite remarkable, given the hallowed place that *Salesman* has assumed in the canon of American theatre, a reputation that has made it a standard item for high-school and college literature courses. The 2011 Broadway revival, directed by Mike Nichols and starring Philip Seymour Hoffman, demonstrates – if there was any doubt –that *Salesman* is one of the postwar American theatre's most enduring successes. In contrast, Kazan's *Streetcar* is reverently ensconced as one of Hollywood's best. It has long occupied forty-seventh place on the American Film Institute's best 100 American films list – an honor roll of

Hollywood's accomplishments on which Kramer's *Salesman* makes no appearance. And so we must count the film a failure not only in Hollywood terms (not much of a moneymaker upon initial release and considered to have no continuing exploitable value). Hollywood's *Salesman* has also contributed nothing to the larger cultural politics in which Miller envisioned his drama playing an important role. Volker Schlöndorff's 1985 television adaptation has many merits, but it is essentially a filmed play (based on the 1984 Broadhurst Theater revival, starring Dustin Hoffman and John Malkovich), and it hardly reached in its initial broadcast the broad viewership that Kazan's *Streetcar* continues to enjoy (there was no theatrical exhibition). Interestingly, the Schlöndorff film is currently available on DVD only in a non-USA Region 2 format.

If there was fault for the failure of Kramer's *Salesman*, it was, in the first instance, Miller's, not the filmmakers, who predictably succumbed to pressures within and without the industry to alter the playwright's vision. Miller simply could not overcome his dislike for the commercial cinema so that he could usefully collaborate on the production. On the other hand, Williams lobbied hard with Kazan to get him to direct the film version of the play for whose Broadway success he had been so responsible; together the pair made sure that producer Charles A. Feldman did not give in to his instincts to turn *Streetcar* into a conventional melodrama. Though Kazan also directed the Broadway *Salesman*, Miller did not solicit his participation in the film project. But bringing the play to the screen also involved surmounting a difficulty that Williams had not been forced to face. Miller's radical politics were not those of desire and its discontents. But, it must be said, the two plays offered different challenges to the prevailing social order, and this had a profound effect on what purchase they would have on the national culture. *Streetcar* was threatening only to the conservative religious or social sensibility of many Americans, with perhaps a solid majority at the time unwilling to grant sex the power that Williams argued it possessed. Miller's theatre was political, not cultural. The film version of *All My Sons* (1948, Irving Reis) could retain, if in a somewhat blunted form, the play's indictment of wartime profiteering, and even its poignant demonstration that the ruthless pursuit of self-interest at the expense of a collectivist ethos blazed a path toward self-destruction; it delivered a message that the American Left at the time received loud and clear. *Salesman* set its sights on a larger and more problematic target. Miller now launched a devastating attack on the myth of what we would now term "branding," the debasingly narcissistic self-fashioning that conveys upon individuals the power to sell through pleasing others. Its thematic center, ironically, was its "likability," which, however elusive, those who serviced a consumer economy had to cultivate and maintain.

This message grew increasingly controversial during the Broadway run as a new Red Scare came to dominate American politics and public opinion. But the filmmakers were confronted by a series of increasingly unfavorable circumstances. Preproduction planning began in the wake of the first Soviet atomic bomb test in 1949, while principal production took place during the escalation of Cold War tensions following the North Korean invasion of South Korea in June, 1950; during that same summer, a grand jury began exploring indictments in the case that would eventually result in the execution of Julius and Ethel Rosenberg for the betrayal of atomic secrets to the Russians. Exploring the supposed communist connections of those in the film industry and arts, the House Un-American Activities Committee (HUAC) was at that time much in the news; Miller would later be called to testify before them, refusing to provide testimony to incriminate others, and earning a place on the industry blacklist as a result. If not yet established as an "unfriendly witness" in 1950, Miller made no secret of his leftist sympathies, and his embrace of what many saw as treasonous politics did not help quell Columbia's anxiety that political troubles would wreck the film's exhibition.

Cohn's agreement with Kramer did not give him veto power over projects, but it seems more than likely he regretted bitterly that the studio had inherited responsibility for this troublesome project from the independent producer, with whom the studio had signed a thirty-six-picture deal. The agreement was canceled after the first eleven of these films, including *Salesman*, proved box-office poison. That "patriotic" groups and self-appointed spokesmen were already grumbling about Miller's play and the film then being made from it clearly influenced Kramer and company. In 1949, for example, A. Howard Fuller, president and founder of the Fuller Brush Company, which depended exclusively on door-to-door salesmen for its retailing efforts, wrote a piece in *Fortune* magazine in which he opined that "Willy is essentially a self-deluded man who has lost the power to distinguish between reality and the obsessions that come to dominate his life." Enthusiasm, Fuller suggests, is essential to sales success, but it can "also destroy and kill," as it does in the case of Willy Loman, who obsesses about being "well-liked."[30] For Fuller, then, Miller's play does not critique an economic system that destroys its most enthusiastic member, but instead offers a cautionary tale about excessive zeal. Screenwriter Stanley Roberts, interestingly enough, came up with a strikingly similar view of Willy's nature and significance; in the film, his dilemma is now no longer seen as, in the words of theatre critic Howard Barnes, driving "its roots deep in the complex structure of contemporary existence."[31]

Intended by Miller as an exploration of the experiences of an American everyman, Kramer's film responded to these political pressures by portraying Willy as mentally deranged, as a mad man whose discontented self-destructiveness distinguished him from his better-adjusted counterparts. This point was not only made within the film itself. Frightened by the possibility of boycotts or protests organized by right-wing groups, Columbia Pictures designed a uniquely self-defeating marketing campaign whose point – to the playwright's increasing horror – seemed to be that Willy was not a typical product of the American system, but an idiosyncratic outlier whose self-destruction could be made the subject of a cautionary tale.

No longer everyman

What did Hollywood see in *Salesman*? The industry's experience with *All My Sons* had been a good one; the film had been praised by critics and rewarded with accolades, even as it proved attractive to filmgoers. Also a profoundly moving family drama, *Salesman* offered Hollywood an even more successful play with much the same materials: a generational conflict between father and son, an understated if profoundly affecting critique of the American dream, and clear, effective dramatic encounters undisrupted by Miller's experiments with objectifying the main character's inner life. Like Joe Keller in *All My Sons*, Willy Loman finally fails to achieve the success promised to the industrious middle-class patriarch who dedicates himself to supporting his family. Loman too is responsible in part, through his own blindness and culpability, for destroying his most valued human connection: the relationship with a favored and adored son. Here was material that could be adapted to fit a then popular series: the social problem film. Early 1950s social problem films were the serious, realist "other" to the dominant series of the era: spectacular blockbusters, which featured casts of thousands, with exotic settings photographed in living Technicolor and in one of the newfangled wide-screen processes such as Cinemascope, and offered escape rather than a confrontation with contemporary discontents.

Perhaps the most famous of the independent producers who mined this area of popular taste was Stanley Kramer. Teamed with the politically like-minded Sam Katz and Carl Foreman (eventually blacklisted for his leftist associations), Kramer achieved a breakthrough success with *Home of the Brave* (1949, Mark Robson), based on the hit play by Arthur Laurents

Figure 3.2 As Willy gets increasingly unstuck in time, he finds himself a constant
companion of long-dead brother Ben (Royal Beal). (frame enlargement)

about anti-Semitism in the armed forces. Collaborating on the screenwriting with Foreman, Kramer daringly changed the film's focus to racism, substituting a black soldier for the play's Jew. Like the other social problem films of the late 1940s, *Home of the Brave* struck a popular chord with an audience conditioned by wartime filmmaking to admire "message" pictures. The social problem film required a typical protagonist who, though victimized or threatened by hostile circumstances, could be depicted as triumphing over them. Though this would change the complexity of Miller's conception, a screen version could have constructed Willy as crushed by a system that discards him despite his years of profitable service to it; he would then be permitted the final gesture of self-annihilation, which could be celebrated as a liberating victory for the common man, who endorses the irony of his own "exchange value" as he looks forward to fulfilling the terms of the life insurance that would, with him dead, sustain the family he could not support while living. Willy, then, would be more typical than aberrant, undone less by psychopathology than by an economic system that uses him up and then heartlessly discards him. This handling of the material would anchor Miller's drama in a realistically evoked contemporary America. And so what critics like Donald Spoto find fault with in the play – the sense that it can seem "humorless" and "relentlessly gray," "oppressive" and "depressing" – would be advantageous, as the film offered up a heroic figure crushed but not defeated by circumstance. Both *Home of the Brave* and *The Men*, Kramer's biggest successes before taking on this project, offer protagonists of this type: a black soldier (James Edwards) ironically "wounded" by prejudice and not enemy fire, who learns to walk again by acknowledging and expressing his anger at whites; a white soldier (Marlon Brando) paralyzed in battle who, through the love of a good woman, learns to overcome the impotence caused by his wound and the not always helpful impersonality of the system that tries to care for him. In both cases, the protagonists' private problems are objectified and solved in a social context; they are not tragic figures, but "cases." The ironic center of Miller's conception, of course, is that much of the real drama of Willy's consciousness cannot by its very nature be made apparent to those around him, family members who are nonetheless deeply affected. Willy can be provided with no more helpful therapist than his own image of his brother Ben, who, in Willy's imagination, urges suicide upon him as a solution for what has gone wrong with his life. Like the protagonists in Kramer's other social problem films, Willy might be allowed dignity and worth even if, as Spoto suggests, he lacks "the heroic qualities that would make his disintegration and downfall authentically tragic."[32] He could still, even as a "case," be a positive character, even if denied the exalted status he achieves in the stage production, where Kazan made it clear that Willy is a tragic figure because, as Richard I. Evans has suggested, he cannot help "believing in what he is forced to rebel against."[33] Even reduced to banal typicality in order to make a political point, he would still express the "tension between a man and his society," which was Miller's intention for him.[34]

But the filmmakers set out on a different, but related, course, one that "melted" that tension. Benedek, clearly following Kramer's wishes, instructed March to "play Willy as a psycho, all but completely out of control, with next to no grip on reality"; the result, the playwright suggests, was that "if he was nuts, he could hardly stand as a comment on anything."[35] For Fuller, Miller's play then does not critique an economic system that destroys its most enthusiastic member, but instead offers a cautionary tale about its excess. Willy Loman is thus neither every man nor every salesman, but rather a deviant case. Instructed by Benedek to use gestures and pacing that communicated a failing grip on reality, March constructed a very different version of the character than had Lee J. Cobb, whose conception of Willy is recorded in the 1966 television version of *Salesman*, directed by Alex Segal, which, even though it abridges the play considerably, preserves the tragic vision of Miller and Kazan and offers a striking contrast to Kramer's adaptation. As Kramer's Willy becomes a pathetic loony, the film deviates from the social problem model, with the result that, in the playwright's words, it draws "the teeth of the play's social contemporaneity."[36]

We'll have no more films that show the seamy side of American life

And yet these concessions to indirect political pressure proved insufficient to prevent the film's exhibition to be troubled by pickets. As Kramer points out, *Salesman* was "the first major film to be picketed by Communist-hunting right-wingers."[37] The specific targets of the protests were, Kramer suggests, himself, Miller, and March, all well known as left-leaning liberals, but even more provocative in his view was the film's implied critique of American culture: "it suggested that American business more often than not was more interested in profits than people."[38] A group called the Wage Earners Committee vowed to picket theatres across the country showing *Salesman*; these right-wingers seemed particularly incensed by Kramer's supposed record of "coddling Reds and pinkos."[39] Worried that they would lose their considerable financial investment in the project, Columbia sponsored the production of a short introduction to the film, to be shown before the start of the main feature in every program.[40] *The Career of a Salesman* seems to have been inspired by (of all people) a university professor, Jack S. Schiff, founder of CCNY's Midtown Business Center, which had recently launched a program in "sales engineering." Schiff became the technical director for the film, and also appears in it as "himself," teaching a class in which he makes the point that a salesman "needs a lot more than personality," scornfully rejecting Willy as "a man with an outmoded and unrealistic philosophy." Hardly true to his own views, Kramer is brought on screen to agree that "Willy Loman is definitely outmoded today," even as he asks viewers to "see this film, *Death of a Salesman*." Shown *Career*, Miller was outraged and (unsuccessfully) sued the studio (he had been promised a percentage of the net profits, thus could argue that his financial interests were harmed by the showing of the film). A deeper wound was that the filmmakers in their adaptation and the studio in its marketing campaign made his play "morally meaningless, a tale told by an idiot signifying nothing."[41]

Eric Johnston, president of the Motion Picture Association of America, proclaimed that in postwar America "we'll have no more films that show the seamy side of American life."[42] Among others, independent producer

Figure 3.3 Confronted with his failures by favored son Biff (Kevin McCarthy), Willy begins to lose touch with reality. (frame enlargement)

Stanley Kramer gave the lie to this fatuous promise, promoting films like *Home of the Brave* and *The Men* that treated subjects which, if not seamy, were troubling and provocative. His *Death of a Salesman* might have done much the same, providing an indelible reminiscence of the play's original production as well, but this was not to be. It is no exaggeration to say, as does Brenda Murphy, that "Willy Loman has become the prime site for working out our deepest cultural conflicts and anxieties about the identity and fate of the salesman. And, being Americans, we are all salesmen in one way or another."[43] But Kramer's film did nothing to further or even deliver that important message.

Endnotes

1 For details see Brooks Atkinson, *Broadway* (New York: Macmillan, 1970).
2 Miller recalls that he shared with Williams a desire to find a form of drama that would engage the Broadway audience of the era: "A number of people, myself included, and obviously Tennessee, were struggling with this dilemma of how to hold an audience, to make them feel something with language that was not exactly familiar . . . What suddenly was encouraging to me was that nobody else could have written *Streetcar*. Here was a piece of writing that belonged to that author and not six others. You could hear a poet's voice in the theatre again. I appreciated that," from Colby H. Kullman, "*Death of a Salesman* at Fifty: An

Interview with Arthur Miller," *Michigan Quarterly Review* 37.4 (1998), 632 (624–634).

3 Arthur Miller, *Timebends: A Life* (New York: Harper & Row, 1987), 180.

4 Ibid., 179.

5 Ibid., 181.

6 Ibid., 179.

7 Ibid.

8 Ibid., 180–181.

9 From Kullman, "*Death of a Salesman* at Fifty," 632.

10 Miller, *Timebends*, 181.

11 For further details of this remarkable story see R. Barton Palmer and William Robert Bray, *Hollywood's Tennessee: The Williams Films and Postwar America* (Austin: University of Texas Press, 2009).

12 Quoted in Murray Schumach, *The Face on the Cutting Room Floor: The Story of Movie and TV Censorship* (New York: Da Capo, 1964), 72.

13 Miller, *Timebends*, 182.

14 Ibid.

15 Ibid., 180.

16 Ibid., 231.

17 For a full discussion of this and related issues see Palmer and Bray, *Hollywood's Tennessee* as well as the chapter on *Streetcar* by Bray in this volume.

18 Miller, *Timebends*, 184.

19 Ibid., 317–318.

20 Ibid., 184.

21 William H. Whyte, *The Organization Man* (New York: Simon & Schuster, 1956), and Sloan Wilson, *The Man in the Gray Flannel Suit* (New York: Amereon House, 1955).

22 He received $100,000 for the film rights to the play, a considerable sum, but substantially less than the $350,000 that Williams received for the rights to *Streetcar*. See Stanley Kramer, *A Mad, Mad, Mad, Mad World: A Life in Hollywood* (New York: Harcourt Brace, 1991), 80.

23 Quoted in Donald Spoto, *Stanley Kramer: Film Maker* (New York: Samuel French, 1978), 76.

24 Quoted in Kramer, *A Mad, Mad, Mad, Mad World*, 79.

25 Philip C. Kolin, "*Death of a Salesman*: A Playwright's Forum," *Michigan Quarterly Review* 37.4 (1998), 591.

26 "Death of a Salesman," *New York Times*, December 21, 1951.

27 Spoto, *Stanley Kramer*, 80.

28 Miller, *Timebends*, 315.

29 Ibid., 314–315.

30 Kevin Kerrane, "Arthur Miller vs. Columbia Pictures: The Strange Case of a Career of a Salesman," *Journal of American Culture* 27 (September 2004), 281.

31 Howard Barnes, "Death of a Salesman," *New York Herald Tribune*, February 2, 1949.

32 Spoto, *Stanley Kramer*, 77.
33 Richard I. Evans, *Psychology and Arthur Miller* (New York: Dutton, 1969), 91.
34 Miller, *Timebends*, 315.
35 Ibid.
36 Ibid.
37 Kramer, *A Mad, Mad, Mad, Mad World*, 81.
38 Ibid.
39 Quoted in Peter Lev, *The Fifties: Transforming the Screen 1950–59* (Berkeley: University of California Press, 2003), 74.
40 The discussion that follows is heavily indebted to Kerrane. All material quoted from *Career of a Salesman* is quoted in Kerrane, "Arthur Miller vs. Columbia Pictures."
41 Miller, *Timebends*, 318.
42 Quoted in Lev, *The Fifties*, 67.
43 Brenda Murphy, "Willy Loman: Icon of Business Culture," *Michigan Quarterly Review* 37.4 (1998), 761.

CHAPTER 4

Elia Kazan's A Streetcar Named Desire

William Robert Bray

In 2011, the arts world acknowledged the centenary of Tennessee Williams's birth and reflected on his vast oeuvre, which is, in both quality and quantity, unrivaled in the American theatre experience. The tributes were many and varied. At home and abroad, academic conferences, popular publications, and numerous theatre revivals (as well as some previously unproduced plays) celebrated Williams's legacy, signalling the continuing appeal of America's great playwright who, for about fifteen golden years from 1945 to 1960, dominated Broadway and brought thousands into movie houses to see his film adaptations. Somehow overshadowed in all the activity was the sixtieth anniversary of the film *A Streetcar Named Desire*.

Perhaps this apparent neglect during the year of its anniversary is owing to six previous decades of attention, for none of Williams's other film adaptations has received either the critical scrutiny or popular acclaim of *Streetcar*. It is listed as the American Film Industry's forty-seventh greatest film and ranks forty-fourth on *Time-Life*'s 100 Best Movies. In 1993, an "Original Director's Version," which restores four minutes of excised material, was released by Warner Bros. on DVD with great fanfare. By some measures, in fact, the picture's awards overshadowed the kudos that the property had won as a play. *Streetcar* premiered on Broadway in 1947 and ran for over two years, with 855 performances. Yet even with this lengthy run and a 1948 Pulitzer Prize for Best Drama, only Jessica Tandy received a Tony Award for Best Actress. On the other hand, the film was nominated for twelve Oscars and won four, including Best Supporting Actor (Karl Malden) and Actress (Kim Hunter), Best Art Direction, and Best Actress (Vivien Leigh). It also became the first film to win awards in three acting categories. With all the accolades, however, came some puzzling snubs as well. Despite Brando's iconic role as Stanley Kowalski, a history-making performance on both stage and screen, the gifted actor lost out to Humphrey Bogart for his lead role in *The African Queen*. *Streetcar* was nominated for Best Picture but was bested by *An American in Paris*, and Elia Kazan was nominated for Best Director but lost to George Stevens for *A Place in the Sun*. Film historians sometimes point to extraneous factors involving the academy voting for 1951. Since Kazan was testifying before HUAC around the time of the balloting, it is often said that his just deserts were denied by Hollywood insiders who were furious with his HUAC involvement and determined to punish him. The awkward controversy over his receiving the Academy's Lifetime Achievement Award in 1999 proved that many in the Hollywood community were still not completely ready to reconcile his artistic accomplishments with what they perceived as his political misdeeds, even almost fifty years later.

The Williams–Kazan axis

Of all the major collaborations in the theatre, perhaps none was more dynamic or fruitful than the relationship between Williams and Kazan. Kazan directed three of Williams's most well-known dramas – *Streetcar* (1947), *Cat on a Hot Tin Roof* (1955), and *Sweet Bird of Youth* (1959), as well as what Kazan called Williams's "beautiful" but "imperfect" play, *Camino Real* (1953).[1] Their collaboration on the film *Baby Doll* (1956) lasted some four years and, as with *Cat*, tested their friendship as well as their individual artistic visions. As Brenda Murphy points out in her brilliant study, *Tennessee Williams and Elia Kazan: A Collaboration in the Theatre*, the relationship between the two artists was far more unique and symbiotic than similar partnerships between directors and playwrights. Murphy describes two models that existed prior to the Williams–Kazan alignment: "the 'symphony model' – director as conductor, merely interpreting the playwright's fixed text – and the 'cinema model' – director as *auteur*, bringing to life the playwright's mere scenario." She goes on to explain,

> The creative interaction between Williams and Kazan, however, was a far more complex process. As soon as he had a recognizable script, Williams would send it off to Kazan for his reaction. Kazan responded with detailed suggestions about how the play might be changed and reshaped. He suggested adding or deleting scenes, emphasizing various themes, developing or changing aspects of characterization, and in general helped to shape the play that finally emerged in the script that went into rehearsal.

Figure 4.1 Director Elia Kazan confers with Mitch (Karl Malden)
as Blanche (Vivien Leigh) listens in.

Furthermore, Williams also challenged the conventional notion of the
so-called "absent author" during production, for in their partnership,
"the director was involved in the play's writing from very early on and
the playwright was involved in the production process throughout its
development."[2]

Given the extraordinary nature of the Williams–Kazan alliance, the
question naturally arises as to how much of *Streetcar*'s script, for both
stage and screen, may be attributed to this partnership – or, more reduc-
tively, what percentage of the glory belongs to the director. Murphy
maintains that with the stage version of *Streetcar*, "Williams was rather
diffident in his first rehearsal period with Kazan. Unlike the later plays they
worked on together, there was little rewriting of *Streetcar* to do during
rehearsals, and Williams generally came by in the afternoon once he had
finished his other work for the day."[3] Other observers paint a different
picture, including drama critic Eric Bentley, who boldly maintained that
since Kazan incorporated so many changes into the play, he should have
been listed as co-author of *Streetcar*. However, in a 1954 letter from Irene
Selznick to Bentley, she writes that she was "appalled" by this assertion

because she "was the first person after Mr. Williams's representative" [Audrey Wood] to read the manuscript, and that she was

> in a position to unequivocally state that not more than a few pages of this play were changed. The only difference between the original manuscript and the play presented in Broadway was the condensation of a tiny part of the final scene. It is so rare as to be almost unique for a play to undergo as little revision or editing as Streetcar.[4]

When Kazan was asked about his written contributions to Williams's plays in a 1962 interview, he responded,

> No, I really haven't. That's not true. That's all been built up – I've never written a word of one of his plays. What I always do with him is to send him a three or four page letter – telling him at the beginning what I think of the play, what I think needs to be done, and what attitude I would take toward the play if I directed it.[5]

Of course, Kazan's laissez-faire description, while perhaps technically correct, belies the director's intense involvement and resulting contributions when transferring Williams's texts to the stage or screen. What bears remembering is that because Williams's understanding about the benefits of working with a genius such as Kazan became more sophisticated with experience, he came more and more to rely upon the director's guidance and opinions throughout the various projects that they shared. In the final analysis, any creative tensions and disagreements between Kazan and Williams over their many projects (and through some of their most fertile years) usually yielded to an affinity and friendship which, at least to some extent, transcended individual ego. In poring through the hundreds of letters between the two, many of which were not available to the public until after Kazan's death in 2003, one must inevitably conclude that their unconventional relationship was in many ways akin to a conventional and successful marriage, with demonstrations of love and anger, joy and despair, condemnations and reprisals, but ultimately comprising a union based upon mutual respect and affection that stubbornly resisted dissolution. Speaking about those who abandoned him after the HUAC hearings, Kazan wrote, "We both felt vulnerable to the depredations of an unsympathetic world, distrustful of the success we'd had, suspicious of those in favor, anticipating put-downs, expecting insufficient appreciation and reward. The most loyal and understanding friend I had through those black months was Tennessee Williams."[6]

Getting Kazan aboard the streetcar

Despite the critical and commercial success of the Broadway play, *Streetcar* was in many ways the most challenging of all the Williams adaptations, even with Kazan eventually taking a very active role in the entire production process. Even though it was presold by its previous success on stage, the play's controversial text, which includes rape, homosexuality, spousal abuse, and pedophilia, proved problematic for film adaptation from the beginning.[7]

With *The Glass Menagerie*, adapted for film in 1950, Williams had maneuvered through the filmmaking process by choosing his battles wisely and sometimes yielding to Hollywood moguls when faced with intractable demands. In turn, Williams learned valuable lessons that would prepare him for future adaptation projects. The learning curve was steep, however, and during the *Menagerie* negotiations the playwright became frustrated and disillusioned. He learned that his idealistic notions of artistic control often gave way to the brazen will of the studio executives. He became distrustful of meddling script doctors and was forced to acknowledge the power of the Production Code Administration and the manner in which its intransigence could, if unchallenged, strip the artistic essence from his proven Broadway successes. This Hollywood education might have given Williams pause to reconsider the difficult process of having another play adapted for the screen, yet less than one full year after the film release of *Menagerie*, *Streetcar* debuted in cinemas across the nation.

After several failed starts, Charles K. Feldman purchased *Streetcar* for $350,000, with an additional $50,000 going to Williams for working with professional screenwriter Oscar Saul to adapt the screenplay. Feldman also signed Kazan for $175,000. The Kazan–Williams film partnership, preceded by their collaboration on the stage play, was an essential part of Williams's artistic vision from the beginning, as Williams intuitively knew that the full potential of the adaptation could only be realized through the dynamic talents of a gifted director such as Kazan. But the director was not even attracted to the play at first reading and had to be eventually convinced by his wife, Molly Day Thacher, to reconsider. Kazan's initial reluctance to become involved in the stage version was immediately assuaged by his first meeting with Williams. As Kazan recalls in his autobiography,

> Tennessee and I took to each other like a shot and without any of the usual gab about mutual friends, tastes, experiences, and so on to bridge the gap. It was a mysterious harmony; by all visible signs we were as different as two

humans could be. Our union, immediate on first encounter, was close but unarticulated; it endured for the rest of his life.[8]

If Kazan had first been reluctant to direct the play, he was even more reticent about taking on the picture. At the time he was Broadway's leading stage director and had recently enjoyed the success of four films: *A Tree Grows in Brooklyn* (1945), *Gentleman's Agreement* (1947), *Pinky* (1949), and *Panic in the Streets* (1950). Financially secure for the time being, Kazan felt that his experience with the stage play had been rewarding enough. Moreover, Kazan had never made a film of a stage play (*Streetcar* would remain the only exception). When first approached by Williams and Feldman to direct the film, Kazan told them that he should not be their first choice. "It would be like marrying the same woman twice. I don't think I can get it up for Streetcar again."[9] Moreover, even though Kazan was never one to back away from a fight, he realized that getting *Streetcar*'s adult content transferred to the screen would be problematic at best and impossible at worst. Sensing that the possibility of collaborating with Kazan was hanging by a thread, Williams wrote the director from Key West in December of 1949, imploring him to accept the job. "Nothing, nothing, *nothing* must stand in the way of our working together on this picture. It will be the beginning of other exciting projects for us together, as I know that the screen is a good medium for us both."[10] With Williams's pleas stroking his ego, Kazan began to look at the opportunity with fresh possibilities for his creative direction. Shortly after a trip to New Orleans, where Kazan was beginning production work for *Panic in the Streets*, the director wrote Williams, expressing his enthusiasm for the project: "I know we can make something really hard and painful out of it . . . I really and truly think that we can make something better than the play of it. I like the few ideas we talked about . . . and I like the idea of somehow making the end harder."[11]

Williams and the patch-work quilt

Once Kazan was under contract, plans moved forward with preparation of the script, which included hiring Oscar Saul. Kazan wrote Williams a letter expressing his confidence in the arrangement, fully believing that Williams would eventually take charge of the project himself and leave the mere tinkering to Saul. At first Williams agreed with the idea of hiring a professional screenwriter who would play a primary role. He wrote Kazan in December of 1949, "I hope you will approve of my so-far passive role in the collaboration. I don't really believe in collaborations as I don't think creative work is done in that way. For that reason I am deliberately standing aside for the time being and letting Oscar go full-steam ahead with his own ideas."[12] However, Williams's passivity soon turned to virtual outrage once he read through Saul's work. Only a month later, he wrote Kazan again: "Oscar Saul has completed his script. I read half of it last night and became disheartened and thrust it under the bed. I had so hoped that I would not have to work at all on this *Streetcar* script but it appears that I shall have to take a hand in it."[13] Once he had seen Saul's script, Kazan concurred with Williams's concerns and listed numerous changes that should be made. At the time Williams was consumed with other projects and extremely reluctant to take a leading role in the revisions:

> I am terrified by the amount of work you still want to be done on Streetcar. Why, honey, it looks like you want me to sit down and write the whole fucking thing over!! The script is going to be the biggest patch-work quilt since the death of Aunt Dinah, and you might as well be reconciled to it. I am going to do my work on it in bits and pieces.[14]

In the end, Willliams did in fact take charge of the rewrite, and his contribution was substantial enough that he received principal credit for writing the screenplay. Saul, with his limited input, was only given credit for the adaptation.

An opening up that fizzles

When Kazan began developing his working continuity for the shooting, he worked for seven months to "open up" the play by shooting scenes at Belle Reve as described by Blanche, including those involving her dying relatives and the drunken soldiers calling her name on the front lawn. He would then shoot her disgraceful departure from Laurel and her arrival at the train station, "materializing out of the cloud of smoke from the old locomotive." To establish Stanley's milieu, Kazan would feature the bowling alley, the various bars he frequented, and the surrounding neighborhood, all shot in order to "create a veritable redneck Kowalski world." He resolved to find the perfect home in the Mississippi Delta for Belle Reve so that the film could be shot on location. But as he read the revised screenplay, he found that "it was a fizzle."[15] Realizing the value of the claustrophobic Kowalski flat that proved so valuable on stage, Kazan reconsidered his intentions to open up the film: "So I went back and photographed the stage play as written."[16] Recognizing that

> the force of the play had come precisely from its compression, from the fact that Blanche was trapped in those two small rooms, where she'd be

constantly aware that she was dangerously irritating Stanley and couldn't escape if she needed to. Everything we'd done to "open up" the play diluted its power.[17]

Rejecting most of the revised continuity, Kazan eventually decided to keep only the brief shots of Blanche's debarkation, the bowling alley, and a scene at Stanley's job in the factory. Kazan also opened up the tableau where Blanche describes Grey's suicide to Mitch by placing it at a night club not unlike the one where her former husband shot himself. For the Elysian Fields apartment set (all the film except for the first few minutes were shot on Warner Bros. lots) Kazan decided to build the walls in sections so that as the film progressed he could compress the space and make Blanche's sense of confinement even more pronounced.[18] He also had a virtual irrigation system installed in the set's walls to make it appear as if they were sweating from the oppressive New Orleans humidity.

The Marlon Brando show

During *Streetcar*'s Broadway run, an unanticipated problem developed as a result of Marlon Brando's dominating stage performance. Even as early as his first reading for the part of Stanley, everyone sensed that the actor possessed a Promethean talent for fitting into the part, as well as a sexual magnetism never before witnessed on the American stage. After auditioning for Williams in Provincetown in the spring of 1947, the playwright wrote Audrey Wood, sparing no superlatives about the actor's ability:

> I can't tell you what a relief it is that we have found such a God-sent Stanley in the person of Brando. It had not occurred to me before what an excellent value would come from casting a very young actor in this part. It humanizes the character of Stanley in that it becomes the brutality or callousness of youth rather than a vicious older man. I don't want to focus guilt or blame particularly on any one character but to have it a tragedy of misunderstandings and insensitivity to others. A new value came out of Brando's reading, which was by far the best reading I have ever heard.[19]

Brando's "humanizing" the part of Stanley, however, turned out to be a mixed blessing. Although Kazan strongly believed that Blanche was the central character of the play, he was forced to admit that Jessica Tandy could not compete with Brando in the Blanche–Stanley battle of the sexes. As Kazan wrote in his autobiography, Tandy's role

> seemed to be a performance. Marlon was living on stage. Jessie had every moment worked out, carefully, with sensitivity and intelligence, just as Williams and I had expected and wanted. Marlon, working "from the

inside," rode his emotion wherever it took him, his performance was full of surprises and exceeded what Williams and I had expected. A performance miracle was in the making. What was there to do but be grateful?[20]

Gratefulness and awe aside, the onstage chemistry between Brando and Tandy evolved into a pheromone-fueled exaltation for audiences watching Brando. His performance exuded cruelty and crudeness, but as with most of his best roles, his sensitivity leavened his brutish dominance. As a result, as Kazan remembered, "what had been intimated in our final rehearsals in New York was happening. The audiences adored Brando. When he derided Blanche, they responded with approving laughter. Was the play becoming the Marlo Brando show? I didn't bring up the problem, because I didn't know the solution."[21]

As the property moved from stage to screen, Kazan's "problem" would be met with another "solution" – to keep nine members of the cast intact, but to drop Jessica Tandy in favor of Vivien Leigh for the role of Blanche. In Kazan's eyes (and those of the financial backers), it was not only Tandy's inability to hold up to Brando; the team needed new blood on the movie set, especially one with star power. Kazan felt some loyalty to Tandy but was also a student of studio realpolitik. He summed up his ambivalence about the altered casting after Charles Feldman and Warners insisted on a new Blanche: "To confess the truth, I'm not certain, looking back, that I didn't want a different actress for Blanche. Feeling stale on the play, I needed a high-voltage shock to get my motor going again."[22]

If Kazan felt "stale" about the project, Brando was even more reluctant to reprise his role for the screen. He had experienced difficulty in keeping the part alive for his two years on the stage. He was trained as a stage actor and was wary of the Hollywood star system and especially of becoming a property of Warner Bros. But the lure of star billing and a $75,000 salary eventually changed his mind. With Leigh replacing Tandy, Kazan initially thought that his problem with "the Marlon Brando show" had been solved. In 1939 Leigh had dominated the screen in *Gone with the Wind*, winning Best Actress for her role as Scarlett O'Hara, and just two years before filming *Streetcar* she had completed a London run of the play as Blanche, directed by her husband Laurence Olivier. But Kazan soon learned that these presumed assets were actually liabilities. Because of her earlier stardom and her classical training, Leigh approached the project with an egotistical swagger, exacerbated by what Kazan thought was Olivier's tone-deaf direction of her part in the play. On the first day of shooting, Kazan asked Leigh to act a certain way, and Leigh responded with, "When Larry and I did the play in London . . ." Kazan would not let this stand. "'But you're not making the film with Larry in Lond' Vivien,' I said. 'You're making it here with us.'"[23] According to took two full weeks to break her away from her theatrical artin consequently, he felt that "the scenes shot in those weeks, if you'll forgive the conceit, are the ones where she appears most artificial, most of the theatre, and most strained."[24]

The key to the production

In preparing for the shooting, Kazan remained determined not to allow Brando's stage dominance to overshadow the character of Blanche, and in doing so he probably referred back to an earlier letter from Williams that the director clearly treasured; one that, in Kazan's words, "became the key to the production for me."[25] Williams wrote, "I remember you asked me what an audience should feel for Blanche. Certainly pity. It is a tragedy with the classic aim of producing catharsis of pity and terror and in order to do that, Blanche must finally have the understanding and compassion of the audience."[26] In his notes from the Final Draft of the Film Script, July 1950, Kazan seemed eager to reinforce Williams's vision and to evoke pity from the film audience by demonstrating "the pain and violence of this story." In order to achieve this end, Kazan became fixated on Blanche's delicate psychological state. As he wrote, "the emotions within this woman, her suffering, her pain, her inner life, can be much better revealed by film than it was [*sic*] on the stage."[27] As a film director, Kazan believed that his job was to transport the Group Theatre's focus on psychological realism from the stage to the screen. As critic John Lahr notes,

> Kazan's rise to directorial preeminence coincided with a crucial psychic shift in American culture … The kingdom of self, not society, became the nation's obsession. Public discourse shifted from the external to the internal: from social realism to abstract expressionism; from stage natural-ism to Williams's personal lyricism, from Marxism to Freudianism. This mutation in the collective imagination suited Kazan's particular directorial skill set, which understood about the subconscious and the power of subtext. For Kazan, the greatest show on earth was the show of human emotions.[28]

Kazan's forte lay in penetrating both the psychological makeup of the acting part as well as that of the actors. According to the director, "My work would be to turn the inner events of the psyche into a choreography of external life."[29] Kazan felt his job was to explore the "core" of the actors. As Arthur Miller wrote in his autobiography, "Kazan's capacity to objectify actors' personalities was really an exercise in clinical psychology."[30] Indeed, Miller's familiarity with expressionistic drama (and probably Kazan's staging of *Streetcar*, which Miller praised) influenced early drafts of *Death of a Salesman*. When Miller began writing the play, he called it "The Inside of His Head," with members of Willy's family existing only as aspects of his own personality. As Miller remembers in his autobiography *Timebends*,

> Streetcar – especially when it was still so fresh and the actors almost as amazed as the audience at the vitality of this theatrical experience – opened one specific door for me . . . With Streetcar, Tennessee had printed a license to speak at full throat, and it helped strengthen me as I turned to Willy Loman . . . I had known all along that this play could not be encompassed by conventional realism . . . [31]

As with Miller, Williams had found in Kazan a director sensitive to his psychologically complex characters, a sympathetic soul who was curious and eager to explore fully Blanche's psyche on screen. Rejecting the reality of representational drama, Williams wrote that

> expressionism and all other unconventional techniques in drama have only one valid aim, and that is a closer approach to truth. When a play employs unconventional techniques, it is not, or certainly shouldn't be, trying to escape responsibility of dealing with reality, or interpreting experience, but is actually or should be attempting to find a closer approach, a more penetrating and vivid expression of things as they are.[32]

With Williams's manifesto of what he called a "new, plastic theatre" that combined screen devices, music, lighting, and mise en scene, all to achieve a unified effect, such tenets carried naturally over from stage to screen.

For the play, as Brenda Murphy writes, "Objectifying Blanche's subjectivity in the stage language meant bringing in the elements of her constructed psychology – a set of experiences and motivations created for her by the director – into action and behavior."[33] Relying on designer Jo Mielziner's formidable talent, the director found that his combination of set designs and lighting "helped to produce the stylized effect that Kazan was after, neither conventional realism nor expressionism, but a new visual environment."[34] Up until his *Panic in the Streets* (1950), Kazan said that "I'd direct actors moving in and out of dramatic arrangements just as I might have done on stage, with the camera photographing them mostly in medium shot." By the time of *Streetcar*, his ongoing education with the camera taught him that "the camera is not only a recording device but a penetrating instrument. It looks into a face, not at a face. A camera can even be a microscope. Linger, enlarge, analyze, study."[35] To project

Blanche's inner self for the film, Kazan would experiment with new shots and angles, above all letting the camera do the work. As his film notes (to himself) advise,

> So crawl into her with your camera. Be free. Don't listen to cutters. You explain to them what you want to get over . . . There is no use in the world in doing Streetcar unless you really make work your idea about "subjective photography," using the camera to penetrate Blanche and then showing the SUBJECTIVIZED source of the emotion.[36]

In a rare one-act draft version of *Streetcar* that the author of this essay located at the Harry Ransom Center of the University of Texas, entitled *Interior: Panic*, Williams takes his expressionistic impulses to another level, as here part of the dialogue is "real," and some is presented as "auditory hallucination," heard only by Blanche. In this play, Williams describes Blanche as becoming increasingly detached from her surroundings, hearing disembodied voices as she moves further into paranoid insanity. Williams provides stage directions that echo Blanche's growing psychosis: "the scene is in a room as it appears to a person on the verge of insanity. Everything is distorted in a similar fashion . . . In fact, nearly everything that occurs on the stage is what is seen, heard, felt, or suspected in a state of hysteria."[37] In his notes on filming *Streetcar*, Kazan seems to have been in complete accord with Williams's vision: "Photograph everything that hurts her. Everything that makes her feel bewildered, helpless, lost, left out. Give the audience the pain she feels."[38] As Williams's one-act and other fragments eventually evolved to the full-length play, Williams wanted to keep in place many of the early expressionistic devices, including all of the hallucinatory voices, but Kazan convinced him to jettison some of this material. For the film, however, both collaborators recognized the necessity of charting Blanche's slipping grip on sanity with probing cameras and sound effects, including the disembodied, echoing voices. Kazan's final notes on the filmscript reflect this emphasis: "See and hear as she hears and sees . . . Blanche is extra aware of sounds. They connote all and evoke emotions. They simply affect her high-strung nature."[39] In fully embracing Williams's idea of subjectivizing Blanche, Kazan believed that "This will make for a new kind of story telling. You tell not the literal facts, as an observer might see them. You bring directly to the screen BLANCHE'S WORLD."[40] It is important to point out, however, that the spectator enters "Blanche's World" not so much by use of the subjective camera per se, i.e., seeing through Blanche's eyes, but rather vis-à-vis cinematographer Harry Strandling's penetrating close-ups and moody chiaroscuro lighting,

as well as soundman C. A. Riggs's haunting voiceovers. These visual and
auditory effects actually allow us privileged glimpses into Blanche's
mind without employing the obvious (and probably less effective) treatment afforded by the camera presenting Blanche's strictly subjective
point of view.

The camera and Blanche's world

One of the film's opening sequences (and the only one shot on location in
New Orleans) helps establish "Blanche's World" by separating her from
the rest of the crowd as she disembarks the train that has brought her to
New Orleans. As passengers greet their loved ones amid the hustle and
bustle of the arriving train, Blanche materializes out of the locomotive's
steam looking bewildered and incongruous to her environment. Kazan's
shooting script supplies the details:

> The space between two trains is filled with blowing steam and smoke.
> Passengers go down the lane between the trains, and a party in Carnival
> costumes are seeing someone off. Passengers from the arriving trains come
> toward the camera. Blanche's figure advances exhaustedly through the night-
> marish tunnel of the station. Everything is in misty focus . . . The flickering
> light from the train windows falls with shuttle-like effect of her face and her
> figure in its mothlike garments. The soft focus clears to a thin mist, like the
> vapor of a steam engine. The opposing crowd through which she struggles to
> move must be created non-realistically. The figures are not even quite
> identifiable as human – perhaps more like rocks in a torrent against which
> she is fighting her way to some source of light and liberation.[41]

As Blanche bends her way toward the Kowalski flat, she dodges puddles as
if walking through a mine field, the raucous noises and lights further
confusing her advancement. When she finally meets up with Stella, the
sisters gather in a bowling alley booth. As Blanche fidgets with her cigarette
and slurps down drinks, low-key lighting and shot/countershots of her
and Stella establish the story involving her departure from Belle Reve
and provide an "uncomfortable spotlight" for her frenetic narrative.
Blanche shields her face with her hands, suggesting her frazzled mental
state but also implying her shame when fabricating the circumstances of
her ignominious departure from Laurel (renamed "Oriel" in the film).
Once they arrive at the apartment, Blanche explains to her sister how she
has lost the plantation, and a medium-shot sequence illustrates the sisters
sparring with both words and body language. As Blanche defensively reacts
to Stella's "accusing" her of losing the home place, a locomotive engine

provides an auditory cue for Blanche's emotional inner state, and she flees the apartment with Stella in pursuit. As she describes their relatives' "long parade to the graveyard," the camera moves beyond Stella's face to fill the frame with Blanche's anguish. Stanley soon arrives, the camera's gaze mirroring Blanche's devouring eyes as she literally sizes up her brother-in-law, who is outfitted in a sweat-drenched, tight-fitting tee shirt, accentuating Brando's gym-ripped physique. With the camera lingering on Stanley, scopophilia is now situated within the female gaze, and cinematic history has been made. As Stanley removes his shirt, Blanche continues her seemingly involuntary fixation with Stanley's body, her dialogue trailing off to a lustful (even if self-consciously shameful) visual appraisal of Stanley's muscular endowment. Shots/countershots ensue, with Stanley constantly shifting his gaze to Blanche's bosom. The sexual tension thus established early in the film, Blanche collapses into a chair to recover her senses as Stanley prods her about her past. When he says, "she [Stella] said you were married once, weren't you?" the lines echo as if from an internal stimulus, and Blanche's anguished visage entirely fills the camera in one of Kazan's efforts to "crawl into her with your camera and your sound." Forced to relive Allan Grey's suicide, Blanche hallucinates hearing the shot in a tortured close-up, putting her hands over her ears as if to stop the sound that still torments her. A light flashing behind her accentuates the trauma, and the scene's tension is then relieved by cutting to the next day.

One of the most interesting and revealing sequences occurs during Stanley's interrogation of Blanche's losing the property. Stella has left the apartment to get Blanche a Coke, providing her sister a chance to flirt with her brother-in-law-executioner. Blanche coquettishly sprays him with her perfume, prompting Stanley to blurt out, "you know, if I didn't know you were my wife's sister, I'd get ideas about you." Here, Blanche, affecting her best southern belle routine, says, "after all, a woman's charm is fifty per cent illusion," but she then tosses her thick southern affectation and drops her voice to a throaty declaration when she says, "but when a thing is important, I tell the truth." In shot/countershot, Stanley continues his inquisition, which leads to a protracted shot of Blanche fondling Allan Grey's billet-doux, further establishing her remorse over his death.

Performance within performance

Later in the film, when Mitch returns to visit Blanche after learning of her sordid backstory (courtesy of Stanley), Blanche's descent into hysteria accelerates quickly. Only *she* hears (but mentions to Mitch) the music – "*What* music?" he responds – and then Blanche hears the gunshot again. A shadowy, blurred background is juxtaposed with a full-frame of Blanche's face as she listens intently to the sounds that only she and the filmgoer can hear. This scene segues into one of the most emotionally violent and painfully revealing moments in the film, when Mitch strips the shade of the light bulb, symbolically discarding all of Blanche's illusions about her age and beauty. Mitch says he wants "realism," but for Blanche, "I want magic!" This is followed by her saying, "I tell what *ought* to be truth," two of the most telling lines in the film. Blanche delivers these lines from a position crumpled on the floor as Mitch, in a dominating position, stares from above. In close shot/countershots depicting Blanche's heavily made-up, aging face, illuminated by the naked bulb and squeezed by Mitch's grip, it becomes painfully clear that Blanche's illusions have been supplanted by ugly reality. As Kazan recalls in his autobiography, "I particularly remember the one [close-up] of the naked light bulb [where] we thrust Blanche's face under its harsh light. She looks patho-logically drawn and aged. This was more telling on film than on the stage."[42] Confronted by the unflattering light, and by Mitch's revelations involving her past, she drops her southern pretense and utters the flat consonants and vowels of a desperate woman under interrogation. In a brilliant symbolic moment, her psychological descent is complemented by a shot from out of the apartment door featuring a spectral woman selling "flowers for the dead" – the exchange between Blanche and this matron underscoring Grey's suicide and symbolically portending her own psychic demise. As the camera peers over the matron's shoulder into Blanche's panicked visage, the brief moment becomes too much to bear, and she slams the door in the vendor's face, shouting, "No! No!" Her voice again flattened and bereft of the southern accent, Blanche describes the history of death at Belle Reve. After Mitch forcefully kisses her (but then says she's not pure enough for marriage), Blanche chases him out of the apartment, screaming and wailing for all the neighbors and passers-by to hear.

In perhaps the most effective portrayal of her psychological disintegra-tion, Kazan shoots a close-up of Blanche hanging onto an outdoor railing as disembodied, echoing voices ask, "Are you all right, lady?" Alex North's frenzied music underscores Blanche's frantic, futile efforts to shut out reality as she slams the shutters and extinguishes the lights. A complete dissociative break is demonstrated in the next cut, which features her in an evening gown and tiara, speaking to imaginary suitors in a lilting, syrupy southern accent. Stanley's return to the apartment startles her into a quick cover-up about an imaginary cruise with an old admirer, Shep Huntleigh.

These five minutes of film, with Leigh moving from shock to madness to a full psychic break, illustrate a feature of her performance perhaps undervalued by critics. Here, as elsewhere, Vivien Leigh is playing Blanche, but Blanche is playing a part also – the distraught southern aristocrat – and rather than Leigh losing sight of her role by slipping in and out of character, it is brilliantly played so that *Blanche, not Leigh*, slips in and out of character. Leigh is an actress playing a part, but Blanche is also an actress playing a part – to recognize this complicated construct is to acknowledge the greatness of Leigh's performance and to help understand why she won best actress for 1951. As Linda Cahir notes, Leigh's classical training and "stylized performance" actually suited her perfectly for playing the role of Blanche. "Essentially, the character Blanche DuBois is an actress in the classical tradition; she assumes, rather than subsumes, a series of roles. Thus, in paradox, Leigh's classical acting, thought to be inappropriate [opposite the Method acting of Brando], speaks to the essence of Blanche DuBois, and in this odd circumstance could be argued to constitute a form of method acting."[43] In assuming the role of innocent belle (and thus acting a part) for Stanley, Mitch, and others, Leigh oscillates between Blanche's actual self and a fabricated mask. James Naremore terms this kind of acting "performance within performance" and notes the relationship between the actor and the audience as well as that of the actor with the other players:

> Sometimes we are as much taken in by these performances as the characters in the drama: sometimes we know that a character is behaving falsely because the plot has given us information; and sometimes we can see indications of deception in a player's expression even when these signs are invisible to others.[44]

Early on in the film, Stanley is keen to these "deceptions" as not only pretense but as actions constituting a threat to Stella's inheritance, and his efforts to determine the facts surrounding the dissolution of Belle Reve result in Blanche's temporary abandonment of her mask, providing what Naremore calls "expressive incoherence." Blanche's sudden shift in tone and affect during the "lay my cards on the table" dialogue precisely demonstrate the kind of acting that affords dramatic irony and emotional richness to the role.[45]

In one of Kazan's most brilliant camera shots adumbrating the rape scene, Stanley pins Blanche to the bed. Here the camera angle shifts to Blanche's subjectivized POV, with the menacing Stanley glaring down like a mad beast. Blanche looks for a means to escape, but she opens the door

Figure 4.2 Stanley (Marlon Brando) pins down Blanche during the rape scene.

Figure 4.3 Blanche's deterioration accelerates after Mitch rejects her as being "unclean."

only to conjure again the apparition of the flower woman. Her desperation leads her into a frantic, discombobulated phone call for help; then Stanley appears in his pajamas. The rest of the scene, including the rape, has also become cinematic history.

At the film's conclusion, as the nurse and doctor arrive and lead Blanche away, most of the dialogue is projected as if Blanche is inside an echo chamber. Her crackup now complete, Blanche is reduced to a writhing mass on the floor, the camera moving into a close-up frame that is shot above the doctor to focus on her helplessly lying upside down.

Interestingly, as Blanche's world begins to turn upside down, Leigh's own grip on sanity became more tenuous as well. Her full investment in the role came at a price, for several biographies have chronicled her psychological instability as she became more and more involved with the part. With Kazan's attempt to bring the picture's main focus back to Blanche's psychological disintegration, and thus arouse some of the pity previously unregistered in the stage play, Kazan found a star who not only fit the role perfectly but unwittingly became a victim of it. Even before the filming began, Leigh's bipolar condition was being accelerated by her run on stage in London. After the play concluded, the actress confessed, "I had nine months in the theatre with Blanche DuBois. Now she's in command of me."[46] Leigh's deterioration was further exacerbated during the filming of *Streetcar*, as she even began mimicking some of Blanche's phrases off set. As she candidly admitted, playing Blanche in the film "tipped me over into madness."[47] Although Leigh and Brando shared the camera in an alliance of mutual respect from start to finish, Brando later confessed that he found her "very much like Tennessee's wounded butterfly. Like Blanche, she . . . was beginning to dissolve mentally and to fray at the ends physically."[48] The heavy price Leigh paid for the role was eventually mitigated by its reward – Best Actress in a Leading Role for 1951. At the twenty-fourth Academy Awards ceremony, however, she was not present to accept the Oscar.

Endnotes

Herrick – Margaret Herrick Library, Center for Motion Picture Study, Academy of Motion Picture Arts and Sciences, Beverly Hills, California
HRC – The Harry Ransom Humanities Research Center, University of Texas at Austin
WB/USC Warner Bros. Archives, University of Southern California
WUCA – Wesleyan University Center Archives, Middletown, Connecticut

 1 Elia Kazan, *A Life* (New York: Alfred A. Knopf, 1988), 495.
 2 Brenda Murphy, *Tennessee Williams and Elia Kazan: A Collaboration in the Theatre* (Cambridge University Press, 1992), 12.
 3 Murphy, *Tennessee Williams and Elia Kazan*, 62.
 4 Selznick to Wood, 1954 (HRC).
 5 William Baer, ed., *Elia Kazan Interviews* (Jackson: University Press of Mississippi, 2000), 40–41.
 6 Kazan, *A Life*, 495.
 7 For the most complete summary of the negotiations among Williams, Kazan, Warner Bros., and the Production Code Administration, see R. Barton Palmer and William Robert Bray, *Hollywood's Tennessee: The Williams Films and Postwar America* (Austin: University of Texas Press, 2009).
 8 Ibid., 334–335.
 9 Ibid., 383.
10 Williams to Kazan, December 1949 (WUCA).
11 Kazan to Williams, n.d. (HRC).
12 Albert J. Devlin and Nancy M. Tischler, eds., *The Selected Letters of Tennessee Williams: Volume II, 1945–1957* (New York: New Directions, 2004), 355.
13 Williams to Kazan, January 27, 1950 (WUCA).
14 Williams to Kazan, February 24, 1950 (WUCA).
15 Kazan, *A Life*, 384.
16 Baer, *Elia Kazan Interviews*, 107.
17 Kazan, *A Life*, 384.
18 Ibid., 384.
19 Elia Kazan, *Kazan on Directing* (New York: Alfred A. Knopf, 2009), 63.
20 Ibid., 343.
21 Ibid., 345.
22 Ibid., 385.
23 Ibid., 386.
24 Ibid., 386–387.
25 Ibid., 330.
26 Ibid.
27 Ibid., 156.
28 Ibid., x–xi.
29 Ibid., xi.
30 Quoted in ibid., xii.
31 Arthur Miller, *Timebends: A Life* (New York: Harper and Row, 1987), 181–182.
32 Tennessee Williams, *Memoirs* (New York: Doubleday, 1975), 134–135.
33 Murphy, *Tennessee Williams and Elia Kazan*, 25.
34 Ibid., 27.
35 Kazan, *A Life*, 380–381.

36 Kazan, *Kazan on Directing*, 156–157.

37 Robert Bray, ed., *Tennessee Williams Annual Review* (2007), 51.

38 (WUCA).

39 Kazan, *Kazan on Directing,* 157.

40 (WUCA).

41 (WUCA).

42 Kazan, *A Life*, 385.

43 Linda Cahir, "The Artful Rerouting of *A Streetcar Named Desire*," *Literature/ Film Quarterly* 22 (1994), 74.

44 James Naremore, *Acting in the Cinema* (Berkeley: University of California Press, 1988), 70.

45 Ibid., 76.

46 Terry Coleman, *Olivier, the Authorized Biography* (New York: Bloomsbury Publishing, 2005), 233–236.

47 Anthony Holden, *Olivier* (New York: Atheneum Books, 1988), 312–313.

48 Marlon Brando quoted in Stefan Kanfer, *Somebody: The Reckless Life and Remarkable Career of Marlon Brando* (New York: Alfred A. Knopf, 2008), 99.

CHAPTER 5

Come back, little scopophile: William Inge, Daniel Mann, and cinematic voyeurism

John S. Bak

Introduction

William Inge's first theatre and film critics were often quick to point out the playwright's reliance upon nostalgic themes to portray a mid-century America unraveling at the seams, yet most only picked through the Freudian baggage that many of his brooding characters carry with them on their journeys through 1950s America. Because Inge so often shouted to audiences through gregarious and heterosexually liberated characters like Bo, Cherie, Hal, Lola, Marie, and Turk, these early critics often ignored those whispers that were his more taciturn, sexually enigmatic characters. And yet, it is precisely in these whispers that Inge's commentaries on postwar psychosexuality in American are most revealing. More recent critics like Ralph Voss, Jeff Johnson, and Robert Combs have turned up the volume on Inge, and what they heard made them declare the "senti-mentalist" Inge dead. The nostalgic playwright, they have concerted, was much more subversive than previously thought. Though not as theatrically audacious or as socially truculent in the 1950s as was his mentor Tennessee Williams (which is one reason why Inge was able to fly beneath the radar for so long), Inge nonetheless chartered the violent and repressed corners of the American heartland through more liminal characters like Virgil Blessing, Gerald Lyman, and Doc Delaney.

If healthy heterosexual appetites were already enough to titillate the silent generation into bouts of "giggly hysteria,"[1] alternative sexualities rocked these interbellumers to their ticky-tacky foundations. Williams celebrated it, Inge intuited it, and Alfred C. Kinsey exposed it. Inge simply negotiated his space between the Williams–Kinsey extremes of sociosexual commentary. In *William Inge and the Subversion of Gender*, Jeff Johnson calls this negotiating "gendermandering": "the intentional undermining of expected gender roles for the dramatic purpose of politically and socially destabilizing social norms."[2] These "gendermandered" characters, in

Johnson's terms, are those that "pretend to essentialist characteristics yet essentially act against type."[3] They are those "potent female characters that exhibit patently male qualities and seemingly dominate male characters that display archetypal feminine traits,"[4] This sex/gender bait-and-switch – a stage technique that Williams, Broadway's then-unrivaled bad boy, had long put into practice – infused Inge's plays with subversive sexual codes and inverted gender patterns that not only escaped the purveyors of the Wales Padlock law but also, and perhaps more importantly, the numerous Broadway audiences that went to see them.

Despite the many inroads Johnson laid into our reading Inge anew, he chose not to deal with the "adaptations or collaborations"[5] of Inge's work, such as the film version of *Come Back, Little Sheba*.[6] And yet, I would add that Daniel Mann's 1952 film adaptation of the play, for which Inge did not write the screenplay but offered suggestions,[7] supplies its own visual equivalent of gendermandering that helped navigate its safe passage through the film industry's Production Code of 1930 (Hays Code), where scenes of "[e]xcessive and lustful kissing, lustful embraces, and suggestive postures and gestures" were prohibited.[8] Mann, director of both the Broadway play and the Hollywood film *Come Back, Little Sheba*, ultimately avoided confrontation with the Code and its ban on suggestive behavior and themes by swapping the play's exploration of sexual transgression for the film's moral message of sexual education. But like Elia Kazan before him, who restituted desire in the Code-censored film version of *A Streetcar Named Desire* through the clever use of visual metaphors of sexual potency and release,[9] Mann filmed *Come Back, Little Sheba* with a visual language of erotic tableaux that reconstitute those themes deemed immoral by the Code. By implicating the audience's voyeuristic role in the play's shadow theme of scopophilia – that is, in deriving pleasure from looking at someone, a phenomenon Laura Mulvey popularized in her 1975 study of filmic voyeurism, "Visual Pleasure and Narrative Cinema," Mann's direction and James Wong Howe's cinematography combine to empower the film's viewers to sympathize with and not denigrate its voyeuristic couple, Doc and Lola. In *seeing* Inge anew, what becomes evident is how the film's marketing and its cinematography supply this visual language of eroticism that counters the film's more nostalgic and sentimental message of lost youth, just as the play's theatrical language had couched its theme of marital dystopia within a "broader social arena of current sexual politics and contemporary expectations of gender."[10]

Part one: "you cannot defy convention or the laws of God"

Come Back, Little Sheba premiered at the Booth Theatre on February 15, 1950 and ran for 190 performances, earning both Sidney Blackmer (Doc) and Shirley Booth (Lola) Tony Awards for their respective performances. Later that year, Hollywood producer Hal B. Wallis purchased the play's movie rights for around $100,000 and – just as Charles Feldman had done with the cast of *A Streetcar Named Desire* – handpicked the play's director Mann and leading actors Blackmer and Booth to reproduce on celluloid the magic they had conjured up on stage.[11] The transfer was not an easy one, given the play's anti-Hollywoodian appeal, as Wallis recalls in his memoirs *Starmaker*:

> Up to now, Paramount executives had agreed with everything I wanted to do, but they were appalled by the idea of filming *Come Back, Little Sheba*. Prepared to accept glamorous men and women in melodramas of the seamy side of life, they were shocked at the thought of making a picture with beaten, unkempt, depressing people [. . .]. But the decision was mine. And I hedged only one bet, casting Burt Lancaster as the husband because of his great box office appeal.[12]

For the same reasons that Vivien Leigh had replaced Jessica Tandy in the role of Blanche DuBois in *Streetcar* the year before, Lancaster was called in to succeed the older Blackmer in the role of Doc, bringing not only a Hollywood cachet to the film, but also a much more complex Freudian element, since Lancaster's Doc was now closer in age to Marie than Blackmer's had been.[13] The play was finally adapted for the screen in 1952,[14] with Inge only offering suggestions to improve Ketti Frings's screenplay.

Initial film reviews, like the theatre reviews, were positive. On December 24, 1952, Bosley Crowther, film critic for the *New York Times*, praised Booth's and Lancaster's "two sterling performances"[15] and described the film as a "vastly suggestive panorama of two pathetically cramped and wasted lives."[16] Most of these early film reviews, like their stage equivalents, focused on the couple's rejuvenation upon Marie's arrival and subsequent consternation when they discover that the co-ed's modern ways of love and petting ran counter to their silent generation's ideas of courtship (despite the fact that Doc and Lola, too, had broken their parents' sexual taboos, resulting in Lola's premarital pregnancy and banishment from her father's house).

Crowther also singled out in his review Mann's "good sense not to tamper too much with the original play of William Inge."[17] Rare is the Broadway play that is not, for one reason or another, altered considerably for the screen, but *Sheba* suffered "no major changes [...] in the story and characterization."[18] There were, of course, the obligatory exterior shots and scenes to flesh out the play, such as when Doc walks Marie part way to school or celebrates his "birthday" at the AA meeting ("one of the nicer bits of Americana in the film,"[19] no doubt inserted to placate the Code's objection to showing alcoholism in films). But each of these scenes served to underline, rather than detract from, the film's themes of familial incompatibility and generational rebellion. Even the bar scene, where Marie and Turk bide their time dancing before returning to the Delaney home to continue their petting, serves only to reiterate Turk's basic narcissism and sexual motives vis-à-vis Marie.[20] The actual "play" does not actually begin until well into the third scene of the film, once the reason for Marie's addition to the household has been established. Beyond the addition of these expository scenes, the film remains faithful to the play, barring, of course, all of those changes mandated by the Code.

For the film to pass the Production Code and receive the blessing of the Legion of Decency, which still exercised a strong influence over Catholic theatregoers and cinema owners in the 1950s, it had to preserve the tacit American double standard that women did not have sex before marriage and those who did were not the ones men wanted to marry (but do still meet in bars). Doc and Lola had in their own day defied such convention: their sexual escapades twenty years ago had landed Lola pregnant and married at eighteen[21] and forced Doc to abandon his medical studies to raise the family that never materialized following Lola's miscarriage. As Lola asks him, "Are you sorry you married me, Doc? [...] I mean, are you sorry you *had* to marry me?"[22] Doc's ambiguous response to her that "you cannot defy convention or the laws of God" carries with it less the volition of love and more the weight of their generation's (and the Code's) injunctions against premarital sex. The couple's offscreen scandal was ultimately accepted by the Code, however, because Doc and Lola did the morally *right* thing in getting married, even if their marriage today is anything but a blessing. Marital strife was seemingly the Code's quid pro quo for having transgressed the societal mores in the first place.

Among *Sheba*'s onscreen scandals that necessitated alteration, the most obvious were Marie's sociosexual transgression and Doc's obsession with the young girl. Marie's sexual license needed to be corralled (not so much that she would become a nun, however),[23] and Doc's fantasies about Marie had to be recalibrated more toward her threatened innocence than her tight-fitting blouse. The solution for both dilemmas was found in the character Turk, who, though sexually aggressive in the play, is not the date rapist he becomes in the film. By making him – and not the flirtatious Marie or the lascivious Doc – the target of public scorn, the film opened up moral space in which to explore Marie's and Doc's psychosexual struggles, while securing safe passage for both through their self-inflicted storms. For these reasons, Turk's sexual overtures in the film appear more callous and calculated so that the audience retained its respect for the innocent girl, a prisoner both to her hormones and to her era's double standards. In the film, for example, Turk has to leave the Delaney house that night for moral reasons and does so via the window so that Doc cannot know he has left. Such alterations to the play allowed Mann to respect the Code's rules concerning the young couple's petting but still justify Doc's drinking binge the following day. When Marie finally decides against sleeping with Turk and instead elopes with her fiancé Bruce the next morning, she upholds decorum and is presumably rewarded with a happy Hollywood ending.

Refocusing Doc's prurient obsession with Marie was more problematic, however. Doc's role in the play as potential lecher to Turk's lothario had to be downplayed of course, but not so much that his drinking binge would appear inexplicable. Turning Doc into an avuncular or paternal figure for Marie, as opposed to Turk's sexual rival, easily corrected the first problem, but it could not satisfactorily address the second one. While a mere denunciation of Marie's loose behavior may have reassured Inge's 1950s audiences that their morals were still in the right place (as well as the hypocrisy that inscribed them), it hardly justified Doc's falling off the wagon. In other words, if the play suggests that Doc's binge is the direct result of his violent jealousy toward Turk's having deflowered Marie (and Marie's recapitulation of Lola's erstwhile promiscuity), in the film Doc is driven back to the bottle simply by the thought that purity, which Marie incarnates for him, had been corrupted – plausible, to be sure, but not bankable as an excuse in itself for convincing 1950s audiences of Doc's relapse.

If there are any number of reasons in the play to explain Doc's alcoholism, Mann's film offers bluntly, if still not obliquely, one: "Alcoholic men drink because they are disappointed." The Code's attitude toward presenting alcoholism in films was unwavering: "The use of liquor in American life, when not required by the plot or for proper characterization, will not be shown." Here, alcoholism was obviously required, but what was Doc disappointed in? While the film avoids a definitive response to this question, it does make it clear why Doc *does not* drink: sexual transgression, imagined or otherwise. This point is made very early in the film's second scene, which is not found in Inge's play. Doc comes down the stairs and asks Lola who it was that had just come in the house, and Lola explains that it was Marie, a girl interested in renting their spare room, which Doc admits that he did not even know was for rent. Lola says that they could use the extra six dollars per month, but Doc says adamantly, "Not the Delaneys." Once he sees Marie, however, he changes his mind. Obviously smitten with the co-ed (what Mulvey calls "fetishistic scopophilia," or transforming the physical beauty of an object into "something satisfying in itself"),[24] Doc is rejuvenated, though his infatuation for her lies above the waistline. While sexual hunger obviously lurks behind Doc's (and Lola's) transformation in the play, Mann characterizes his infatuation for Marie as a schoolboy crush, as if he was trying to recover the youth he and Lola were denied when moral codes locked them in a marriage for which neither was ready or perhaps even wanted.[25]

Through this rather tame exposition to the screenplay, Mann reinforces the play's romanticized Doc and soft-pedals the prurient one, resulting in a one-dimensional character whose eventual relapse to the bottle is finally explained in terms of his disgust with seeing all that is pure and innocent in this world corrupted. Though hardly a satisfying reason by modern epistemologies for justifying one's self-destruction on the screen, lugubriosity nonetheless worked in the film because Inge had weaved it in the play in the first place to help gendermander Doc's response to Marie's beauty. In adapting the play for the screen, Frings cleverly manipulated Doc's spiritual idealism in the play into a ready-made escape-hatch for explaining his alcoholic relapse and his feelings toward Marie in the film. In short, since such a reading was already present in the play, all that was needed to satisfy the Code was to build up cathedrals to the romantic Doc and sweep the prurient one under the proverbial rug.

For all of these reasons, *Sheba* the film is much more a product of its censored times than the play. Crowther's comment about the film's appeal in his second review a fortnight later not only evinces this truism but helps provide the de facto interpretation that locked the play for decades into the sentimentalist box that it had struggled to unhinge: Wallis and Mann combined to create a motion picture "that amazingly holds the eye, as well as stirs the emotions with a build-up of tender sympathy."[26] No doubt, the film's recapitulation of the American double standard on sex before marriage, which the play problematizes, secured that "tender sympathy." As Ralph Voss notes, "[t]he film version of *Sheba* became [. . .] far more popular and better known than the Broadway play had been,"[27] if only because its nostalgia appealed to a wider audience than the play had done. Consequently, Inge's reputation for years as America's sentimentalist playwright remained, if not static, at least consistent.[28] As noted earlier, recent research by Voss, Johnson, and Combs into the cold case surrounding *Sheba*'s sentimentality have revealed a much more subversive Inge at work,[29] but one of the repercussions of their inquiries has been a widening epistemological gap in Inge criticism between the play's and the film's aesthetic appeals and sociopolitical renderings of an era, a gap I would argue that is not as marked as it may first appear.

As Robert Combs has noted in a recent article, the adults in the play *Sheba*

> have no acceptable solutions for the problems they are facing in midlife. They are as lost as their children, perhaps more so. Marie and Turk have little trouble circumventing sexual prohibitions in *Come Back, Little Sheba*. But Doc and Lola agonize voyeuristically, because they are unable to articulate their complex feelings about frustration and desire.[30]

Barring a remake, any film adapted from a play remains in aspic, the evolution of its interpretation beholden to each era's willingness to revisit, rediscover, or reinvent it; a play, on the other hand, is resuscitated by each new actor's delivering its lines, director's building upon past performances, or dramaturge's measuring its critical pulse. *Sheba* needed all of this, as well as a general thaw in the nation's mores, to have its more salacious side fully explored, evidenced in a recent production that lends full currency to Combs's interpretation. In his review of the 2008 revival for the *New York Times*, theatre critic Ben Brantley applauds the play's "surprising virtues" in its frankness with respect to sexual transgression, alcoholism, and marital incompatibility, problems audiences are more willing to confront today than in the 1950s because they reflect the norm rather than the exception to contemporary American life.[31] As Brantley writes, since the play was "about s-e-x from the zipped-up 1950s" and how "the pursuit of primal instincts derails everyday lives[,] [it] could easily tilt toward giggly hysteria" for today's audiences.[32] Thankfully, Brantley concludes, the 2008 production did not. For many contemporary film reviewers and audiences, Mann's film had tilted, appearing today no more than "a soggy period piece" of a bygone era.[33]

Despite the film's datedness and being out of joint with respect to the current critical discourse on Inge's play, there is still no denying its sexually charged visual language. Mann's film was indeed ripe for its times, when sex was poised to make the transition from the bedroom to the living room (or at least to the screening room). If Americans did not openly talk about sex in the 1950s, privately they could not shut up about it, or so Alfred

Kinsey proclaimed. Hollywood understood this about *Sheba* back in 1952 and realized that it could still capitalize – within the Code's limits, of course – on the play's oozing sensuality, one fact alone that establishes the film's closer affinities with the play. No doubt that fact had played into Wallis's decision to replace the aging Blackmer with the younger, more alluring Lancaster. Any play that shouted the word "s-e-x" in repeated whispers as *Sheba* had done on Broadway was ideal fodder for the double standard of Hollywood's sexual economy that enticed patrons into the cinemas with sex, then subsequently teased them like many a high-school co-ed.[34]

Part two: "if it's all right for a woman, it oughta be for a man"

On the surface, the film version of *Come Back, Little Sheba* respected the Code's tradition that (sexual) virtue be rewarded and transgression punished by empowering Marie to ward off her date rapist and "learn her lesson" about what happens to "loose" girls. The more the film's script became domesticated, however, the more its visual language heightened the play's erotica. Perhaps Mann learned the lesson himself from watching Elia Kazan and Tennessee Williams fight Joseph Breen and the Code with regard to their rapist Stanley's necessary "punishment" in the film version of *A Streetcar Named Desire*.[35] Mann might also have learned from Kazan and Williams that there were ways around the Code if a director was clever enough at cinematic legerdemain. If Kazan could rejuice a Code-neutered *Streetcar* through suggestive visual metaphors and camera angles, could not Mann also breathe transgressive sexual life back into a play that was recast by Hollywood's moral majority? Mann achieved this aim by playing upon one of the play's original themes – voyeurism – and using it to reestablish certain sexual codes that the Code had not rubber stamped.

Lola and Doc are as electrified in terms of their roles in Marie's sexual awakening as Marie is herself. If in the play Lola nearly pimps for Marie, allowing her a stage on which to discover her sexuality (all the while knowing and eventually preparing for her fiancé Bruce's arrival the next day), the film's Lola comes off as being nothing more than a nostalgic busybody. Love was, after all, denied her and Doc, whose years have "vanished into thin air,"[36] just like Sheba and Mrs. Coffman's lilacs.[37] Yet her gaze toward the young couple in a passionate embrace is anything but innocent and announces clearly Lola's voyeuristic intentions (albeit romanticized) throughout the film. Doc's role with respect to Marie is more troubling, however. Is he indeed reliving through Marie that time of sexual innocence denied him in his preemptive marriage to Lola discussed earlier (not surprisingly, Doc refuses to shoulder or even share the blame for Lola's pregnancy or for his having given up his medical studies to become a chiropractor)? Or is he as predatory as Turk in his predilections toward Marie? The play, of course, buries these questions in Freudian hypothesis. The film version, though, brings it more to the fore once the significantly younger Lancaster replaced the older Blackmer in the role of Doc. The younger Doc is still no competition for Turk (or even Bruce) with regards to Marie's affections, but that does not remove the stigma of Doc's furtive leers and fetish fondling of Marie's private objects. If such topics were conventional on the Broadway stage, they were still taboo on the Hollywood screen in 1952, and Mann exploited the voyeuristic theme present in the play in order to intimate answers to those questions that the Code demanded be suppressed.

When Marie invites Turk home to sketch him for the Athletic Games poster, for example, Lola in the play is presented as being maternal in her doting affections for the future lovers. Mann problematizes this domesticated image of Lola in the film, however, having just used the sexual subtext of the "Taboo" radio program in the previous scene to establish her repressed erotic desires. Lola's looks in this sketching scene, then, are anything but innocent, despite the fact that the film attempts to portray them as such on a surface level. Thus, when Marie tells Turk to "take off [his] clothes"[38] and proceeds to sketch him, as Millie does Hal in *Picnic*,[39] desire is anything but nipped in the bud. As the play makes implicit, Marie decides against sketching him in the art studio, a neutral place where nudity is not eroticized. Instead, she brings him home and sketches his semi-naked body in the living room, just outside her bedroom, where they end up later that same evening. Just as Lola studies the Milkman's "physique study"[40] for "life class,"[41] Marie studies Turk, though in the film we are made to believe that both women only admire the beauty of the classical Greek statues that the two men represent for them.[42] Of course, Turk is a javelin thrower, instead of a hurdler (a pole-vaulter was apparently out of the question, even for Inge), and the phallic broom which Lola offers him allows Mann the opportunity to substitute visually the phallus castrated from the film's script. More importantly, the film's visual language lets Mann turn Lola from simple admirer to obsessive ogler.

In the play, for instance, Turk admits to Marie that Lola, who "*peers*" at him, makes him "feel naked."[43] Inge made it clear that Lola's gazes were only matronly on the surface. While it was understandable by the Code's

Figure 5.1 Lola ogles Turk's javelin. (frame enlargement)

standards to suggest a young Marie's fascination with Turk's physique (her respectful sexual education again), it was unacceptable to have Turk visibly arouse a middle-aged woman.[44] Yet aroused Lola is, and openly so, if only for a brief second, devouring his metonymic broomstick with her eyes.

"Didn't she ever see a man before,"[45] Turk complains in both the play and the film, and Marie, her hands again suggestively groping his chest, rejoins playfully, "not a big beautiful man like you." He responds in the film by grabbing her violently and admonishing her: "You know, you are going to get yourself into a lot of trouble." Turk's strong words, which foreshadow his attempted date rape later in the film (there is no "trouble" comment in the play since Marie *is* complicit), quickly redirect our attention away from Lola's gaze and onto the couple's rising sexual agon.

As such, the innocence behind Lola's spying on the "spooning" kids is subtly called into question in the film. In the film's promotional poster, Lola is relegated to the background, gazing secretly at the young lovers' embrace, just as Doc is, but her expression is no more motherly than his is paternal or avuncular. In several shots from the film, for instance, we see this pattern repeated: Lola lurking in the background, while the lovers play out their seduction scene. Whether from behind a cracked door or a veiled

Figure 5.2 Lola (Shirley Booth) as voyeur, admiring Turk (Richard Jaeckel) and Marie's (Terry Moore) petting. (frame enlargement)

window, Lola is seen "observing" Turk and Marie kissing. In one shot, Lola is "*standing by the doorway where she can peek at them.*"[46] The slit made by the door, or the parted folds in the second shot's window veils, was a frequent cinematographic trick to represent the hymen, and Lola's endearing smile (like Doc's with the perfume salts later) does little to disarm the violation of her – and by extension our – voyeuristic act.

In an act of *mise en abyme*, as Laura Mulvey has shown, Lola enjoys looking at the couple as much as we enjoy the gaze ourselves because it allows us to stare at the couple's love scene *and* see others doing it, too, which removes the stigma of our own voyeuristic acts by acknowledging its universal appeal. With a smile or not, Lola's voyeurism (and our own) still is illicit, though Mann removes its essential stigma by contrasting it with Doc's voyeurism.

Part three: "you *were* the first one, Daddy, the *only* one"

In Inge's play, Lola's gendermanding, like Marie's, is handled directly and unashamedly. In Mann's film, though, he needed to find a similar visual language to depict Doc's sexual frustration. Just as the "jungle tom-toms" of Lola's exotic "Taboo" radio program in the play are meant to suggest that she confronts her demons to tame them, Doc's listening to the "Ave Maria" on the radio while "fondl[ing] Marie's scarf" (or sniffing her bath salts, as in the film) is intended to paint a much darker Doc unwilling to fess up to his own sexual dysfunctions. The play exploits that darkness to its fullest extent, where his admiration for the "*ethereal beauty*"[47] of the two Maries combats – or camouflages – the deep-seeded sexual desire he harbors for the co-ed. But Mann's Doc, like his Lola, is fully sanitized in the screenplay, and Doc's ambiguous admiration for Marie in the play becomes essentially a romanticized one in the film. For reasons related to the Code's stand against inferring that "low forms of sex relationship are the accepted or common thing" or "stimulat[ing] the lower and baser element," Mann turns the play's shadowy Doc, whose alcoholism is sparked as much by his disgust for his miserable life as it is by his lust for Marie, into a romantic shell of a man, whose alcoholism is ignited by a sense of having been cheated out of life's sublime offerings. Again, though, Mann counters this psychologically reductive Doc with a voyeuristic double that subtly captures in him, as Mann had done with Lola, a prurience forbidden by the Code.

For Inge, what makes Doc in the play a shadowy figure is his weakness in admitting to or confronting his dark thoughts about Marie. If anything, what saves Lola from a similar bout with alcoholism is her honest (or ignorant) attempt to locate releases for her sexual frustration. Unlike Doc in the play, Lola is a voyeur, and proudly admits to it, since for her the purpose of her observing nature is to admire young love and not the sex that it leads to (though that is implicit). When Turk returns in Act 1, and he and Marie are "*spooning behind a book*," Lola "*stands silently watching*" them and breaks out in a "*broad, pleasant smile*."[48] She even invites Doc to "[c]ome and look," but he angrily refuses. She then insists: "Just one little look. They're just kids, Daddy. It's sweet."[49] But Doc denies his own voyeuristic tendencies: "Stop it, Baby. I won't do it. It's not decent [just as he says her opening Marie's telegram was not decent] to snoop around spying on people like that. It's cheap and mischievous and mean."[50] Lola insists that she does not spy on Marie to be "mischievous and mean,"[51] just as she had not seen her steaming open the telegram as being a form of spying.[52] Lola even points out Doc's double standard:

> You watch people make love in the movies, don't you, Doc? There's nothing wrong with that. And I *know* Marie and I like her, and Turk's nice, too. They're both so young and pretty. Why shouldn't I watch them?[53]

Doc's voyeurism is public, not private like Lola's, and sanctioned (appropriately enough) by the cinema. To be sure, Doc in the play does not spy directly on Turk and Marie and does not even know that Turk spent the night, only that Turk was in her room late: "I heard her; it was after midnight [. . .] I thought I heard a man's voice."[54] Once Doc hears Turk laughing like a "*sated Bacchus*" in Marie's room the following morning, he faces the truth, and the "*lyrical grace, the spiritual ideal of the Ave Maria is shattered*"[55] for him. Running into Turk later as he tries to make his escape and sharing with him a "*moment of blind embarrassment*"[56] only serve to accentuate Doc's obsession with the girl's deflowering. Were Doc as gregarious as Dr. Lyman in *Bus Stop*, it is not beyond reason that he would eventually make a play for Marie himself, instead of simply taking pleasure in fondling her personal objects.[57] Lacking Lyman's slick tongue (and Lola's logorrhea), Doc turns instead to the bottle to quell his desire.

Inge's two-faced Doc was, of course, difficult to sell in Hollywood. Frings recognized the problems early on in the adaption process and opted for the disillusioned Doc rather than the dysfunctional one. Though neutered of his sexual potency, the film's Doc was still an effective troubled alcoholic. Inge biographer Ralph Voss notes that Mann, a lot like Inge himself, "was still a young director then" and, in direct contrast to Kazan, was "probably not inclined to push any Hollywood envelopes." As such, Mann did not try to show "anything beyond suggestiveness by 1952 standards [so] that the code people had[n't] any complaint."[58] And yet, there are moments in the film when a visual language – a gesture, a look, a camera angle – does recall the play's darker Doc that Frings marginalized, just as Mann had captured Lola's sexual frustration. Two of the most striking examples concern Doc's fetishism and his own bout of voyeurism in scenes not found in the play.

From the very beginning of the film, it is obvious that Marie is the altar upon which Doc sacrifices his material attachments to this world. When he runs to the bathroom, after having just witnessed that sacrosanct image of her threatened in the scene where she is sketching the semi-naked Turk, Doc calms his palpitations with Marie's perfumed bath salts in a bottle that foreshadows the whiskey bottle to which he will turn later when his image of the "Ave Maria" is completely shattered. Doc's fondling of the bottle of bath salts is accompanied by a schmaltzy harp air that is meant to underscore the romanticism of his perception of Marie as innocence incarnate and to clarify for us that Doc's intentions are, as far as Marie is concerned, purely aesthetic or nostalgic.

Figure 5.3 Doc (Burt Lancaster) and his psychological crutch. (frame enlargement)

While the perfume is innocent enough here in suggesting Doc's need for beautiful things, the fact that they are bath salts and in the bathroom complicates that romantic signifier. Mann could have had Doc smell Marie's scarf (though that, too, would be unsettling), for example, but instead he places Doc in the same room where a naked Marie daily sprinkles the salts over the bathwater that she will slip into. That the scene is not in the play and that its message could have been established in ways less erotic was surely not lost on Mann.

The second scene, which again was not part of Inge's play but which, like the bathroom scene, eroticizes the film's overall visual language, takes place just prior to the end of Act 1, when Marie and Turk spend the night together. In the film, Marie is denied this night of passion, for reasons discussed earlier, so Doc could not find out the next day that Turk had not in fact spent the night, as Doc discovers in the play that he had. Mann and Frings knew that they needed to have both Doc and the audience see Turk entering Marie's room at night, but only the film's audience sees him leave moments later by the bedroom window, disgusted that Marie will not put out for him. The result is a moment of cinematic voyeurism that satisfies this narrative dilemma and puts a new spin on Doc's honesty, recalling Doc's earlier rebuke of Lola's spying on the young couple kissing.

When Lola asked Doc earlier, "They're so sweet and nice, why shouldn't I watch them," he does not have an answer: "I don't know, Baby, but it is not nice."[59] Such voyeurism lies at the heart of the dramatic *and* cinematic experiences, for we, too, are watching "young people making love in the movies" as Doc does and, moreover, watching Doc watch the couple, just as we had earlier watched Lola watching the couple. When is voyeurism an acceptable social act and when isn't it is one of Inge's more probing questions in *Sheba*. Mann's film unquestionably toys with this same question, and it is in his suggestive answer that he restores Doc's darker side.

Freud defined scopophilia in *Three Essays on Sexuality* and in *Instincts and Their Vicissitudes* as a pre-genital autoeroticism that generates pleasure from looking at someone. In "Visual Pleasure and Narrative Cinema," Laura Mulvey applies this theory to instances of filmic voyeurism where women are objectified on screen for the pleasure of male audiences. Taken to its extremes, Mulvey writes, scopophilia "can become fixated into a perversion, producing obsessive voyeurs and Peeping Toms, whose only sexual satisfaction can come from watching, in an active controlling sense, an objectified object."[60] The cinema is a perfect locus for such an act because the "extreme contrast between the darkness in the auditorium (which also isolates the spectators from one another) and the brilliance of the shifting patterns of light and shade on the screen helps to promote the illusion of voyeuristic separation."[61] It is no doubt this "illusion of voyeuristic separation" that pleases Doc when he goes to the cinema (and audiences when they attend Inge's play) to look in on "a private world"[62] of "young people making love in the movies." But scopophilia also fulfills a secondary role, that of ego recognition, an act of self-preservation by identifying with a particular figure on the screen. In filmic language, Mulvey explains,

> one implies a separation of erotic identity of the subject from the object on the screen (active scopophilia), the other demands identification of the ego with the object on the screen through the spectator's fascination with and recognition of his like. The first is a function of his sexual instincts, the second of ego libido.[63]

In terms of Lola's (in the play and in the film) and Doc's (only in the film) voyeurism, it might be said that Lola's is more representative of Hollywood's and the Code's principle of cinematic pleasure in that it creates as its goal a hero worshipping which helps formulate or reconstruct the fragile or damaged ego, among whom Lola's certainly can be counted.

By extension, the spectator's observation of Lola watching Turk and Marie serves essentially to help the audience identify with Lola's ego-struggle and gain its sympathy in her struggle to recover what has been lost or denied her for the last twenty years – her child, her dog, and her husband's love and respect. By contrast, Doc's voyeuristic moment does not create a similar object–subject–spectator relationship, and what it leaves the audience with is the discomforting feeling of having also violated the young couple's intimacy.

We are no doubt meant to empathize with Doc's own ego-struggle upon the sudden discovery in this scene of the couple outside Marie's bedroom, evident in Doc's frowning and the lowering of his eyes as he slinks his way up the stairs. Mann rightfully avoids the subjective camera angle here and has us instead concentrate on Doc's shocked and disappointed response to what he observes, just as Mann earlier had us focus on both the couple and Lola, and then on Lola's nostalgic smile. But Doc here is clearly *not* taking pleasure in watching Turk seduce Marie as Lola does, and it pains him to see the two together – in this place and at this time of the night. Lingering outside Marie's door before climbing the stairs, and all but peeking in through the keyhole for a better look (as he had accused Lola of doing), Doc fails to achieve the object–subject–spectator triad of voyeurism, since we know that his intentions in the act are not as naïve as Lola's. Doc is more culpable than she is simply because he *knows* better than she that one should not spy on someone else and, in doing so, *admits* as much to the illicitness of his acts.

Furthermore, the dark of the nighttime setting where Doc makes his hapless discovery reproduces the cinema's "illusion of voyeuristic separation." As a result, the epistemological gap between Doc and the spectator narrows radically. We are no longer observing Doc watch Turk and Marie, as we had done with Lola, but rather are *watching* Doc and Turk and Marie ourselves. If Lola spied on Turk and Marie during the daytime and when they were in more "public" spaces like the living room or the sidewalk, we are now spying (along with Doc) on their love-making in a more intimate setting. The residual effect is much more erotic than at first appears to the casual spectator, for instead of witnessing the love scene through his eyes and adopting his thoughts subjectively, we are positioned behind him, looking over his shoulder and thus being as much a voyeur as he is.

This object–subject–spectator relationship in the film supplies the needed sexual indeterminacy surrounding Doc's infatuation with Marie and the audience's duplicity in engendering that indeterminacy, which the play *Sheba* makes more explicit. Inge's and Mann's gendermandered Doc, then, both "pretend to essentialist characteristics yet essentially act against type":[64] in the play by cloaking his prurience toward Marie in clerical garbs; in the film by vicariously making love to Marie through surreptitious acts of smelling and gazing.

Conclusion: from "I'll fix your eggs" to "It's good to be home"

When Wallis came knocking and eventually purchased the film rights to *Come Back, Little Sheba*, Inge was at first scared about what Hollywood would do to his play. He saw firsthand the damage it wreaked on Williams after its disastrous adaptation of *The Glass Menagerie*, and no doubt felt a similar experience awaited him: "I remember [. . .] going into the screening room to see the movie of 'Come Back, Little Sheba,' with a dreadful feeling of apprehension. It was a scary experience."[65] His fears were not warranted in the end, as he confessed to Michael Wood:

> They [cinematic techniques] make you conscious of the vast freedom of the camera as compared with the close economy of playwriting. I kept telling myself, "It all looks so easy." [. . .] [T]he camera plays on Miss Booth's face and we see its wistful expression of melancholy and immediately we have a feeling for Lola's unrealized youth and her present emotional immaturity. We felt this, too, in the play, but the camera gives it a stamp of definition.[66]

Mann also felt the initial pangs of apprehension, and this was before his relationship with Wallis began to sour. He knew the play's sexual potency intimately and no doubt wondered how he would remain loyal to it and to Inge, given Frings's Code-driven needs to sanitize the screenplay. But any film director, even one not posing as a self-styled *auteur*, as Mann says he was not,[67] must try and make the material his or her own. Kazan certainly did that with the film version of *A Streetcar Named Desire*, and Mann was not much different with *Sheba*. In his interview with Michael Wood, Mann admits: "There was something about the nature of the energy that I got from what Bill had written and given me to use that meshed with my theory in acting: where the writer ends, the director begins, and where the director ends, the actor begins, and where the actor ends is where the audience begins."[68] The spectator's role was essential to the interpretive process, and in that theory Mann found a way to negotiate the film's dual necessities to remain loyal to Inge's play but satisfy Hollywood's expectations.

Hollywood, of course, helped manage this transition through its publicity of the film. But as any reader knows about book covers, promotional posters (like today's trailers) are made to dupe or at least tease audiences into entering into the economic exchange of pleasure for money. Mann also recognized that, if he were to respect his two masters, he needed to broker a visual language that would restore the play's subtext of sexual frustration and transgression. In other words, he had to fill in the missing subtext that turned a play of failed marital coitus that ends "I'll fix your eggs" into the feel-good movie of renewed marital quietus that ends "It's good to be home." Since Mann had felt that the cinema's voyeuristic role was key to interpretation, and the play already made ample use of voyeurism as a suggestive theme of social transgression, it was perhaps ineluctable that he would use voyeurism in dialogical ways: references to it made in the textual language of the play are exploited more fully in the visual language of film. As a result, no matter how much the contents of the film version of *Come Back, Little Sheba* appear dated now, its style will remain in vogue as long as desire and its repression continue to haunt the human condition.

Endnotes

1 Ben Brantley, "So Quiet You Can Hear a Heart Stop," *New York Times* January 25, 2008. Available at http://theater.nytimes.com/2008/01/25/theater/reviews/25sheb.html?ref=theater (March 20, 2010).

2 Jeff Johnson, *William Inge and the Subversion of Gender: Rewriting Stereotypes in the Plays, Novels, and Screenplays* (Jefferson: McFarland, 2005), 20.

3 Ibid., 8–9.

4 Ibid., 21.

5 Ibid., 7.

6 Jackie Byars argues in *All that Hollywood Allows: Re-Reading Gender in 1950s Melodrama* (Chapel Hill: University of North Carolina Press, 1991) that Mann's film tends to follow a "rigid narrative structure" (115), where the woman as moral center overcomes her "deviance" in order to maintain or create "a domestic order, a family" (118).

7 In the film version, Inge was happy that "all my suggestions had been used." Quoted in Ralph Voss, *The Life of William Inge: The Strains of Triumph* (Lawrence: University Press of Kansas, 1986), 125.

8 All references in this essay to the Code's regulations to "Govern the Making of Talking, Synchronized and Silent Motion Pictures" come from www.artsreformation.com/a001/hays-code.html (October 20, 2011).

9 Though some two minutes of the film version of *Streetcar* containing these metaphors or innuendos were eventually cut from the final version due to pressure from the Catholic Legion of Decency, many others, such as the breaking of the mirror during the rape scene or an ejaculating fire hose in the jump cut that immediately follows, passed undetected.

10 Johnson, *William Inge and the Subversion of Gender*, 8.

11 Thomas F. Brady, "Wallis Acquires Inge Play for Film; Buys 'Come Back, Little Sheba' for a Reported $100,000 – Seeks Blackmer, Booth," *New York Times*, June 26, 1950. Amusements 31.

12 Hal Wallis and Charles Higham, *Starmaker: The Autobiography of Hal Wallis* (New York: Macmillan, 1980), 123. Wallis describes later his break-up with Mann in terms similar to those Mann voiced in his interview with Michael Wood.

13 Blackmer was eighteen years older than Lancaster, and Shirley Booth was fifteen years his senior, which made Doc's desire toward Marie more problematic in the film.

14 The *New York Times* review of November 16, 1952 produced stills from the film that had yet to open at the Victoria Theater in New York.

15 Bosley Crowther, "Shirley Booth, Burt Lancaster Team Up in 'Come Back, Little Sheba,' at the Victoria," *New York Times*, December 24, 1952, 13.

16 Ibid. To add to her Tony for best actress on the stage with her performance of Lola, Booth also won the Academy Award for Best Actress, a Golden Globe, the New York Film Critics Circle Award for best actress, and the *Prix d'interprétation féminine* at the Festival de Cannes 1953. The film won best international "dramatic film" (*Prix international du film dramatique*) and was nominated for but did not win the *Palm d'Or*. Terry Moore received her only Academy Award nomination for the role of Marie Buckholder.

17 Crowther, "Shirley Booth," 13.

18 Voss, *The Life of William Inge*, 125.

19 Crowther, "Shirley Booth," 13.

20 To emphasize his philandering nature, the film has Turk flirting with a blonde, who is "drooling" over him, while dancing with Marie.

21 William Inge, *Four Plays* (New York: Random House, 1958), 14.

22 Ibid., 32–33. Page references to the published play appear in endnotes. Quotations that carry no page reference are those taken directly from the film and not found in the play.

23 As such, Crowther found Terry Moore's Marie "strik[ing] precisely the right note of timeless and endless animalism" (Crowther, "Shirley Booth," 13) in her character's needs to challenge the era's sexual mores yet preserve her virginity for her future husband, Bruce.

24 Laura Mulvey, "Visual Pleasure and Narrative Cinema," in *Film Theory and Criticism: Introductory Readings*, ed. Leo Braudy and Marshall Cohen (New York: Oxford University Press, 1999), 840.

25 To ensure that Doc's obsession for Marie does not appear deviant, Mann has him repeatedly mumble "pretty Lola," and not "pretty Marie," during his detox at the city hospital.

26 Bosley Crowther, "Stage to Screen; A Consideration of Three New Movies, All Derived from Notable Plays," *New York Times*, January 11, 1953, Drama xi. Crowther adds in this second review that, despite *Sheba*'s "confined and minute view of a dismal domestic situation that plainly has little pictorial range" where its two main characters are locked in "a slow foot-race with

bathos and boredom to their graves" (Crowther, "Shirley Booth," xi), it made the successful transition from stage to screen.

27 Voss, *The Life of William Inge*, 125.

28 As Brantley writes, "By the late 1960s Inge's small, tidy canvases seemed unlikely candidates for posterity compared to the more grandly scaled work of Williams and Miller. His Freudian take on repressed American sexuality was regarded as archaic; so was his careful, paint-by-numbers dramaturgy" (Brantley, "So Quiet You Can Hear a Heart Stop," n.p.).

29 Lola and Ed Delaney, for instance, evolved in *Sheba* from minor characters in *Farther off from Heaven*, Inge's first play about the couple's "barren and unhappy marriage, devoid of all 'sex'" (Voss, *The Life of William Inge*, 85). Lola, based on Inge's eccentric aunt, even represents "two of Inge's most frequent thematic concerns – loneliness and sexual frustration" (ibid., 87).

30 Robert Combs, "Oh, Those Kids! Vanishing Childhood Innocence in the Adults of William Inge," *American Drama* 13.2 (Summer 2004), 68.

31 Proof of the play's continued success among audiences can be seen in the 1974 musical *Sheba* by Clint Ballard, Jr. (music) and Lee Goldsmith (book and lyrics) and in the 1977 television version of the play, which aired on NBC and starred Laurence Olivier, Joanne Woodward, and Carrie Fisher (directed by Silvio Narizzano and produced by Granada Television).

32 Brantley, "So Quiet You Can Hear a Heart Stop," n.p.

33 Ibid., n.p.

34 For more on Hollywood's double standard regarding sexuality, see Tanya Kryzwinska, *Sex and the Cinema* (New York: Columbia University Press, 2006); Tom Dewe Mathews, *Censored: The Story of Film Censorship in Britain* (London: Chatto & Windus, 1994); and Eric Schaefer, *"Bold! Daring! Shocking! True": A History of Exploitation Films, 1919–1959* (Durham: Duke University Press, 1999).

35 For more on this, see Nancy Tischler, "'Tiger – Tiger!': Blanche's Rape on Screen," in *Magical Muse: Millennial Essays on Tennessee Williams*, ed. Ralph F. Voss (Tuscaloosa and London: University of Alabama Press, 2002), 50–69; R. Barton Palmer, "Hollywood in Crisis: Tennessee Williams and the Evolution of the Adult Film," in *The Cambridge Companion to Tennessee Williams*, ed. Matthew C. Roudané (Cambridge University Press, 1997), 204–231; and my "'Stanley made love to her! – by force!': Blanche and the Evolution of a Rape," *Journal of American Drama and Theatre* 16.1 (April 2004), 69–97.

36 Inge, *Four Plays*, 32.

37 Ibid., 49.

38 Ibid., 23.

39 Ibid., 113–114.

40 Ibid., 21, 24.

41 Ibid., 23.

42 Jealous of the attention directed toward Turk, Doc feels that Marie should paint a "cathedral" or a "sunset" (ibid., 26) – two images of the sublime

spirituality associated with the "Ave Maria." His mother had a "cathedral in a sunset" on the mantelpiece over their fireplace (ibid., 6). Later, Bruce and Marie, after their engagement, do watch the "sun rise" together over the lake (ibid., 62), suggesting a potential return of her "Ave Maria."

43 Ibid., 24.

44 The film curiously (given the times) upholds one of the play's more radical lines. In response to Marie's comment that Turk has "got to take off his clothes" (ibid., 23), Lola responds: "If it's all right for a woman, it oughta be for a man" (ibid., 23, 26). Perhaps Marie's retort that "men are always more proper" (ibid., 23) was seen by the Code as the proper correction to Lola's "impertinent" comment.

45 Ibid., 24.

46 Ibid., 42.

47 Ibid., 29.

48 Ibid., 36.

49 Ibid., 37.

50 Ibid. Doc's response is probably a reference to the spying taking place in America at the time, fueled by Joseph McCarthy and the HUAC witch-hunts, as much toward communists as toward homosexuals like Inge himself.

51 Ibid., 38.

52 Ibid.

53 Ibid.

54 Ibid., 43.

55 Ibid., 44.

56 Ibid., 46.

57 Ibid., 11, 44.

58 Excerpted from an email to the author, March 15, 2010.

59 Inge, *Four Plays*, 38.

60 Mulvey, "Visual Pleasure," 835. Traditionally, it is the woman who supplies the cinematic object of male desire, though Inge plays with this notion of "*to-be-looked-at-ness*" by making Turk the object of both female and gay male desire.

61 Ibid., 836.

62 Ibid.

63 Ibid., 837.

64 Johnson, *William Inge and the Subversion of Gender*, 9.

65 Murry Schumach, "Inge Sets Limits as Film Scenarist; Playwright Refuses to Adapt Own Works to Screen," *New York Times*, August 25, 1961, 17.

66 Michael Wood, "An Interview with Daniel Mann (the Director of Inge's First Success and His First Failure)," *Kansas Quarterly* 18.4 (Fall 1986), 16.

67 Ibid., 15.

68 Ibid., 9.

CHAPTER 6

The Big Knife: *Hollywood's "fable about moral values and success," a movie about the movies*

Christopher Ames

Success ... has been the most painful affair in my life.
Clifford Odets, *The Time is Ripe*

Mr. Tavenner: Did you meet with all of those persons as members of the Communist Party; that is, those you have named up to the present time?

Mr. Odets: Yes, sir.
from the HUAC hearings, May 1952

"Based on a play by Clifford Odets" appears prominently in the credits to the 1955 Robert Aldrich film *The Big Knife*. Hollywood proudly featured an adaptation of a work by the well-known playwright, even if it was an attack on Hollywood. And the credits remind us that we cannot respond to the play or the film without invoking the multiple myths surrounding the playwright. Clifford Odets was many things: a successful leftist playwright, a Hollywood screenwriter and director, a romantic figure who consorted with a variety of New York and Hollywood celebrities. His fame was cloaked in powerful American myths. Odets was the golden boy whose tremendous early success was followed by disappointment in later life. He was a New York writer who sacrificed his allegiance to Broadway for the riches of Hollywood. And he was a former communist who decided to inform on his colleagues under the pressure of the House Un-American Activities Committee (HUAC) investigation. These three powerful myths intertwine to color how we view *The Big Knife* and its morally tortured lead character, Charlie Castle (Jack Palance).

When a play about Hollywood becomes a Hollywood film, a host of self-referential elements emerge. And though the time span between the play (1949) and the film (1955) is quite small, that intervening period includes the premature death by heart attack of John Garfield (the lead in the play) following his persecution by HUAC, and Clifford Odets's cooperative testimony providing names to the same government

Figure 6.1 Aldrich's film begins with a revealing establishing shot
of Hollywood's off-kilter opulence. (frame enlargement)

inquisition (both in 1952). These factors make the reception and experience of the film fundamentally different from that of the play, even though
the dialogue differs very little.

The Big Knife is set in the playroom of actor Charlie Castle's Beverly
Hills home. Through acts spread over three days in the course of a week,
various figures visit Charlie: his wife, Marion (Ida Lupino); a gossip
columnist (Ilka Chase); his publicist (Paul Langton); his agent (Everett
Sloane); his publicist's wife (with whom he has had an affair – Jean
Hagen); a Hollywood starlet named Dixie Evans (Shelley Winters); and
Stanley Hoff (Rod Steiger), the head producer of Charlie's film studio. The
plot emphasizes Charlie's moral dilemma. His wife says she will leave him
if he signs the new contract from his studio that would tie him to them for
seven years. She believes that Hollywood and working in films has sapped
Charlie's artistry and integrity; she longs for a return to New York and a
more authentic life. Even though the contract is worth millions and
includes final script approval, Charlie is willing to forego it – except that
producer Stanley Hoff has information to blackmail him into signing.

On an earlier Christmas Eve, Charlie killed a child in a hit-and-run
drunken car accident. The studio (with Charlie and Marion's cooperation)
arranged for his publicist to take the fall and serve six months in jail. Faced
with the possibility of not only losing his livelihood if he doesn't sign the
contract but perhaps going to jail and losing all his accrued wealth and

possessions to lawsuits, Charlie caves into pressure from Hoff and his stooge Smiley Coy (Wendell Corey) and signs the contract near the end of Act 1. Marion plans to leave him with his best friend, an idealistic writer, Hank Teagle (Wesley Addy), who has proposed to Marion.

Between Acts 2 and 3, Marion and Charlie reconcile and appear happy together in spite of Charlie's having signed the contract. But Odets introduces another wrinkle. Unbeknownst to Marion, Charlie wasn't alone when the accident occurred. A young starlet, Dixie Evans, was in the car with him; the studio bought her off with a $300-a-week contract. But lately she's been getting drunk and threatening to tell the story. It appears that only attention from Charlie – or perhaps marriage to him – will quiet her. Frustrated at being ignored by Charlie and the few in the studio who know what happened, Dixie confronts Hoff in his office (offstage), and he beats her savagely. Faced with this situation, Hoff's aide proposes to Charlie a plan to silence Dixie by poisoning her. Charlie refuses to go along with murder and brutally confronts Hoff. Hoff vows to ruin him, but Charlie ultimately stands up for his principles. Hoff leaves, and Charlie goes upstairs to take a bath and kills himself in the bath by slitting his wrists. Just before his suicide is discovered, his wife learns that Dixie Evans has been struck by a city bus and killed while walking drunkenly across Sunset Boulevard. The play ends with Marion screaming for help and water from the overflowing bathtub pouring through the ceiling. Idealist Hank Teagle (Wesley Addy), explicitly compared to Horatio, describes Charlie's suicide as a "final act of faith."

The pain of success

Like the book Hank Teagle is writing, *The Big Knife* is "a fable about moral values and success." But critics and audiences have been uneasy with the terms of the moral dilemma. Robert Aldrich recounts his father's blunt criticism of the premise: "'Tell me one thing. Am I to understand that [Castle's] choice was to take or not take $5,000 a week?' I said, 'Yes.' 'Well then, you'll never have a successful picture.' I asked, 'Why not?' 'Because there is no choice.'"[1] Other critics were equally uncomfortable with the lack of motivation for Marion's rejection of the contract, particularly since Odets goes to great pains to show that the studio has responded to Castle's call for more say in the roles he is given. Compared to the working-class dramas of Odets's early plays, *The Big Knife* seems to pivot around an artificial moral quandary of a privileged central character. Bosley Crowther described the movie devastatingly in the *New York Times* review: "a group of sordid people jawing at one another violently."[2]

But, like so many writers lured to Hollywood, Odets was writing about what he knew. The moral crux of the play depends on understanding the cultural clash between the New York literary scene and Hollywood, Odets's career-long fascination with success and failure in the American ethos, and, finally, the multiplicity of individual moral crises engendered by the investigation of communism in Hollywood. As Aldrich says simplistically but revealingly in an interview: "Well, of course, [Hoff] is McCarthy."[3] One is tempted to add that Castle is Odets.

When *Time* magazine put Odets on its cover on December 5, 1938, it captioned his picture: "Down with the general fraud!" The article explains that Odets defines the general fraud as "the American Dream, the Cinderella formula, the success story (presumably his own)."[4] Odets was reacting to the popular mythology of the rags-to-riches narrative, captured in Horatio Alger's novels and their countless imitators. Just as comedies end with marriage, so too did these narratives end with the hero capturing his dreams of materialistic success. Odets examines what happens after putative success. The sly parenthesis in the *Time* article – "presumably his own [success]" – reminds us how Odets was haunted throughout maturity by the promise and praise heaped upon him in youth. Odets was intrigued with how his literary reputation altered how people reacted to him: "being famous cuts one off from all normal intercourse."[5] Odets's success and the country's economic progress out of the Depression also distanced him from the working-class themes of his early successful plays. His play *Golden Boy* also can be read as a fable about artists choosing between theatre and film, but the parable is still acted out in the setting of a working-class ethnic family. *The Big Knife* moved Odets into territory more like the world in which he moved in Hollywood, of actors, agents, and producers.

Odets, not surprisingly, never matched his 1935 achievement of having four successful plays running simultaneously on Broadway, but current critical estimates would acknowledge the value of his later plays. As a Hollywood screenwriter, he met with considerably more success than most writers who moved west. With screen credits on seven films, including high-quality productions such as *Humoresque* and *Sweet Smell of Success*, writer/director credits on two solid films (*None but the Lonely Heart* and *The Story on Page One*), and with four of his plays converted by others into motion pictures during his lifetime, Odets was a skilled and successful Hollywood writer. But that is not how he or the critics perceived the latter part of his career. Rather, he was characterized as someone who squandered a great playwriting talent on Hollywood work for hire and was never wholly relevant afterwards. That narrative of decline and artistic compromise sets the stage for actor Charlie Castle.

Castle's dissipation and the tawdry Hollywood characters who surround him underscore the message that what looks like tremendous success in our culture is often vapid and compromised. At the start of the film, the gossip columnist interviewing Charlie Castle reminds him that "The first time we met all you'd talk about was the New Deal ... What do you believe in now?" "Health, hard work, rare roast beef – and good spirits," Charlie responds, raising a liquor bottle. *The Big Knife* reveals how the dream of material success turns individuals into commodities: thus Charlie Castle is owned by Hoff, and the contract struggle emphasizes how Charlie's material success has limited his options in life.

Similarly, the film demonstrates how Hollywood commodifies sexuality in two ways: the casting couch (Dixie Evans) and the sexual opportunities created by wealth and fame (Charlie's affair with Connie Bliss, his agent's wife). The poignancy of Dixie's character emerges in her frank exchange with Charlie about what the people in the studio "do and say": "You'd have to be a girl with a good figure to know!" she says, adding, "I'd rather see a snake than a Hollywood producer." Odets ends Act I of the play with Charlie taking Connie upstairs to bed. Odets puts Charlie at the unsavory center of the sexual dynamics of stardom and explicitly associates Hollywood with infidelity. Charlie's affairs are the most blatant manifestation of Marion's (and the film's) assertion that Hollywood has compromised his moral character. And Dixie's secret presence at the fatal accident becomes the plot point that turns the story toward its tragic conclusion with her death and Charlie's suicide.

Charlie's suicide is the dark conclusion of his ascent to Hollywood stardom. The scene of Marion's screaming for help as the water from Charlie's bath pours through the ceiling parallels such dark moments as Willy Loman's suicide and Jay Gatsby floating dead in his pool. *The Big Knife*, like most Hollywood fiction, participates fully in the oppositional literature attacking the myths of the American Dream.[6]

In the film of *Golden Boy*, a scene opens with a shot of an enormous floral display, on which appears a single word: "Success." The flowers are a gift from the mobster backer of Bonaparte's fighting career, a figure clearly parallel to Stanley Hoff as the unscrupulous wealthy employer who views his employees as property, who "owns" them. This is a crucial identification, and it points to how *Golden Boy*, but more especially *The Big Knife*, grows out of the fascinating literary migration of the 1930s and 1940s in which established writers on the East Coast of America went to Hollywood to write for motion pictures. The alienation of the screenwriter was precisely this awareness of being owned, of participating in work for hire rather than creating art. The combination of the explosion of talking pictures with the decline of publishing, magazines, and live theatre during the Depression led a surprising number of novelists, playwrights, and journalists to relocate to Hollywood and work various lengths of time as film writers. The genre of the "Hollywood Novel" grows entirely out of this literary relocation, and transplanted writers also wrote memoirs, journalistic accounts, and plays drawing directly upon their experiences on the West Coast.

From New York to Hollywood

As Richard Fine has summarized, the role of the writer in Hollywood was profoundly different from that of the New York-centered publishing world and Broadway. The difference was most profound for novelists, who typically worked in solitude and then consulted with sympathetic literary editors in the process of revising a work. Though writers had to compromise with publishers in order to get into print, they retained control over their work through the final galleys and into the copyright on published material, which bore their names as sole authors. None of this was true for writers contracted to studios: they wrote on assignments, and other writers (including unpublished producers) would typically rewrite their work; they had no control over the final product and often received no formal credit or acknowledgment for work they wrote. Further, they did not have in Los Angeles the extensive literary community or the high esteem granted writers in Manhattan. Hollywood writers chafed against their lack of autonomy and artistic control and their subservience to producers, who often treated intellectuals with scorn.

Playwrights naturally had a little more experience with collaboration: they knew that their work was not complete until it was produced, directed, and acted. Still, playwrights typically were involved through all those stages of production, and their final say over whether a word was altered in the script was protected by the Minimum Basic Agreement, first negotiated by the Dramatists' Guild in 1927.[7] Playwrights were just as jarred by entering into work-for-hire relationships as fiction writers were. And this different artistic environment – with story conferences and multiple rewrites by different writers – combined with the primacy of anti-intellectual producer bosses to create a world in which writers felt their talents were belittled. As Fine puts it, "Writers [in Hollywood] were completely stripped of . . . their autonomy – their basic right of legal ownership and creative control of their work. Without this right, they were not writers in their own estimation, but hacks."[8]

This alienation was reinforced by the content of the movies themselves. While most writers in Hollywood were struck by the power of film as a narrative medium, they recognized that movies were mass entertainment and thus characterized by formula and sentimentality. Writers were often angry not to get screen credits, but they were at times equally embarrassed to receive credits for films vastly different from what they had originally written. Hollywood writers saw themselves as contributing to the art of the mediocre, a sentiment expressed in Charlie Castle's denunciation of the movies in the stage version of *The Big Knife*: "Don't they murder the highest dreams and hopes of a whole great people with the movies they make? This whole movie thing is a murder of the people."[9] Not surprisingly, these lines are omitted from the film. Nevertheless, writers were drawn to Hollywood because the pay so greatly exceeded what they could earn in Depression-era publishing and playwriting. By the early 1930s, publishing houses had seen sales decline by as much as 60 percent, and magazines had cut their size in half and slashed what they paid for short stories. Broadway was hit even harder: "Fifty fewer plays opened on Broadway in 1930 than the year before, and by the start of the 1932 season, only half of the legitimate theatres in New York were open."[10]

Not only was Broadway losing playwrights to motion pictures, it was losing actors as well. And, at the height of the Depression, it was also losing audiences to the much less expensive motion pictures. Charlie Castle despairs, "The theatre's a bleeding stump. Even stars have to wait years for one decent play."

Writers in Hollywood felt guilty about betraying their talent, and playwrights like Odets became concerned that they were abandoning colleagues as well. Of the several hundred already established writers who worked for Hollywood studios in the 1930s and 1940s, Odets was the one whose struggles concerning writing for film were most publically played out in the press. New York newspapers and magazines such as *Vanity Fair*, *Time*, *Life*, the *New Yorker*, and the *New Republic* all discussed his peregrinations between coasts, invoking all the by then stereotypical themes. Odets himself wrote articles about why he wrote in Hollywood and when and why he was returning to writing for the stage. Odets was the most publicized embodiment of the artistic and moral dilemmas of the literary migration to Hollywood because of his being cast as the most promising playwright of the time and because of the prominence of his leftist politics in his work and public persona: how was the author of *Waiting for Lefty* going to flourish writing for righty?

Odets made several trips to Hollywood. His first was in 1936, following the commercial failure of his play *Paradise Lost*. As the hottest and most avowedly political playwright in New York, hailed as the theatre's "great white hope," Odets's acceptance of a $2,500 per week contract from Paramount was big news. The *New York Times* subtitled its article: "Proletarian Playwright on $2,500 a Week Talks Like a Bourgeois Shaw."[11] A comical profile in the *New Yorker* refers to him "surrender[ing] to the gold of Hollywood" and "carrying five-hundred-dollar bills around in his pocket," yet remaining "unfailingly interested in the plight of the masses."[12] Odets publically defended his actions, however. He noted that he contributed a share of his earnings directly to the Group Theatre, helping sustain them in a difficult period. And Odets argued that movies could be an effective medium for his art.

For a proletarian playwright, the elite nature of Broadway posed a problem: weren't the moving pictures perfectly suited to reach the masses with work that illuminated their struggle? "I believe that you can create entertainment and still tell the truth," he asserted in the 1936 *Times* article, adding, "I believe that my ideas can be put over in pictures."[13] When he returned from his first Hollywood tour to debut *Golden Boy* on Broadway, *Life* heralded his "return from Hollywood to write his best play" and concluded that "Hollywood, contrary to prediction, had not broken Clifford Odets. It had matured his art, disciplined his style, taught him to tell a story, helped him to become indisputably as good as the best the U.S. theatre has to offer."[14]

But when Odets returned to New York in 1948 from a later Hollywood sojourn, he was far less sanguine about the possibilities of filmmaking: "Is it still news that a Hollywood movie is born on the stone floor of a bank? And that this celluloid dragon, scorching to death every human fact in its path, must muscle its way back to its natal cave, its mouth full of dimes and nickels?" He answers his own questions bitterly, concluding that movies have to be "as accessible as chewing gum, for which no more human maturity of audience is needed than a primitive pair of jaws and a bovine philosophy."[15] It is in this later mood (and year) that Odets wrote *The Big Knife*.

Odets's vacillation regarding Hollywood exemplifies the mixed motives that many writers felt about their dual careers. Hollywood enriched him not only through work for hire, but by purchasing the rights to his plays for treatment by other writers. *Golden Boy* was financed not only by Odets's labors in Hollywood but by his selling the rights to the play to Hollywood for $5,000. What *Life* sees as Hollywood having "taught [Odets] to tell a story" may be the complex sense that he was now writing for two very different audiences.[16] So when Odets's bitter anti-Hollywood play was released as a motion picture in 1955, he offered yet another strained defense of Hollywood artistic integrity to promote his work in film. Thus the remarkable document "In Praise of a Maturing Industry" in the *New York Times*, which identifies *The Big Knife* as the best of the film adaptations of his work. To make this argument, Odets had to assert that Hollywood had changed dramatically in the last decade. He argued plausibly that competition with television had led Hollywood "more and more to screen subjects of realism and importance."[17]

As Odets's ambivalence about screenwriting work played out in popular magazines and newspapers, the myth of the prostituted Hollywood writer was codified. Odets transformed that myth into corrupted actor Charlie Castle, and Robert Aldrich turned that play into a Hollywood-on-Hollywood film crystallizing the multiple ironies of the self-critical and self-celebrating genre. One consequence of that irony was the complaint that writers who satirized Hollywood excesses were hypocritically profiting from an industry they disparaged, a familiar criticism raised against both the play and film versions of *The Big Knife*. That criticism was coupled with a critique of Odets turning his focus away from the working class to study the trials of the rich and famous. "[*The Big Knife*] never reaches beyond Odets' own dilemma. Everyone attacks Hollywood, particularly those who have been its best-paid hirelings. No one has yet made the attack significant."[18] That is, some critics reached the same conclusion that Robert Aldrich's father did.

But viewing *The Big Knife* in the rich context of the American film industry reveals Hollywood as a cultural force, a power that justifies it as a literary subject. Odets argued this explicitly in an unpublished rebuttal of a negative review of the play: "Hollywood is the very glass and symbol of high success the wide world over ... so many people in Hollywood ... [are] so unmoved morally by the rotten fruit of that work ... Hollywood is purveying a steady diet of bon-bons to a great people who are hungering for the simple bread of a spiritual life."[19] Aldrich similarly notes:

> You can't work here and not be fascinated by it, but there is also a saying that what happens in California this year will happen in the rest of the country in two years. And if that's true what happens in Hollywood is going to happen in California in two years ... You can see social and political

issues in the white heat of the cauldron of what makes Hollywood work
much sooner than you will see them in the rest of the country. In *Big Knife*,
Odets saw them early on.[20]

HUAC and the art of the moral crisis

The pathos in *The Big Knife* does not revolve primarily around the critique
of Hollywood. There is a more specific historical context for the emotional
crises of the play: the investigations of the House Un-American Activities
Committee into the influence of communism in motion pictures that
implicitly acknowledged the cultural influence of Hollywood. Like so
many plays – and particularly those from the mid twentieth century –
The Big Knife revolves around a moral dilemma facing the central character. We have seen that Charlie Castle's moral crisis is rather contrived, but
the contrivances make sense when we view them through the lens of
Hollywood under HUAC and the blacklist. Castle can sign Hoff's contract
and enjoy continued prosperity and fame as a movie star but lose his self-
respect and his wife. Alternatively, Charlie can refuse the contract, but, in
doing so, he risks losing his ability to work in Hollywood as well as
chancing imprisonment for his role in the drunken car accident. Those
risks parallel the challenges facing Hollywood employees who refused to
cooperate with HUAC: blacklisting in Hollywood (but not Broadway) and
a possible jail term and fine for contempt of Congress. Odets's plot
contrived a moral situation parallel to the dilemma that Odets (as well as
colleagues Elia Kazan and John Garfield) would face in 1951 and 1952.

The Big Knife was written and produced on stage between the two
HUAC Hollywood investigations of 1947 and 1951–1952. The investigations of 1947 focused on the Hollywood Ten, who were indeed blacklisted
and imprisoned for refusal to cooperate. Odets did figure in the first round
of investigations, though his public testimony would come in the second
round. After the first round of HUAC hearings, the studio bosses capitu-
lated to the external pressure and blacklisted the Hollywood Ten and made
it clear that they would not employ communists or any persons charged
with contempt by the committee. So as Odets wrote *The Big Knife*, the
threat of further investigations and intimidations was very much hanging
over his head.

The testimony of Clifford Odets to HUAC in May, 1952 is painful
reading.[21] Odets attempts to educate the committee about the purity of his
motives and those of others who saw the Communist Party as offering
hope to America in the height of the Depression. But he is confronted

repeatedly with questions about his participation in an intellectual delegation to Cuba, signing this or that petition, writing an article with pro-communist sensibilities, supporting drives for left-wing causes, and so forth. He answers cooperatively, though he often doesn't recall details. There is a lengthy, almost comical back-and-forth discussion over reviews of Odets's plays in communist publications, with Odets citing negative notices and the committee citing positive ones. Ultimately, of course, he does what he had decided to do to save his Hollywood career: he provides names that the committee already had. The committee was not interested in gaining information from Odets; rather (as with Kazan) they were interested in the publicity value of his cooperation, and with the fact that they were able to get a prominent leftist playwright and screenwriter to endorse publically their agenda by cooperating and naming names.

In Kazan's view, the testimony ruined Odets: "Naming his old comrades deprived Odets of the heroic identity he needed most. I don't believe he was ever again the same man."[22] Kazan's comments occur in the context of his justification of his own very similar cooperation, and thus they are difficult to interpret. Kazan saw his cooperation as justified by his own ideological position and his willingness to endure the scorn of his colleagues. He argues, however, that Odets had neither his belief that investigating communists was necessary nor his willingness to lose face with the left. In other words, Kazan argues that he was doing something he believed was right, while Odets was doing something he believed ultimately to be immoral. Kazan's lengthy discussion of his own choice (and the defiant advertisement he ran in the *New York Times* after his testimony) reveals a lot about the moral complexities facing everyone touched by the HUAC investigations, even if one ultimately rejects Kazan's self-justifying apologetics.

Odets justified his testimony by arguing that his moments of upbraiding and challenging the committee counterbalanced his ultimate cooperation, and he sent copies of his testimony to some friends, fearing they had judged him from the headlines and not his full testimony. His closest friends, however, saw the justification sympathetically as financial necessity: he had divorced Bette Grayson and was raising two children by himself, one with expensive medical needs. He felt acutely that his current stage work could not sustain him economically, and he accepted the painful compromise of cooperating with a committee that he believed was intruding on fundamental American freedoms. The dramatic struggles of Charlie Castle reflect the moral challenges that Odets experienced throughout the period. By making Charlie a stage actor come to

Hollywood, Odets increased the financial stakes and the glamour, distanced his own experience somewhat from the play, and drew as well on the similar struggles of the man he cast as lead in the play, John Garfield. Director Abraham Polonsky said of Garfield, "The Group trained him, the movies made him, [and] the blacklist killed him."[23]

From stage to film

Robert Aldrich's film of *The Big Knife* was his first independently produced movie, shot in sixteen days for a cost of $400,000 and enabled by the willingness of actors to accept deferred payments. Thus the film reflected Aldrich's own frustrations with Hollywood producers as well as those of Odets and Garfield. The resonance between Aldrich and Odets is powerful enough that a key critical work on Aldrich, *Body and Soul: The Cinematic Vision of Robert Aldrich*, begins with a full chapter on "Odets and Aldrich," even though the making of *The Big Knife* and a brief acquaintance in the early 1940s are the only literal connections between the two. Williams makes a convincing case that Aldrich's work expresses an Odets-like sensibility in a different medium and slightly later time: "Using the legacy of Clifford Odets, Aldrich developed a cinema that would clash by night and day with the delusionary mechanisms of a system he was part of and attempted to change."[24]

Aldrich saw *The Big Knife* as one of his best films, even though it was not a critical or financial success.[25] Aldrich had wanted to direct *The Big Knife* for several years. He wrote the first version of the adapted screenplay and worked with writer James Poe on subsequent drafts. Compared to most adaptations, the changes to Odets's play are minimal. Aldrich does a few things to "open up" the single set play: a few brief glimpses of Castle's pool and gardens, a brief scene at the beach house where Marion and Billy are staying, a scene of Hank Teagle and Marion in Hank's car, a brief glimpse of Castle shooting publicity stills at the studio, and an equally brief glimpse of Monty Ritz's party next door as Dixie Evans takes a phone call from Charlie. These minor changes reduce the staginess, but they still preserve an important element of the play's scenic construction: that the entire play unfolds in Charlie Castle's stage-like playroom, as various Hollywood denizens come to persuade and tempt him. The brief scenes outside of Charlie's playroom insert crucial elements of Hollywood iconography: the swimming pool, the privileged backstage glimpse of the studio, the beckoning Pacific Ocean, and the frivolous excess of the Hollywood party. In addition, Aldrich brings on screen an offstage event only alluded to in the stage directions, the screening of an old Charlie Castle film for dinner guests at Charlie's house, thus introducing one of the classic self-referential symbols of Hollywood-on-Hollywood films, the "framed screen."[26]

A variety of minor changes respond to the sensitivities of the Production Code, though the Code was just beginning to give way in mid-1950s Hollywood. The coinage "weirdy" is used instead of "bitch"; Hoff tells Castle that he has "thrown away" a kingdom instead of "pissed away" the same. More significantly, the story of Marion's abortion (which occurs during the two weeks of the play but ends up having relatively little importance to the plot) is eliminated. More interesting are the changes that make oblique allusions in the play clearer. When Marion and Charlie discuss the superficiality of Hollywood films, Marion offers a list of artistic directors and includes Elia Kazan on the list. When Charlie complains about the quality of his film roles, he is reminded that this isn't the Mercury Players or the Group Theatre. And Hank Teagle makes explicit the allusion to Shaw's "The Quintessence of Ibsenism" in his denunciation of Castle as a half-baked idealist.

Aldrich's most important contributions come in the introduction of the boxing motif, the use of unusual canted camera angles and noir lighting, and the casting and development of Marion, Dixie, and Hoff. The opening of the film immediately sets it in a film noir context. An extreme close-up of Castle with his head buried in his hands in a rictus of anguish is set against Saul Bass titles, a jarring soundtrack, and a voiceover that tells us that this is Bel Air and "Failure is not permitted here." The opening of *The Big Knife* rapidly assembles the by-now familiar elements of film noir: dark lighting, modernist music and titles, voiceover, and the individual in anguish or despair.

Aldrich adds the character of Nick, an athletic trainer (Nick Dennis), and shows Charlie at the opening of the film sparring with Nick in boxing clothes. References to boxing, sore muscles, and rubdowns run through the play, and when we see an old Charlie Castle film being shown, it is a boxing film. The boxing background works in two important ways. First, it establishes Castle as a fighter so that the various individuals that come through the door of his Beverly Hills playroom become so many sparring partners. In the movie, Charlie goes various rounds with these partners and antagonists, reaching his nadir when he kneels before Hoff to sign the contract and his zenith when he stands up to Hoff in the final round. Aldrich may also have been intentionally echoing *Golden Boy*, in which the hero must choose between boxing and the violin, a decision representing the choice between vulgar Hollywood and refined Broadway.

Figure 6.2 Dressed appropriately in a boxer's robe, Charlie (Jack Palance)
does combat with the studio personnel intent on getting him to sign another
contract: Smiley Coy (Wendell Corey), Stanley Hof (Rod Steiger),
and Nat Danzinger (Everett Sloane). (frame enlargement)

The film role of Charlie Castle was intended for John Garfield, who
played it on Broadway. But he died in 1952 of a heart attack following his
travails with HUAC. Aldrich offered the part to Burt Lancaster, but ended
up with Jack Palance instead. Palance was fresh from having performed
Stanley Kowalski on Broadway as a vacation substitute for Marlon Brando,
and he brings a similar brooding intensity to the role of Castle. What Tony
Williams calls the play's "male hysteria"[27] is counterbalanced by the
nuanced performance of Ida Lupino, who seems to understand fully
Marion's role as the core of reason and morality in a world spinning into
irrationality and immorality. She communicates a love for Charlie Castle,
though that love is often mediated through her love for the earlier, more
idealistic Charlie Cass (Castle's birth name). The vibrancy of her performance, and Aldrich's care in lighting and costuming her so that she looks
appealing but more sensibly dressed than Dixie or Connie, help cover up
one of the weaknesses of the play: the lack of explanation for Marion and
Charlie's reconciliation between Acts 2 and 3. Aldrich's choice to have
Hoff's secret recording of Marion and Hank play at the end of the film and
reveal Marion's loyalty to Charlie and the audience strengthens her declaration of love and forgiveness in the face of revelations about Charlie's
affairs with Dixie Evans and Connie Bliss (the latter revelation having been
added by Aldrich).

Through much of the film (and play), Marion is absent, however, and the rational and loving world she represents is missing as well. Hollywood comes to Castle embodied in a variety of grotesque figures. Charlie's moral quandary is played out in his increasingly frustrated and cynical responses to their various entreaties. The structure reinforces the idea that Castle's moral failings are to some extent Hollywood's, that he has become a cog in the system he chose. Three elements lead Charlie Castle ultimately to stand up to Stanley Hoff and his values: the influence and love of Marion; his sympathy and identification with Dixie Evans; and his repulsion at the immoral self-righteousness of Hoff. Aldrich succeeds in working with Lupino, Winters, and Steiger to make Charlie's transformation – and the film – dramatically effective.

Casting Shelley Winters as Dixie Evans must have seemed obvious, for her career began in an uninspiring series of roles as cigarette girls in B pictures, the very roles that her character complains about. Winters's recent success in *A Place in the Sun* has obvious parallels to her role in *The Big Knife*. She also brought her experience in the Actors Studio to Aldrich's production. Her combination of a high-pitched voice, baby-talk locution, an ample figure, and platinum-blonde hair allows her to be typecast as the starlet, but the play gives her a deeper role. Winters researched the film by hanging out at Schwab's drug store and chatting with call girls. While the movie was being filmed, she flew back to New York to confer with Lee Strasberg about the part, which Aldrich affirmed (in Winters's recollection) provided the film's pivotal scene. In this key scene, she flirts with Castle, but shows also how desperately she longs to be taken seriously and how exhausted she is from the travails of the casting couch. Like Smiley, Buddy, and Hoff, Castle fears that she may broadcast what she knows about the Christmas Eve incident. But, more profoundly, Castle *identifies* with her as someone who is owned by Hoff. The victimization of Dixie Evans is of a piece with the entire system that creates mass entertainment through hired employees, and that ideological realization comes when the logic of Hollywood dictates that she be killed, a plan that Smiley Coy communicates to Charlie and which leads to Charlie's revolt against Hoff and Hollywood. The plan offends Charlie not only because it is murder but because "That pathetic little girl is my friend." That line, delivered powerfully in the film by Palance, reminds us that loyalty to one's friends – often at the expense of support and employment from the studios – was one of the key values in how people responded to the HUAC investigations. Winters explicitly affirms in her memoir that she viewed her role in those terms: "*The Big Knife* was my personal salute to the angry and gifted, great, sad and sweet

John Garfield. It was also my personal tribute to my many friends who had
been so brave facing that truly un-American HUAC Committee."[28]

The most memorable characterization from *The Big Knife* is Stanley
Hoff, Rod Steiger's exaggerated and bitterly comic interpretation of a
Hollywood studio head. As Aldrich relates, the characterization was drawn
heavily from Harry Cohn, but without Cohn's foul-mouthed vocabulary
and with the addition of Louis Mayer's sentimentality and ability to cry on
cue. The caricatures were widely recognized in Hollywood and clearly
resented by Cohn, who expressed his displeasure to Aldrich and Odets in
no uncertain terms. But beyond straight caricature, Odets, Aldrich, and
Steiger create an enduring depiction of the most despised figure in the
Hollywood system, the self-important, uneducated producer. Steiger's
hammy performance captures the self-righteousness of the ruthless self-
made man. And the overplaying suits the part, since Hoff takes each
meeting as an occasion to perform a mélange of sentimental reminiscence,
avuncular advice, and intimidating tycoon. Steiger's performance is surely
the inspiration for Michael Lerner's similar turn in the Coen brothers'
Hollywood film *Barton Fink* (based loosely on Clifford Odets).[29] Odets
gives Charlie and Marion the lines that critique Hoff's hard-won preten-
sion, as Charlie asks, "Were you never told that the embroidery of your
speech is all out of proportion to anything you have to say?" And Marion
brings the meeting to a halt when she asks, "Mr. Hoff, can't you stop
talking about yourself?"

The scene resolves with the mutual raging of Hoff and Castle and
Castle's existential choice to break with Hoff and kill himself. In a fine
moment, Castle's agent Nat ends his career by denouncing Hoff to his
face: "one of the meanest, dirtiest skunks that God ever put breath into."
As Aldrich notes, however, "[Hoff] is McCarthy." In that context,
the heroic denunciations of the studio head – and Steiger's satiric
performance – fall into the category of wish fulfillment, the kind of
thing one wishes one had said to a bully. The equivalency that Aldrich
draws reminds us how, through the blacklist, the studios were wholly
complicit with the HUAC investigations and the culture of paranoia and
suspicion.

Charlie's suicide is called by his friend and rival Hank Teagle "a final act
of faith," and it seems clear that Odets meant the gesture heroically
(though Aldrich was uncomfortable with that reading). Odets was doubt-
less drawing on his personal and literary experience in seeing suicide as the
existential solution to a choice in which all other alternatives represent
unacceptable compromises. It appears that Odets's first serious romantic

Figure 6.3 Charlie and Marion (Ida Lupino), their relationship and lives shattered, embrace his suicide. (frame enlargement)

partner killed herself and their child when marriage seemed impossible.[30] *The Big Knife* had also run on Broadway alongside Arthur Miller's *Death of a Salesman*, which is probably the best-known suicide in American dramatic history. Teagle's Horatio-like eulogy for Charlie Castle – "He killed himself because that was the only way he could live" – is omitted in the film version in favor of a more florid final peroration about love. In either case, the lines must have had poignancy in 1955 after the premature death of John Garfield and the career-saving testimonies of Kazan and Odets.

The Big Knife reveals the complex intertwining of art, mass entertainment, and politics in postwar America. The political climate did not allow a film or play to criticize directly the poisonous effects of blacklisting and the organized persecution of communist sympathizers. But a surprising number of plays and films by a small group of writers and directors created a dialogue about that climate of suspicion and moral crisis: *The Big Knife*, *The Crucible*, *On the Waterfront*, *A View from the Bridge*, *Kiss Me Deadly*, and *Sweet Smell of Success*.

The melodrama of *The Big Knife* on stage and screen is complexly implicated in the context of the time in which playwright and screenwriter Clifford Odets grappled with his unfulfilled promise, his turning from Broadway to Hollywood, and his anguished capitulation to the bullying of the blacklist. The movie furthers an artistic dialogue among writers, directors, and actors all affected by the dynamics of McCarthyism and expressing that dynamic in the moral fables of their time.

Endnotes

1 Alain Silver, "Interview with Robert Aldrich," in *Robert Aldrich Interviews*, ed. Eugene L. Miller, Jr. and Edwin T. Arnold (Jackson: University Press of Mississippi, 2004), 56.
2 Bosley Crowther, "Screen: 'The Big Knife,'" *New York Times*, November 9, 1955, 41.
3 Silver, "Interview," 58.
4 "Clifford Odets – Down with the General Fraud," *Time*, December 5, 1938, 47.
5 Clifford Odets, *The Time is Ripe: The 1940 Journal of Clifford Odets* (New York: Grove Press, 1988), 187.
6 Though many books have been written about the Hollywood novel, the best survey of typical themes and attitudes remains the doctoral dissertation Carolyn See, "The Hollywood Novel: An Historical and Critical Study," University of California at Los Angeles, 1963.
7 Richard Fine, *Hollywood and the Profession of Authorship, 1928–1940* (Ann Arbor: UMI Research Press, 1985), 35–36.
8 Ibid., 127.
9 Clifford Odets, *The Big Knife* (New York: Dramatists Play Service, 1976), 70. All other quotations are from the film.
10 Fine, *Hollywood and the Profession of Authorship*, 75.
11 "Mr. Odets is Acclimated: Proletarian Playwright on $2,500 a Week Talks Like a Bourgeois Shaw," *New York Times*, May 3, 1936, x4.
12 John McCarten, "Revolution's Number One Boy," *New Yorker*, January, 22, 1938, 21–22.
13 "Mr. Odets is Acclimated," x4.
14 "Odets Returns from Hollywood to Write His Best Play," *Life*, January 17, 1938.
15 Clifford Odets, "On Coming Home: Writer Tells Why He Left Hollywood," *New York Times*, July 25, 1948, xi.
16 "Odets Returns from Hollywood to Write His Best Play," *Life*.
17 Clifford Odets, "In Praise of a Maturing Industry," *New York Times*, November 6, 1955, x5.
18 Allan Lewis, *American Plays and Playwrights of the Contemporary Theatre* (New York: Crown Books, 1988), p. 112. Cited in Albert Wertheim, "Hollywood as Moral Landscape in Clifford Odets' *The Big Knife*," in *Hollywood on Stage: Playwrights Evaluate the Culture Industry*, ed. Kimball King (Garland: New York, 1997), 44.
19 Cited in ibid., 47, but note that Wertheim cites this comment as supporting the universal reading of the play. I take it to be Odets's defense that his important particular – Hollywood – has broader significance.
20 Pierre Sauvage, "Aldrich Interview," in *Robert Aldrich Interviews*, 102.
21 Communist Infiltration of Hollywood Motion Picture Industry: hearing before the Committee on Un-American Activities, House of Representatives, 82nd Congress, first session, 1951, volume 8. www.archive.org/details/communistinfiltro8unit.

22 Elia Kazan, *A Life* (New York: Knopf, 1988), 134.

23 Cited in Brian Neve, "HUAC, the Blacklist, and the Decline of Social Cinema," in Peter Lev, *Transforming the Screen: 1950–1959* (New York: Charles Scribner's Sons, 2003), 75.

24 Tony Williams, *Body and Soul: The Cinematic Vision of Robert Aldrich* (Lanham, MD: Scarecrow Press, 2004), 25.

25 Silver, "Interview," 57.

26 For a fuller discussion of the concept of the framed screen, see Christopher Ames, *Movies About the Movies: Hollywood Reflected* (Lexington: University Press of Kentucky, 1997).

27 Williams, *Body and Soul*, 193.

28 Shelley Winters, *Shelley II: The Middle of My Century* (New York: Simon and Schuster, 1989), 68.

29 See R. Barton Palmer, *Joel and Ethan Coen* (Champaign: University of Illinois Press, 2004), 114–131.

30 See Margaret Brenman-Gibson, *Clifford Odets: American Playwright: The Years from 1906 to 1940* (New York: Atheneum, 1981), 135–141.

CHAPTER 7

Adapting Lorraine Hansberry's sociological imagination: race, housing, and health in A Raisin in the Sun

Martin Halliwell

The full screenplay of Lorraine Hansberry's landmark play of 1959, *A Raisin in the Sun*, was first published in 1992, over a quarter of a century after Hansberry's untimely death from cancer at age thirty-four. A substantially cut version had been used by Canadian director Daniel Petrie in the 1961 Columbia film of *A Raisin in the Sun*, which featured actors from its first Broadway run at Barrymore Theater (March 1959 to June 1960), directed by Lloyd Richards and starring Sidney Poitier as the anguished Walter Lee Younger and Claudia McNeil as the matriarch Lena Younger. Petrie's film retains many of the dramatic conventions that helped Hansberry's play win the New York Drama Critics Circle Award two years earlier, but we only see outside of the claustrophobic interior of the Youngers' Chicago South Side apartment on five occasions: we see Walter's begrudging work as a chauffeur; three bar scenes; and a scene featuring the white Chicago neighborhood where the family intend to move. Apart from these breaks in the unity of place, Petrie's film closely follows the play's directions, dialogue, and action. However, as this essay discusses, the full screenplay enabled Hansberry to develop her exploration of dramatic and cinematic space and to further her interest in sociological and cultural ideas by adding scenes that focus sharply on racial and social inequality.

The publication of the original screenplay was a sustained attempt on behalf of her husband Robert Nemiroff to establish Hansberry as a writer of substance, particularly as she published only three plays in her lifetime. In the mid 1980s, Nemiroff noted that 40 percent of Hansberry's screenplay had been cut in the 1961 film, including a number of additional scenes that "expand our understanding of ... the realities of the ghetto the Youngers are struggling to transcend and, most strikingly, anticipate the revolution in black and national consciousness the next decades would bring."[1] Not only does this statement confirm Hansberry's status as a pioneer of African American theatre, but it positions her within a broader history of sociological enquiry and political struggle, as emphasized by her work on Paul Robeson's campaigning newspaper *Freedom* in the early 1950s and the text she supplied for the 1964 study *The Movement: Documentary of a Struggle for Racial Equality*, published in the face of "tumultuous black ghettoes, with verminous tenements and crumbling schools."[2]

Nemiroff's comment was partly his attempt to rescue Hansberry from criticism that *A Raisin in the Sun* adhered too closely to conventional dramatic forms that subordinate the black struggle to a universalistic story that has closer links to Arthur Miller's *Death of a Salesman* (1947) than to black culture. Hansberry encouraged this connection in her essay "Willy Loman, Walter Younger, and He Who Must Live," written for the *Village Voice* in 1959, in which she stressed that *A Raisin in the Sun* is essentially "a play about an American family's conflict with certain of the mercenary values of its society," rather than one that tackles "the Negro question" head on.[3] But the publication of the full screenplay demonstrated that Hansberry had a strong sociological imagination: the screenplay adds new dialogue, explores race relations in public spaces, and emphasizes the intellectual role of the African nationalist Joseph Asagai, one of two suitors of Beneatha Younger, the high-spirited twenty-year-old daughter who is studying to be a doctor. Beneatha is torn between the advances of George Murchison, a respectable middle-class African American with material prospects, and Asagai, who has come from a Nigerian township to (what we assume is) the University of Chicago. Asagai reminds Beneatha of her African heritage, teases her for her "assimilationism," and later asks her to return to Nigeria with him, but there are hints that Asagai would only end up subordinating Beneatha to a power differential based on gender rather than race. This incipient feminist dimension never comes into full view in the play, though, primarily because Hansberry conceived it as a family drama, before shifting in the screenplay to prioritize Walter's psychological development. As well as considering these shifting perspectives, we need to frame the play in terms of Hansberry's interest in sociology and urban planning in order to better understand the themes of class, education, housing, and race relations that shape the Youngers' family life.

The publication was also Nemiroff's riposte to the criticism that this play, like other postwar plays involving African American actors, did not really challenge theatrical boundaries. In a 1961 essay, "Theatre: The Negro In and Out of It," James Baldwin argued that he had "rarely seen a Negro actor really well used on the American stage or screen, or on television" and that one could attend a whole Broadway season "without ever being moved, or terrified, or engaged."[4] Baldwin's criticism was levelled at conventional cultural forms and the minstrelsy tradition (of which Hansberry was also critical), but also a theatre of "nerve-wracking *busyness*" and "self indulgent mannerisms" that delimited acting styles for black performers. Baldwin did not comment directly on *A Raisin in the Sun*, sparing his criticism for plays by Reginald Rose and Edward Albee, but he believed that stasis was as true of black plays as white, such as the theatrical version of Richard Wright's novel *The Long Dream*, adapted for Broadway by Ketti Frings that ran for only five performances in February 1960. In another 1961 essay, "Is *A Raisin in the Sun* a Lemon in the Dark," Baldwin argued explicitly that Hansberry's play was flawed because of the centrality of Lena's "stock" role as a black matriarch, and he wished that her character had "been written with greater ambiguity."[5] Nevertheless, a few years later, in his affectionate essay "Sweet Lorraine" (1969), he reflected on the play's first Broadway run, noting that he had "never in my life seen so many black people in the theater" and had "never before . . . had so much of the truth of black people's lives been seen on the stage."[6]

The radical playwright Amiri Baraka's criticism that *A Raisin in the Sun* was part of the "'passive resistance' phase" of the Black Arts Movement would have stung Nemiroff even harder. Baraka thought the play was off-focus in its class depiction and lacking intimate engagement with the lives of ordinary blacks: "we thought her play 'middle class' in that its focus seemed to be on 'moving into white folks' neighborhoods,'" when most blacks were trying to pay their rent in ghetto shacks."[7] This is a slightly odd view for two reasons. First, the range of characters in *A Raisin in the Sun* span different historical experiences (Lena was born in the South in the 1890s, Walter in Chicago in the 1920s, Beneatha early in World War II, and Travis after the war), whereas Baraka's play *Dutchman* (1964) depicts only one African American character, Clay, who is a representative type and is fatally seduced by a shape-shifting white prostitute on the New York Subway. Second, both working-class and middle-class audiences intermingled during early performances of *A Raisin in the Sun*. However, like Baldwin, Baraka tempered his opinion by the mid 1980s: he recognized his inability to see that the Youngers represented the "black majority," and he credited Hansberry for depicting "a family on the cutting edge of the same class and ideological struggles as existed in the movement itself and among the people."[8]

One could go further and say that class is as much a central theme of *A Raisin in the Sun* as race, because as many postwar social scientists were discovering, it was hard to separate the one from the other, particularly within urban ghettos. It was this sociological interest that led Hansberry to add new scenes to the screenplay that explore Chicago housing and depict the Youngers' interactions within and beyond their neighborhood. These scenes did not make the final cut, partly because they would have extended the film to well over two hours, and partly, as Judith Smith observes, because the producer David Susskind thought that these extra scenes, especially those dramatizing white paternalism and the plight of black workers, "might be racially provocative and drive away white audiences."[9] Although Hansberry stated publically that Petrie's film was a successful realization of her play, its cinematic conservatism (Aram Goudsouzian comments that it looks like "a photographed stage production" holding "the same shot for minutes, awkwardly pulling the camera in and out") and the decision to exclude Hansberry's additional scenes would have been disappointing.[10] For example, it is clear from the screenplay that she was deeply interested in the relationship between race, housing, and health – an interest she is likely to have gained from sociological studies such as the 1939 report *Mental Disorders in Urban Areas*, St. Clair Drake and Horace Cayton's *Black Metropolis* (1945), which focused on the intersection of race, class and economics in the development of Chicago's South Side, and E. Franklin Frazier's *Black Bourgeoisie* (1957), which explored how psychological responses (oppression, self-hatred, guilt, and delusions) often stem from economic roots.[11] Given that the South Side had been a ghetto since the late 1910s and had witnessed periodic racial violence, Hansberry was able to draw on her parents' and her own childhood experiences. This combination of sociological scholarship and personal experience helped Hansberry to understand that the urban ghetto often imprisons its inhabitants and raises "various enormous questions of the social organization around them which they understand in part, but only in part."[12]

In assessing the sociological importance of *A Raisin in the Sun*, this essay will examine the connections between Hansberry's published play, the unfilmed screenplay, and Petrie's 1961 film adaptation, sparing brief comments for the 2008 film version of *A Raisin in the Sun*, directed by Kenny Leon and based on the 2004 Broadway revival starring Sean Combs as Walter and Phylicia Rashad as Lena. Leon's film arguably makes better use of cinematography than the 1961 film, and includes extra details from Hansberry's screenplay; most notably the ominous twitching curtains of the Youngers' new white neighbors; a scene where we see Lena asserting herself while grocery shopping; George Murchison's dismissive reaction to Beneatha's career plans; and Ruth's nervous visits to a backstreet abortionist. Leon's film and Bruce Norris's spin-off play *Clybourne Park* (2010), which projects Hansberry's milieu forward by fifty years, might both be interpreted as ripostes to the cultural limitations of Petrie's film, drawing out race and gender politics more strongly than the 1961 adaptation was able to achieve.

Hansberry was interested in the historical and social realities of inner-city Chicago from a young age; reflecting on her Chicago upbringing in the 1930s, she commented that "I think you could find the tempo of my people on their back porches. The honesty of their living is there in the shabbiness."[13] This is perhaps romanticized nostalgia for her parents' southern childhood – her father Carl grew up in Mississippi, her mother in Tennessee – and later fed into her dramatic interest in space and light as signifiers of well-being. Hansberry thought that the South Side harbored a mixture of shabbiness, dirt, and weariness on the one hand, and resolve and determination on the other. She considered her childhood to be ordinary, but noted that her family was more affluent than her neighbors due to her father's success in banking, Carl's activist work for the NAACP, and his successful legal challenge to Chicago housing segregation in the early 1940s when he tried to move the family to a predominantly white neighborhood. The black intellectual Harold Cruse actually characterized the family as "prosperous, upper middle-class" (her father founded his own bank on Lake Street), and he criticized Hansberry for never having experienced the "misery, humiliation, violence and resentment" on display in Richard Wright's *The Outsider*.[14] But, in fact, Hansberry positioned herself against Wright's brand of protest fiction: writing a review in *Freedom* (April 1953), she expressed the suspicion that Wright's deeply alienated characters did not speak to the broad cross-section of urban family life and that Wright abandoned dignity in favor of existential "nothingness." In contrast, her parents' migration stories from the South and her schooling within the segregated Chicago system attest to the typicality of her childhood.

It is clear that the theme of health in *A Raisin in the Sun* derived from Hansberry's interest in the relationship between housing and well-being. Her own middle-class family treated sickness "sternly, impersonally and carefully," but in this regard her childhood was quite different from the more deprived areas of the Chicago ghetto characterized by poor sanitation and high-density residences. Working as a public health nurse in the South Side during the 1950s, Bonnie Bullough saw instances where rats killed children and, in one case, "chewed the hand of a small black newborn infant in a dug-out basement under a dilapidated row house."[15] When she tried to intervene, Bullough was told that public officials could do nothing about the rats, nor offer alternative accommodation for such a poor black family, leading her to conclude that "poverty, discrimination, and an inadequate health care delivery system [was] an impossible combination."[16] And not only was infant mortality a major issue in the Chicago slums, but alcoholism was widespread among poor and unemployed black men: following the war the number of liquor stores rose significantly in black residential areas, and there was a dramatic increase in cirrhosis among non-whites after 1950.

A Raisin in the Sun does not directly represent slum deprivation, even though the Youngers' apartment is described as a "rattrap" and Beneatha's plans to be a doctor are, in part, driven by her desire to make whole broken bodies.[17] Critics have noted that this lack of explicit representation of the black ghetto might have contributed to the film's lukewarm reception in Europe, even though it was selected for the Cannes Film Festival.[18] Nevertheless, despite this deliberate omission, the play subtly links class, space, and health. A lack of opportunity leaves the characters empty and purposeless, such as Lena's deceased husband, who used to "slump down" on the couch vacantly every night, and Walter Lee, who talks about the empty future in terms of existential dread "hanging over there at the edge of my days. Just waiting for me – a big, looming blank space – full of *nothing*. Just waiting for me."[19] Perhaps to counteract this psychic diminution, Walter rather grandiosely sees himself as a "giant" in a world of ants and a "volcano" ready to explode, but there is a distinct possibility that this explosion might not lead to positive change but rather a shrivelling up of Walter's being, like the "raisin in the sun" of Langston Hughes's poem, from which the play takes its name.[20] There is the sense that Walter might be a Prometheus figure – as he is called mockingly by George Murchison (a feature emphasized in Petrie's film, but omitted from the 2008 version) – but he does not understand George's classical reference, and it might refer to his role as an over-reacher or one likely to be punished for his actions, rather than a hero stealing fire from the gods.

Against Walter's feelings of despair and disappointment, the first act of the play and film depict the family excitedly awaiting the life insurance cheque of $10,000 from Walter Sr.'s death, which promises to dramatically reshape their future. It is significant that Walter Lee dreams of opening a neighborhood liquor store and his sister Beneatha studies to become a doctor at a time when there were very few opportunities for women, particularly black women, other than in ancillary medical work and nursing (a profession that Walter believes to be more fitting for Beneatha). Walter thinks that a liquor store is his first step to economic success and enhanced respect, but he is seduced by slogans such as "money is life," and he cannot see that his dream of owning a liquor store in the South Side ghetto will feed off the misery of others.[21] This is in contrast to the potential intellectual and social freedoms of Beneatha's aspiration to become a giver of health. We cannot be entirely sure whether Beneatha will sustain her interest in medicine, but her plans precede the insurance windfall, she is serious in her studies, and she can diagnose, in part at least, the family's condition by pronouncing rather pretentiously, "we've all got acute ghetto-itus."[22] In fact, Walter and Beneatha represent the poles of illness and health, particularly as Walter suffers from a deep-seated neurosis which links his problematic parental relationships, the deleterious effects of capitalism (he says "I want so many things that they are driving me crazy"), and the possibility that alcohol might be negatively affecting his relationships with his wife Ruth and their son Travis: Ruth exclaims "let him go on out and drink himself to death!" he goes missing for three days, and in the film we see Walter dive out of the apartment to the bathroom to be sick.[23] The play does not make explicit that Walter is suffering from mental health issues, but his lack of self-respect, his beleaguered ego, his drinking habit, and his economic delusions make this a tacit theme, cleverly realized through Sidney Poitier's performance in Petrie's film. As the remainder of this essay argues, Walter's psychological development is the key to understanding the narrative trajectory, but so too is the physical environment in which this plays out.

The opening of the play is crucial in this regard. The scene is early morning in a Chicago South Side apartment at an undisclosed moment between World War II and the late 1950s, but most likely the mid 1950s (Leon's 2008 film adaptation and the first half of Norris's *Clybourne Park* are clearly situated in 1959). Had Hansberry's dating been more precise – either before or after *Brown vs. the Board of Education* made separate but equal facilities unconstitutional in 1954 – it might have triggered a more politicized play. However, the fact that ghetto conditions did not radically change through the 1950s – and that Martin Luther King, Jr.'s march on segregated housing in the Chicago suburbs in 1966 was the most troubling stage of the Civil Rights campaign in terms of white backlash – signifies gradual rather than radical change.

At the outset Hansberry provides a detailed description of the interior of the apartment. The opening sentence – "The Younger living-room would be a comfortable and well-ordered room if it were not for a number of indestructible contradictions to this state of being" – introduces a spatial and psychological register which is subtly carried through the description.[24] We have evidence of the care taken to choose the furniture, but "the once loved pattern of the couch upholstery" is now hidden "under acres of crocheted doilies and couch covers which have themselves finally come to be more important than the upholstery." This is a patchwork room signifying a family that is making-do but struggling to stay organized due to a lack of space and, as we soon find out, the news of another baby that will worsen the cramped conditions. The "tired" furnishings and "weary" carpet are not countered by Lena's attempts to sanitize the room: "everything has been polished, washed, sat on, used, scrubbed too often," almost as if the attempt to keep a clean house has hastened its dreariness. There is a kitchen area, but this small space hints at exploitation, as the "landlord's lease" has permitted him to market the apartment as having a separate kitchen. Not only is the room claustrophobic, but its lack of light suggests an inability to grow, symbolized by the struggling plant which Lena tends near the "single window" of the kitchen area through which light "fights its way." With two bedrooms for five inhabitants – one for Lena and Beneatha, the other for Walter and his wife Ruth (with their son Travis sleeping on the weary living-room couch) – the apartment is barely large enough to sustain its current occupants. Recalling Hansberry's belief that the porch is an important part of American family life, there is no porch or balcony from which they can view the wider world, rather just a room of "depressing uniformity."

In the screenplay Hansberry describes the apartment in a similar manner, but she includes sociological details, this time starting from the outside and using the camera as an optical device to "inspect" the Youngers' living conditions.[25] The camera initially focuses on a medium-sized apartment building at early morning before panning across the third-floor apartment and through the "tiny" single window. The brick building is "city-stained ... old enough, for the Middle West, but it is not a tenement. It would be a reasonable place to live but for overcrowding."[26] Interestingly, the apartment is described as having a "disease," linked to overcrowding rather than the "deterioration" of the building itself. We find out more about the multiple uses of the single room, how it had been used for Beneatha when her father was still alive, and how Travis had to sleep behind a screen in Walter Lee's and Ruth's room, leaving the family "bitterly antagonized by it for many years." Other factors are made more explicit in the screenplay, including the high rents of ghetto apartments, the family's ambition to improve itself by putting Beneatha through college, the fact that this is a working-class house with "worn" rather than "dirty" things, and that Lena has chosen items for the apartment "culled" from her southern memories mixed together with a "general American lower-class appreciation for the glossy."[27] In fact, Lena's abhorrence of barrenness has led to her acquiring a collection of ornaments that worsen the clutter; the description changes tone from sociological neutrality to personal distaste for a "truly grotesque frosted glass bowl," other "objects d'horror all over the place," and a "huge and bald-faced" television set. The restricted light source in the room is emphasized, but so too is the fact that this is Lena's apartment: Ruth "might have affected the choice" of a few items like a coffee table; Beneatha's influence on the apartment is "meager," amounting to "scattered random objects" that reveal her interest in anatomy and culture; and, tellingly, there is no mention at all of Walter's personal items.[28] The final image before the camera focuses on Ruth is of Lena's struggling plant, "small and miserable-looking ... in which her imagination, alone in the universe, has invested a spirit of heroism."[29] Hansberry's intention was for the camera to shift between objective and subjective perspectives: moving from an exterior establishing shot to the apartment interior, panning freely over the furnishings before resting on the plant as the only "natural" feature of the apartment, a feature that is subjective in that it signifies Lena's aspirations for her family. Just as the apartment is an index of its inhabitants' psychology, so the plant's health is closely linked to a family struggling with itself.

Petrie's film takes some, but by no means all, of these cues. In fact, the opening shots of the film do not concentrate on the claustrophobic clutter, evoking a psychological rather than a sociological register. Our first image is a close-up of Walter Lee (Poitier) sleeping in bed with his arm resting against his forehead. We see Walter open and shut his eyes when the alarm rings, while Ruth (Ruby Dee) arises and shakes Travis as he sleeps on the couch. Their room is separated from the lounge by sliding doors, but it has a substantial window through which the morning light shines, and sunlight illuminates the lounge when Ruth pulls open the blind in the kitchen area. She encourages Walter to rise by opening the bedroom blind, letting light shine directly on Walter's sleeping face – a mirror image of Travis a few moments earlier. With the screen between bedroom and lounge still open, the initial scene takes place with two natural light sources that make the apartment brighter and airier than Hansberry's play or screenplay. Indeed, the screenplay emphasizes the smallness and dinginess of the bedroom: "The light which comes in [the bedroom] window is also interrupted as if another structure intercepts part of it and perhaps throws a distinctive shadow into the scene."[30] Such shadows are entirely absent in the film's opening sequence, and the lightness of the room is accentuated by the opaque glass window in the apartment door which, together with the imposing fridge, porcelain sink, and white net curtains, creates a brighter environment than the two text versions. The set is cramped for space, especially when three or more characters are on screen, but the fact that *Ebony* magazine is visible on the lounge coffee table suggests that the apartment in the film lacks Hansberry's attention to working-class detail: *Ebony* speaks more to Beneatha's outlook and ambitions than to Lena or Ruth.

Character detail in the 1961 film also departs from the screenplay. Walter's face is our first image in the film, whereas the screenplay documents the apartment, shows Ruth standing by the stove feeling ill (we later learn she is pregnant), dramatizes her frustration and anger at Walter's indolence, and reveals Walter scrambling for a cigarette before we see him in full view. Sidney Poitier's face is relaxed as he lies sleeping; only a hint of bewilderment breaks the repose when he wakes momentarily and then falls back to sleep. On arising, his body is "taut" and "lithe," and his face is both "handsome" and "concentrated," smoothing over the "intensity" that Hansberry wished to project.[31] This is perhaps a hangover from the earlier dramatic performances, during which Hansberry complained that Poitier's performance needed more "strength and anger."[32] In the original play Walter is described as a "lean, intense young man in his middle thirties, inclined to quick nervous movements and erratic speech habits and always in his voice there is a quality of indictment."[33] Poitier tries to embody Walter's restlessness, with movements that combine both kinetic and latent energy. This is visually demonstrated in the scene from Act 1 (see Figure 7.1), in which Walter pleads with Lena to allow him to invest in a liquor store; the strong vertical line of the door frame separates the two characters, both physically and generationally, from one another. The angle of Poitier's head, the intensity of his eyes, and his beseeching hands are framed against the front door, in contrast to Lena's stoic, upright profile outlined by the kitchen area in the background.

Many of Walter's lines hint at resentment as he thrashes out at the three women in his life, but Poitier's delivery rarely echoes the "erratic speech habits" of Hansberry's play, as a marker of a mind that cannot grasp the complexity of things or perceive what Richard Wright in *Native Son* called the "white mountain" that defines Walter's horizon.[34] These tacit pressures contribute to Walter's agitation and lead him to distraction in the play. The symptoms, rather than the causes, are most in evidence, leading Beneatha to throw insults at her brother: she calls him "mad," a "nut," and "an elaborate neurotic," but she pulls back from her diagnosis that he is psychotic: "Brother isn't really crazy yet" (this and other insults are

Figure 7.1 Walter (Sidney Poitier) challenges Lena's (Claudia McNell) authority.

spared in the film).[35] Even Lena detects Walter's neurotic behavior, and sometimes reduces him to inarticulacy as he "starts to speak several times."[36] When Walter rebuts her questions, Lena elaborates: "Something eating you up like a crazy man . . . You get all nervous acting and kind of wild in the eyes" (lines included in the film).[37]

Walter Lee's neurotic condition is exacerbated by a tight net that binds the apartment's claustrophobia to his demeaning work as a rich white man's chauffeur. His dreams of breaking out of the South Side ghetto are single-minded, but his choice of opening a liquor store actually drives him further into a ghetto mentality. In the play and film Walter feels jealous of, and undermined by, Beneatha's college education, and he believes that the cards are stacked against him – feelings that are intensified by the lack of male company at home. He displays clear signs of psychic damage, but he is far from the extremely alienated character we see in Wright's *The Outsider*, where Cross Damon carries deep scars of self-hatred and intense distrust toward everyone around him, including his mother. On this count Hansberry did not escape criticism. The "violence, brutality and strong behaviour" we see in Cross Damon derives directly, according to

Harold Cruse, from "the black ghettos" as "the spawning ground for every psychological manifestation of spiritual alienation."[38] Cruse criticized Hansberry for failing to face "social realities," but he was writing in the late 1960s (at the same time as Baraka), when a drama of "hope" and "affirmation" (as Jacqueline Foertsch calls *A Raisin in the Sun*) had less potential following King's assassination than it did in either 1959 or 1961.[39]

But that does not mean that Hansberry or Petrie ignore the scars which the family members bear and which lead them to pursue different goals that tug in opposite directions. One further social-scientific study is important in this regard. In 1951, psychiatrists Abram Kardiner and Lionel Ovesey published a groundbreaking text on African American mental health, *The Mark of Oppression*, based on twenty-five psychodynamic case studies.[40] Taking their cue from E. Franklin Frazier's argument in *The Negro Family in the United States* (1939), that pathology often stems from family disorganization, Kardiner and Ovesey contributed significantly to the discussion of personality damage and how institutional racism can promulgate racial inferiority, self-hatred, and psychotic aggression. Frazier pointed out the dangers of delinquency, desertions, and broken homes, writing in the late 1940s that "life among a large proportion of the urban Negro population is casual, precarious, and fragmentary. It lacks continuity and its roots do not go deeper than the contingencies of daily living."[41] This sense of fragmentation was particularly acute, according to Franklin, in urban localities, where the conditions are not unlike the loss of roots experienced by immigrants, but are exacerbated by poverty, unsanitary living conditions, and inadequate health services. Kardiner and Ovesey focus on this potent combination of racism, poverty, and social stigma, but we should note that when *The Mark of Oppression* was republished in 1962 it began with a more upbeat message: in the eleven years since the first edition, the grassroots energies of the Civil Rights Movement had given them confidence that deeply ingrained inferiority complexes could be unseated.

The themes of disorganization and oppression are deeply ingrained in *A Raisin in the Sun*. Lena is desperate to keep her family together: she scrubs the room to give it dignity; she reminds her adult children to respect each other, and, at times, she overcompensates for the loss of her husband by keeping order in an unruly household. Lena's faith is sometimes her bulwark and refuge but at other times prevents her from appreciating Beneatha's assertion of secular faith in human endeavour or in understanding Walter's view of mercantilism. Lena's plan to move to Clybourne Park, an exclusively white suburb of Chicago, might be the most selfless

Figure 7.2 Walter drinks alone.

ambition in the play – she chooses the house to keep the growing family together. Alternatively, however, it could be seen as equally self-serving, because Lena wants to remain in control of the family's destiny: for example, she is firmly against Ruth's initial plan to seek an abortion, regardless of the family's economic plight or cramped living conditions. Lena can be seen as the most practical character, but the play raises questions about how carefully she has thought through the plan to move to a white neighborhood and why she gives Walter the remaining $6,500 when half of it was earmarked for Beneatha's education. We could say that Lena tests Walter's sense of responsibility, but, given that he has been acting erratically and has been drinking for three days, the play suggests that he is incapable of making rational decisions about investing a substantial sum of money. In this respect, the bar scenes – taken directly from Hansberry's screenplay – are pivotal in Walter's development. We do not see the exact shot depicted in Figure 7.2 in the second of the bar scenes, but similar camera angles in this brief scene visualize Walter's self-absorption as he stares into a glass of whiskey; the light shining off the glass, the watch, and the mirrored wall jars with his dashed aspirations.

The film makes a few modifications to the third bar scene from Hansberry's screenplay. Lena arrives at the bar realizing that she needs to rescue Walter from brooding; she does not knock the drink out of his hand, as the screenplay intended, and she replaces "controlled fury" with stern resoluteness. However, once Lena and Walter move away from the bar counter into a booth the dialogue resorts to the screenplay. Emerging from his drunken stupor, Walter asks Lena why she left the South, and he likens his desire to run a liquor store to her physical train journey from the Deep South to Chicago. Hansberry had envisioned a montage sequence of hands earlier in the film, and in this scene Walter's hands were intended to remind Lena of her dead husband's, filling her with a mixture of "exhaustion" and "new determination."[42] The filmed scene actually focuses more intently upon Poitier's and McNeil's faces than their hands, but the emphasis remains: Lena puts her hand gently on Walter's as he slumps on the table, and when she presents him with the money she says, "I'm putting it in your hands."

If the 1961 film avoids – for both racial and dramatic reasons – a more panoramic view on Chicago, then it takes other cues from the screenplay's depiction of Walter's fragile mental health. When, three days earlier, Lena announces that she has placed a down payment on the Clybourne Park house, we see Walter react by squeezing and smashing a glass in close-up as he tries to contain his rage. In this scene Walter is positioned at the edge of the frame, as Hansberry intended, but his mixture of "incredulity and hostility" is replaced with a telling image of Walter slumped senseless in a chair with his hand bandaged. He then verbally explodes, accusing Lena of "butcher[ing] up a dream of mine," before disappearing for three days.[43]

This is the point where the film pulls back from an ambitious, but fascinating, sequence through which Hansberry tried to dramatize the tangled psychological and sociological roots of Walter's neurosis. Following Lena's revelation and Walter's leave-taking, we see a single shot of him in the bar. The screenplay then depicts Walter driving at speed, before stopping at Chicago's steel mills and stockyards, and then wandering aimlessly round the Loop with "his blues ... now in total possession of him."[44] Beginning with an image of Walter slumped on the curb "in the early-morning shadow of the Negro Soldier's monument" (the 1928 Victory Monument commemorates the heroism of an African American regiment in World War I), we see him stumbling upon a black nationalist street orator who speaks to an African American crowd about the oppression of white rule. Hansberry also intended to include Asagai, who listens intently to the orator (in contrast to Walter's blank response), and Murchison, who ironically drives by in a European sports car. Given that the film crew experienced hostility during the filming of the Chicago location scenes, it is not surprising that Petrie excluded this sequence, but it would have provided more depth to Walter's despair than do the solitary drinking scenes.

Walter's state of mind and his turbulent emotions are best demonstrated by a brief analysis of two climactic scenes. The first of these scenes is when Walter realizes that his father's inheritance has been squandered, and the second follows the denouement, when Walter changes his intention to accept the bribe offered by Karl Lindner in an effort to keep the Youngers away from Clybourne Park.

The first scene depicts Walter's friend and business partner Bobo entering the apartment, anxious and worried after the liquor store deal has fallen through. Walter is in an elated mood, full of expectation, and the scene proceeds as Bobo nervously tells Walter and Ruth that Willy has run off with the money. When Walter finally absorbs the gravity of the situation, he is incredulous – "halted, life hanging in the moment," as the play describes it.[45] In the film he grabs Bobo's jacket and threatens him; Bobo backs away, and Walter menacingly follows him into the corner of the room. At this point the acting shifts from realism to expressionism to dramatize Walter's temporary psychosis: threatening orchestral music intrudes, and a series of sharp camera cuts emphasize his wildly agitated face and his jerky body as he lurches around.

The space of the apartment is just as important in this scene as Walter's disturbed behavior. In the screenplay Walter turns "madly, as though he is looking for Willy in that very room," and he speaks in snatches "wandering around the room," before crumpling to the floor "as Ruth just covers her face in horror."[46] The film heightens the drama by having Lena and Beneatha enter just as Walter screams at Bobo "that money was made out of my father's flesh." Walter is startled to see Lena standing near the kitchen table; as she steps forward, her body blocks our view of the withered plant (suggesting that this is a family in decline) at the moment that Walter crumbles to the floor in agony. In the play Lena is senseless and barely recognizes her son, while the screenplay depicts Lena beating Walter in the face. The film mirrors the play here, pulling back from physical violence to suggest that for Lena the agony is internalized. Her voice slowly rises in intensity as she remembers her husband's drudgery; she pleads to God to give her strength, and the camera fixes on her tired body as she towers over her abject, crouching son, before the scene ends with Walter despairingly grasping at Lena's waist.

Walter's redemption comes in the final scene of the play, in which he refuses Lindner's bribe. He has already debased himself in front of the family by acting out an imaginary, but humiliating, scene of subjection to white supremacist rule (Sean Combs's Walter more obviously adopts a Jim Crow voice in the 2008 film). Aghast, Beneatha exclaims "where is the bottom!" and Lena tells her son that "We ain't never been that dead inside."[47] Walter's voice falters as he rehearses "the show" he will put on for Lindner; the screenplay emphasizes his "enormous agitation" as he mumbles and quarrels with himself, and ends with Walter breaking down, before leaving the room.[48] By the time Lindner arrives Walter has composed himself, but he seems to have regressed to the slow and uncertain approach of "a small boy." He begins his speech awkwardly, the showman of the rehearsal replaced by a broken man at a loss for words. While describing his family's work, Walter remembers his father's violent reaction when confronted with racial abuse. He pulls Travis toward him, and this memory stimulates a psychological shift as he moves from describing his family as "very plain people" to being "very proud people" who will not be paid off.[49] Walter straightens his body as he reaches the moment of refusal, and the scene ends with Travis showing Lindner the door.[50]

The closing scene that follows soon after shows the family preparing themselves, once more, to leave the apartment for Clybourne Park just as Lena comments to Ruth that Walter has "come into his manhood today."[51] The play ends ambiguously, but with the focus entirely on Lena. As the family call to her below, she stands alone in the apartment; a "great heaving thing rises in her and she puts her fist to her mouth," before casting "a final desperate look" around her at the "walls and ceilings."[52] She leaves the apartment and then re-enters momentarily to grab her plant. We can read into this scene either Lena's misgivings about the family's move or her disbelief that she is finally leaving this ghetto rat trap. Perhaps realizing that this should also be Walter's moment, Hansberry's screenplay and the film shift the focus slightly, making Walter and the apartment agents in this final scene. Just as Lena is filled with "a deep heaving emotion," so Walter reappears in the doorway. They exchange views about the economics of the new house (with Lena possibly returning to work), before Walter picks up the plant and "puts it in his mother's hands."[53] The two leave together as Walter outlines his future business plans. This action provides a less ambiguous resolution than the play does, with the suggestion that Lena and Walter are now equals. The film, though, reintroduces ambiguity. Just as the final moment focuses on Lena's leave-taking and her connection to the plant, so we see Walter standing silently in the stairway outside. We might interpret this choice of direction to imply that Walter has moved beyond the confines of the apartment and cheerfully accepts the family's future. However, the dual perspective – Lena as an active agent in the foreground, Walter standing still with head bowed in the background – might suggest that the power dynamic of the family has not shifted and that Walter still remains a potentially unstable presence, confirming James Baldwin's reading that Walter walks straight out of one rat trap into "a greater one."[54]

As this essay has discussed, these three versions of *A Raisin in the Sun* – the play, screenplay, and the 1961 film – inflect Walter's psychological development in different ways. Walter mocks "the sociology and the psychology" that George Murchison studies at university, but it is precisely these two dimensions – not as dry disciplines, but as lived realities pertaining to housing and health – that Hansberry wished to develop in her screenplay, exploring the apartment further, moving out into the Chicago streets, and probing into Walter's psyche.[55] The hints of Walter's psychopathology are explored more deeply in the screenplay, but remain in the cinematic framing of Poitier's embodiment of Walter – a theme that is carried further in Bruce Norris's *Clybourne Park* via acts of homicide and suicide. While Petrie's film adopts some of the new emphases in Hansberry's screenplay, it also holds back in key respects, for both racial and dramatic reasons. However, particularly in the two climactic scenes discussed here, the film retains the ambiguities of the original play that Hansberry's screenplay sought to resolve. For this reason, despite its inability to grasp the full scale of Hansberry's sociological imagination, the 1961 film remains a strong reading of *A Raisin in the Sun*.

Endnotes

1 Lorraine Hansberry, *A Raisin in the Sun: The Unfilmed Original Screenplay*, ed. Robert Nemiroff (New York: Signet, 1994), xvii.

2 Ronald Segal's introduction to *A Matter of Colour: Documentary of a Struggle for Racial Equality in the USA*, text by Lorraine Hansberry (London: Penguin, [1964] 1965), 4.

3 Lorraine Hansberry, "Willy Loman, Walter Younger, and He Who Must Live," *Village Voice*, August 12, 1959, 8.

4 James Baldwin, "Theatre: The Negro In and Out of It" (1961), in *The Cross of Redemption*, ed. Randall Kenan (New York: Vintage, 2011), 19.

5 James Baldwin, "Is *A Raisin in the Sun* a Lemon in the Dark" (1961), in ibid., 31.

6 James Baldwin, "Sweet Lorraine" (1969), in Lorraine Hansberry, *To Be Young, Gifted and Black*, adapted by Robert Nemiroff (New York: Vintage, 1995), xviii.

For similar comments on 1950s film see Hansberry, "The Mystery of the Invisible Force: Images of the Negro in Hollywood Films" (originally written for the student magazine *New Foundations*, 1951), quoted in Hansberry, *A Raisin in the Sun: The Unfilmed Original Screenplay*, xliii.

7 Amiri Baraka, "A Critical Reevaluation: *A Raisin in the Sun*'s Enduring Passion," in Lorraine Hansberry, *A Raisin in the Sun and The Sign in Sidney Brustein's Window* (New York: Vintage, 1995), 19.

8 Ibid., 20; Baldwin, "Sweet Lorraine," xviii.

9 Hansberry, *A Raisin in the Sun: The Unfilmed Original Screenplay*, xxxi; Judith E. Smith, *Visions of Belonging: Family Stories, Popular Culture, and Postwar Democracy, 1940–1960* (New York: Columbia University Press, 2004), 323.

10 Aram Goudsouzian, *Sidney Poitier: Man, Actor, Icon* (Chapel Hill: University of North Carolina Press, 2004), 187.

11 See Hansberry, "What Could Happen Didn't," *New York Herald Tribune*, March 26, 1961.

12 Hansberry, *A Raisin in the Sun: The Unfilmed Original Screenplay*, 5.

13 Hansberry, *To Be Young, Gifted and Black*, 17.

14 Harold Cruse, "Lorraine Hansberry," in *The Crisis of the Negro Intellectual* (New York: New York Review Book, [1967] 2005), 269.

15 Vern L. Bullough and Bonnie Bullough, *Health Care for the Other Americans* (New York: Appleton-Century-Crofts, 1982), 4.

16 Ibid., 6.

17 Lorraine Hansberry, *A Raisin in the Sun* (London: Methuen, [1959] 2001), 28.

18 See Margaret Wilkerson's introduction to Hansberry, *A Raisin in the Sun: The Unfilmed Original Screenplay*, and Goudsouzian, *Sidney Poitier*, 187.

19 Hansberry, *A Raisin in the Sun*, 28.

20 Ibid., 62.

21 Ibid., 53.

22 Ibid., 41.

23 Ibid., 52, 51.

24 Ibid., 9. All quotations in this paragraph are from p. 9.

25 Hansberry, *A Raisin in the Sun: The Unfilmed Original Screenplay*, 4.

26 Ibid., 4.

27 Ibid., 5–6.

28 Ibid., 7.

29 Ibid.

30 Ibid., 8.

31 Ibid., 9.

32 Goudsouzian, *Sidney Poitier*, 170–171.

33 Hansberry, *A Raisin in the Sun*, 10–11.

34 Richard Wright, *Native Son* (New York: Harper, [1940] 1992), 443, 447.

35 Hansberry, *A Raisin in the Sun*, 22, 32.

36 Ibid., 50.

37 Ibid., 51.

38 Cruse, *The Crisis of the Negro Intellectual*, 272.

39 Jacqueline Foertsch, "Against the Starless Midnight of Racism and War: African American Intellectuals and the Anti-Nuclear Agenda," *Philological Quarterly* 88.4 (Fall 2009), 419–424.

40 See Abram Kardiner and Lionel Ovesey, *The Mark of Oppression: Explorations in the Personality of the American Negro* (Cleveland, OH: Meridian, [1951] 1962), ix.

41 E. Franklin Frazier, *The Negro in the United States* (New York: Macmillan, 1949), 636.

42 Hansberry, *A Raisin in the Sun: The Unfilmed Original Screenplay*, 142.

43 Hansberry, *A Raisin in the Sun*, 68; Hansberry, *A Raisin in the Sun: The Unfilmed Original Screenplay*, 127.

44 Hansberry, *A Raisin in the Sun: The Unfilmed Original Screenplay*, 129.

45 Hansberry, *A Raisin in the Sun*, 94.

46 Hansberry, *A Raisin in the Sun: The Unfilmed Original Screenplay*, 176–177.

47 Hansberry, *A Raisin in the Sun*, 107–109.

48 Ibid., 109.

49 Ibid., 111.

50 Ibid., 112.

51 Ibid., 114.

52 Ibid., 114.

53 Hansberry, *A Raisin in the Sun: The Unfilmed Original Screenplay*, 206.

54 Baldwin, *The Cross of Redemption*, 33.

55 Baldwin, "Is *A Raisin in the Sun* a Lemon in the Dark," 62.

CHAPTER 8

Double vision: the film adaptations of The Children's Hour

Neil Sinyard

When producer Sam Goldwyn was told that *The Children's Hour* was unsuitable for filming because the two main characters were alleged to be lesbians, he is said to have replied: "No problem – we'll make them Americans." True or not, this priceless Goldwynism does allude to one important aspect of the 1936 film adaptation of Lillian Hellman's play: namely, that the material would have to be substantially altered to accommodate the Hays Code, which at that time regulated issues of morality permissible on screen. Goldwyn was compelled to change the title to *These Three* and also forbidden to publicize the film as an adaptation of the play, though he cannily and accurately calculated that the critics would do that for him anyway.

By the time of the play's gathering notoriety, Hellman was under contract to Goldwyn and had contributed to his film *Dark Angel* (1935); and it was she who had suggested that, for her next project, she should adapt her play for the screen. Hellman fully recognized that some adjustment would be needed, arguing that the play was not about lesbianism but about the power of a lie; and on that basis, the nature of the accusation could be changed without fundamentally altering the play's main theme. She was also pleased when Goldwyn assigned his new contract director, William Wyler, to the project, for she had seen Wyler's film of Elmer Rice's Broadway success *Counsellor-at-Law* (1933) and been impressed. She and Wyler were to become not only artistic collaborators but life-long friends.

The Children's Hour was Lillian Hellman's first play. Her partner, Dashiell Hammett, had first suggested the idea to her, recommending that she read William Roughead's book of notorious criminal case-histories *Bad Companions* (1930) and particularly a case-history called "Closed Doors" about a Scottish school in 1810 that had been forced to close because of a child's accusation of an alleged lesbian relationship between its owners. Hellman updated the action to the 1930s and set the play in Lancet, sixty-three miles outside of Boston. (The title, incidentally, derives from the 1859 poem of that name by Henry Wadsworth Longfellow.) In the play, two young schoolteachers, Karen Wright and Martha Dobie, are accused of having a lesbian relationship by a malicious schoolgirl, Mary Tilford, whose grandmother ensures that the parents of all the other girls are informed and the pupils withdrawn from the school. When the teachers sue her for slander, they lose the case. Eventually, Mary's lie is discovered, but not before Karen has broken off her engagement to the grandmother's nephew, Joe, and Martha has disclosed to Karen that she now realizes she is indeed in love with her. Out of anguish at the trouble she believes she has caused, Martha commits suicide. First produced by Herman Shumlin in the Maxine Elliot Theatre in New York on November 20, 1934, the play had caused a sensation and ran for a record-breaking 691 performances. Despite its success, the play had been passed over for a Pulitzer Prize (the New York critics in retaliation promptly formed their own Drama Critics Circle and gave it their prize), and had been banned in Boston and Chicago.

In *These Three*, the play's lesbian slander has now been changed to the accusation that Martha (Miriam Hopkins) is in love with Karen's fiancé Joe (Joel McCrea) and that Mary has seen them together late in Martha's room in a compromising situation. The revelation of Martha's forbidden love for Joe comes after she has been talking of her childhood and turns to discover that he is asleep; she motions to touch him, but then withdraws her hand and sits down in a chair to watch him. The camera pans to the window, where a storm is raging, and then there is a fade to black to indicate a passage of time. There is also an earlier scene when Martha is decorating the house and where her excitement at Joe's arrival (she takes off her glasses and straightens her hair) and her evident disappointment when he moves off to find Karen (Merle Oberon) would make little sense if the film's surrogate and subversive strategy were to suggest Martha's secret love for Karen. It is clear that Wyler was not attempting to circumvent the Production Code but playing straight with the alternative dramatic situation that Hellman contrived.

These Three is also notable as marking Wyler's first collaboration with the cameraman Gregg Toland, whose photography, particularly his mastery of composition in depth, was to have a massive influence on Wyler's visual style, because it served his preference for long takes over elaborate montage and multi-plane shots where different acts and actors can be shown in the frame without cutting. The two got on famously and developed what was to become one of the most celebrated director–photographer partnerships of the classical Hollywood era, seen at its finest in another Hellman adaptation, *The Little Foxes* (1941), and Wyler's masterpiece, *The Best Years of Our Lives* (1946). The camera work is relatively unobtrusive in this film, though there are occasional striking moments, as when the camera stealthily and ominously closes in on Mary hiding in the shadows and spying on Martha in her distress.

Apparently, some of the adults in the cast grumbled at the amount of time Wyler was devoting to Bonita Granville in the shaping of her performance, but it certainly paid off. Every gesture and movement seem characteristic and revealing of a child who revels in her power over others as well as her boundless capacity for mischief. The character's alarming, diabolical intelligence is superbly conveyed by Granville, who gives a well-nigh definitive performance of the child-horror and was rightly nominated for an Oscar. One writer who was bowled over by Granville's performance and the film was the novelist Graham Greene, at that time the most incisive film critic in the UK and still the most quoted of all film critics of that era; and it would be worth dwelling on Greene's review as representative of the general critical appreciation. In his review in the *Spectator* (May 1, 1936),[1] he was critical of the opening ten minutes or so for its quaintness and sentimentality; and he thought the happy ending in Vienna, which sees Karen reunited with Joe, softened the play's conclusion. However, Greene was most impressed by the presentation of the world of childhood in the film, which he thought had "never been represented so convincingly on screen, *with an authenticity guaranteed by one's own memories*" (my italics).

"The more than human evil of the lying sadistic child," he went on to observe, "is suggested with quite shocking mastery by Bonita Granville. It has enough truth and intensity to stand for the whole of the dark side of childhood, in which the ignorance of the many allows complete mastery to the few."[2] He was almost equally impressed by the performance of Marcia Mae Jones as Rosalie, whom Mary is blackmailing into doing her bidding after discovering Rosalie's theft of a bracelet. The deep impression made on him by *These Three* can be felt in some of his future works: for example, in his 1938 novel *Brighton Rock*, where the virginal evil and psychological sadism of the young gangster Pinkie has echoes of Mary. His screenplay for Carol Reed's *The Fallen Idol* (1948) would also be full of echoes of *These Three*, both narrative and visual. There is a striking situation in that film where the little boy, like Rosalie in the confrontation scene, is surrounded by questioning and intimidating adults, is unsure whether to lie or tell the truth, and becomes fearful of the consequences. *These Three* had an enormous personal resonance for Greene. That it could move deeply a critic notoriously difficult to please and often disdainful of mainstream Hollywood cinema is a tribute to the power and artistry of the film.

Given this critical and commercial success, it might seem surprising that Wyler was interested in remaking it twenty-five years later under the play's original title. His most recent film, *Ben-Hur* (1959), had been a commercial success, but it did nothing for his artistic reputation. After a decade of McCarthyism and blacklisting in Hollywood, he undoubtedly felt that the play's indictment of intolerance and its atmosphere of accusation and social hysteria were even more timely. There is an interesting exchange in Rui Nogueira's 1971 book-length interview with the great French director Jean-Pierre Melville when Melville is praising James Garner as the great champion of underplaying in contemporary American cinema. "But he's very bad in Wyler's *The Loudest Whisper* [the UK title for *The Children's Hour*]," suggests Nogueira, to which Melville retorts: "Nothing's bad in that film. It's a masterpiece. Your lack of taste appals me!" When Nogueira suggests that the "masterpiece" is actually Wyler's first version of the material, *These Three*, Melville is equally dismissive. "You're wrong," he says flatly. "Do you think Wyler would bother to re-make a successful film? It's because he knows he failed the first time that he made the second version."[3]

This exchange encapsulates the critical divide over the 1961 version. Like Nogueira, many in the critical fraternity were unimpressed. Wyler was later to express regret that he had ever made the film.[4] By contrast, a fellow filmmaker, Jean-Pierre Melville, thought the film a magnificent portrayal of its particular middle-class society. The fact that Wyler's cinematic peers thought more highly of the film than the critics, incidentally, is also indicated by the fact that his direction was nominated for a Director's Guild award and that the film was nominated for five Oscars: Best Supporting Actress (Fay Bainter, who probably should have won), Best Black-and-white Photography, Best Costume Design, Best Art Direction, and Best Sound. When Nogueira expressed a preference for the first version over the second, he was reflecting a widely held view and one shared by Lillian Hellman herself. By contrast, Jean-Pierre Melville contended that a great director would only remake an earlier film of his if he thought he could improve on the original.

The play's basic plot outline has been restored by Wyler and the screenwriter, John Michael Hayes. In the 1936 version, the accusation of infidelity never seemed a big enough lie to account credibly for the individual and social outcry that followed. In restoring the original lesbian

Figure 8.1 Karen (Audrey Hepburn) and Martha (Shirley MacLaine) are partners in the management of a residential school, but, living together, share a daily intimacy that Wyler's camera often captures in the 1962 version of Hellman's play. (frame enlargement)

accusation, Wyler was both consciously challenging Hollywood's Production Code at that time and giving dramatic sense to the material, only to find that many critics thought it was, in his words, "much ado about nothing."[5] What must have been hurtful was that many critics were not just negative but condescending. Leading the assault was the influential Bosley Crowther, who in his *New York Times* review (March 15, 1962) described the film as old-fashioned and unconvincing. "It is hard to believe," he wrote, "that Lillian Hellman's famous stage play ... could have aged into such a cultural antique in the course of three decades as it looks in the new film version."[6] Publications such as *Time, Newsweek*, and the *New Yorker* took a similar line, while in the UK the British Film Institute's *Monthly Film Bulletin* dismissed it as "dead as mutton," and the highly regarded Penelope Gilliat in the *Observer* witheringly classified it with "one of those Hollywood films that give one the feeling that they must have been made entirely in the girls' powder room."[7]

Perhaps worst of all for Wyler was the fact that Lillian Hellman disliked the film, feeling that it was too respectful to the play. Wyler had invited her to adapt the play herself, but her writing and teaching commitments and, not least, the death of Dashiell Hammett in 1960 made that impossible, and her role was reduced to that of screenplay advisor. How much

that situation affected her response to the film would be difficult to say,
but she cannot have been pleased by the fact that much of the animosity
was aimed at the play also: that is, the film was attacked as inadvertently
exposing the weaknesses of a source that now looked dated and over-
wrought. The early 1960s was a period when the kind of Ibsenite, well-
made plays of writers such as Hellman, Arthur Miller, and Terence
Rattigan were decidedly out of fashion in favor of the more experimental
absurdist dramas of writers such as Beckett, Pinter, Albee, and Ionesco.
Nevertheless, to describe the work as a "cultural antique," as Bosley
Crowther did, was surely overstating the case. A more recent critic,
John C. Tibbetts, has described Crowther's misgivings and Wyler's
gloomy acceptance of the criticism as "misguided" and rightly insisted that
"allegations of homosexuality among teachers is indeed a volatile issue, as
today's newspaper headlines continue to attest."[8]

One has to allow for differences of taste that might be irreconcilable.
But it is important to defend the film from misrepresentation. When
Caroline Latham stated that "the picture ends with Karen's fiancé ...
walking her away from the cemetery into the Hollywood sunset that
suggests the eventual dawn of happiness,"[9] this is simply wrong, a misunderstanding of a narrative detail that undercuts the author's implied
criticism of the film's sentimentality. In fact, in what might be Wyler's
homage to the famous last shot of *The Third Man* (1949) by his friend
Carol Reed, she walks past the waiting hero without even looking at him.
If there is to be an "eventual dawn of happiness" for Karen – and one
sincerely hopes there will be – then the film makes it absolutely clear it will
not involve her former fiancé. Bernard F. Dick proposed a reading of the
ending that was not so much inaccurate as eccentric. "Karen is no longer
the stylish creature who has to be 'kept up' in the latest fashions," he wrote,
alluding to a line early on in the film. "She is wearing flats, an ill-fitting
cloth-coat and a beret. The camera tracks in for a close-up of a face that has
grown mannish ... Here then is the film's one original contribution to its
source: the possibility that Karen may also be a lesbian."[10] Quite apart
from his dubious stereotypical assumption about what a lesbian looks
like – and Hepburn's face, in the film's glorious final close-up, does not
look in the least "mannish" to me – his costuming point is bizarre. As
Karen is in mourning and leaving a funeral, one would hardly expect her to
be displaying the latest in fashionable attire.

John Michael Hayes had adapted the play for the screen and, in Dick's
view, "when Hayes deviates from Hellman, it is generally for the worse."[11]
Rather, Hayes's selective deviations invariably improve on the original,

strengthening both narrative structure and character motivation. As one would expect from the screenwriter best known for four excellent screenplays he had written for Alfred Hitchcock, he is alive to the elements of suspense, and his script is also wittier than that of the play, notably at the expense of Martha's aunt, Lily Mortar (Miriam Hopkins), an unemployed actress helping out at the school because Martha cannot support her financially in any other way. The aunt's scenes with Martha have a comic edge that always have the potential of careening into something more serious. In an early scene invented by Hayes for the film, when Aunt Lily is taking ages to dry some glasses in the kitchen after Open Day, Martha asks if she could speed up the process. "I do not aim for speed," Aunt Lily replies with the attempted grandeur of a Sarah Bernhardt, "I aim for perfection in life." "Well, could you perfect a few more?" asks Martha, plaintively, but the aunt now cries off with a headache; and it is evident that her presence is becoming something of an irritation, particularly to Martha. In the play it is Karen who wishes Aunt Lily to go, but in the film it is Martha who is especially sensitive about her presence. This shift of emphasis gives extra tension to their exchanges and an additional ambiguity to Martha's rage at her aunt's accusations. It also adds a layer of irony to Karen's comment to Martha, "You worry about her too much," since it is Aunt Lily who sets up the chain of events that will wreck Martha's life. "I've worked my fingers to the bone, to the very bone!" she exclaims theatrically to Martha at a later stage, when she feels she has been snubbed by Joe and Karen. Martha's response (drolly acted by Shirley MacLaine) is to lift her glasses quizzically to inspect her aunt's allegedly overworked fingers before returning, unimpressed, to her marking. In the equivalent scene in the play, when Martha is pressing her aunt to leave the school and offering her money to do so, the aunt's response is to say, "I'd scrub floors first," to which Martha responds mildly, "I imagine you'll change your mind." In the film, Hayes makes Martha's response much more cutting: "You'll change your mind after the first floor." Shirley MacLaine delivers the line with such pointed hostility that one senses it might precipitate something more serious, as indeed it does. Stung, the aunt will lash out at Martha with her accusations about her attitude to Joe, the argument will be overheard, and the first stages of the tragedy will be set in motion.

One crucial addition Hayes makes to the play is a scene between Aunt Lily and Mary's grandmother, Mrs. Tilford (Fay Bainter), when the latter has been horrified by Mary's whispered accusation about her teachers and is seeking either corroboration or denial. While she clatters about with her inexpertly packed suitcase, Aunt Lily's thoughtless but emphatic confirmation of Mary's use of the word "unnatural" to describe Martha's feelings for Karen – and going on to characterize these feelings as "insane devotion" – is, unhappily, precisely the evidence Mrs. Tilford needs. In the play, when Mrs. Tilford says to Joe, "You know very well that I wouldn't have acted until I was absolutely sure," the line does not ring true, for there is no indication that she has made sure. Because of Hayes's additions, the line carries more weight and conviction, for Mrs. Tilford has been swayed not only by the fact that Aunt Lily has been dismissed from the school but by the fact that the aunt – and adult, not a child – confirms what Mary has said. And so Mrs. Tilford would credibly feel she could not have acted otherwise.

Another significant structural change occurs in the finale, when Hayes puts Martha's suicide *after* Mrs. Tilford's disclosure of Mary's lie and not before, as in the play; and also has Martha present when Mrs. Tilford makes her apology and offers help to compensate for the damage caused. This change intensifies the irony, for one wonders what would have happened if Mrs. Tilford had called before Martha's heartbroken declaration of love for Karen: might they have been able to continue their relationship as before? Bernard F. Dick's description of Martha's suicide as "a gratuitous action or gesture of defeat"[12] does scant justice to the sensitivity of Shirley MacLaine's performance, and particularly her last look at Karen through the window, so delicately accompanied by Alex North's exquisite main theme, which floats into irresolution, with dissonant chords signalling a foreboding of what will soon happen. However tragic and misguided, Martha's suicide is an act of unconditional love, a self-denying sacrifice that will clear the way for her beloved's new start. (And incidentally, the fact that Martha hangs herself in the film rather than shoots herself as in the play also seems more plausible: it would surely be unlikely, not to say irresponsible, for a girls' school to have a gun conveniently lying around.) In shifting the sequence of events at the end, Hayes responds to a criticism that Hellman herself had made: that the ending was too drawn-out and that the true climax should have been Martha's suicide.[13]

Hayes's skill as a screenwriter is evident from the start. Rather as in his classic screenplay for *Rear Window* (1954), all the essential elements of the subsequent drama are set up in the opening ten minutes: the close friendship between the two teachers, Karen and Martha, and the happy atmosphere at the school; the wickedness of the child Mary and her tormenting of her nervous friend Rosalie; Mary's close relationship with her grandmother Mrs. Tilford; and the futile fussiness of Lily Mortar,

Martha's aunt who is nominally helping out at the school but seems neither use nor ornament. All of this is established during a school opening day to which the girls' parents have been invited. The atmosphere seems light and happy, and indeed Alex North's original title music for the film was a set of variations on the children's nursery rhyme "Skip to My-Lou." (When it is quoted later in the film, its use is more sinister and ironic.) This initial first statement of the main theme (at this stage without any darker orchestral colorations) stops before the credits are completed, and the mood changes as a rather mysterious tracking shot takes us toward the school building, where we can faintly hear the sounds of a piano recital.

Typically, Wyler enriches the opening with moments of humorous observation: a father dozing off during the recital and being first embarrassed, then amused, when Martha notices; Aunt Lily conducting the piano performance with a gusto that seems more distracting than helpful and will lead to a final wrong chord; Karen doing her tour round the girls' bedrooms at night, and casually tapping the lid of a basket and saying, "Alright, bedtime," knowing without looking that one of the girls will be hiding in there (she is right). However, there are also undercurrents of tension whose significance is later to become apparent. Mary's salacious reading matter before bedtime reinforces the idea of her unpleasant precocity. Aunt Lily's strident uselessness is at this stage funny, but might soon begin to grate, and one already senses Martha's exasperation with her. There is the slight, awkward pause when Martha describes the moment she first saw Karen ("I remember thinking – what a pretty girl"), and her words are made to hang momentarily in the air. It is one example among many where one can see how Wyler's dramatic instincts and his sense of timing have sharpened since *These Three*. Another example would be the moment when Karen catches out Mary in her lie about where she picked the flowers for Aunt Lily when she arrives late for class (unlike in the play and in *These Three*, we actually see Mary taking the flowers from the trash can so we are in no doubt about her lie). Wyler's camera angle – Mary in the foreground of the frame arranging the flowers and studiously avoiding Karen's gaze – and Audrey Hepburn's subtly probing repetition of the line "Where did you get them, Mary?" have much more tension than the equivalent moment in *These Three*.

A sense of unease beneath the normality and easy informality of the opening also emerges when Karen's fiancé, Dr. Joe Cardin (James Garner), unexpectedly arrives while Karen is upstairs settling the girls down for the night and Martha is tidying up alone in the kitchen. Martha's mood perceptibly changes. Ostensibly, it might be because she and Karen were planning to go for a walk, and Joe's arrival probably upsets that plan. It expresses itself in her (arguably justified) irritation at the way Joe is helping himself to some of their food and drink when he must know their resources are stretched. When she makes a sarcastic reference to this and Joe comments that she has been a little sharp with him lately, Martha seems a little taken aback and stares at her reflection in a pan, noticing a blemish on her chin. "Maybe it's me," says Joe. "Maybe it is," replies Martha. Wyler's framing of Joe at this point, a slightly shadowy figure under the solitary light, leaves a feeling of disquiet. It is a significant moment not only because of subsequent narrative developments, but also because of the repetition of the word "maybe," which is to become a very significant word in the latter stages of the film. When their relationship is in peril and Joe has to insist that he believes Karen's denial of a lesbian relationship with Martha, Karen replies, softly, "Yes, maybe you do"; it is one of the loveliest moments in Audrey Hepburn's performance, resting her cheek in Joe's hand and imbuing the tenderness of her voice with just the faintest tinge of doubt. In confessing her love for Karen, Martha will use the word "maybe" no fewer than five times, as if her depression and feelings of guilt have pushed her toward a deduction about her sexual nature that may be true, but then again may not. Shirley MacLaine's heartbreaking rendering of Martha's agony of confusion, torment, and self-disgust would be difficult for any subsequent actress in the role to match.

James Garner's performance has been criticized, but he is less mono-lithically noble than Joel McCrea in *These Three* and certainly takes more risks, bringing the character near to the point of tears at one stage and subtly suggesting Joe's insensitivity beneath the character's likeability and charm. The impression is that the length of his engagement to Karen (two years) might have subconsciously given rise to more doubts about her than he realizes. There is a particularly striking moment when he first hears about the lesbian accusation from Karen after she and Martha have burst into Mrs. Tilford's house, and he demands to know why his aunt has made such a claim. "Because it's true," she replies. At this point one might have expected a reaction shot of the accused, but Wyler's first reaction shot is that of Joe, swivelling around in mental turmoil, as if a seed of doubt has been planted amidst the revulsion and shock. From that moment onwards – and however hard Joe tries to be steadfast and loyal to Karen – something irrevocable has happened. His frustratingly long engagement has suddenly been given a nightmarish explanation that will forever cast a shadow over their relationship.

Before the lesbian accusation, there is a scene in Joe's car with him and Karen (not in the play) where they agree to marry. It is an interesting variation on a scene in *These Three*, where Joe's attempt at the fair to tell Karen he loves her has been continually thwarted and put him in a bad mood. There the scene was played largely for comedy that then leads to romance as Karen accepts his proposal of marriage; but in the remake, the scene is more troubled. Joe's bad mood shades into boorishness; and his mockery of Karen's ideal of domesticity (nicely acted by Garner) is potentially, and embarrassingly, hurtful. Indeed, it will be Karen who obliquely proposes to him ("Can we have a baby twelve months from now?"), and it seems to be an impulse in response to Joe's mood. The impact of the decision will have massive repercussions, prompting a fierce outburst from Martha when Karen tells her about the upcoming wedding that will awaken Mary and lead her to spy on the two as Karen leaves Martha's room, pausing to kiss her on the cheek. Wyler's ominous close-up of Mary at this point, as the shadow from the closing door casts a diagonal darkness across her face, tells us all we need to know about what the girl's rancid imagination could make of what she has seen. The scene in the car closes on a romantic note. The two embrace, and in close-up Karen says, "Oh, how I love you," before whispering in Joe's ear, "love you, love you, love you, love you." Audrey Hepburn's acting at that point seems so natural that one could almost feel that the moment was improvised; and yet Hayes and Wyler were also probably aware of its dramatic irony, where a whispered declaration of love in a car is to be contrasted and indeed displaced by Mary's later whispered and hateful lie to her grandmother in her limousine.

Although in this later scene – perhaps the most chilling in the film – Hayes sticks closely to Hellman's dialogue in the play, the change of setting from the grandmother's study to the limousine in which she is returning Mary to school is particularly effective. It adds to the sense of claustrophobia because in the limousine the grandmother cannot easily escape from the relentless insinuations of her granddaughter, whose "motiveless malignity" (to borrow Coleridge's phrase about Iago) begins to puncture the grandmother's defenses. The change of setting also introduces an additional ingredient of suspense: the element of time. As the limousine draws closer to the school, Mary realizes that time is running out if she is to persuade her grandmother that she is not to return. Consequently, the tempo of her accusations quickens; the insinuations become a little more extreme, and when she senses that the word "unnatural" seems to be pressing on an uncomfortable nerve, she plays that for all it is worth. As she whispers her poison into her grandmother's ear, Wyler cuts to the front of the car so that we see the imperturbable chauffeur, unaware of the drama being played out behind the glass; the sound has dipped but abruptly rises again as the grandmother lowers the glass and shouts to the startled driver, "Stop the car!" and the car screeches to a halt. Wyler's gradation of the soundtrack from whisper to shout to screech becomes a kind of aural jump cut to simulate the spread of Mary's lie in terms of both its speed and the hysteria it generates.

Karen Balkin had been cast as Mary on the strength of her performance of the evil child in a Texas production of *The Bad Seed*. Although she does not have the dark, needle-sharp menace that Bonita Granville brought to the role in *These Three*, she does make a convincing, pouting, spoiled school bully. Indeed, Mary's unhappiness at school and her incessant mischief might stem precisely from her limited intelligence and might make her lies more credible. As her grandmother says, "How would a child her age know of such things? She could hardly invent them." Part of the tension of the scene in the limousine comes from the fact that Mary, in her desperation at not wanting to go back to school, seems only belatedly to pick up the significance of what Mrs. Mortar has said about Martha. When told earlier by her classmate about the argument between the two, Mary has asked, "What did she mean, unnatural?"; and she has clearly not said anything about any of this to her grandmother the previous evening. It is only in the limousine that Mary makes the connection: that Mrs. Mortar was not talking about Martha's jealousy of Karen but about her jealousy of Joe. Facially and vocally, Karen Balkin conveys this dawning realization extremely well, suggesting not only the girl's alarm at the substance of the accusation but simultaneously her sense that this might be the opportunity she has been looking for. On seeing her grandmother's increasing discomfiture at the word "unnatural," she presses her advantage. We have already seen how Mary, like many bullies, has the knack of spotting someone's weak spot and probing it until it hurts. It is this gift that gives her dominion over the wretched Rosalie (finely played by Veronica Cartwright), whose theft of Helen Burton's bracelet, which Mary has twisted from her grasp, is not an isolated aberration as she claims but part of an ongoing kleptomania. Wyler's presentation of Mary is unusually blunt, going for straightforward nastiness over nuance, and Karen Balkin delivers what he requires. For example, when Karen tries to make Mary admit her deception over the flowers for Mrs. Mortar, Audrey Hepburn plays the scene with a gentleness and humor that would have won over all but the most irredeemable of souls, so there is a real frisson when Mary

Figure 8.2 Mrs. Tilford (Fay Bainter) is shocked by what her niece (Karen Balkin) tells her about Karen and Martha. (frame enlargement)

sticks to her story. Karen Balkin's unblinking glare is so intimidating that it forces the teacher to her feet in shock at the girl's defiance.

The great confrontation scene in the grandmother's house gives the clearest indication of Wyler's development as a director. His direction here has a new dimension of cinematic maturity, being more fluent in structure and movement, more expressive in terms of composition, and with a surer sense of pacing and suspense. Only in the comparative performances of the two girls might *The Children's Hour* yield to its predecessor, but even here the visual presentation is more imaginative. For example, Wyler builds Rosalie's entry very carefully, showing her changes of mood as she descends the staircase, first happy, then nervous as she notices the unexpected presence of her teachers in the house, but then even more apprehensive as Wyler switches the camera angle and Rosalie finds herself staring into the face of her nemesis, Mary. Earlier in the scene, when the grandmother imperiously commands the teachers to leave the house as if their very presence is contaminating the atmosphere, she turns her back on them and looks out of the window. Wyler replicates that composition later in the film, when Mary's lie has been discovered, suggesting how the grandmother is recalling the earlier moment and digesting the full horror of what she has done. This kind of structural and visual parallelism, favored by

Hayes and Wyler, might appear to some as overly schematic, but it can be seen as a concise and intelligent strategy to emphasize something of great importance in the film: namely, it invites us to reflect not only on people's actions but the consequences of those actions as well. When, after discovering the truth, the grandmother tells the protesting Mary to "Be still!" one feels that the command has all the more venom behind it (and it visibly terrifies Mary) because it recalls the same phrase that Martha had used when the child began her web of lies at her house. The grandmother's demand resonates with all the horror of words that have come back to haunt her.

If there is a primary difference in the confrontation scene in the two films, it is surely felt in the level of performance. The acting in *The Children's Hour* is, to borrow Isabel Quigly's apt description, "awe-inspiring."[14] Consider the performances of Shirley MacLaine as Martha and Fay Bainter as the grandmother. In *These Three*, Miriam Hopkins as Martha plays the scene capably on a consistent note of quiet and bewildered sincerity. Shirley MacLaine's characterization has more variety, attack, and emotional instability, recalling the aunt's warning about Martha's temper. Consequently, the dramatic temperature of the scene is significantly raised. When MacLaine insists to the grandmother that the accusation "is not true, it's just not true," she not only gives an edge of anger to her denial, but cuts across the grandmother's path to confront her and, as it were, throw the accusation back in her face. In *These Three*, when Martha catches out Mary in her lie about seeing the guilty partners through the keyhole ("There is no key-hole on my door"), Wyler tilts the camera up toward Martha, and Miriam Hopkins states the line almost calmly to the grandmother. In the remake, MacLaine is forceful enough to ram home the point on her own, stating the line first quietly as recognition of the lie dawns, and then shouting it in the child's ear, again as if hurling the lie back at its source. In comparison with Hopkins's, MacLaine's performance is pitched at a more intense dramatic level: along with her role in *The Apartment*, this seems to me her greatest performance on film.

Similarly, Fay Bainter as the grandmother takes the material onto another dramatic plane. Whereas in *These Three*, Alma Kruger's grandmother suggests a kind of stubborn integrity, Fay Bainter imbues Mrs. Tilford with a blend of righteous conviction and moral indignation that is frightening to behold. When Karen tells her they have nothing left but the dirt she has made of them, the grandmother snaps back, "The dirt you have made for yourselves!" Fay Bainter delivers the line direct to the camera with a ferocious sense of outrage and revulsion. The grandmother's later discovery of Mary's falsehood turns her not into a wicked figure but into a tragic one. Her precipitous fall from the moral high ground is steep indeed; and Wyler, ever sensitive to the dramatic use of place and space, stages it as a literal fall, taking place at that area by the door where she stood when she originally summoned Rosalie to confirm Mary's story. At that point, Karen had said, "You deserve whatever you get, Mrs. Tilford," to which the old lady replied quietly, "I don't know, maybe it is what I do deserve." There is the word "maybe" again. We never learn what the grandmother does when she follows the terrified Mary up the stairs presumably to exact some form of punishment, but her look says it all: each has become the other's mutual hell.

As for Audrey Hepburn, Douglas McVay was one of the few critics to recognize what he called her "greatest 'Greek tragedy' performance."[15] In *The Children's Hour*, her delivery of a line time and again brings a lump to the throat through its almost musical sadness, like her gently caressing utterance of the film's last line, "Goodbye, Martha, I'll miss you with all my heart." Earlier, as Martha is about to confess her love for Karen, who, preoccupied with her grief over Joe's departure, is only half listening, Karen says, almost to herself, "I'm cold." This simple line is not in the play, but, as delivered by Hepburn, with her arms wrapped around herself to keep herself warm, it becomes not simply a statement of fact but a shiver of premonition: the quiet, flat tone suddenly changes the temperature of the room. Later, after the grandmother's visit where she has offered reparation for the damage caused by the girl's lies, Karen goes up to see Martha in her room. "Martha, I'm going away someplace to begin again," she says, and Martha begins to nod in resigned acceptance, before Karen adds: "Will you come with me?" Karen is signalling her forgiveness and indicating it makes no difference to their friendship. It is one of the most poignant additions to the play, for it allows us to appreciate Karen's rejection of Martha's self-condemnation and (implicitly) her absolute rejection of the prejudices of a society whose values have caused Martha such suffering. The irony now is that it might be the very kindness of Karen's gesture – so sensitively acted by Hepburn – that prompts Martha to commit her ultimate act of self-sacrifice and, as it were, set her friend free.

Hepburn is at her absolute finest in the scene of Martha's suicide. Wyler and screenwriter Hayes contrive what is arguably the dramatic highlight of Hepburn's career. Leaving Martha to sleep in her room, Karen walks in sunlight to the entrance of the school, recalling a similar walk earlier in the film by Martha before the tragedy has struck. One can almost feel the fresh air on one's cheeks after the prolonged confinement in the school. Hearing

Figure 8.3 Martha's guilt over the break-up of Karen with her fiancé Joe
(James Garner) prompts the confession of deeply hidden feelings
of attraction and jealousy. (frame enlargement)

Aunt Lily calling for Martha and getting no response, Karen begins to retrace her steps, and almost imperceptibly the tension begins to grow. Wyler cuts to a point-of-view panning shot as Karen looks up toward Martha's window and senses something is wrong. She breaks into a run, her face communicating, in McVay's phrase, "by every nuance of her expression her dawning suspicion and panic at what may have happened."[16] Wyler maintains the tension by keeping her in close-up during the run and deploying a series of jump cuts (brilliantly edited by Robert Swink) that reflect the agitated heartbeat of someone hurtling toward the worst nightmare she can imagine. When she rushes up the stairs, one might subliminally recall the similar shot of her excitedly running up the stairs to give Martha the news of her upcoming wedding: a chilling parallelism that links the first stage in the drama with its tragic conclusion. As Karen tries to break down the door, Wyler cuts to a shot inside the room and to the fulfillment of our fears: an overturned chair, a shadow on the wall slightly swaying. When Karen bursts in, she breaks down at what she sees and slumps to the floor, moaning, "Martha ... Martha ...": a crescendo of panic now modulates to a diminuendo of pain.

The Children's Hour deals with, in Oscar Wilde's phrase, "the love that dare not speak its name." Indeed, the word "lesbian" is never used in the film, though it was never used in the play either. The film has been attacked by subsequent commentators for not giving a more positive and progressive depiction of homosexual experience. For example, Harry Benshoff and Sean Griffin have written:

> In *The Children's Hour*, a schoolteacher hangs herself after her lesbianism is exposed. In *Advise and Consent* (1962), a promising young politician takes a razor to his throat when a past homosexual relationship threatens to come to light ... Homosexuality was understood as a tragic flaw linked to violence, crime, shame and more often than not, suicide. At best these films called for pity and sympathy for people who could not help suffering from the "illness" of homosexuality.[17]

That seems to be an obvious oversimplification. As dramatized by Wyler and Hayes, Martha's suicide has a much more complicated motivation. More so than the play, the film makes it clear that Martha's disclosure makes no difference to Karen's devotion to her friend. One could hardly argue that in this film homosexuality is "linked to violence, crime and shame" since the relationship between Karen and Martha is the most sympathetic in the film. What passes for a "normal" response to their relationship is seen unequivocally as bigoted and cruel.

That was then, this is now? Hardly. As I write these words nearly half a century after the film's release, one of the lead stories in my morning national newspaper concerns a leading political figure feeling compelled to reveal intimate details of his married life to scotch rumours about a gay affair with a political aide; and an article in the Women's Section of the paper has the subtitle: "Why don't we admit it is still hard to be gay?" It is clear that the issues raised by Wyler's film not only had resonance at the time but remain relevant. And, of course, homosexuality is not the only issue in both film and play. *The Children's Hour* is a text about lives destroyed through deceit, unjust accusation, collective hysteria, bigotry, and intolerance. It is also about wickedness across generations, about the varieties of love, and about the pressures and prejudices that can distort it or destroy it, but which it can also rise above. It speaks to the human condition, and the 1961 adaptation is a masterwork from a great director at the height of his powers. Jean-Pierre Melville was correct.

Endnotes

1 Graham Greene, *The Pleasure Dome: Collected Film Criticism* (London: Secker & Warburg, 1972).
2 Ibid., 72.

3 Rui Nogueira, *Melville on Melville* (London: Secker & Warburg, 1971), 94–95.

4 Gabriel Miller, ed., *William Wyler Interviews* (Jackson: Mississippi University Press, 2010), 140.

5 Ibid., 71.

6 Axel Madsen, *William Wyler: An Authorized Biography* (London: W. H. Allen, 1974), 160.

7 Christopher Tookey, *The Critics Film Guide* (London: Boxtree, 1994), 129.

8 John C. Tibbetts and James Welsh, *Encyclopedia of Stage Plays on Film* (New York: Facts on File, 2001), 52.

9 Caroline Latham, *Audrey Hepburn* (New York: Proteus, 1984), 84.

10 Bernard F. Dick, *Hellman in Hollywood* (Toronto: Associated University Press, 1982), 82.

11 Ibid., 44.

12 Ibid., 47.

13 Jackson Bryer, ed., *Conversations with Lillian Hellman* (Jackson: Mississippi University Press, 1986), 131.

14 Tookey, *The Critics Film Guide*, 129.

15 Douglas McVay, "The Goddesses," *Films and Filming* 135 (1965), 16.

16 Ibid., 17.

17 Harry M. Benshoff and Sean Griffin, *America on Film* (Oxford: Wiley-Blackwell), 323.

CHAPTER 9

Sidney Lumet's family epic: re-imagining Long Day's Journey into Night

Mary F. Brewer

Eugene O'Neill began writing *Long Day's Journey into Night*, considered by many critics to be his most sublime play, in 1939, completing it in 1941. According to Stephen Black, one of O'Neill's motives for creating the play was therapeutic: to understand why his family had behaved as they did[1] and, thereby, to resolve some of his familial demons. The autobiographical thrust of the play accounts for a host of its dramatic elements. The setting reproduces that of the O'Neills' summer home: Monte Cristo Cottage in New England. The events depicted in the lives of the Tyrone family represent O'Neill's loosely disguised remembrances of his family – his thespian father James O'Neill, his mother Ella, who suffered from drug addiction, and his elder brother Jamie, an alcoholic. The character of Edmund (given the name of O'Neill's dead brother) stands in for the playwright himself.

Biographies of O'Neill stress the appalling state of his physical, mental, and spiritual health after finishing *Long Day's Journey*. Arthur and Barbara Gelb speak of O'Neill being tortured by the agony of reliving his painful past, combined with feeling guilty at laying bare the secrets of others, which eventually plunged him into depression.[2] Sensitivity about staging his family's life history delayed the play's publication and production, as did O'Neill's concern that its subject-matter would not be appropriately received in wartime America. In a letter to his son written in April 1941, O'Neill expressed his satisfaction with the artistry of *Long Day's Journey*, suggesting that along with *The Iceman Cometh* it would rank among the finest things he had written. However, he insisted also that he did not want either play to be made public "at this crisis-preoccupied time," because "[t]hey could not be understood. Not their real meaning or truth."[3]

Indeed, it is doubtful whether O'Neill envisioned *Long Day's Journey* ever being produced beyond an early draft stage; this may account for its decidedly literary qualities, such as long prose passages that would not appear out of place in a novel, and the extended citation of poetry. While

Figure 9.1 The morning pleasantries passed between Mary Tyrone (Katharine Hepburn) and James Tyrone, Sr. (Ralph Richardson) mask the problems of recurrent addiction that mar their family life. (frame enlargement)

O'Neill did authorize his publishers to release the play twenty-five years after his death, he insisted that he never wanted it produced. Notwithstanding, the play was published in 1955, only two years after O'Neill's death, at the behest of his widow Carlotta. Also, she gave permission for its theatrical production, and its stage premier in Stockholm, Sweden, followed a year after its publication in February, 1956.[4]

Following the Stockholm production, the play opened in New York. The Broadway show enjoyed reasonable commercial success for a serious (i.e., non-musical) drama, running for 144 performances. Critically, it was a triumph, hailed as one of the most important plays in American, and perhaps world, dramatic history; as the *New York Times* reported in 1956, "*Long Day's Journey into Night* has been worth waiting for. It restores the drama to literature and the theatre to art."[5] In addition to the 1957 Pulitzer Prize, *Long Day's Journey* won the New York Drama Critics Circle Award, as well as a Tony Award for best play. The play's critical accolades, conjoined with O'Neill's status as America's premier dramatist, and, I would argue, the play's novelistic elements, made it an attractive proposition for adaptation to film.

The director Sidney Lumet acquired the film rights to O'Neill's play, and his adaptation of *Long Day's Journey* was released by one of the smaller Hollywood studios, Republic Pictures. It premiered at the Cannes Film Festival in 1962, where it received good reviews. Five months later it was released in New York, but US reviews, while generally positive, were more mixed, and, despite the publicity attendant upon Katharine Hepburn's Oscar nomination for best actress, it was viewed as a box-office failure. Feeling that the original 174 minute running time was too much of an endurance test for viewers, the distributor cut the film by an hour for its second commercial run, but this butchered version proved no more attractive to viewers than Lumet's original.[6] In this essay, I focus on the director's original cut because this is now the standard issue in which the film is available to audiences.

The opening credits of Lumet's film make clear that what follows is meant to be a production of O'Neill's masterpiece, with the playwright's name mentioned twice. The cast are described as appearing in O'Neill's drama, and the playwright is named as writer, with Lumet's identification as director coming only at the end. The credits allude to how O'Neill's play and Lumet's film cross-fertilize one another. While postmodern theory has called into question the traditional hierarchy that privileges literature over film, in 1962, the filmmakers noticeably capitalized upon the play's critical status, and O'Neill's, to bolster that of the film.

Of course, over time the relation between the play and the adaptations it has generated has become dialectical, with the prestige of the original augmented by a series of filmed copies.[7] Arguably, Lumet's film, although it was released in VHS format in 1998 and remains available in DVD, has not been as influential in this context as later prestige projects for television, such as Michael Blakemore and Peter Woods's 1973 film for ABC, or Jonathan Miller's more controversial interpretation in 1987 for Showtime network. Lumet's *Long Day's Journey* does not feature in critical lists of landmarks in modern film, nor is it ranked among the director's most outstanding contributions to film.

Though he was already reasonably well known, following films like *Twelve Angry Men* (his first, in 1957), Lumet was still at a fairly early stage of his directing career when he took on the project. He acquired permission to adapt the play largely on the back of his respectful and highly praised 1960 television adaptation of O'Neill's *The Iceman Cometh* for CBS. This success, Frank Cunningham notes, gave O'Neill's executors confidence in Lumet as a safe pair of hands to handle O'Neill's *magnum opus*.[8] In *Making Movies*, Lumet's retrospective on his career, he discusses his approach to adapting *Long Day's Journey*, which is nothing short of reverential. "Sometimes a subject comes along and . . . is expressed in such great writing, is so enormous, so all-encompassing, that no single theme can define it . . . I am very lucky to have had a text of that magnitude in my career."[9]

Lumet continues: "I found that the best way to approach it was to ask, to investigate, to let the play tell me."[10] Hence, it becomes clear why Lumet did not choose a screenwriter for his film, but rather used O'Neill's play script. According to the director, "the only adaptation made for the screen was to cut seven pages of a 177-page text" during the three-week rehearsal period before filming began.[11] Lumet's aim in adapting O'Neill's play, then, was to transpose it to film – to mirror as closely as possible the stage play. In fact, what Lumet creates is a commentary on O'Neill's work. In other words, although the film remains faithful to the spirit of O'Neill's play, Lumet takes creative license on a number of fronts, including dialogue cuts, setting, and character, which, in turn, impact the work's tragic theme and how viewers may respond to it.

As documented by Donald Costello, from the 2,849 lines of dialogue in the play, Lumet cut 749 lines, amounting to over 25 percent of the play's language.[12] Costello suggests that Lumet's judicious use of cinematic technique allowed him to cut without seeming to do so. Indeed, critics of the film frequently commented on its close fidelity to O'Neill's text. *Variety* reported that, except for a "few cuts ... otherwise it is as O'Neill wrote it,"[13] while *Time* magazine called it a "photographed play,"[14] a designation to which Lumet strongly objected. While Lumet admitted that the film's "theatrical origin was easily identifiable,"[15] he insisted that "What makes *Long Day's Journey* a film rather than a color photographed stage play is a fifth character ... the camera."[16]

In an interview with Lumet, William Sipple records the director's belief in the advantage that the camera offered the film medium over the stage: this "is not limited to presenting 'wide, open spaces,' but in bringing the audience into the film and its action, so as to experience each nuance of gesture, facial expression and motion, all of which are lost to the majority of the theatre audience."[17] This essay will explore the intertextual relation between O'Neill's stage play and Lumet's film version of *Long Day's Journey*. My aim is to determine what the film says to the viewer that the play does not reveal to the spectator and vice versa. How does Lumet's reworking of O'Neill's dramatic material, whether involving dialogue cuts, camera use (close-ups, point-of-view shots, panning), or changes in mise en scène, work to enhance the meaning of O'Neill's dramatic language and intentions? Where and how does the film utilize these elements with the result that they take on meanings distinct from O'Neill's stage version?

As the opening credits to *Long Day's Journey* roll, they are over-scored by André Previn's musical theme, with its disturbing, uneven tempo; the piano music produces a slightly menacing air, perfectly in keeping with the idea of a descent into darkness that is encapsulated in the film's title. By choosing to shoot in black-and-white, Lumet further parallels the stark world in which O'Neill encases his characters, the bleakness of which appropriately echoes their spiritual lives. Consequently, the opening sequence has a jarring effect because its environment produces an entirely contrapuntal mood.

In this opening scene, the camera pans across a peaceful, sun-drenched vista. We watch a maidservant exit a weathered, but large and imposing, cottage, and cross over lush, manicured lawns; behind her, the camera takes in a marina dotted with pleasure craft, before slowly moving to capture James and Mary Tyrone as they stand on their front porch. Lumet's location filming places the Tyrones' cottage, and the couple themselves, in a picturesque setting, which gives the impression of bourgeois conventionality. The viewer is led to expect that the occupants of the cottage will resemble the normative middle-class American family. Lumet even compares the high-key lighting he uses in this scene with that of the fluffy, maudlin *Andy Hardy* movies, a series of comedy films celebrating idealized American family life that began in the 1930s.[18]

Considering Lumet's pledge to fidelity, the first scene stands in odd contradistinction to that of the play. O'Neill's stage directions describe the interior of a holiday cottage on a summer morning in 1912. Sunlight streams in, illuminating a miscellany of worn chairs, tables, and overflowing bookcases that fill the living room of the cottage. James Tyrone, his wife Mary, and their grown-up sons, Jamie and Edmund, are just finishing breakfast. Yet, this commonplace domestic setting, redolent of so many American dramas of domestic realism, is immediately revealed to be a façade. As Tyrone and his wife emerge center stage from the back parlor, the spectator receives a clear sense from their verbal and nonverbal exchanges that they stand poised on the threshold of an emotional journey of devastating proportions, one which will prove in startling contrast to their routine surroundings.

O'Neill establishes an emotionally claustrophobic atmosphere on stage, which complements the characters' tumultuous, but repressed feelings. He never allows his audience to see beyond the walls of the family's first-floor living room. In contrast, Lumet affords the imagination of the film viewer a much more expansive scope, presenting the characters within a variety of interior and exterior settings. By taking them out of their stifling environment, he creates an atmosphere that is out of tune with their lived experience.

When transplanted into a brilliant natural setting, they are temporarily but plainly altered. The viewer does not sense them to be the same isolated beings as those first encountered by the dramatic spectator. The first time we see Mary and James on film, Mary is performing the polite, feminized task of serving her husband a cup of coffee. Her opening words, "Thank heavens, the fog is gone," represent a cut of more than two pages of dialogue from scene one of O'Neill's drama. Instead of immediately hearing about a litany of family troubles – Mary's pointed criticism of James for unsound property speculations, Edmund's illness, Tyrone's apprehensive observation of Mary (spying, she feels) for signs of nervous tension – the viewer overhears a heightened moment of playful and prosaic marital banter, as Mary gently admonishes James for keeping her awake the night before with his snoring louder than the foghorn.

The cuts in speech, combined with the genteel setting and activity, and the initial good-natured humor that seems to mark the pair, reinforce the light tone established in the opening panoramic sequence. Lumet's idyllic representation of the pair creates a very different understanding of the characters' personalities and the nature of their relationships than what is conveyed in O'Neill's play. For instance, it allows the possibility of reading Tyrone as a typical "old curmudgeon" type. His initial grumbles could be mistaken for mock-resentment, and his ensuing complaints about his sons' habits and political opinions may be interpreted as the usual generational differences and disagreements that may be found within most families.

This process of normalization continues when Mary and Tyrone are joined by their sons. The scene moves onto the lawn leading down to the sea, where the family shares a laugh over a story that Edmund tells about a neighbor. Once again, by allowing the characters to move outside of the dark, interior confines of their original setting, different nuances of psychology are suggested. Here, the eye-catching, brightly lit surroundings, and the level gaze of the camera, give rise to a false sense of family harmony. When the family laughs at James, their mockery may seem good-humored, rendering his stinginess a harmless, if annoying, trait. As a result, Edmund's ensuing irruption of temper toward his father generates a moment of surprise, whereas O'Neill's intention at this point is already to reiterate that Edmund's angry volatility marks his, and his family's, status quo.

Thus, the way that Lumet employs mise en scène differs markedly from his source material, with the result that the correlation of commonplace domestic-realist surroundings, and family relationships that flow along easy and familiar lines, become established in the viewer's mind. The film's expression of characters' personalities, states of mind, and relationships at this point is at odds with the thrust of the play's thematic intentions, and while I would not wish to tax the film too much with the burden of fidelity (albeit invited by Lumet), its radical departure from the play in the opening scenes leads to confusion surrounding the film's genre.

O'Neill's *Long Day's Journey* is a tragedy, and one of the elements that gives the play its emotional punch is how the playwright draws upon classical antecedents to reinvent tragedy for a modern audience. *Long Day's Journey* is shorn of spectacle and rank, as well as the terror and hope that the possibility of divine intervention lends to classical tragedy. In its place, the drama highlights the absurd propensity for the common woman and man to create their own suffering; consequently, the sense of impending tragedy that is self-made, but nonetheless inescapable, depends upon the inner fabric of the Tyrones' lives and the lies and self-delusions that propel their conflicts.

Drawing upon psychoanalytic theory, Zander Brietzke contends that "libidinal energy" characterizes the play's inner fabric. O'Neill's nuclear family "isn't about parents and children, but about parents and grown, over-grown, clearly sexually active men. The family sleeps in close proximity to each other; the sons are too old and too big to live in such rooms and in such close quarters to their parents."[19] Although Lumet's adaptation is not wholly insensitive to the play's Freudian overtones (consider how the film shows Mary's compulsion to touch Edmund and their psychological co-dependency), the theme is much less pronounced than in O'Neill's story, where a strong current of oedipal desire and tension underscores the tragic nature of the characters' relations throughout. Andrew Dix helpfully points out that this dissonance may be due also to the Motion Picture Production Code lingering on until 1968.[20] In any case, the altered setting, mood, and characterization created in the beginning of the film do not sit logically with the Tyrone family's competitive oedipal propensities, which serve to approximate classical tragedy's sense of the relentless nature of fate. To the contrary, the sense of wholesomeness established at the outset fit more with a tradition of bourgeois realism than tragedy.

When the film violates the boundaries of the play's physical settings, reducing the connection between external surroundings and internal mindsets, another result is that personality appears less fixed. If the characters' states of mind may be perceived, like the shifts in setting and lighting, as possibly changeable, then the notion of repetition, so crucial to the core meaning of O'Neill's play (and to much of the script that Lumet retains) is significantly reduced in narrative and thematic importance. What the characters have done and said, and felt, in the past, wholly

Figure 9.2 The Tyrone sons Edmund (Dean Stockwell) and Jamie (Jason Robards, Jr.)
make common cause in their alcoholism and worry about their mother.
(frame enlargement)

determines their present for O'Neill. When Tyrone exasperatedly pleads
with Mary to: "For God's sake, forget the past!" she responds:

> Why? How can I? The past is the present isn't it? It's in the future, too.

> We all try to lie out of that, but life won't let us.[21]

Michael Manheim describes Mary at this point as having regressed to her
"ritual of addiction." This ritual entails the reliving of certain life events
such as her marriage, childbirths, and illness. It demonstrates how her
identity is rooted entirely in her past, and Manheim notes her belief "that
her past is fated to be repeated."[22] James, Edmund, and Jamie also play out
specific obsessive rituals, theirs compounded by addiction to alcohol. The
family's ritual traits, governed by a sense of "mysterious determinism," to
borrow a phrase from Norman Berlin,[23] form the thematic skeleton of
Long Day's Journey.

The prospect of character mutability introduced by Lumet, however,
with its sense of a melodramatic descent from light to darkness, pulls this
skeleton out of alignment. Consider that only after Edmund recounts the
story about the neighbor (one-third of the way into O'Neill's first act) does
the viewer get a clue about Mary's history of ill health. Conversely, O'Neill

sets up the first point of comparison between Mary the morphine addict and Mary in recovery during the play's initial lines (cut by Lumet). The first thing the theatre spectator learns of is Tyrone's pleasure in Mary having *regained* her good looks. "You're a fine armful now, Mary, with those twenty pounds you've gained."[24]

As the play begins, the characters are positioned at the start of a new day and, at the same time, each character is *in medias res* of his or her particular ritual of addiction and despair. As O'Neill's drama unfolds, events are governed by a series of patterns characterized by hope, struggle, despondency, resurgence, but ultimately defeat. The sharper dichotomy between past and present that marks the film, in contrast, sets up a melodramatic sense of impending disaster; this tension creates a distinct emotional impact on the viewer from O'Neill's ritual repetition that stems from his tragic form: pity without the awe, one might say. Thus, the element of mutability adds further to the sense of confusion surrounding the film's genre because its awkward citation of realist and melodramatic elements do not fit within O'Neill's tragic format.

Just as the characters' mental landscape is firmly defined at the outset of O'Neill's *Long Day's Journey*, the fixity of their psychological and emotional patterns is mirrored throughout in their physicality, or rather their lack of it. The play is remarkable for the fact that nothing really happens, especially given its length. However, the fact that the characters engage in limited physical movement is essential to highlight their mental turmoil. Linda Seger points out that one of the reasons filmmakers find adapting plays a challenge is because they tend to use dialogue to explain ideas, often privileging character over the events of a story.[25] This is certainly true of *Long Day's Journey*, which stages the philosophical beliefs and feelings of the Tyrone family.

In a sense, language is action in the play; that is, action is symbolically articulated through language, as in classical tragedy, with those acts that reveal the causes underlying the characters' emotional problems having occurred in the past. Stillness, then, is the essence of *Long Day's Journey*, with long passages of stage time centering on speech between two or more of the actors, frequently while seated. The state of motionlessness allows an audience to carry out a deep analysis of O'Neill's complex dialogue, especially the verse elements; this, in turn, lends the language fuller power to achieve a visceral effect upon the spectator.

Lumet shows some awareness of how powerful the still focus of O'Neill's work can be in the film's final scene, where James and Edmund are alone playing cards. He symbolically frames James during his monologues, first for ninety seconds, and then for three and one-half minutes; the latter, Costello notes, in a single shot, uninterrupted by even the reaction of Edmund.[26] Too often, though, Lumet strives for liveliness in his film, which is problematic, especially where he tries also to retain O'Neill's dense and emotionally intricate dialogue. Here I refer to the actors' movements, gestures, and facial expressions within the film's various settings.

The kind of action and the style of performance that Lumet brings to the viewer's attention sometimes shift the emphasis away from the covert substance of the characters' dialogue. In other words, when the actors are involved in a series of constant movements and activities, unrelated to the meaning of the dialogue or undetermined by it, the nature of their communication is subtly redefined, and it detracts from the psychological implications and emotional intensity of their discussions, rendering the dialogue less forceful in its impact on the viewer.

A prime instance occurs in the gardening scene featuring Jamie and his father. In the play, the actors make a simple exit from the living room, upon Tyrone announcing, "The way to start work is to start work."[27] Any ensuing dialogue or action that occurs between James and his son in the garden, except that which is represented later, briefly reported by Jamie, does not feature in the spectator's conception of the play. In Lumet's adaptation, the dialogue between father and son that immediately precedes their exit from the stage is transposed from the living room to a walk outdoors that leads to an invented setting, a large garden outbuilding, where we watch the men gather and prepare the tools for gardening.

The dialogue in this scene relates to each man's fears, resentments, needs, and jealousies, of each other and, most importantly, of Mary. The need to protect her from learning the true nature of Edmund's illness and the possibility that she has succumbed once again to morphine use is laid bare for discussion, but these significant issues are not amplified to the same degree in Lumet's set-up as they are in O'Neill's original staging, where the men remain confined to the living room. In the film, the feelings underlying the words exchanged between them are obscured beneath the surface mask of mundane and casual activity, and by filming the scene in three different spaces, beginning on the lawn, moving to the edge of the porch, and then into the outbuilding, the viewer's concentration as well as the continuity of each character's speech is broken, with the effect that the dialogue appears less noteworthy.

Further, the general tendency of Lumet's characters to be in motion often masks the meanings that attach to characters' "*unconscious habits of speech, movement and gesture*" as written by O'Neill.[28] Bennett Simon remarks upon how the gestures mime the themes in the play,[29] but, when the film does not follow this alignment, it makes the physical signs of emotions less remarkable and removes a good deal of their power to convey relevant meaning to the viewer. On stage, each time Mary touches her hair, for example, this small gesture cites the history of her drug addiction, while also forcing its memory into the present for her family, who watch her along with the audience. It points also to the protracted and recurring nature of her emotional turmoil. When Mary proves unable to keep her hands still in the film, then, this gesture no longer conveys as effectively her shame about her addiction. Bosley Crowther's 1962 review in the *New York Times* picked up on this: he described Hepburn as "tricky and uneven" in the role – "probably because she has too much to do in the moments of deepest anguish."[30]

The realization of numerous ordinary activities on film, and the corporeal animation that attends their performance, therefore, frequently come at the expense of the film's thematic and characterological cohesiveness. Obviously, in this regard Lumet is following the conventions of realist filmmaking, but by animating O'Neill's script along the lines of conventional realism, the film runs counter to one of the playwright's key objectives – to tell the story of the Tyrone family within the terms of what Jean Chothia terms "real realism," which is tied to O'Neill's conception of tragedy.

Speaking about his play *Welded*, O'Neill argues that the term "realistic" is used too loosely in the theatre: "When I spoke to you of the play as a 'last word in realism,' I meant something like 'really real,' in the sense of being spiritually true, not meticulously life-like – an interpretation of actuality by a distillation, an elimination of most realistic trappings, an intensification of human lives into clear symbols of truth."[31] As Chothia explains, "real realism" expresses the qualities in O'Neill's writing that are rooted in recognizable places, times, and characters, *as well as an intense focus on metaphysical being and the implications of the character's speech in relation to that core being* (italics mine).[32]

Given how often they sit unnaturally alongside O'Neill's dialogue, characters, and dramatic objectives, the question of what motivates Lumet's "action sequences" arises. It is possible that the director was driven by commercial ends. Although the film was made on a small budget of under $500,000 (thanks to the cast and director taking basic Equity wages), nevertheless, it needed to recoup the cost of production, advertising, and distribution, and a film that meets the expectations of viewers used to realism on screen would be more likely to do so.[33]

The film's unevenness with regard to corporeal and psychological consistency and generic principles may also relate to a cultural struggle that was taking place in the American film industry at the time of its production. In the early 1960s, the industry was concerned with holding onto its audience, which was being threatened on one side by the increasing monopoly of television as popular entertainment and, on the other side, by the growing attractiveness of European avant-garde imports, the French New Wave cinema for example, especially among younger filmgoers.[34] Lumet's film shows signs of this struggle: its scenic slices-of-life give the audience something of what it would be comfortable watching, even though it might not always accord with the artistic demands of the script; concomitantly, its subject-matter resembles less of what audiences were used to watching at home, or at the American cinema, and more like the challenging material that constituted the subject of European art films.

The attempt to balance traditional film style with alternative topical elements intensifies the sense of generic unevenness also with regard to perspective or point of view. Lumet is on record as expressing his disappointment with the Broadway production of *Long Day's Journey* because it focused on the father–son relationship between James and Jamie, while for him Mary and Edmund form the center of O'Neill's play.[35] Yet, the dual relationship between Mary and Edmund never fully materializes as the film's focus. Rather, the perspective on events and actions is derived mainly from Mary's point of view: both the cuts in dialogue and the way in which Lumet shoots Hepburn contribute to Mary's dominating the filmic narrative.

There is no protagonist in O'Neill's *Long Day's Journey*, and if there is a spokesperson for the playwright, it would be Edmund; yet, the subjective camera Lumet applies to Mary defines her as the key figure in the narrative. Mary's dominance is seen most clearly in the film's ending, where, before the camera pans back on all four characters and they become smaller and smaller, Lumet uses two extreme close-up shots of Mary, before the screen dissolves to black. In thematic terms, this overly privileges her emotional perspective on what has happened in the past and/or what is taking place in the present. In terms of genre, it ties the film further to the conventions of Hollywood realism, for by converting Mary into a leading character the viewer is provided with a central figure through whom the story may be more easily accessed/followed, and with whom the viewer is encouraged to identify.

The problem of Mary's domination is exacerbated by Lumet's choice of actor. Lumet contends that he sought "not just stars, but *giants*" to play the

Figure 9.3 In a striking set-up using deep focus, Sidney Lumet demonstrates
how the family aligns itself as night approaches. (frame enlargement)

O'Neill characters, while being aware of the problems associated with integrating the very strong personal qualities an actor of this stature brings with those of the character being played: "If you've got a major star, you've got that strong personal quality seeping through in every performance," he states.[36] Without doubt, Hepburn was the leading star in a stellar cast that featured also Ralph Richardson and Jason Robards (reprising his Broadway role).

Richard Dyer argues that "the powerfully, inescapably present, always-already-signifying nature of star images more often than not creates problems in the construction of character, potentially destroying the unity of a film."[37] I would not suggest that Hepburn as Mary destroys the film's coherence, but her star image is a problem that the film never overcomes, despite Lumet's awareness of the risks involved in casting "giants." Crowther puts it this way: "A little less of Miss Hepburn would help the film."[38] While Lumet admits that "Hepburn is allowed a few lapses in which her own personality dominates that of the character,"[39] in fact, too often her established persona not only amplifies the perception that *Long Day's Journey* is the story of Mary Tyrone, but also skews the viewer's perception of the character.

Dyer categorizes Hepburn as exemplifying "the independent woman type," a film persona she cultivated throughout the 1930s, 1940s, and 1950s in classic vehicles such as *Adam's Rib* (1949) and *Pat and Mike* (1952). Conversely, O'Neill writes Mary as a very self-contained figure, a quality that is ideally exemplified in Constance Cummings's performance of Mary in Blakemore and Woods's adaptation. Cummings's restrained approach brings out Mary's fragility, propensity for delusion, and what O'Neill describes as her "*simple, unaffected charm,*" "*shy convent girl youthfulness,*" and "*innate unworldly innocence.*"[40]

In contrast, most of Hepburn's gestures, physical motions, and vocal expressions, regardless of the director's faith in the heightened advantages of film, misrepresent important aspects of Mary's character rather than deliver a privileged insight into O'Neill's work that Lumet claims to offer. Hepburn produces an overly hyperactive performance, which is unable to compensate the film for her persona established over decades of screen time. This is evidenced by reviewers' reactions. The *New York Post* remarked that "some viewers will be stopped short by her remembered mannerisms of voice, laughter and tooth."[41]

Hepburn claimed to take the same approach to the play as Lumet. She shared his reverence for O'Neill and explained that she "wanted to play it without really acting it. I did not want to be fascinating or colorful or exciting. I just wanted to keep out of its way and let it happen."[42] While Hepburn's theatre background would have meant that she was aware of the different acting styles appropriate to stage and screen, judging from what the viewer sees, her comment about not offering an over-enlarged portrait of character seems disingenuous. I do not mean that O'Neill's characterization of Mary lacks fluidity, or that the text cannot be refocused successfully, for Miller's adaptation certainly proves otherwise. Rather, the problem lies in both the director's and actor's continued assertions that what they are offering represents a presentation of *Long Day's Journey* on film – a claim to fidelity that itself continually reinscribes the privilege of O'Neill's original text.

From the outset, Hepburn plays Mary with a startling degree of vigor and emotional dynamism. Her misplaced physical and emotional energies are most remarkable when she responds to Edmund's suspicion about her relapse into addiction; Hepburn moves from a figure of maternal nurturer, who fusses about her son's appearance and comfort, to a fractious antagonist. Her hand-wringing, eye-rolling, vocal acrobatics and the frantic circles she makes around the room (the camera circling with her) reach a climax when she screams at Edmund, "Stop suspecting me!" Carey describes her at this moment as "clasping, rubbing and wearing her hands like a latter-day Lady Macbeth," which leads to his reading the character as "an emotional vampire who uses her addiction to subjugate and terrorize her family,"[43] a vision, I suggest, that O'Neill would struggle to recognize as his creation.

The dominant mood of the scene as played by Hepburn is strident, whereas the expressive register of O'Neill's Mary ranges across a much wider compass of feelings. In her encounter with Edmund, O'Neill variously describes her as dull, pitiful, stricken, uneasy, bitter, helpless, sharp, with her most intense emotional state portrayed as a "strange undercurrent of revengefulness," the latter summed up in a single line: "it would serve all of you right if it was true!" The principal difference in Mary's presentational styles in the play, according to O'Neill, is that sometimes she appears more "*a little withdrawn from her words and actions,*" while delivering her lines in a more detached "*voice and manner.*"[44]

The breadth of Mary's mind-states points to the complex and paradoxical nature of her psychological makeup, a facet of character that does not emerge as fully via Hepburn's more monochromatic demeanor. Hence, Hepburn's performance of Mary strikes another odd note in Lumet's expressed endeavor to reproduce faithfully O'Neill's play, bearing a resemblance more to Jonathan Miller's avowed radical interpretation of Mary as a "typical maternal tyrant."[45] Perhaps Lumet's choice of Hepburn was guided by the inclination of 1960s filmmakers and producers to invest great hopes in "star power" to lure viewers away from their televisions and back into the cinema.[46]

Although the anger and hysterical bitterness of the above scene has the potential to evoke a strong emotional response in the viewer, this is not the principal way in which the play challenges the spectator's emotional resilience. Berlin remarks on the strains that O'Neill creates for an audience, as they are forced to "listen to the talk of members of a family for four hours, stuck in a room . . . physically entrapped as the characters are entrapped."[47] In contrast, the film lasts 2 hours 54 minutes, which, though lengthy by Hollywood standards, departs from the kind of emotionally exhausting experience O'Neill provides, especially considering Lumet's tendency to enliven the atmosphere as already discussed.

Lumet justified the reduced running time by arguing that the "use of close-ups would make those moments [the script cuts] clearer sooner."[48] Indeed, there are moments when Lumet's camera work superbly augments the viewer's understanding of character. In the brutal, yet poignant final confrontation between Edmund and his father, Edmund declares his hatred of James for caring more about money than his family. His charge provokes James into explaining how his anxious need to save money is rooted in his dire childhood poverty. As they exchange barbs, the scene comprises a series of close-ups and medium shots, interspersed with reaction shots; together these facilitate the viewer's heightened identification with the characters' anguish, the camera wonderfully highlighting how James and Edmund react to the other's vindictive or plaintive language as if to a body blow. Yet, as Robert Scholes and Robert Leland Kellogg argue, although close-ups may reveal more of a character's psyche than can be managed on stage, "in narrative only . . . is the inward life of characters really accessible."[49]

Lumet's close-up shots cannot entirely compensate for how the decreased demand on the viewers' attention alters their overall emotional response to the events and characters depicted. Brietzke explains that in order to have an emotional experience at the end of the play, the audience must be "exhausted."[50] He contends that "the length of the play is essential to show . . . a variety of perspectives in order to gain sympathy for every character and to see how they are all caught in familiar relationships of love and hate from which they cannot escape"[51] and where "any one account of what happened must be interpreted in terms of who says what to whom and under what circumstances."[52]

Brietzke's argument is especially relevant to the final scene. However, because Lumet makes the deepest cuts to O'Neill's text in the fourth act, especially to the poetic dialogue, not only is the viewer's emotional experience of the scene altered, but also his/her understanding of the men's confessions is compromised. Manheim argues that the final act is "the all important one because it shows the men of the family reaching one to another as deeply as people ever do."[53] Yet, this reaching out to confess is not done in a direct manner.

First, the men are heavily intoxicated, and in their drunkenness lay the truth that they cannot speak to each other under the constraints of sobriety. Secondly, much of the truth about their feelings is revealed only through quotation. James quotes his idol Shakespeare; Edmund quotes Baudelaire, Dowson, and Swinburne; Jamie quotes Swinburne and Wilde. The men's language is saturated with other literary allusions to Kipling, Zola, Rossetti, and Nietzsche.

The poetry O'Neill chooses has several functions within the narrative. Sometimes it comments upon what is happening on stage, as when Jamie quotes the stage directions from *Hamlet* – "*The Mad Scene. Enter Ophelia!*" – and Mary enters for the last time. In other instances, the poetry is used as a psychological mask (primarily for James) or as a means of voicing the men's feelings that they cannot find their own words to express (Jamie and Edmund). What the spectator understands through the poetic dialogue – that its removal leaves vague for the viewer – is how the men's internal responses vary regarding the family's dysfunction, especially their perception of Mary's addiction, and how their responses gesture toward the nature of their future.

Edmund employs Baudelaire's poem to reveal his intention to always be "so drunk you can forget."[54] It is through Jamie's recitation of Swinburne's "A Leave-taking" that his brusque and cavalier veneer is finally stripped, revealing that he, rather than Edmund, is the more fragile of the two brothers. Compared to O'Neill's verse, the film's realist mode means that the viewer does not get the full sense of what a crushing defeat Mary's loss to morphine represents for Jamie, for s/he does not hear his bitter lament at his mother's neglect of him and preference for Edmund, captured in the lines "and though all men seeing had pity on me / She would not see."[55] Moreover, in the film, the final argument between Jamie and Edmund does not rise much above personality conflict, when, Frederic Carpenter suggests, in order to attain the level of tragedy to which O'Neill aims, their quarrel should illuminate "the conflict of two philosophies of life." Carpenter recognizes how the conflict between the cynical negations preached by Jamie and the tragic transcendence of these negations, which lie at the heart of all Edmund's dramas,[56] is tied directly to their poetical philosophies.

Chothia makes a similar point about the significance of the final act, demonstrating how poetry speaks to Edmund's "beliefs which reach beyond the private turmoil" of his family.[57] These beliefs are what give Edmund some chance, however small, of transcendence through sympathetic understanding. Albeit small, this sense of hope is a vital component of *Long Day's Journey*.

Defending his play *Diff'rent* in 1921, O'Neill presented his concept of tragedy:

> It is the meaning of life – and the hope. The noblest is certainly the most tragic. The people who succeed and do not push on to a greater failure are the spiritual middle-classers. Their stopping at success is the proof of their compromising insignificance.
>
> Only through the unattainable does man [*sic*] achieve a hope worth living and dying for – and so attain himself. He with the spiritual guerdon of a hope in hopelessness, is nearest to the stars and the rainbow's foot.[58]

It is regrettable, then, that the cuts and alterations made by Lumet, especially in the crucial final act, produce a film that lacks this sense of hope, perhaps another reason for its lackluster performance at the box office being so far removed from Hollywood's commonplace resolutions. It would be difficult to project the need, intention, or ability to "push on"

Figure 9.4 The film begins with sunny exteriors and ends with this tableau of a family
swathed in a darkness that grows ever more threatening. (frame enlargement)

upon the four figures that gradually dissolve into darkness in the film's
final tracking shot. Rather, Lumet's *Long Day's Journey* leaves us with an
overall sense of pessimism, a condition explicitly rejected in O'Neill's "play
of old sorrow, written in tears and blood."

Endnotes

I am grateful to Andrew Dix and Imelda Whelehan for their insightful and very
helpful comments on early versions of this essay.

1 Stephen A. Black, *Eugene O'Neill: Beyond Mourning and Tragedy* (New Haven:
   Yale University Press, 1999), 446.
2 Arthur Gelb and Barbara Gelb, *O'Neill* (London: Jonathan Cape, 1962), 836.
3 Eugene O'Neill, "To Eugene O'Neill, Jr. April the 28th, 1941," in *Selected
   Letters of Eugene O'Neill*, ed. Travis Bogard and Jackson R. Bryer (New Haven:
   Yale University Press, 1988), 517.
4 O'Neill's dedication read: "For Carlotta, on our 12th Wedding Anniversary."
5 B. Atkinson, "Long Day's Journey into Night: New Stature for American
   Theater," *New York Times*, August 11, 1956, accessed July 21, 2010, www.eoneill
   .com/artifacts/reviews/ldji_times.htm.
6 Gary Carey, *Katharine Hepburn: A Biography* (London: Robson, 1983), 203.
7 Robert Stam and Alessandra Raengo, "Introduction: The Theory and Practice
   of Adaptation," in *Literature and Film: A Guide to the Theory and Practice
   of Film Adaptation*, ed. Robert Stam and Alessandra Raengo (Oxford:
   Blackwell, 2005), 8.

8 Frank Cunningham, *Sidney Lumet: Film and Literary Vision*, new edn. (Lexington: University Press of Kentucky, 2001), 123.

9 Sidney Lumet, *Making Movies* (New York: Alfred A. Knopf, 1996), 14–15.

10 Ibid., 15.

11 Ibid., 32.

12 Donald P. Costello, "Sidney Lumet's *Long Day's Journey into Night*," *Literature Film Quarterly* 22.2 (1994), 79.

13 *Variety* staff, "*Long Day's Journey into Night*: Review," January 1, 1962, accessed June 1, 2009, www.variety.com/review/VE1117792690.html?categoryid=31&cs=1.

14 Lumet, *Making Movies*, 89.

15 Ibid., 89.

16 Sidney Lumet, "On a Film Journey," *New York Times* (October 7, 1962), 7.

17 William L. Sipple, "William L. Sipple on the Films of *Long Voyage Home* and *Long Day's Night*," *The Eugene O'Neill Newsletter* 7.1 (1983), accessed July 21, 2010, www.eoneill.com/library/newsletter/vii_1/vii–1c.

18 Lumet: "I wanted to start it off as lightly and brightly as an Andy Hardy movie." Dale Luciano, "*Long Day's Journey into Night*: An Interview with Sidney Lumet," *Film Quarterly* 25 (1971), 21.

19 Zander Brietzke, "Too Close for Comfort: Biographical Truth in *Long Day's Journey into Night*," *The Eugene O'Neill Review* 25.1–2 (2001), www.eoneill.com/library/review/25–1.2/25–1.2d.

20 Andrew Dix, email message to the author, September 31, 2009.

21 Eugene O'Neill, *Long Day's Journey into Night* (London: Nick Hern, 1993), 50.

22 Michael Manheim, "The Transcendence of Melodrama in *Long Day's Journey Into Night*," in *Perspectives on O'Neill: New Essays*, ed. Shyamal Bagchee (University of Victoria, 1988), www.eoneill.com/library/on/manheim/ldj_els.

23 Norman Berlin, "The Late Plays," in *The Cambridge Companion to Eugene O'Neill*, ed. M. Manheim (Cambridge University Press, 1998), 91.

24 O'Neill, *Long Day's Journey*, 3

25 Linda Seger, *The Art of Adaptation: Turning Fact and Fiction into Film* (New York: Henry Holt, 1992), 159.

26 Costello, "Sidney Lumet's *Long Day's Journey into Night*," 86.

27 O'Neill, *Long Day's Journey*, 21.

28 Ibid., 2.

29 Bennett Simon, *Tragic Drama and the Family: Psychoanalytic Studies from Aeschylus to Beckett* (New Haven: Yale University Press, 1988), 189.

30 Bosley Crowther, "*Long Day's Journey into Night*," *New York Times*, accessed July 21, 2010, www.eoneill.com/artifacts/reviews/ldjf_times.htm.

31 O'Neill, *Selected Letters*, 155.

32 Jean Chothia, *Forging a Language: A Study of the Plays of Eugene O'Neill* (Cambridge University Press, 1979), 32–33.

33 *Variety* reported that the film was shot for $400,000, while Lumet suggests alternately $435,000 and $495,000.

34 Paul Monaco, *The Sixties: 1960–1969* (Berkeley: University of California Press, 2001), 3.

35 R. Bean, "The Insider: Sidney Lumet Talks to Robin Bean About His Work in Films," *Films and Filming*, June 1965, 13.

36 Lumet, *Making Movies*, 67.

37 Richard Dyer, *Stars* (London: British Film Institute, 1979), 146.

38 Crowther, "*Long Day's Journey into Night.*"

39 Bean, "The Insider," 13.

40 O'Neill, *Long Day's Journey*, 2.

41 Homer Dickens, *The Films of Katharine Hepburn* (Secaucus, NJ: The Citadel Press, 1973), 180.

42 Carey, *Katharine Hepburn*, 203.

43 Ibid., 202.

44 O'Neill, *Long Day's Journey*, 31.

45 The audio interview may be found on *Long Day's Journey into Night*, directed by Jonathan Miller, USA. Image Entertainment, 1987, DVD, 170 mins.

46 Monaco, *The Sixties*, 120.

47 Berlin, "The Late Plays," 89.

48 Lumet, *Making Movies*, 32.

49 Robert Scholes and Robert Leland Kellogg, *The Nature of Narrative* (Oxford University Press, 1966), 171.

50 Zander Brietzke, *Aesthetics of Failure: Dynamic Structure in the Plays of Eugene O'Neill* (Jefferson: McFarland, 2001), 140.

51 Ibid., 234.

52 Ibid., 235. (This takes on even greater relevance in Lumet's film considering how the role granted to Hepburn skews the viewer's understanding of perspective.)

53 Michael Manheim, "The Stature of *Long Day's Journey into Night*," in *The Cambridge Companion to Eugene O'Neill* (Cambridge University Press, 1988), www.Eoneill.com/library/on/Manheim/ldj-Cambridge.htm, accessed April 11, 2013.

54 O'Neill, *Long Day's Journey*, 79.

55 Ibid., 109.

56 Frederic I. Carpenter, *Eugene O'Neill* (Boston: Twayne, 1979), 157.

57 Chothia, *Forging a Language*, 178.

58 Oscar Cargill, N. Bryllion Fagin, and William J. Fisher, *O'Neill and His Plays: Four Decades of Criticism* (New York University Press, 1970), 104.

CHAPTER 10

Hollywood's Who's Afraid of Virginia Woolf?: breaking the code

David Lavery and Nancy McGuire Roche

Who's Afraid of Virginia Woolf? and censorship

[*Who's Afraid of Virginia* Woolf was] the Fort Sumter of film censorship.
                                                                Jack Valenti

American cinema of the 1960s pushed against and broke down the censorship codes of previous decades. Fueled by European New Wave, art-house, exploitation, underground, and cult films, a new cinema evolved that ruptured many of the traditional narratives of Hollywood. As the decade progressed, particular films began to constitute a seismic undercurrent in cinema. One of the most important of these was Mike Nichols's *Who's Afraid of Virginia Woolf?* (hereafter *WAVW?*).

In America the Motion Picture Production Code of 1930 (hereafter MPPC) was the primary agent of film censorship from the early 1930s until 1968, when the film ratings system was first employed after a decade of films challenged previously adhered-to rules. The rise and fall of the MPPC reflected the moral and political climate of the nation during the era of its power. From the early years of the twentieth century, American church and state closely watched the rise in popularity of film and debated its merit as a valuable instrument for controlling the ideas and feelings of its viewers, a barometer of American morals, as well as entertainment for the masses. The MPPC, also referred to as the Hays Code, after its first administrator, William Hays, would become a powerful delineator of these purposes.

The Hays Code's ascension to power and the tale of its demise provide a fascinating look at American culture in two very disparate decades. With its off-color language, references to marital infidelity, and alcoholic excess, *WAVW?* reflected many of the aspects of American culture that the MPPC, a document which held authority over the creative process of an entire generation of American film, sought to ban. Under its power, the rules by which films could be created were established, and consequently narratives mythologizing certain aspects of American society were allowed, while others were repressed. *WAVW?* helped to liberate American cinema from this repression.

Movies arrived in America in 1895 and by the early years of the twentieth century had become the most popular form of entertainment for the lower classes in America. The popularity of motion pictures and concern regarding their thrall over the masses developed simultaneously; in 1907, less than a decade after film arrived in America, the city of Chicago passed the first law to regulate content. Thus began a delicate balance of power between the authority of the state and the local police, those who produced films, and those who consumed them. As Francis Couvares observes, "Censorship battles reveal the bonds and cleavages in society by mobilizing people's emotions and sometimes their political energies in defense of values and commitments and in opposition to adversaries perceived to be dangerous and alien."[1]

In *Pre-Code Hollywood: Sex, Immorality, and Insurrection in American Cinema, 1930–1934*, Thomas Doherty delineates many of the factors which preceded the MPPC:

> A technologically complex, capital-intensive business dependent on circuits of national distribution, the motion picture industry around 1920 came to describe not just a location but also an economic practice. The vertical integration of motion picture production, distribution, and exhibition – in which a single corporate entity produced, sent out, and screened the film product – crystallized into the mature oligopoly of the Hollywood studio system.[2]

Hollywood was more than a technical production system at this point. As Doherty theorizes, it was also a "moral universe."

The saga of the Movie Production Code began in 1922, when movie production companies founded a trade association, the Motion Picture Producers and Distributors of America, and appointed Will Hays its director. The rise to power and eventual domination of the Hays Office, Doherty maintains, gave a few individuals control over the diegesis of American cinema. He points out that the Golden Age of Hollywood, a period of roughly thirty years, both began and ended with the Hays Code. Not only did the progenitors of movie censorship finally triumph with the Depression raging at the door of America; they continued to control the entertainment of its populace until the 1960s destroyed the moral conventions which had fueled and fed it.

As President of the Motion Picture Producers and Distributors of America, Hays worked to keep the peace between a film industry which continued to churn out images of "wild youth, dancing daughters, straying wives and dark seducers"[3] and the moral vanguard which opposed them. In 1930, however, the MPPC, written by Father Daniel Lord, a Jesuit priest, and a Roman Catholic, Martin Quigley (the editor of the trade paper *Motion Picture Herald*), spelled out in very specific terms film topics which would be allowed or rejected. Doherty postulates that at the very heart of the Code was the morality of the Roman Catholic Church:

> Their amalgam of Irish-Catholic Victorianism colors much of the cloistered design of classical Hollywood cinema ... deference to civil and religious authorities, insistence on personal responsibility, belief in the salvific worth of suffering, and resistance to the pleasures of the flesh in thought, word, and deed.[4]

Through the MPPC, Quigley and Lord sought to control the morality of America's visual entertainment. Like the early Victorian censors, they were most concerned with proper role models for youth, the "protection" of women, and plots which demonstrated the futility of crime. As a form of internal policing, the Motion Picture Producers and Distributors of America controlled Hollywood, which now answered to the capitalists behind the industry rather than the studios, producers, or directors – that is, the creative forces behind the movies.

To head this office, Will Hays appointed another Roman Catholic, Joseph Breen, who would remain in this position from 1934 to 1954. Breen believed that film was a force which could steer the moral zeitgeist of America, and he never faltered in his course. Starting in 1934, the Catholic Legion of Decency organized boycotts of films that did not meet Code standards, and a fine of $25,000 was levied against any theatre showing a film without MPPC approval. It would not be until Breen left office in the mid 1950s that cracks would appear in the foundation of the Code.

The demise of the Hays Code was brought about by changes in the social climate of America, but it was instigated by a number of specific films that reflected massive changes in society. Throughout the 1950s and into the turbulent 1960s, America's youth had evolved to a darker, intellectual force that considered revolt as a means to have their opinions heard. From Martin Luther King, Jr.'s march on Washington to the novels of the Beat writers Jack Kerouac and William S. Burroughs, young people began to resist the status quo. As protests against segregation escalated in the South in the early 1960s and student protests against the war in Vietnam became common events, the decade became more tumultuous.

From their living rooms, Americans could watch images of villages being burned, Vietnamese children on fire, and the return home of the body bags of American soldiers. Live broadcasts of children in Selma, Alabama, being blasted with fire hoses in 1963 and rioters at the 1968 Democratic convention being beaten by police would deeply affect American ideology and sensibilities. By the mid 1960s Hollywood could no longer ignore the social and political turmoil of the era. The upheaval of the 1960s and an increasing distrust of both church and state were reflected in the subject matter of 1960s films like *WAVW?*, which, while questioning the traditional standards and prescriptions of institutions such as marriage, became one of the most important movies of the 1960s rebellion against the Hays Code, and perhaps the film most singularly responsible, for both moral and financial reasons, for its demise.

The rise of New Hollywood started in the mid 1960s as major production companies such as Warner Brothers, United Artists, Columbia, and Twentieth Century Fox began to lose money. When these corporations could no longer own motion picture theatres, they could no longer control what was shown there. Suddenly, there was no guaranteed audience. As Leff and Simmons explain, "By the 1950s ... major studios [were] increasingly placing their emphasis on distribution and thinking more globally. Earnings abroad for the Hollywood majors, in fact, surpassed their domestic revenues for the first time in 1958; that trend continued every year throughout the 1960s."[5] The number of feature films made in the US markedly decreased as well. Monaco notes that studios such as Paramount, which had once created as many as a hundred films a year, dropped their production rates to fifteen annually for the duration of the 1960s.

As the number of movies declined, production risk for each motion picture exponentially increased. The need for movies such as *WAVW?* to achieve ratings approval by the Production Code Office became more crucial. The financial pressure for approval of high-budget films (and *WAVW?* was at the time the most expensive black-and-white film ever made), as well as the appointment of the more liberal Jack Valenti as the head of the MPAA, helped to instigate the liberalization of the Hays Code and emancipate American film. But these boundaries had to be tested.[6]

Much like the auteurs of the European new waves, American directors began to acquire more power over their work and its content, which they used to create "stylistically diverse and narratively challenging films that were much more tuned in to the social and political climate of the era."[7] Working from an award-winning play that challenged the mindset of

American morality, first-time director Mike Nichols accomplished something far more daring in the end. In 1966, and under Hays Code stipulations, he used *WAVW?* as a weapon to challenge MMPA standards.

Edward Albee's *Who's Afraid of Virginia Woolf?* debuted on Broadway in October of 1962. Long before Nichols became director of the film, Geoffrey Shurlock, the more liberal successor to Joseph Breen as chief enforcer of the MMPC, had already announced in a memo to Jack Warner the proper path to bring *WAVW?* to the screen when it was still only a stage play: get rid of all the profanity and all the sexual implications[8] – in other words, he believed it to be "unfilmmable."[9]

Shurlock's successor, Jack Valenti, characterized by Richard Schickel as "an old Texas liberal"[10] who had worked in the Johnson administration, a man who deemed the Hays Code "draconian" and would later give us our current MPAA ratings code, had been on the job only a month when production of *WAVW?* fell into his lap. Valenti would in retrospect describe the film as "pioneering . . . in pushing the boundaries" and recalls its impact as "the Fort Sumter" of film censorship as a welcome development.[11]

At Nichols's insistence no "clean cover shots" – frames without profanity or visual suggestiveness to-be-used-if-needed – were filmed during production,[12] making the possibility of a later censored version virtually impossible. No longer worried as it had been in the past by the potential commercial curse of a bad rating by the likes of the Catholic Church's Legion of Decency, Warner threatened to send the film into theatres unrated.[13] The movie went out with a "for adults only" warning – Warner's suggestion – creating, in effect, the "R" rating two years before it would become a reality.[14]

A final breakthrough for *WAVW?* would come in February of 1966, when, under the influence of a more open-minded, liberal Catholicism, the Legion of Decency approved an initial proposal for a ratings system. It would not be until later that spring, however, that a confluence of events allowed *WAVW?* to continue toward release: Valenti was drafted as head of the Production Code Administration; Warner Brothers voluntarily instituted a "no one under 18 policy" for the film's distribution; and Jack Warner engineered a meeting with the National Catholic Office, which begrudgingly approved the film uncut but restricted for viewers under eighteen years of age. "The vote," Leff and Simmons observe, "sent an emphatic message to Hollywood. With classification, motion pictures and free expression could co-exist."[15]

In the end, *WAVW?* was granted an exemption from the Code, and Quigley announced in *Motion Picture Herald* that the "Code is Dead." Within a month Jack Valenti unveiled a new Production Code, and by fall: "Even *Alfie*, a Paramount import with an abortion sequence, won approval from an Association review board."[16] *Alfie* (1966, Lewis Gilbert), which contained an abortion scene when the MPPC specifically forbade the topic of abortion, was given a rating of A-IV, "morally unobjectionable for adults – with reservations,"[17] the precursor to the rating system's "Suggested for Mature Audiences."

The wheels of change were in motion. Jack Valenti, it seemed, had seen the value in films that appealed to young moviegoers as they began to constitute a large audience in the 1960s, and, to prove him correct, *WAVW?* won five Academy Awards.

Adapting *Who's Afraid of Virginia Woolf?*

If you were married to Martha, you would know what that means. But then, if I were married to your wife, I would know what that means, too . . . wouldn't I?

George to Nick in Who's Afraid of Virginia Woolf?

Married couples are not saints, and sin is not some error which we may renounce one of these days in order to adopt a more accurate truth. We are unendingly and incessantly in the thick of the struggle between nature and grace; unendingly and incessantly unhappy and then happy. But the horizon has not remained the same. A fidelity maintained in the name of what does not change as we change will gradually disclose some of its mystery: beyond tragedy another happiness waits. A happiness resembling the old, but no longer belonging to the form of the world, for this new happiness transforms the world.

Denis de Rougemont, Love in the Western World

Jesus Christ. I think I understand!

Nick in Who's Afraid of Virginia Woolf?

Thirty-eight seconds into the 1966 film adaptation of Edward Albee's controversial play *Who's Afraid of Virginia Woolf?* George (Richard Burton) and Martha (Elizabeth Taylor) emerge from a lit doorway in a college building. Dressed in overcoats at this late hour (George notes that it is 2:00 a.m.) on this clearly autumn evening, the couple walks slowly home. During their three-minute-and-eleven-second credit-sequence stroll, we learn the names of the cast and crew of the movie we are watching. George Segal (Nick) and Sandy Dennis (Honey) completed the cast. The cinematographer was Haskell Wexler. Ernest Lehman produced and wrote the screenplay. The score poignantly accompanying George and Martha's nocturnal perambulation was Alex North's; Richard Sylbert designed the production; Sam O'Steen edited. Mike Nichols directed.

Figure 10.1 The on-the-make young professor Nick (George Segal), accompanied by wife Honey (Sandy Dennis), is the focus from the beginning of the after-party get-together hosted by his older colleague George (Richard Burton) and his predatory wife Martha (Elizabeth Taylor). (frame enlargement)

As with most credit sequences, we may watch with divided attention as we settle down in our seats and sample the popcorn, assuming the passing moments, in this case approximately 2.5 percent of the film as a whole, are probably dispensable, mere backdrop to obligatory onscreen titles informing the audience (with varying degrees of cinephile recognition) who did what. This extramural scene, however, one of several in the movie (such as George and Nick's backyard discussion and the sojourn to the roadhouse) transpiring outside George and Martha's claustrophobic "dump" of a house, could not be more important in understanding the adaptation from stage to screen of *WAVW*?

Before George and Martha enter their house, before she declares it to be "a dump," before she tells her husband he makes her want to "puke" and proclaims "I swear . . . if you existed, I'd divorce you"; before George brings a trick rifle out of the closet and pretends to shoot his wife in the head; before he announces his intention to have her committed, we have seen, in being privy to these moments of long-married pedestrian (literally) intimacy, that George and Martha, though unquestionably "sad, sad, sad," actually love one another. They are a couple, as we learn in the first post-credits scene, when they begin to "exercise what's left of their wits," that knows how many teeth each other has and finds laughter in that knowledge. On the DVD commentary/dialogue with fellow director Steven Soderberg on the special edition DVD set (hereafter Soderberg/Nichols), Nichols goes out of his way to contest those who fail to understand this facet. Every director of a movie, like every director of a play and oral interpreter of a poem, imposes his or her interpretation upon a text, "reading" it in a certain way. For Mike Nichols, *WAVW?* is a profound love story.

Warner Brothers had acquired the rights to Albee's scandalous but successful play[18] for $500,000[19] soon after it debuted in 1962, hiring Ernest Lehman, best known for his early-in-the-decade adaptation of *West Side Story* (1961), to produce.[20] All sorts of George and Martha pairings were initially considered: George Hill and Uta Hagen (the original Broadway actors), Bette Davis[21] and James Mason, Jack Lemmon and Patricia Neal.[22] Famous actors turned down roles in the play: Henry Fonda said no to George, and Robert Redford passed on Nick.[23] Before Broadway director Nichols (winner of two Tonys)[24] got the assignment – his first as a film director – Fred Zinnemann (*High Noon* [1952], *From Here to Eternity* [1953]) and John Frankenheimer (*The Manchurian Candidate* [1962]) were considered.[25] In the end it was Elizabeth Taylor who got Nichols the assignment.[26] Lehman insisted on Taylor, and Taylor demanded Nichols.

Nichols had known Burton from Broadway and had visited him (and Taylor) in Italy when the world's most famous, most tabloidized couple was filming *Cleopatra* (1963, Joseph L. Mankiewicz,) at CineCittà Studios. Once the Burtons showed interest in taking on George and Martha, that possibility drove the film's preproduction. They wanted Nichols to direct, but that became a possibility only after he received permission from producer Lawrence Turman, who had him under contract to do *The Graduate* (1967).[27] Nichols would sign on for $250,000,[28] and his contract granted him three months to learn directing prior to the beginning of production in March 1965. "I wasn't entirely sure how a camera worked," he admitted.[29] As a director's first film, the result deserves mentioning in the same breath with the most famous of all initial outings: Orson Welles's *Citizen Kane* (1941).

A great film customarily presents itself to the world as a *fait accompli*, when in fact scores of battles must be won, and correct decisions made, in preproduction and behind the scenes, in order for it to become a work of cinema worth remembering. Nichols's clashes – with cinematographer Harry Stradling, Lehman (sarcastically deemed by Nichols as the "so-called writer-producer who was neither producer nor writer"),[30] with the Production Code and motion picture censorship – were many, but he won most of them.

Once Nichols took the helm on a production shot at Warner Brothers Studios in California and on the campus of Smith College in Massachusetts,[31] the studio assigned him a crew that included the sixty-four-year-old Stradling, an Oscar-winning cinematographer, perhaps best known for his

Figure 10.2 Mike Nichols frequently uses unbalanced compositions to suggest the uncertainty of the personal relationships the film probes. (frame enlargement)

work on *A Streetcar Named Desire* (1951, Elia Kazan), who would clash often with the novice director. Unimpressed when Nichols required him to consider Fellini's *8½* (1963) and the work of French *Nouvelle Vague* directors Truffaut and Godard as visual models, Stradling rebelled at Nichols's partiality to filming in black-and-white.[32] The director's insistence on the passé mode of photography was not merely aesthetic, of course: black-and-white would go a long way toward masking the age differences of actors and characters. After suggesting that Nichols film in color and then print in black-and-white, Stradling was fired[33] and replaced with soon-to-be legendary cinematographer Haskell Wexler, fourteen years Stradling's junior.

Wexler concurred with Nichols that black-and-white was more "visceral" than color,[34] and his contributions to the film were, in Richard Schickel's estimation, "immense."[35] *Time*'s film critic would take special note of Wexler's use of hand-held camera (360 shots; for example, of George and Honey dancing and Honey cavorting "like the wind") and the film's admirable use of gray: Schickel praises the film as "as good a piece as night shooting as I've ever seen." Not surprisingly, *American Cinematographer* would do a cover story on *WAVW?*,[36] and Wexler would win an Oscar for the film.[37]

Nichols's stand-off with producer and credited screenwriter Lehman was equally significant and more protracted (he worked with Lehman for at least two months on the script).[38] Lehman had already written versions with no obscenity,[39] but Nichols encouraged him "to go for close to broke."[40] The veteran screenwriter had developed some peculiar notions, however – ideas Nichols saw as more appropriate to *Whatever Happened to Baby Jane?* (Robert Aldrich, 1962) than *WAVW?*

Lehman, it seems, was briefly intrigued by the in-the-air-at-the-time notion (firmly rejected by Albee) that George and Martha were gay, and in his first version of the script the couple's imaginary son was in fact real and had, at the age of eighteen, hanged himself in a closet his parents had then sealed forever.[41] Nichols was especially appalled by one version of Lehman's script that had George coming across dogs having sex while out for a walk. Lehman's cautionary directive that "This must be beautifully shot" failed to convince Nichols of its value.[42] The man ultimately credited as the film's author "wasn't suited to the Albee stuff, and he wasn't used to being a producer," as Nichols would recall. By his own admission the young director did not "have the patience" to compromise with either Stradling or Lehman. "I would get pissed off and probably be rougher than I needed to be."[43] The finished script rejected almost all of Lehman's questionable revisioning.

Although the final film bears Nichols's imprimatur through and through, it is worth noting that, as Harris observes, *WAVW?*'s director was treated rather badly in postproduction. Not only did Warner Brothers refuse his desire to replace Alex North's music with André Previn's, it banned Nichols from the editing room in the final days.[44]

When all was said and done and *WAVW?* was in the can, Jack Warner supposedly remained alarmed that "My God, we've got a $7.5 million dirty movie on our hands."[45] The concern was unnecessary: the film would be the second-highest grossing of the year, taking in (according to the Internet Movie Data Base) $28,000,000 in the US and over $40,000,000 worldwide and garnering thirteen Academy Award nominations.[46]

Even Albee would approve. Although the playwright was initially "a little upset by the casting," finding "Elizabeth . . . twenty years too young and Richard about five years too old," in an interview for the DVD he admits that the film was "pretty damn good" and fairly represented his play, and he would praise Taylor's performance as "the best work she's done on film."[47]

Watching Nichols's film with Albee's play in hand,[48] we take note of many differences that provoke several questions.

- The hilarious slovenliness of Taylor's Martha – she puts a chicken leg she has been gnawing on back in the fridge, throws debris in the fireplace, stuffs dirty clothes under the blanket on their bed – is not in the play, not even in stage directions. Was Taylor improvising? What role did Nichols play in the blocking?

- Dialogue – about their respective number of teeth, their six-year difference in age, "guts," the who's afraid of Virginia Woolf joke from the party (chanted now by Martha while straddling George), the soon-to-arrive guests, the chewing of ice cubes, George's status as a "Poor Georgie-Porgie, put-upon pie," the need for a "big sloppy kiss" – takes place in the upstairs bedroom and on the bed prior to Nick and Honey's arrival. No location is stipulated in the text.
- Martha's "Screw you" in the play at the entrance of the guests becomes "Goddam you" in the film.[49]
- A discussion of Martha's drinking habits (24) is not in the film (hereafter NIF).
- George's insistence that he looks older than he is (35): NIF.
- Discussion at several points in the play (37–41, 65–68, for example, or 71–75) of chromosomes and genetic engineering (resulting from the realization that Nick is a biologist and not "in the math department"): NIF.
- George's rambling comments on being a professor and his father-in-law and running the History Department (38, 40–41): NIF.
- George's suggestion that Martha is her father's "right ball" (47): NIF.
- Martha's admission that she has no sense of humor (76): NIF.
- An extensive discussion of Martha's childhood (77–80): NIF.
- George and Nick take their somewhat abridged rambling discussion – about the boy who drank "bergin," Honey's false pregnancy and her father's money, and historical inevitability (89–117) – outside, underneath a tree in the yard.
- The surprising revelation from George that "Martha has money too. I mean her father's been robbing this place blind for years" (107): NIF.
- Nick's drunken realization that his plan to start "plowing pertinent wives" should start with Martha – "I bet your wife's the biggest goose in the gangle . . . gaggle" (114) becomes in the film the decidedly more obscene "your wife must have the widest, most inviting avenue of all."
- George's discourse on China (166): NIF.
- Martha's extensive fantasia about their boy (220–223): for the most part NIF.

Most of these departures are logical enough. *WAVW?*'s three-hour running time[50] required significant cutting, and it seemed only natural to eliminate

Figure 10.3 Escaping the claustrophobia of George and Martha's "dump" of a house at
a local roadhouse, Nick and Martha dance lasciviously while George prepares for
a game of "Get the Guests" (frame enlargement)

tangential orations on history and biology. Getting out of the house was
likewise an understandable move, intended to open out the narrative in a
manner impossible on stage, and Nick and Martha's laughably dated
dancing at the roadhouse could just as well have misfired in the house as
out. To contemporary ears, changing "Screw you" to "God damn you"
might not seem to decrease potential offensiveness but evidently did meet
the needs of the time, as did the reluctance to identify Martha as one of her
father's testicles. And if having George envision Martha as "the widest
most inviting avenue of all" is indeed more sexually suggestive, the phrasing
is the sort of double entendre that would not be objectionable today.

But why diminish, as the Nichols version arguably does, our complex
understanding of Martha? In his dialogue about the film with Soderberg,
Nichols not only insists, as we saw earlier, that George and Martha are
truly in love and Nick and Honey clueless about its true nature; he is
emphatic, too, that, despite appearances (one of the play's major themes),
George is the couple's better half. Take note that Martha's moving
confession to Nick that her husband is the only man who ever made her
happy does make it into the film intact:

> There's only been one man in my life who's ever made me happy. You
> know that? One ... George. My husband ... George who is out some-
> where there in the dark. Who is good to me. Whom I revile. Who can keep

learning the games we play as quickly as I can change them. Who can make me happy and I do not wish to be happy. Yes, I do wish to be happy. George and Martha. Sad, sad, sad. Whom I will not forgive for having come to rest. For having seen me and having said ... "Yes, this will do." Who has made the hideous, the hurting ... the insulting mistake of loving me. And must be punished for it. Sad, sad, sad. Some day ... some night ... some stupid liquor-ridden night I will go too far. I'll either break his back or I'll push him off for good, which I deserve.

Martha may insist that all the men she takes to her bed (both play and film suggest that her fling with Nick is hardly unprecedented) are "all flops. I am the Earth Mother and you are all flops," but she is anything but an Earth Mother. As Nick finally comprehends ("Jesus Christ, I think I understand this"), George and Martha are incapable of having children; this Earth Mother is not fertile. When Nick inquires just prior to his exit "You couldn't have ... any?" George generously replies "*We* couldn't," and Martha chimes in (with, as the stage directions indicate, "a hint of communion"), "*We* couldn't." But it is Martha, not George, who has invented an imaginary child to fill the void in her soul; Martha whom George threatens to have committed (and could well be successful if he did so); Martha whose delusions must be exorcised this very night.

How can any reader, or any viewer, watching the quiet, terribly moving, almost wordless final scene, in which Martha quietly pleads to bring back her boy, even after he has been put to rest in the third act's mass for the dead (a request her husband gently denies), still not grasp George and Martha's impenetrable tenderness and profound love? In one of the final chapters of his *Love in the Western World*, de Rougemont, reminds:

> Nature is said to have required several hundreds of thousands of years for the selection of those species which now seem to us adapted to their surroundings. And yet we have the presumption to suppose that all of a sudden in the course of a single life we may solve the problem of the adaptation to one another of two highly organized physical and moral beings.[51]

Who's Afraid of Virginia Woolf? – play and film – is a too-close-for-comfort, almost too intimate, imaginary record of one momentous night of marital adaptation.

Endnotes

1 Frances G. Couvares, *Movie Censorship and American Culture* (Washington, DC: Smithsonian Institution Press, 1996), 3.

2 Thomas Doherty, *Pre-Code Hollywood: Sex, Immorality, and Insurrection in American Cinema, 1930–1934* (New York: Columbia University Press, 1999), 4.

3 Ibid., 6.

4 Ibid., 6.

5 Paul Monaco, *The Sixties: 1960–1969* (Berkeley: University of California Press, 2001), 10.

6 For a comprehensive account of the back and forth of financial and moral concerns in the American film industry see Jon Lewis, *Hollywood v. Hard Core: How the Struggle over Censorship Saved the Modern Film Industry* (New York: NYU Press, 2000)

7 Yannis Tzioumakis, *American Independent Cinema* (New Brunswick, NJ: University of Rutgers Press, 2006), 170.

8 "*Who's Afraid of Virginia Woolf?*: A Daring Work of Excellence," *Who's Afraid of Virginia Woolf?* DVD. Warner Bros., 2006. (Henceforth "Daring.")

9 "*Who's Afraid of Virginia Woolf?*: Too Shocking for It's [*sic*] Time," *Who's Afraid of Virginia Woolf?* DVD. Warner Bros., 2006. (Henceforth "Shocking.") Film historian Drew Caspar insists that Shurlock was nevertheless sympathetic to the idea of bringing *WAVW?* to the big screen ("Shocking").

10 Ibid.

11 Ibid.

12 Ibid.

13 Ibid.

14 The example of *The Pawnbroker* (Sidney Lumet, 1964), a very serious film about a Holocaust survivor which received a certificate despite an uncensored brief scene of nudity, was very much on everyone's minds as *WAVW?* went into production. Its passage opened the door for serious films like *WAVW?* that included possibly objectionable material (Mark Harris, *Pictures at a Revolution: Five Movies and the Birth of the New Hollywood* [New York: Penguin, 2008], 174–176).

15 Leonard J. Leff and Jerold L. Simmons, *The Dame in the Kimono: Hollywood, Censorship, and the Production Code from the 1920s to the 1960s* (New York: Grove Weidenfeld, 1990), 258.

16 Ibid., 269.

17 Harris, *Pictures at a Revolution*, 235.

18 Albee mirthfully recalls his favorite review – one that labeled *WAVW?* "a play for dirty-minded women" ("Daring") – as the sort of scornful notice that virtually guarantees audience interest.

19 Harris, *Pictures at a Revolution*, 73.

20 The most comprehensive account of the making of *WAVW?* is to be found in Mark Harris's *Pictures at a Revolution*, a source to which we are tremendously indebted here. The DVD set also provides helpful interviews and featurettes about the production as well: "1966 Mike Nichols Interview," "Elizabeth Taylor: Intimate Portrait," "*Who's Afraid of Virginia Woolf?*: A Daring Work of Excellence," "*Who's Afraid of Virginia Woolf?*: Too Shocking for It's [*sic*] Time." The Soderberg/Nichols commentary is likewise invaluable.

21 Albee recalls talking to Warner and remarking that he looked forward to seeing Bette Davis do an imitation of Bette Davis in the opening scene ("Daring").

22 Harris, *Pictures at a Revolution*, 73.

23 Both had similar reasons for opting out. Fonda's agent rejected George as a "no-balls character" (Harris, *Pictures at a Revolution*, 73) (Fonda was Albee's first choice as George ["Daring"]), and Redford found Nick too much a toady for his taste (Soderberg/Nichols).

24 Nichols had received two Tony Awards for directing *Barefoot in the Park* (1964) and *The Odd Couple* (1965).

25 Harris, *Pictures at a Revolution*, 73.

26 Ibid., 74.

27 According to Harris, Turman's generosity had an ulterior motive: he wanted Nichols to learn his craft on *WAVW?* before doing his film (ibid., 74).

28 The stars, of course, were paid much more, Taylor earning $1.1 million and Burton $750,000 (ibid., 118).

29 Ibid., 74.

30 Ibid., 118.

31 Ibid., 116.

32 Ibid, 100–101. Albee agreed with Stradling. His comment upon learning that *WAVW?* would be in black-and-white: "how bizarre" ("Daring").

33 Harris, *Pictures at a Revolution*, 102; Soderberg/Nichols commentary.

34 "Daring."

35 Ibid.

36 Ibid.

37 As Mark Harris reports, Nichols and Wexler were not entirely *sympatico*: "Nichols was irritated by Wexler's slowness, but supported his work when the studio didn't think the rushes looked good" (ibid., 118).

38 "Daring."

39 Nichols recalled that "Ernie . . . changed 'you son of a bitch' to 'you dirty lousy dot dot dot' . . ." He remained convinced, ever, that "disguising profanity with clean but suggestive phrases is really dirtier" (Harris, *Pictures at a Revolution*, 29).

40 Ibid., 99.

41 Ibid., 99–100.

42 Ibid., 118.

43 Ibid., 100. "You would think that as a director, slowly, as you got to be a geezer, you would become more and more irascible," Nichols once observed, until you ended up like George Cukor, screaming at Candice Bergen and Jacqueline Bisset for an entire movie [*Rich and Famous*]. But with me, it was the other way around. I started out as a prick on the set. Not to the actors much, but by and large to everybody. I don't know who I was then or what was happening. And I got nicer as time went by. But I was a prick" (ibid., 102).

44 Ibid., 185.

45 Ibid., 183.

46 *WAVW?* earned a nomination in every possible Oscar category, the first motion picture ever to do so: Best Actress in a Leading Role (won by Taylor), Best Actress in a Supporting Role (won by Dennis), Best Art Direction/Set

Decoration, Black-and-white (won by Sylbert and George James Hopkins), Best Cinematography, Black-and-white (won by Wexler), Best Costume Design, Black-and-white (won by Irene Sharaff), not to mention Best Actor in a Leading Role (Burton), Best Actor in a Supporting Role (Segal), Best Director (Nichols), Best Film Editing (O'Steen), Best Music, Original Music Score (North), Best Picture, Best Sound (George Groves), and Best Writing, Screenplay Based on Material from Another Medium (Ernest Lehman).

47 "Daring."

48 The text we used was the original 1962 paperback (page numbers in the text refer to it). Another edition, "revised by the author for the 2005 Broadway Revival," is the only version now in print.

49 On the DVD, the widow of editor Sam O'Steen reconstructs her husband's post-synching of the three-syllable "goddam you" over the recorded two-syllable "screw you" ("Shocking").

50 Websites for recent productions estimate the play's duration at three hours and fifteen minutes, including intermissions.

51 Denis de Rougemont, *Love in the Western World*, trans. Montgomery Belgion (New York: Harper and Row, 1956), 303.

CHAPTER 11

Sex, lies, and independent film: realism and reality in Sam Shepard's Fool for Love

Annette J. Saddik

There's not a movie in this town that can match the story I'm gonna tell.

Eddie, *Fool for Love*[1]

While Sam Shepard is probably best known as one of America's most celebrated playwrights, his accomplishments as an actor, director, musician, and writer of screenplays, poetry, and prose make him a unique figure in the American theatre. Born in 1943, Shepard started out as an actor, touring with a theatre group after leaving his home town of Duarte, California, in 1962, and moving to New York City in 1963. He developed a passion for rock music, and from 1967 to 1970 he was the drummer for the "amphetamine rock band" The Holy Modal Rollers (a.k.a. The Moray Eels). In a 1971 program note, Shepard asserted his connection with music in what has since become a well-known statement: "First off let me tell you that I don't want to be a playwright. I want to be a rock and roll star."[2] Yet despite his attraction to a career in music, Shepard first made a name for himself as an experimental playwright, becoming "the unofficial star of the alternative theatre scene."[3]

From the beginning of his career, Shepard was interested in exploring the innovative dramatic forms that emerged in Europe after World War II and took root in the off- and off-off-Broadway American theatre during the 1960s and 1970s. Infusing these new forms with a particularly American character, Shepard became active in such downtown experimental theatres as Café Cino, La MaMa E.T.C., and Theatre Genesis, where he got his start in 1964 with his early plays *Cowboys* and *The Rock Garden*. The off- and off-off-Broadway theatre scene was particularly interested in exploring the period's concern with personal freedom and authenticity apart from political oppression in order to locate an individual essence, or "reality," outside conformist social roles, an issue that became one of Shepard's primary themes. Writing mostly one-act plays, Shepard's early successes were in the avant-garde theatre. He won his first three OBIE Awards (Off-Broadway Theater Awards) for *Chicago, Icarus' Mother,* and *Red Cross* in 1966, as well as a fourth for his first full-length play, *La Turista,* in 1967. He continued to distinguish himself off-Broadway with OBIE Awards for *Forensic and the Navigator* and *Melodrama Play* in 1968, and for *The Tooth of Crime* in 1973.

Shepard never abandoned his interest in music, however, and he often managed to combine multiple talents in his work. Many of Shepard's plays are presented with the style and energy of a rock concert. In 1974, he insisted that music in the theatre "adds a whole different kind of perspective, it immediately brings the audience to terms with an emotional reality."[4] Shepard wrote songs for several of his plays; the influence of jazz, rock 'n' roll, and country and western music is present both in the rhythms of his dialogue and in his direct use of live bands and music in his productions. *The Tooth of Crime,* for example, is heavily influenced by rock 'n' roll, and Shepard wrote the music for the play himself, instructing that the opening song should have a sound that resembles "Heroin" by the Velvet Underground.[5]

Not content working only in the mediums of music and drama, Shepard also went on to write various collections of poetry and short stories (*Hawk Moon* in 1973, *Motel Chronicles* in 1982, and, later, *Cruising Paradise* in 1996, to name a few), as well as several screenplays. He had early screenwriting credit on the films *Me and My Brother* (1968) and Michelangelo Antonioni's *Zabriskie Point* (1970), Antonioni's first film set in America with a counterculture theme. He went on to write the screenplay for Wim Wenders's *Paris, Texas* (1984), which won the prestigious *Palme d'Or* at the Cannes Film Festival. Throughout the 1970s and 1980s Shepard focused mainly on playwriting and acting, writing what are considered some of his major plays – *Buried Child* (1978), *Curse of the Starving Class* (1978), *True West* (1980), *Fool for Love* (1983), and *A Lie of the Mind* (1985) – and establishing himself as an actor in films such as *Days of Heaven* (1978), *Frances* (1982), *The Right Stuff* (1983), *Country* (1984), *Crimes of the Heart* (1986), *Baby Boom* (1987), and *Steel Magnolias* (1989). Shepard has been unusually successful in various artistic mediums, winning the Pulitzer Prize for *Buried Child* in 1979, and earning an Academy Award nomination for Best Supporting Actor in 1983 for his portrayal of Chuck Yeager in *The Right Stuff.* He continued to work in film and theatre throughout the 1990s and 2000s, and remains active in both today.

Shepard's experimental plays are often characterized by truncated and fragmented dialogue, highly symbolic language, and characters lifted from the mythic discourses of Hollywood film and the American West, rock 'n' roll, and literature; they often concern themselves with the question of "authentic" identity in connection with the slippery nature of role playing, and it is the cowboy out on the Western desert, or his contemporary counterpart, the rock star, who is at the center of this mythology. His more mature full-length plays continue to struggle with these issues and more deeply explore the balance between obligation and freedom, the limits of individualism, and what it means to be a family, particularly in plays such as *Buried Child*, *True West*, and *Fool For Love*. In all three of these plays, memory and identity are called into question, and the "natural" connections that are supposed to accompany family ties are precarious, as human relationships prove unstable. In *Buried Child*, Dodge does not recognize his own grandson who has returned to the family home, asking him "Who are you to expect anything? Who are you supposed to be?"[6] In *True West*, "Mom" returns home to find her two sons in heated conflict and the house trashed, claiming that she doesn't "recognize it at all."[7]

It is in *Fool for Love*, however, where the cycle of heredity and the nature of family ties occupy the forefront of the play's mythology. The "Old Man," a non-realistic character that exists only in the minds of his children, May and Eddie, represents memory, history, and the determinism of blood relationships. He occupies a place on the side of the stage, observing and commenting on the action. Yet he is similarly dissociated from his past and his kin, claiming that neither May nor Eddie "look a bit familiar" to him, and that he does not recognize himself in either one of them. He "can't even remember the original circumstances" of their births, and insists they "could be anybody's" children.[8] Family connections are presented in the play as a myth with no real origin and no substantial value, yet their burden is keenly felt.

Fool for Love was first produced in San Francisco at the Magic Theatre in February 1983 and moved to New York for an off-Broadway run at the Circle Repertory Theatre in May of that year. Perhaps because of its intense emotional content, suspenseful atmosphere, and potential for melodramatic action, this was the first of his plays that Shepard decided to adapt for the screen. The film of *Fool for Love* was released in 1985, starring Kim Basinger, Harry Dean Stanton, Randy Quaid, and Shepard himself in the role of Eddie.

When the film premiered, the critical reception was generally negative, often faulting director Robert Altman's misguided decision to turn the play into a realistically motivated melodrama centered on two feuding lovers. Some, like Andrew Sarris at the *Village Voice*, were unequivocal in

Figure 11.1 The run-down motel where the action unfolds provides a fitting visual correlative of the disorder from which the film's characters suffer. (frame enlargement)

their condemnation, writing that "Quite simply, a very effective play has been stretched out into a very ineffective movie ... What was ritualized, stylized, or merely mentioned on the stage has been rendered with a brooding 'realism' on the screen."[9] Similarly, Scott Rosenberg of the *Boston Phoenix* felt that "For some reason, the sounds of conflict are muted in the Robert Altman screen adaptation of *Fool for Love* ... Whoever is behind this transformation (Shepard wrote the screenplay and takes the role of Eddie, and he handpicked Altman to direct the project), it's deadly – it lets all the pressure out of the piece, and the material goes flat." For Rosenberg, the result of the film's failed attempt at turning Shepard's "flamboyant poetic images" into a more conventional feature film that approaches Hollywood realism was that, ultimately, "Everything in the play that was solid melts away."[10]

There were some exceptions to this sort of reaction, such as Sheila Benson of the *Los Angeles Times*, who complimented Shepard and Basinger's performances (critical responses were mixed on this account), and also applauded the film's quasi-realistic treatment: "Altman's most inspired stroke is to people this trailer court with a mixture of real and memory figures, to have time flow as effortlessly as his camera." Benson felt that "In transferring [*Fool for Love*] to the screen, director Robert Altman has rolled up his sleeves and, for starters, let the two lovers breathe. Out of the one room that served to remind us only too well of a cage, their bone-jarring, wall-rattling assaults on each other now range all over this crummy neon-pueblo trailer court."[11] Overall, however, the critics agreed with Don Shewey's assessment that Altman "perversely took a play set in a tiny motel room made claustrophobic with erotic tension and spread it out

Figure 11.2 The "reunion" between the former lovers Eddie (Sam Shepard) and May (Kim Basinger) has its combative moments. (frame enlargement)

over the desert sky,"[12] and felt that opening up the action to the outside diluted the intense relentlessness and sense of being trapped that defined the atmosphere of the play.

The first words of the play's stage directions indicate that "This play is to be performed relentlessly without a break."[13] The setting is constructed in dark, dingy colors that attenuate an atmosphere of decay. This is a very physical, loud play that relies on the sounds of banging, slamming, hitting, and throwing, and the intensity of passion and frustration comes across in this "relentless," claustrophobic atmosphere. Language is punctuated with action, as when May asks Eddie about his affair with the Countess and, before he responds, he "bangs his head into the wall. Wall booms,"[14] or when May emphasizes her assertion that she will kill both Eddie and the Countess with two separate knives by slamming the wall with her elbow for each, as the "Wall resonates."[15] Language cannot contain or express the desire, violence, and emotion of the characters, which spills out and explodes into physical gesture. Eddie is constantly performing for May, but his cowboy persona is frustrated in the tiny motel room, and he resorts to roping the bedposts in a pathetic parody of a cowboy, doing backflips across the stage and crashing into the walls.[16]

The film does not match the play in terms of physical intensity. The action is opened up to the neon-lit motel grounds, the restaurant, and the vastness of the desert, so the characters are no longer trapped physically. As a result, they are also no longer trapped by emotion, desire, and memory to the same extent as in the play. Instead of being stuck in the motel room and roping the motel bedpost, Eddie ropes the jukebox in the restaurant, and outside he rides his horse in circles, roping a garbage can and dragging it noisily around the parking lot. Another way in which the action is opened up is through the use of flashbacks that punctuate the characters' recollections, visualizing memory. Moreover, memory freely roams around the motel grounds as characters from the past occupy the space of the present, interacting in a way that makes the trappings of memory seem less oppressive. Therefore, a different physical emphasis operates in the film – the visual representation of memory and emotion through flashback scenarios and additional characters strewn throughout – to replace the physical intensity of the play.

In a 1993 interview, Shepard acknowledged that while the film "attempted to move into a certain kind of emotional terrain that was true to itself," he didn't "think it eventually succeeded at it."[17] The play, however, does succeed in eliciting the powerful "emotional terrain" that Shepard was after, and one main reason for this is that, unlike the film, it resists sacrificing the power of myth to psychological narrative and visual authentication. While the style of the film is not strictly realistic, but rather employs a "mixture of real and memory figures," it is certainly much more realistic than the play in its goals, as it attempts to restrain the play's poetic truths in favor of a focus on the melodramatic aspects of the more superficial "story."

What David J. DeRose has argued about Shepard's *Buried Child* – that it "proves to be a Möbius strip of contradictory memories and realities that never comes to narrative resolution" – can be said of several of Shepard's plays, and certainly applies to *Fool for Love*.[18] In this play, the present is defined through a past accessible only through unreliable memory and emotional impressions, dependent upon competing narratives. Therefore, present reality is called into question. Reality exists only in the mind, in what we believe to be truth, and this is the only truth that counts, since it is the basis for motivation and action. The Old Man, who has the last word, emphasizes this attitude, as he ends the play "pointing into space, stage left" at an invisible picture of country singer Barbara Mandrell on the wall: "Ya' see that picture over there? Ya' see that? Ya' know who that is? That's the woman of my dreams. That's who that is. And she's mine. She's all mine. Forever."[19] The ending of the film, however, cuts off the Old Man's speech, embracing closure rather than ambiguity and subjectivity. Eddie drives off in his truck, promising to return, even though May knows

Figure 11.3 The play's metadramatic character, the "Old Man," plays a substantially different role in the film, as incarnated by Harry Dean Stanton. (frame enlargement)

that "he's gone." Martin has the last word as he calls out for May, who has already packed her suitcase and is walking off into the desert night. The focus is on the lovers and their turmoil as they part once again, perhaps for the last time, perhaps not.

Through its emphasis on realistic motivation and narrative detail, flashbacks that serve to locate "truth" in visual representation, and a bias toward closure, the film version of *Fool for Love* ultimately resists the play's conclusion that reality is effectively based "in [the] mind."[20] The result of imposing a realistic bias on such an impressionistic play is an uneven film that seems to want, like the play, to make a comment on the unreliability of memory, the inaccessibility of the past, and the flexibility of truth, yet only winds up presenting a pseudo-realistic narrative that seems to reinforce superficial expectations of truth, reality, and representation, and still manages to leave the audience confused and unsatisfied. As Tennessee Williams – a playwright whose influence on Shepard is well noted – stated in an interview in 1974, "Sometimes the truth is more accessible when you ignore realism, because when you see things in a somewhat exaggerated form you capture more of the true essence of life . . ."[21]

The film's promises of a conventional plot and intriguing characters are evident in its promotional descriptions that highlight the more sensational aspects of the story – a tumultuous love affair and a "tragic secret" that will be revealed. The "secret," of course, is that the lovers (May and Eddie) are actually half brother and sister, and the Old Man is their father. While in the play incest can be seen as a metaphor for the fated, inescapable bond of love as something that is not freely chosen, the film's summary on IMBb (Internet Movie Database) reduces *Fool for Love* to a soap opera about a "complicated" love triangle: "May is waiting for her boyfriend in a run-down American motel, when an old flame turns up and threatens to undermine her efforts and drag her back into the life that she was running away from. The situation soon turns complicated." This account of the "plot" is not only reductive, but emphasizes the superficial, less interesting aspects of the script. The description of the film on the Netflix jacket likewise exemplifies the focus on a realistic (and scandalous) storyline: "Rugged drifter Eddie (Sam Shepard) turns up at the dilapidated El Royale Motel in New Mexico with an eye toward wooing his former flame, May (Kim Basinger), a blonde hottie who waitresses in the bar. Over the course of a single night, the lovers argue endlessly, gradually revealing the tragic secret behind their former affair. Randy Quaid co-stars as a rival for May's affections. Director Robert Altman's [*sic*] adapts Sam Shepard's hit Broadway play."

In these descriptions, the film is pandering to Hollywood standards of psychological realism, providing a specific, realistic context for the action, and providing background information that exists in the play only marginally, if at all (May is described as a waitress in a bar, for example, and we see her working as the film opens). Eddie is predictably "an old flame" and "a rugged drifter" who arrives to disrupt the domestic peace of May and her "boyfriend," or at least the "rival for [her] affections." A clear goal is stated, and the revelation of a "tragic secret" is highlighted, complete with a "blonde hottie." Rather than serving as the witness/audience to the competing narratives of May, Eddie, and the Old Man, as he did in the play, Martin becomes an important character in his own right as a rival suitor, creating a love triangle that was not an important aspect of the play's "emotional terrain." While the play contains only the four principal characters (May, Eddie, Martin, the Old Man), Altman added seven other characters to the film version – May's mother, Eddie's mother, teenage May, teenage Eddie, young May, the Countess, and Mr. Valdez – which also serves to focus on the details of the storyline and adds to the realistic portrayal of the action. Characters who were simply mentioned in the play, or younger/past versions of the main characters, appear as part of the action in the present or in flashbacks.

In keeping with a realistic bias, Netflix's description of the film turns the actual shooting location (New Mexico) into the fictional location, giving it a specificity of setting and action that the play does not warrant. While the desert setting is important in the play, the stage directions simply state that it takes place in a "Stark, low-rent motel room on the edge of the Mojave Desert,"[22] which mainly occupies Southern California, but also parts of Nevada, Utah, and Arizona. Yet the film's 1986 poster for the Cannes Film Festival lists the play's location as the Mojave Desert, leaving the location the same as the play's. The most curious description, however, comes from the official Cannon Films 1985 promotional materials for the film. While it is interesting that Netflix conflates the film's fictional and actual locations, Cannon's sensationalistic Production Notes borrow from both the *play's* stated location and the film's actual shooting location, claiming that the setting is "New Mexico's Mojave desert": "*Fool for Love* is the fiery, interpersonal drama of Eddie and May, two people challenging their complex, mysterious and intriguing love affair on the hot fringes of New Mexico's Mojave desert." Since this is apparently an error, as the Mojave does not spill out as far east as New Mexico (and there is no evidence that this is an Ionesconian move toward surrealistic contradiction), the attempted specificity of this description results in a sloppy conflation, leaving us with neither the specificity of realism nor the broadness of symbolism. While this minor error may not seem central to an analysis of the film, it is indicative of the film's haphazard collusion of realistic detail and fictional imagination, as well as a seemingly random borrowing from the play that illustrates a lack of commitment to some consistent vision, which is one reason the film does not succeed artistically.

The film begins with Eddie driving his truck down the road, a picture of May taped to his car's visor, as Sandy Rogers's song "Let's Ride" plays on the radio.[23] There is no dialogue for the first five minutes, only images and music. The first words belong to May, insignificant leave-taking chatter with Mr. Valdez as she leaves the restaurant/bar where she works. She sees Eddie's truck coming up the road and runs into her motel room to pick up the clothes on the floor and straighten things up. The film provides a realistic context for Eddie's arrival, and presents May for the first time in her day-to-day professional and domestic life. In the play, by contrast, no context for the action is provided before we are thrown into the dialogue of May and Eddie's relationship. The first words are Eddie's: "May, look. May? I'm not going anywhere, see? I'm right here. I'm not gone" (which, of course, is later contradicted when he leaves her again).[24] The action begins in the thick of things, *in medias res* with no background information. We are focused on these two people in the motel room in their moment. May first appears sitting on the edge of the bed "facing audience, feet on floor, legs apart, elbows on knees, hands hanging limp and crossed between her knees, head hanging forward, face on floor. She is absolutely still and maintains this attitude until she speaks."[25] May does eventually take this posture in the film, but only well into the dialogue during the confrontation with Eddie, after their relationship has been established.

Another significant difference between the play and the film is that while they both create an interdependence of past and present, this contradiction is realized in the film through "extra" characters plucked from memory, which is not very useful and only serves to confuse the audience. Past and present exist simultaneously in the film on a visual level. May as a child of perhaps three years old, her mother as a young woman, and a younger version of the Old Man are guests in another of the bungalows and roam about the motel grounds simultaneously with the characters and the action in the present. This can be difficult to follow in the beginning if the viewer is not familiar with the play. May even interacts with both herself as a child and the Old Man in one scene: May, as a little girl, is playing on the swing set; Eddie runs off, creating a commotion. Adult May looks at the little girl, who is reacting to the ruckus. Eventually, May goes over to the little girl and hugs her. The mother comes out and calls for the girl; she runs to her mother. May lies on the ground as the Old Man walks over and tells his story of a memory involving May as a little girl, her mother, and himself, while a flashback visualizes his narration. May listens to him and reacts to his story, which does not occur in the play. Not until this moment in the film do we fully realize that the family in the next bungalow are May, her mother, and the Old Man. Yet despite the anti-realism of this juxtaposition of past and present (which does not really work), the motel rooms are each free-standing bungalows, and the viewer is led to peer in the windows as a voyeur in the true fashion of domestic realism.[26]

The symbolic and emotional impact of having the past and present exist simultaneously in the same space was more successfully achieved in the play by the evocation of the past through narratives of memory, and through the presence of the Old Man, who sits on the side of the stage in a rocking chair and clearly "exists only in the minds of MAY and EDDIE," even though he "treats them as though they all existed in the same time and place."[27] In the film, however, the Old Man seems to be more of a realistic character, living in a trailer behind the motel. He rummages through Eddie's truck, apparently looking for liquor, prompting Eddie to run out and chase him away, yelling, "Hey, what the hell you doin' in that truck?" The Old Man comes across as a bum walking around the property, making eye contact and interacting often with May and Eddie, which is not the case in the play, "even though they might talk to him directly and acknowledge his physical presence" at times.[28] While Vincent Canby's review in the *New York Times* applauded Altman's transformation of the Old Man into a realistic character, he seems to miss the point: "Extremely effective, however, is the way in which the Old Man, who is a phantom in the play, now exists as both the owner of the El Royale Motel and as the quarrelsome, ghostly parent. Also very good is the use to which Mr. Altman puts the El Royale's other guests who, on occasion, become memory figures."[29] One problem with this assessment is that the Old Man hardly appears as the "owner" of anything, much less a motel. Another is that the only other guests at the motel are the younger versions of the Old Man, May's mother, and May, who consistently, rather than "on occasion," exist as "memory figures." Rosenberg's comment on this point is much more on target:

> It was clear, on stage, that the old man existed in a different dimension from the rest of the play; he was outside its frame – he may even have been its artist, with all the action existing inside his head. This is the sort of ambiguity Shepard's identity-bending family sagas depend upon. Altman tries to recreate this enigma with frequent cutaways to Stanton, who lurks in the margins of the film like a burglar. But the device doesn't work on screen; Stanton comes off as a vagrant invading the story instead of as a metaphysical participant in its creation.[30]

The Old Man is part of the action of the film, a character wandering around, ignored apparently because of his social marginalization rather than because of his subjective existence.

The truth that exists in the mind is visualized and validated in the film, giving it a reality of its own, apart from individual consciousness. The film's flashbacks serve as one of the most significant differences between the play and the film, as they run simultaneously to a character's recollection of past events, with image and language often contradicting each other. Yet while the flashbacks are technically an anti-realistic device and seem to blur the boundaries between reality and imagination, they actually serve a realistic purpose in their privileging of *one* narrative that reveals or counts as *the* truth. They also serve to set the past in a more specific place and time through period fashion, car models, and other props (a picture of President John F. Kennedy on the wall of Eddie's mother's house shown at the end of May's story, for example, when May's mother goes to the door to confront Eddie's mother). Therefore, despite the juxtaposition of past and present in the film, its effect is still ultimately more realistic than the play's because it offers a visual confirmation of truth through flashbacks.

Rosenberg writes: "What's meant as epiphany comes across as conventional flashback, and Altman only adds more muddle by introducing disparities between what we're told by the speaker and what we see on the screen. He must want to undermine the unreliability of memory; but our ability to process mysteries has already been overextended, and these fussy alienation effects just irritate."[31] While in both the play and the film truth rests on contradictions, in the film language is subordinated to image, and "seeing is believing," as the images, or flashbacks, become a reliable indicator of the truth. The emphasis is on the visual, on "speaking without words," as in Eddie's description of his memory of seeing a drive-in movie screen in the distance while walking with his father one night: "It was Spencer Tracy. Spencer Tracy moving his mouth. Speaking without words. Speaking to a woman in a red dress."[32] Likewise, in the film of *Fool for Love*, silent images of the past speak without words and create meaning outside of language. They contradict the characters' narratives and illustrate how they misremember defining moments of their lives.

In the Old Man's recollection of a family car trip that he relates to May, for example, he claims that May was crying and that her mother was asleep, but the flashback does not show either of those things to be the case. The unreliability of memory is therefore effectively illustrated. However, since visual evidence is often considered proof, the flashbacks do seem to provide a final, authentic version of truth. Memory *is* unreliable, but in the play we are left without a final answer as to whose story, if anyone's, is accurate. Even gendered versions of truth take on particular significance; the Old Man pleads with Eddie to counter May's story at the end: "I wanna' hear the male side a' this thing. You gotta represent me now. Speak on my behalf. There's not one to speak for me now!"[33] In the film, the flashbacks solve that dilemma and at some level resolve the contradictions between language and image; truth is revealed, which is in fact one of the central goals of dramatic realism and, conversely, the sort of revelation that anti-realistic presentation, and the play version of *Fool for Love*, actively resists.

Other significant contradictions between language and image occur in Eddie's story. For example, Eddie claims that the Old Man gave him the first sip from the bottle after taking him to the liquor store to get it. In the flashback, this does not happen; not only does the Old Man not offer Eddie the first sip, but Eddie never even drinks from the bottle. This serves to point out that Eddie's memory is unreliable as well. Other examples of contradictions in his story occur when Eddie claims they walked in silence; and yet, in the flashback, the Old Man is clearly talking as they walk down the road. Eddie also says that the Old Man was crying, but he was not. No character is immune from misremembering; no language is a reliable source of truth. Some details are accurate in Eddie's story, and some are not. Memory, as always, is selective. The curious thing is that Eddie strongly emphasizes the Old Man's offering him the first sip – he says it twice, with emotion; it was an important event to him, and stuck in his memory as highly significant. The fact that he misremembers this moment makes the contradiction even more powerful. Even the most vivid memories that shape our lives can turn out to be lies.

When Eddie recounts his version of his family's relationship with his father, another significant difference between the flashback and the narration occurs. Eddie claims that the Old Man drove a Studebaker, and the Old Man interrupts him to protest that the car was, in fact, a Willys-Knight, not a Studebaker, and that he never even owned a Studebaker. In the flashback, we see the car pull up to the house, and as the Old Man (in the present) is protesting that it was a Willys-Knight, there is a close-up of the hood ornament, which seems like the classic 1950s spacecraft/jetfighter ornament of a Studebaker, and is clearly not the figure of a knight that characterized the Willys-Knight hood ornament. Moreover, the two car models look very different, and even if the viewer could not identify the Studebaker with certainty, Willys-Knight cars were only in production from 1914 to 1933,[34] and any model would look archaic in the context of the 1960s, which is, given the fashion, the portrait of Kennedy, and the "present" time period of the film, when the flashbacks take place. The Studebaker, on the other hand, was in business until 1966,[35] and fits in well within a 1950s or 1960s background. The average viewer, therefore, seems led to believe that Eddie is correct, that the car was indeed a Studebaker. Closer investigation of the car model, however, reveals that the car in the film is neither a Studebaker nor a Willys-Knight, but actually a 1955 Pontiac Strato Streak.[36] While this detail would signify that neither the Old Man's nor Eddie's memory is correct, it is unlikely that the film's viewers would be expected to identify the specific model of the car beyond the choices given, and so the intention was probably to imply that the car was a Studebaker, the closer of the two options. The fact that the film used a Pontiac in the flashback, however, remains curious, but perhaps this was simply a practical choice that says more about independent film budgets and availability than about the film's philosophy.

This scene occurs a bit differently in the play. Eddie and the Old Man contradict each other as well, but the Old Man insists that the car he owned was a Plymouth. One reason for altering this in the film may have been that a Willys-Knight, to the average viewer, differs much more from a Studebaker than a Plymouth does. Plymouth began making cars in 1928, was a very popular model throughout the 1950s, and remained in business in some capacity until 2001.[37] While it would be reasonable to visually confuse a Plymouth with a Studebaker in the film, a Willys-Knight is such an old-fashioned model that to confuse it with a Studebaker seems highly unlikely. The film therefore definitively makes the point that Eddie is correct about the car in question. In the play, however, we have no way of telling whose story, if either's, is true.

The flashbacks also tend to represent emotion visually. For example, in one flashback we see Eddie as a teenager lying in bed, pining, lovesick for May, and his arm is in a cast, but this injury is never given a specific context. It seems, therefore, that even his emotional pain is given a physical, visual manifestation. The two mothers are also seen in the flashbacks as full characters in their own right. Their visual scenarios indicate a bias in terms of the intensity of May's mother's passionate obsession for the Old Man, whereas Eddie's mother seems more resentful and resigned. Once again, there is a need to locate truth in the visual, and these representations of the past become the final word. In the play, the attitudes and emotions of characters in the past are left to our imaginations, and we only have access to them through the language of the characters' narratives, which remain primary. We are left with competing narratives and no final revelation, no version that is authenticated, and no definitive closure. The accuracy of both past and present events therefore remain open-ended.

Both the play and the film seek to comment on the symbiotic relationship of truth and lies, the process of constructing truth, and the creation of art. *Fool for Love* blurs the boundaries of the binary oppositions we take for granted – truth/lies, reality/imagination – and offers us art, or "stories," as a lie that serves to access a deeper truth. The play's philosophy on truth, lies, and the representation of reality is best articulated by Eddie, when he responds to Martin's observation that "making up" stories "would be lying," by insisting that "No, no. Lying's when you believe it's true. If you already know it's a lie, then it's not lying."[38] The overdetermination of language makes this statement somewhat ambiguous: Who is the "you" in the sentence? Is it the audience of the story, or the teller/creator? In other words, is "you" the one making up the story or receiving it?

The more likely meaning seems to indicate that "you" refers to the audience, the person receiving the story. In this case, Eddie is implying that if the audience of the story is under the impression that it is the truth, and it is not, then that is a lie. If, however, the audience is aware that the story is "made up" and not the literal truth, then it is not a lie. What is it, then? It's art. Yet if Eddie intends the "you" to refer to the person *telling* the story, the statement becomes slightly more complicated. In that case, according to Eddie, if the storyteller believes that the story is true, then it is inevitably a lie, presumably because language can never contain or articulate the whole truth, and *Fool for Love* demonstrates that "truth" is based on perspective. In the film, we see this point illustrated when the stories the characters tell are contradicted by the visual record. They *think* their stories are true, but they are lies – unintentional lies, but lies nonetheless.

In either case, the point is that "truth" is always tied to perception, perspective, and emotion, and can therefore never be fully accessed. According to Eddie's logic, truth is also dependent on intention – which is key when it comes to the tricky question of lying – and focuses on the primacy of perspective. For example, if someone says the sky is green, and for whatever reason really believes it is green, is this a lie? Yes and no. Yes, because it is not objectively true by consensus; and no, because the intention was to make a true statement. But the truth has still not been articulated. At some level, all "truth," or reality, involves a willing suspension of disbelief.

Fool for Love is an exploration of the malleable nature of truth, the limits of realistic representation, and the value of storytelling, or art, in accessing truth(s) beyond the surfaces that "reality" offers us. Yet because the film stylistically embraces the goals of dramatic realism, a mode of representation based on surfaces, it often contradicts its philosophical goals, and therefore fails at key points where the play succeeds. As unreliable as the memories of all the characters may be, the film offers a visual record, an answer we can turn to in order to find "truth," or at least some revelation at the close of the narrative. Ultimately, however, the real is unattainable and cannot be located, since truth is fluid and subjective. It exists in individual consciousness, like the Old Man's marriage to Barbara Mandrell, the woman he is "actually married to . . . in [his] mind." As he tries to explain to Eddie, "that's realism," a truth that is not based on the real.[39]

Endnotes

1 Sam Shepard, *Fool For Love and Other Plays* (New York: Bantam Books, 1984), 51.
2 Stephen J. Bottoms, *The Theatre of Sam Shepard: States of Crisis* (Cambridge University Press, 1998), 66.

3 Matthew Roudané, Introduction to *The Cambridge Companion to Sam Shepard*, ed. Matthew Roudané (Cambridge University Press, 2002), 3.

4 Bonnie Marranca, ed., *American Dreams: The Imagination of Sam Shepard* (New York: Performing Arts Journal Publications, 1981), 201.

5 Ibid., 203.

6 Sam Shepard, *Buried Child*, in *Sam Shepard: Seven Plays* (New York: Bantam, 1984), 89.

7 Sam Shepard, *True West*, in *Sam Shepard: Seven Plays*, 59.

8 Shepard, *Fool for Love*, 40.

9 Andrew Sarris, "The Selling of Sam Shepard," *Village Voice*, December 10, 1985.

10 Scott Rosenberg, "*Fool for Love* gets the star treatment on screen," *Boston Phoenix*, January 7, 1986.

11 Sheila Benson, "Eddie & May: Fools for 'Love'," *Los Angeles Times*, December 6, 1985.

12 Don Shewey, *Sam Shepard* (New York: Da Capo Press, 1987), 191.

13 Shepard, *Fool for Love*, 19.

14 Ibid., 24.

15 Ibid., 23.

16 Ibid., 33–34.

17 Carol Rosen, "Emotional Territory: An Interview with Sam Shepard," *Modern Drama* 36.1 (1993), 1–11.

18 David J. DeRose, *Sam Shepard* (New York: Twayne Publishers, 1992), 99.

19 Shepard, *Fool for Love*, 57.

20 Ibid., 27.

21 Tennessee Williams, Interview with Cecil Brown, 1974, in *Conversations with Tennessee Williams*, ed. Albert J. Devlin (Jackson, MS: University Press of Mississippi, 1986), 264.

22 Shepard, *Fool for Love*, 19.

23 Sandy Rogers, who wrote several songs for the film, is actually Shepard's sister.

24 Shepard, *Fool for Love*, 21.

25 Ibid., 20.

26 The bungalow windows in relation to the voyeurism of realistic representation have a particular significance with respect to May's body in the film. May is seen through the window as she undresses and walks around, and Eddie watches her for a long time, which does not happen in the play. When the men leave the room to go to the bar to talk, we see her walking around in her slip. Perhaps this is motivated by a need to account for why it takes her such a long time to join the men at the bar (she's changing clothes), or an excuse to see Kim Basinger in various stages of dress, but the voyeurism is unmistakable.

27 Shepard, *Fool for Love*, 20.

28 Ibid., 20.

29 Vincent Canby, "Screen: Shepard's 'Fool for Love,'" *New York Times*, December 6, 1985.

30 Rosenberg, "*Fool for Love* gets the star treatment on screen."

31 Ibid.
32 Shepard, *Fool for Love*, 49.
33 Ibid., 54.
34 http://clubs.hemmings.com/clubsites/wokr/gallery/wk_hist.htm.
35 http://studebakermuseum.org.
36 My thanks to Tom Abbett and Larry Hecht at Fast Lane Classic Cars in St. Charles, Missouri, for identifying the car model.
37 www.timelessrides.com/wiki/plymouth.
38 Shepard, *Fool for Love*, 45.
39 Ibid., 27.

CHAPTER 12

Actor, image, action: Anthony Drazan's Hurlyburly (1998)

Laurence Raw

David Rabe (1940–) began his graduate studies at Villanova University in Pennsylvania, which were interrupted when he was drafted into the army in 1965. He spent the majority of active service in Vietnam and later returned to Villanova, earning his MA in 1968. The Vietnam experience provided the basis for a trilogy of plays, *The Basic Training of Pavlo Hummel*, *Sticks and Bones*, and *Streamers*. *Sticks and Bones* won the Tony Award in 1972 for best performance by a leading actor by Tom Aldredge, who played a Vietnam veteran coming to terms with blindness. Al Pacino won the same award for his performance in *The Basic Training of Pavlo Hummel*. The three plays depict the ruthlessness and horrors of battle and the effects of war on those involved, combatants and non-combatants alike. Rabe is especially interested in the male psyche: the Vietnam plays are structured around protagonists who try to come to terms with new constructions of manhood and their own identities in terms of such constructions. Although the plays have war as their background, Rabe is careful to place his protagonists against a society that is often separate from that war: the home in *Sticks and Bones*, personal backgrounds and pressures in *Basic Training* and *Streamers*. By combining life in the barracks with life outside, Rabe suggests that the soldiers' inherent violence in one environment is the product of the other.

Images of manhood associated with violence and aggression are repeatedly foregrounded, not only in the Vietnam plays but also in later works such as *Goose and Tomtom* (1978) and *Hurlyburly* (1984). Rabe's characters constantly fail to live up to the ideals of manhood that the American media promotes, yet they cannot forge alternative constructions for themselves. Hence their violence; it represents the futile gesture of characters under fire, imprisoned by cultural expectations that complicate rather than help them define their identities.

Like other contemporary American playwrights such as David Mamet and (to a lesser extent) Sam Shepard, Rabe is concerned less with social issues per se than with how those social concerns impinge on the human psyche. Hence he is not interested in writing well-made plays with a coherent beginning, middle, and end; rather he aims to find a form of writing congruent with the ways in which human minds work. Actors are thus encouraged to free their minds from extraneous considerations and turn all their concentration on the objective – in this case, the meaning of Rabe's plays. To understand how they work, they should appreciate that dramatic language frequently functions as a means of obfuscation rather than communication: while the male characters crave the security of group identity (excluding females, of course), they find it impossible to express their feelings to one another. As with Mamet, Rabe's plays are written in sparse, intense language that sums up their alienated lives. In a 1995 interview Rabe commented on this experience, having returned from Vietnam: "It wasn't just that I couldn't reach my family. I couldn't reach *anybody*. People would listen attentively, but not understand a thing."[1] Rabe shows that this experience persists, even among those men who apparently lead prosperous lives. They remain lost souls, leading half-lives fueled by alcohol, drugs, and casual sex.

Critical reaction to Rabe's plays has been predictably diverse. Viewing the original New York production of *Hurlyburly* in 1984, Richard Schickel celebrated the dramatist's achievement in showing how "words have begun to fail. The vocabulary in which his [Rabe's] people speak, a jargon derived from televised reductions of reality and popularised psychology, leaves them without the tools they need to know their own minds, let alone the complexities of their shared existence."[2] However, Robert Leiter, writing in the *Hudson Review*, obviously expected to see a well-made play with a coherent beginning, middle, and end; and was obviously disappointed with this "overly long, unconvincing [piece], muddled in thought and filled with bombastic language masquerading as the height of realistic speech," written by someone who was "never much of a thinker, nor the most skillful of technicians."[3] Twenty years later, the *New York Times* felt that theatregoers attending the New Group's revival of the play – with Ethan Hawke in the lead – would be most likely to experience "a heady buzz of excitement and clarity" in a production which gave the lie to the theory that "you have to like characters to be engaged by them."[4] However, *Variety* rehearsed the familiar criticisms voiced by conservative drama critics in describing the play as fundamentally "rudderless ... a punishing marathon."[5]

Anthony Drazan's 1998 film version drew equally conflicting reactions. Chris Chang in *Film Comment* congratulated the director for "preserving the integrity of the original and fleshing it out with cinematic language" – for example, mobilizing face-to-face confrontations with moving cars, dueling cellphones, and a variety of Los Angeles locations.[6] However, Schickel believed that the play's subject-matter seemed dated in the post-Reagan era, while the characterizations, "no matter how passionately rendered, [seem] more like exercises for an acting class rather than something we can connect with."[7]

Such criticisms are only to be expected: *Hurlyburly* deliberately frustrates our expectations of a coherently structured dramatic narrative involving complex characters. Instead, Rabe treats his characters as objects existing solely in relation to themselves rather than to the other dramatis personae (which explains the play's lack of a structural rudder which might posit some kind of relationship between the characters). In the afterword, Rabe explained what he was trying to do:

> [T]he play is its own expression . . . No one in it knows what it is about. It has no character who is its spokesman . . . no character understood the nature of the events in which he [*sic*] was involved, nor did anyone perceive "correctly" their consequences. Beat by beat, then, the play progressed with each character certain about the point of the event in which he was involved, and no two characters possessing the same certainty, while beneath these abundant and conflicting personal conceptions was the event whose occurrence moved them on to what would follow, where they would each be confidently mistaken again.[8]

The action consists of discrete sequences, wherein the characters try to come to terms with shifting (and frequently unforeseen) circumstances: Donna's unannounced arrival in Eddie's house, the competing struggle for Darlene's affections between Mickey and Eddie, Phil's divorce and subsequent death. Our attention focuses on the ensuing "thrusts of emotion, the threatening surges of the force of feeling, as if the play [and its characters] were one huge personality at war with itself."[9] The play places considerable vocal and technical demands on its actors: when Eddie and Mickey recall their treatment of Bonnie's six-year-old daughter, Rabe's stage directions ask them to reflect on whether the memory was "funny or horrible."[10] Such directions not only distance the spectator from the character, but the character from the emotion as well. Hence actors need to draw upon techniques of speech and gesture they might have previously neglected, as Rabe suggests in a note to his 1969 play *Sticks and Bones*:

> What is poetic in the writing must not be reinforced by deep feeling on the part of the actors, or the writing will hollow into pretension. In a more "realistic" play, where language is thinner, subtext must be supplied or there is no weight. Such deep support of *Sticks and Bones* will make the play ponderous.[11]

Figure 12.1 The dissolute lives of movie executives Mickey (Kevin Spacey) and Eddie (Sean Penn) hit a new low when they hook up with a homeless waif (Anna Paquin), who has just been picked up by their friend Phil (Chazz Palminteri). (frame enlargement)

Since its premiere, many celebrated actors have taken up the challenges posed by the text of *Hurlyburly*: William Hurt, Judith Ivey, Harvey Keitel, Christopher Walken, Sigourney Weaver, Sean Penn, and Ethan Hawke. The play has also become a favorite source of audition pieces for amateur and professional companies alike.[12]

Superficially, *Hurlyburly* might seem ripe for cinematic adaptation, as it reveals the extent to which the medium of cinema – especially cartoons – permeates mid-1980s Californian culture, which in Eddie's view has become two-dimensional, peopled with "Cardboard cutouts bumping around in this vague, you know, hurlyburly, this spin-off what was once prime-time life."[13] In an introductory essay to one of Rabe's drafts for the screenplay, director Anthony Drazan claimed that *Hurlyburly* "had endless depths ... You could dive as deep as you wished into the feelings, the ideas, the layers within David Rabe's play and never hit bottom."[14] Nonetheless, we are faced with specific methodological issues in considering how and why Rabe altered the text while transforming it into a screenplay. Any judgment based on fidelity issues seems spurious, implying that Rabe sought the kind of coherence in the screenplay that was conspicuously absent from the stage version. He had no need to sustain "the integrity of the original" (recalling Chris Chang's observation in the *Film Comment* review), as the play deliberately repudiates the notion of structural integrity. I recommend instead that we should examine the performances in Drazen's adaptation of *Hurlyburly*, concentrating on how the six-strong cast – led by Sean Penn and Kevin Spacey – communicate the characters' emotional and physical isolation through speech and gesture, and how Drazan evolves a cinematic style (predominantly comprising close-ups, shot/reverse shots, two-shots, and tracking shots) to support them. Drazan himself claimed that this was the kind of approach that he and Rabe decided to adopt in bringing the play to the screen: "[We wanted to turn it] into a real movie, not just a filmed play. But how the hell do you actually do that? . . . What David and I decided to do, boldly or foolishly, was to go back into *Hurlyburly* scene by scene and find new ways – through . . . character – to make the piece distinctly cinematic and as resonant as it had been on stage."[15] My analysis will draw upon Rhonda Blair's theory of acting based on cognitive neuroscience, which calls for actors both on stage and screen to "create more consciously a living string of both cascading and anchoring images that draw on sensory, affective and explicit memory, and to connect this with a detailed kinesethetic score that supports the body-mapping of these images."[16] In this model performances are not judged according to a predetermined standard of "truth" or "believability," but are rather approached as a collection of choices and behaviors – "a process, rather than a discrete entity, a motivated movement, rather than a gloss of feeling."[17] "Character" as a fixed entity is no longer sufficient as a way of interpreting a role, as actors adapt to or try to make sense of different contexts (as indicated through dialogue, as well as acts and scenes). Blair's theory seems particularly apt for a film like *Hurlyburly*, whose characters spend their time trying – and mostly failing – to cope with shifting circumstances, without any idea of what will happen next. More importantly, I suggest that critical attention needs to move beyond the confines of the text to other aspects of the mise en scène (particularly performance) as a way of understanding *how* and *why* this modern American classic has been adapted to the screen.

Blair's theory requires actors to engage image, language, and action in their characterizations; to address the issues of "what," "where," "when," "who," and "why," through a play's language, and to use this information to interface with other actors. She cites the example of Hamlet's "To be or not to be," in which the actor's goal should be to develop "a detailed score, a stream of images . . . that puts the play into the actor's body as vividly and immediately as possible." By such means, the focus of attention shifts away from Hamlet's "psychology" or motive and on to "a stream of images that come from or reside in the body."[18] The same process applies to modern American plays, as well as classic drama: Blair recounts her experiences of working on Rebecca Gilman's *Boy Gets Girl* (2000) at the Echo Theatre, Dallas, in which she challenged the cast "to have a specific stream of sensory and kinesthetic images to carry them through each scene, as well as specific images in mind prior to entering for any scene."[19] Rather than look for coherence within characters, the actors created a cascade of images for themselves – visual, aural, experimental – that helped them understand every phrase of dialogue they were expected to deliver. Such images might be contradictory, or even random, with little apparent connection to one another, but they helped the actors develop a series of "character-memory images, an updated and recontextualized version of sense and affective memory, [that] provided color and urgency to her [one actor] engaging with her fellow-actors."[20]

Drazan's film of *Hurlyburly* offers the actors numerous opportunities both to create and dramatize that mental "filmstrip" of images. Eddie (Sean Penn) calls Mickey (Kevin Spacey) on the car-phone, and admits that while "Darlene and I have no exclusive commitment to each other, of any kind whatsoever, blah-blah-blah," he wants Mickey to "have a little empathy for crissake."[21] Penn begins this speech by coming out onto the balcony of his apartment, smiling and speaking his lines calmly, as if acknowledging Mickey's right to go out with Darlene ("Darlene and I have no exclusive commitment . . ."). This calm is rapidly replaced by a mood of desperation, suggested first by the gabbled delivery of the phrase "blah-blah-blah," followed by the next line "have a little empathy," where each word is enunciated in a high-pitched whine. As he speaks, Eddie paces up and down the little balcony, as he desperately tries to sustain his self-control. He continues: "I bring this very *special lady* to meet my roommate, my best friend . . . I'm just trying to tell a story here, nobody's to blame."[22] Eddie speaks the first four words of this speech in measured tones, but his emotions get the better of him: the phrase "special lady" is delivered in a high-pitched scream. He recovers some of his composure in the line "nobody's to blame," but we can understand his fragile state of mind from his body language, as he clasps and unclasps his left hand, while using the right hand to talk on the phone. Mickey berates Eddie on the phone while driving to work: "I mean, couldn't you have said, 'no?' Couldn't you have categorically, definitively, said 'no' when I asked? But you said – 'Everybody's free, Mickey.' I mean that is what you said."[23] Mickey speaks the line "Everybody's free, Mickey" in a derisive voice, as if parodying Eddie's statement. The action cuts back to Eddie on the balcony, his whole body throbbing with emotion, yet at the same time unable to respond to Mickey's jibe. This short sequence, lasting no more than two minutes, reveals how Eddie and Mickey remain isolated from one another; rather than addressing important issues face to face, they avoid them by means of snatched conversations on mobile phones. At the same time we realize that both men try to keep talking as a means of avoiding despair; hence Eddie's use of the meaningless phrase "blah-blah-blah," or Mickey's needless repetitions ("But you said ... I mean that is what you said").

In a later sequence, Phil (Chazz Palminteri) pursues Eddie into a grocery store, as he tries to find out whether the friendship between the two of them can be sustained. Eddie grabs a bottle of wine off the shelves, turns toward Phil, and hisses, "Sometimes I get like I'm angry when I get excited,"[24] with a stress placed on the word "get." Phil responds aggressively: "Because you're absolutely one hundred per cent right in everything you're saying."[25] As the two men stalk round the store, it seems as if they are fighting rather than trying to reconcile with one another. Eddie turns round to Phil and shouts, "You gotta do it [tell his wife about wanting to have a baby], Phil!" emphasizing the point by poking his index finger in Phil's chest. However, Phil lacks the will to do so, as indicated by his delivery of the phrase: "I know that and I will, w-without a doubt, but I just wanna know ... what kinda latitude I have regarding our friendship, you know, er- er- if my mind gets changed." The pauses in the line betray Phil's weaknesses; despite his physical size (he towers over the diminutive Eddie as they walk round and round the aisles in the store), he cannot set his mind to anything. Eddie turns round and screams, "You're a GROWN man, you asked me, I'm telling you, TELL HER!" His face screws up in pain as he tells Phil, "our friendship is totally IRRELEVANT here!"[26] The sequence ends up with the grocery store manager (David Fabrizio) intervening, and nearly getting beaten up by Phil for his pains. Phil walks out, leaving Eddie to apologize rather sheepishly to the manager for the disturbance they have caused.

Although Eddie starts the sequence in a position of strength, his basic character flaws emerge – for example, in the phrase "our friendship is totally IRRELEVANT here," where his facial expression suggests precisely the opposite. If Phil were to leave, Eddie would be condemned once more to isolation. The same is also true of Phil, who treats his friendship with Eddie as more important than patching up relations with his wife. However, both men are incapable of admitting their true feelings; they remain emotionally inarticulate, despite their endless chatter. Their frustration is evident in their facial expressions: Eddie contorts his face at Phil, while

Phil stares wide-eyed as Eddie walks away from him down the grocery store aisles, as if unable to contemplate the prospect of isolation.[27]

The entire cast – particularly Penn – work hard to create a "filmstrip" of contrasting tones and gestures to communicate their characters' states of mind. For some reviewers at least – notably Richard Kelly, writing in the British journal *Sight and Sound*, who likened Penn's "nerve-straining demeanour" to "a return to a dry well"[28] – the performances might seem too intense, but they underline the significance of Blair's preoccupation with the action of the moment. Penn suggested in a 1999 interview with talk-show host Charlie Rose that this approach to characterization helped him understand Eddie's futile desire to break free of "the bubble" of isolation on account of his inability either to communicate directly or sustain a lasting relationship.[29]

Blair recommends that actors have to acknowledge "the feeling that arises in the moment of the acting," inspired by the imagery in the dialogue.[30] This feeling has no need of consolidation through a back-story; it is vivid enough on its own. In the speech above, for instance, the feelings are made manifest through individual speeches. The full stop separating Eddie's first two statements emphasizes his pleasure at recalling Bonnie's exotic dances ("That's her trip."). Mickey concurs through the two-word sentence using the vocabulary of theatre reviewers ("Critically acclaimed"), which is given a sexual orientation in the next phrase, "The next best thing is she's up for anything." The effect of this exchange in performance depends on the actors having very specific images in their minds – of Bonnie dancing, the range of "services" she can provide, both on and off the floor, and their childlike fantasies of a woman willingly fulfilling their patriarchal and sexual desires. Such fantasies stimulate their recollection of Robbie Rattigan and Bonnie in the back of the limousine: Artie's interjection ("The airport?") stimulates them to describe the experience as comprehensively as they can. The syntax – a mixture of long and short sentences, frequently beginning with personal pronouns ("*She's* a fuckin' critic," "*He* looks at her" [italics mine]) – suggests that their memories come easily and fluidly.

However, the mood changes once Eddie remembers Bonnie's six-year-old child, who was also in the back of the car ("Oh Christ, the kid!"). What matters here is the depth of feeling communicated through the invocation ("Oh Christ"), the pause between the words "Christ" and "the," and the exclamation mark ending the phrase. Mickey is equally traumatized by the memory, despite his best efforts to exonerate himself ("I was blotto, personally blotto"). Eddie and Mickey's dialogue has been inspired by another cascade of images: Rattigan's expression of sexual satisfaction; Bonnie's face and lips as she performs the act of oral sex; the child's expression of mental and sexual abuse; and Eddie and Mickey's feelings of culpability and revulsion.

Penn and Spacey use a combination of verbal and nonverbal strategies to dramatize this "filmstrip" of images; in his description of Bonnie at the club, Penn pauses between the words "bitch" and "who" in the line, "This is a bitch who dances artistically naked," to suggest a careful choice of words. Mickey nods his head in approval, and delivers the next line as a throwaway ("With a balloon"). Both men visualize themselves as a comedy double-act indulging in sexual banter: as Eddie begins the airport story, Mickey doubles up with silent laughter and sips his whiskey. Meanwhile, Eddie relishes the innuendo of the word "relax" in the phrase "We wanted to *relax* him on the drive back to town" (italics mine). They seem to be in control of both past and present; they hired Bonnie to give a television star fellatio in the back of a limousine; and they experience the pleasure of recounting the story for an admiring (male) audience comprising Phil and Artie. Mickey takes a pause of one or two beats between the phrases "He reaches over and unzips his fly," and "He looks at her," and momentarily assumes the role of Rattigan experiencing oral sex, his eyes looking up toward the ceiling, his fists clenched. Eddie beams with pleasure at the memory; at last, it seems, he has established control over his life and those involved in it – especially women. Mickey grins and observes, "welcome to LA" – an expression of sublime contentment as he alludes to the louche pleasures available in California. He sits back in his armchair and lights a joint – a fitting example of one of these pleasures.

Within moments, however, the atmosphere changes, as Eddie looks down at the ground and mumbles the words, "The look on the kid's face." The two of them look guiltily at each another, and Eddie spits out the word "catatonic," which forces Mickey to look at him. Their masculine sense of strength has evaporated, as they mutually confront the horrific memory of the child's expression. In Blair's terms, they communicate their feelings, which in her view represent "emotion made conscious ... The great degree of interpretation used in translating emotional and bodily stages into feeling reinforces the idea that the actor must think creatively and adventuresomely in imagining a role, and in responding to and using emotion and feeling [suggested by the moment]."[31]

Blair implies that her theory of acting transcends different media – theatre, film, or television; as she suggests in her foreword, it is conceived as a series of ideas helping actors probe "more deeply into the poetry and mystery of what it means to act and, thus, what it means to be human."[32] Nonetheless, we should at least speculate on how her ideas might be applied to the collaborative medium of film adaptation. There is no doubt that film actors have an important role in the adaptation process; Linda Hutcheon suggests that they "embody and give material sense to the adaptation" – even though she doubts whether they are "conscious adapters" or not.[33] Quoting the novelist Michael Ondaatje, she claims that to a certain extent actors can "bring their individual sense and senses to the characters and give them those glances and gestures that come from their own imagination." However, their interpretations are significantly shaped by other creative contributors – for example, the screenwriter, the director, the film editor, or the producer.[34] Bearing these caveats in mind, perhaps the best way to consider how Blair's theory might work is to analyze a specific adaptation in terms of its *skopos*. This term – drawn from the Greek word meaning "purpose" – was coined by German scholars of translation studies such as Hans Vermeer, Katherina Reiss, and Christiane Nord during the 1970s. It determines what kind of relationship exists between texts, intertexts, and paratexts in any translated or adapted work. Vermeer in particular argues that the *skopos* of a work can be determined through a tripartite theoretical framework comprising: (a) the *process* – focusing on the goals of the adaptation/translation; (b) the *mode* – looking at the content or the form of that adaptation/translation; and (c) the *result* of that adaptation/translation, observing in particular the audience's response.[35] The *skopos* of Drazan's adaptation of *Hurlyburly* places particular importance on the actors' contribution: its *process* was inspired by previous stage productions of the play (especially that of Sean Penn, who had played Eddie in the Los Angeles revival of 1998), as well as by Rabe's suggestions – expressed in the afterword to the published text – that the play shows the characters existing only in relation to themselves, rather than to a coherent dramatic structure. The *mode* of Drazan's adaptation depends on its *process*: attention focuses not on plot-development, but rather on the characters' spiritual and emotional isolation. The *result* depends on whether we have taken the *process* and *mode* into account, while formulating our judgments. I would argue that Drazan, Rabe, and the cast made a conscious decision to focus on individual performances – not because the cast contained bankable names (even though Penn and Spacey might come into that category) but because the entire creative team conceived Rabe's play as predominantly character-driven. All other elements in the adaptation – plot, fidelity issues, mise en scène, editing – assume a subordinate role. By applying Blair's ideas to *Hurlyburly*, we might conclude that the adaptation deliberately foregrounds the actors' capabilities to create a detailed performance score by applying their creative talents to the cues suggested by the screenplay. It is Drazan's responsibility to create the kind of filming style that reveals this process most effectively.

For example, the sequence where Eddie and Mickey recount their experiences with Rattigan begins with a series of shot/reverse shots, set against the nondescript background of Eddie's Los Angeles apartment. Any interruptions from Phil or Artie are also shot in close-up, with specific attention paid to their facial reactions; the more lurid the story, the better they like it. As Mickey speaks, the camera tracks him moving round the room, becoming more and more animated; like Phil and Artie, we eagerly await to find out what he will do or say next. Drazan cuts to brief close-ups of Phil and Artie: Phil clenches his fists in anticipation; Artie's brow furrows slightly, as he wonders whether the story is a little off-color. The pace quickens as the story reaches its climax, with a further spate of shot/ reverse shots between Mickey and Eddie. However, the pace slows down significantly once Eddie recalls the sight of Bonnie's daughter. Drazan's camera lingers on Eddie and Mickey in close-up, as they wordlessly contemplate the consequences of their actions. We hear their disembodied voices still talking to one another, but do not actually see them speak. In the background, the sound of background music trills away. The close-ups become tighter and tighter, until Eddie and Mickey's faces fill the screen: Drazan eventually provides us with some kind of relief by cutting to medium close-ups of Phil and Eddie's horrified faces as they understand the full implications of the tale.

Through the repeated use of close-up, Drazan almost literally places his characters under the microscope; they remain imprisoned by the camera lens, with every facial movement subject to close scrutiny. Their physical and emotional isolation is emphasized by the absence of two-shots; although they are sitting together in the same room, enjoying the pleasures of hard drugs and alcohol, none of them can relate to one another in any meaningful way.

Sometimes Drazan employs more surreal techniques to make the same point. Later on that evening, Eddie and Artie are left alone in the apartment, both stoned out of their minds. Both of their faces are seen in surreal close-up: Eddie lying down on the floor, and Artie standing up, peering at him through a filthy glass-topped coffee table adorned with white stains, a pack of razor blades, and the latest copy of *Variety*. Drazan cuts to a long close-up from Artie's point of view: we see Eddie lying flat on the floor through the glass of the table, while on the right Artie's hands and half of

Figure 12.2 Phil and Eddie share a cocaine addiction as well as women. (frame enlargement)

his face are visible, as he continues the conversation. Drazan switches to
another point of view from Eddie's perspective; we see Artie's face on the
left of the frame and Eddie's grinning reflection through the stained glass
on the right. Drazan switches between these two point-of-view shots as the
conversation progresses: Artie protests, "We're having a confrontation
here, goddam it!" but Eddie's sole response is to burst out into peals of
laughter. Incensed, Artie storms out of the apartment. The sequence ends
with an aerial shot, looking down on Eddie, a pathetic figure stretched out
on the floor under the table, his face picked out by a light coming from the
open front door. Drazan's use of reflections emphasizes the disconnection
between the two characters; they would rather talk through a table littered
with domestic trash rather than contemplate a direct face-to-face exchange.
Artie's statement "We're having a confrontation" is painfully ironic; the
glass actually *prevents* them from having a confrontation. By such means
Drazan underlines Rabe's observations that the characters in *Hurlyburly* are
"confidently mistaken" in their world-views.

In the film's concluding sequence Drazan employs a variety of strategies
to suggest isolation. Eddie is once again photographed in close-up, staring
in despair into the middle distance. His attempt at committing suicide by
jumping into the pool turns out to be a farce; the water is too shallow, and
Donna (Anna Paquin) unexpectedly returns to his house, forcing him to
climb out, soaking wet, to welcome her. Rather surprisingly, Drazan
introduces a two-shot showing Donna and Eddie; but all we can see in
the frame is Donna sitting on the sofa and Eddie's headless torso on the left,
reminding us once again of his inability to sustain a face-to-face conversation. Throughout the sequence the relentless quacking of the television can
be heard on the soundtrack, as Eddie surfs through various channels
broadcasting hard news, human-interest stories, and live football games.
Chris Chang's comment aptly sums up its function in the mise en scène:
"All he [Eddie] really wants is a late night partner in meaninglessness."[36]

Drazan's mode of "powerhouse filmmaking," foregrounding the actors'
performances, assumes that every gesture is significant: "Spacey nails every
twisted laugh with elegant precision, but it's Penn who digs deepest as
Eddie confronts what's left of his conscience. As an actor, Penn is as good
as it gets."[37] This kind of actor-centered adaptation is nothing new, but
Drazan gives it a contemporary (i.e., late-1990s) spin. We can understand
this more clearly if we consider how the structure and performance-style of
Hurlyburly differ from earlier adaptations – for example, some of the 1950s
versions of Tennessee Williams's plays. Christine Geraghty argues that Elia
Kazan's film of *A Streetcar Named Desire* (1951) eschews the shot/reverse

Figure 12.3 Phil's funeral brings his friends together but does nothing to halt their self-destructive predation. (frame enlargement)

shot technique, particularly in sequences involving Stanley Kowalski (Marlon Brando) and Stella (Kim Hunter). Rather, Kazan makes use of the two-shot, in which the two actors are either parallel with one another or in a diagonal line with one closer to the camera. Audiences feel as if they are viewing the film from outside, "in a manner that preserves the distance of the theatre audience while lending it the closeness of camera."[38] We are inside the proscenium arch, so to speak, but not implicated in the point of view of either character. However, once Blanche Dubois (Vivien Leigh) enters, Kazan introduces alternative shot-structures – including point-of-view shots and shot/reverse shot close-ups – so as to draw the audience more into the relationship between the two characters. Kazan uses close-up to emphasize the back or profile of a character, so as to sustain the spatial distance of theatre.[39] Such strategies confirm that the film tries to stage a play by means of cinema. Within this framework, both Brando and Leigh create a pattern of "looks and proximity" that draws attention to the actors' bodies and movements and heightens the impact of their physical presence on screen.[40] On the other hand, in Daniel Mann's film of *The Rose Tattoo* (1955), our attention seldom departs from Anna Magnani's central performance: "Long takes and medium shots offer the viewer a position . . . [promoting] appreciation of the gestures, expressions and vocal registers that signify feeling. What we participate in is the unfolding of a performance that is in many ways excessive, uncontained by the film's narrative."[41]

Whereas *Streetcar* takes great pains to emphasize the film's origins in the theatre, *Hurlyburly*'s basic lack of narrative structure renders such questions irrelevant. It does not matter whether what we see is a play or a film; the text is its own expression. Like Kazan, Drazan ensures that we remain cognizant of the actors' physical presence on the screen, but Drazan refrains from emotional identification with their patterns of "looks and proximity." He employs a mixture of shot/reverse shots as well as occasional two-shots to underline the distance – both physical and emotional – between characters. Such techniques are reminiscent of *The Rose Tattoo* (where Magnani's central characterization seems to exist independently of the narrative, as well as the actors surrounding her). *Hurlyburly* treats its characters not as sympathetic subjects but as objects functioning in relation to themselves rather than to others. The actors look for this kind of reaction, as they neither look one another in the eye nor solicit the audience's attention through close-ups. (An example of this might be Eddie's close-up in the final sequence, discussed above, where he stares into the middle distance.)

It is in this area of acting technique that *Hurlyburly* significantly differs from the earlier Williams adaptations. Geraghty suggests quite rightly that "Method" acting exerted a powerful influence over Hollywood films during the 1950s; in *Streetcar*, for instance, Brando's performance "involved representing a theatrical experience for cinema in a way that drew attention to its origins ... the power and brutality of Brando's erotic force is carried as much by movement and proximity as by 'the gaze.'"[42] This kind of acting, Geraghty believes, "is often a source of pleasure and a matter for judgment."[43] While Magnani is not a Method actor per se, her performance in *The Rose Tattoo* is distinguished by its variety of tones, ranging from "melodramatic expressiveness" to "a deft comic manner more in line with romantic comedies of the 1930s and 1940s."[44] In both films there is an emphasis on coherence, with each gesture and vocal inflection designed to illuminate a character's psychology, and consequently produce some kind of reaction from the audience. In *Hurlyburly*, however, the actors create deliberately incoherent characterizations in which gestures and vocal inflections are conceived as responses to the action of the moment, rather than any predetermined view of the roles they play. By means of such techniques, derived from cognitive neuroscience, they try to demonstrate that "the 'self,' insofar as it something we experience, is dynamic and fluid ... Though it is a unit, it is not unitary ... the self is a 'dramatic ensemble.'"[45] Their performances recall the sentiments expressed by Walt Whitman in "Song of Myself" (1860):

There is that in me – I do not know what it is –
but I know it is in me . . .
Do I contradict myself?
Very well then, I contradict myself.
(I am large, I contain multitudes) (parts 50–51)

In many ways this approach to acting and performance in film adaptation is characteristic of an era that has witnessed great advances in understanding brain structure, processes, and consciousness. Blair comments that "Definitions of personhood, reason and emotion are being rethought in light of new information about brain structure and neurochemical processes, and how these manifest in consciousness and behavior."[46] More importantly many actors now "define their focus [in rehearsal and performance] as experiential and emotional, rather than factual or critical, and resist being analytical or technical."[47] Rather than searching for a coherent interpretation of the characters they play on screen, they discover alternative, often contradictory constructions of the "real" or the "truthful" in their performances, in a context where "popular forms, media and technologies keep shifting the ground of what we understand those [terms] to be."[48] Drazan's film of *Hurlyburly* provides an ideal opportunity for the cast to pursue such explorations, with its pronounced lack of structure and characters perpetually unable to come to terms with a media-dominated American culture of the late 1990s, in which concepts of truthfulness, sincerity, and friendship no longer seem significant.

Endnotes

1 David Rabe, "Hurlyburly," in *Hurlyburly and Those the River Keeps: Two Plays by David Rabe* (New York: Grove Press, 1995), 196.
2 Richard Schickel, "Hurlyburly," *Time*, July 2, 1984, accessed December 12, 2010, www.time.com/time/printout/0,8816,926691,00.html.
3 Robert Leiter, "Theater Chronicle," *Hudson Review* 38.2 (1985), 297–298.
4 Ben Brantley, "Theater Review: *Hurlyburly*," *New York Times*, April 21, 2005, B7.
5 David Rooney, "Hurlyburly," *Variety*, January 31, 2005, 6.
6 Chris Chang, "Hurlyburly," *Film Comment* 34.6 (1998), 77–78.
7 Schickel "Hurlyburly."
8 David Rabe, "Afterword," *Hurlyburly* (New York: Grove Press, 1985), 169–170.
9 David Rabe, "Afterword," *Sticks and Bones* (New York: Samuel French, 1987), 164.
10 Rabe, "Hurlyburly," 272. Rabe revised the play after its New York performance for a revival at the Trinity Rep in 1986, and rewrote it once again

following his own 1988 Los Angeles production. This version was published by Samuel French and reissued by Grove Press.

11 Rabe, "Afterword," *Sticks and Bones*, 226.
12 Rooney, "Hurlyburly," 6.
13 Rabe, "Hurlyburly," 299.
14 Anthony Drazan, "Introduction," in David Rabe, "Screenplay: *Hurlyburly*," December 1996, unpublished typescript, 1.
15 Ibid., 2.
16 Rhonda Blair, *The Actor, Image and Action: Acting and Cognitive Neuroscience* (London: Routledge, 2008), 81.
17 Ibid., 82.
18 Ibid., 89.
19 Ibid., 91.
20 Ibid.
21 David Rabe, "First Draft Screenplay: *Hurlyburly*," March 1, 1996, unpublished typescript, 31.
22 Ibid., 31–32.
23 Ibid., 32. The screenplay departs slightly from Rabe's play at this point: in the published version Mickey's last line reads "That's what you said" (Rabe, "Hurlyburly," 172).
24 Rabe, "First Draft Screenplay: *Hurlyburly*," 67.
25 The play adds the phrase "without a doubt" after the word "absolutely."
26 In another version of the screenplay this line was written as "Our friendship doesn't matter here" (Rabe "Screenplay: *Hurlyburly*," December 1996, 43).
27 In the final act of the play Eddie insists that at all times that "I don't know what I mean, but I know what I'm saying" (Rabe "Hurlyburly," 262). This comment sums up the characters' predicament perfectly; there is little or no relationship between their utterances and the meanings they hope to communicate through such utterances.
28 Richard Kelly, "Hurlyburly," *Sight and Sound* 10.5 (2000), 51.
29 "A Discussion About the Film *Hurlyburly*," *Charlie Rose*, January 20, 1999, accessed December 21, 2010, www.charlierose.com/view/interview/4484.
30 Blair, *The Actor, Image and Action*, 93.
31 Ibid., 68–69.
32 Ibid., xiv.
33 Linda Hutcheon, *A Theory of Adaptation* (London: Routledge, 2005), 81–82.
34 Ibid., 82.
35 Laurence Raw, "The *Skopos* of a Remake: Michael Winner's *The Big Sleep* (1978)," *Adaptation Advance Access*, November 24, 2010, accessed December 24, 2010, http://adaptation.oxfordjournals.org/content/early/2010/11/24/adaptation.apq019.full.pdf+html, 2.
36 Chang, "Hurlyburly," 78. However, Donna seems oblivious to its pernicious effect, as she tells Eddie how great it is "when people [like herself and Eddie] know what each other are talking about."
37 "Holiday Goodies in Small Packages," *Rolling Stone*, December 24, 1998, 171.

38 Christine Geraghty, *Now a Major Motion Picture: Film Adaptations of Literature and Drama* (Lanham, MD: Rowman and Littlefield, 2008), 79.
39 Ibid., 80.
40 Ibid., 82.
41 Ibid., 87.
42 Ibid., 82.
43 Ibid., 84.
44 Ibid., 90.
45 Blair, *The Actor, Image and Action,* 54.
46 Ibid., 3.
47 Ibid., 5.
48 Ibid., 23.

CHAPTER 13

David Mamet brings film to Oleanna

Brenda Murphy

The two epigraphs that Mamet printed in the published version of *Oleanna* suggest the failed utopian ideal that the play dramatizes. The first explains the play's title, which has confused audiences and reviewers since its earliest production. The epigraph is from a folk song that Mamet knew from childhood:

> Oh, to be in *Oleanna*,
> That's where I would rather be.
> Than be bound in Norway
> And drag the chains of slavery.[1]

These lines describe a failed utopian community that was founded by the Norwegian musician Ole Bull and his wife Anna, thus the name, Oleanna. The community failed because the farmland that was to support it proved rocky and infertile. In an interview about the film adaptation on National Public Radio, Mamet added two lines that he remembered as being from a rendition by the Kingston Trio[2] that suggest a deeper irony than the epigraph does: "Little roasted piggies go running through the city streets / Inquiring most politely if a slice of ham you'd like to eat." He added, "the utopia in the song was a land development and the utopia in the movie is academia."[3] The other epigraph, from Samuel Butler's *The Way of All Flesh*, describes the seemingly happy state of mind sustained by children who grew up in the poisonous air of the back alleys of nineteenth-century London. Even if children are unhappy, "very unhappy – it is astonishing how easily they can be prevented from finding it out, or at any rate from attributing it to any other cause than their own sinfulness" (Epigraph, n.p.).

As Mamet has indicated, the application of these epigraphs to *Oleanna* is straightforward. The play, set in an American university, is ostensibly about the failed ideal of academia, the dream of an intellectual community in which knowledge is imparted from teacher to student in a generous,

238

disinterested, and humane way, for the good of all. In John, a fortyish assistant professor on the brink of being awarded tenure and preoccupied with buying a house on the strength of his new job stability, and Carol, a student who has been made desperate by her imminent failure of his course, the play presents two hopelessly self-absorbed people who feel oppressed by the academic power structure as it inhibits their efforts to succeed in the world outside academia. At the same time they exploit that power structure as much as they can to achieve their own ends.

The three-act play consists of three meetings between John and Carol in which one character is attempting to get something from the other character, who has all the power in this particular exchange. In the first act, Carol comes to John, ostensibly for help with his course in Education. Actually, she is trying to achieve two things. She hopes that John can give her some sort of magical key into the mystifying language of academia that has so far defeated her so that she can get good grades, earn a degree, and, as she says, "get on in the world" (12). More immediately, she hopes to get her grade changed. The meeting is constantly interrupted by phone calls to John, which are ostensibly about a glitch in the real-estate deal that could cause him to lose his house, but instead turn out to be a ruse to get him to a surprise party to celebrate his imminent tenure confirmation.

Essentially, John and Carol carry on parallel monologues in the first act, each expressing anxiety because their personal ambitions are being thwarted by the entity that holds power over them in the context of the academic system: John, as Carol's professor, and "The Bad Tenure Committee," as the body that is deciding on John's future career (and consequently his material well-being and that of his family). Although John's interest is piqued when he feels a kinship with Carol in her anger and her belief that she is stupid, he is so deeply self-absorbed that he can only project his sense of his own youthful self onto her. Thus an inevitable misunderstanding occurs when John proposes to take off the "artificial structures" of teacher and student and to start the course over, promising Carol an "A" if she will come back and meet with him a few more times. John thinks he is living his own principles, being a true educator, breaking out of the restrictive conventions of the system and taking the extra step to help his student. Carol, it turns out, reads the situation differently.

In Act 2, the balance of power has shifted. John has asked Carol to come to his office so he can answer the charges she has brought against him to the tenure committee, charges which accuse him of being elitist and of wasting time in "nonprescribed, in self-aggrandizing and theatrical *diversions* from the prescribed *text*," maintaining that these diversions "have taken both sexist and pornographic forms" (47). In this confrontation, John's attempt to overwhelm Carol with the jargon that had defeated her in Act 1 no longer works, as she now has her own linguistic power base, the feminist language she has learned from her unnamed "Group." John's self-serving attempt to reorder the terms of the exchange by appealing to Carol to "agree that we are both human" (53) fails when he reveals (through a phone conversation she overhears) that he is only interested in "dealing with the complaint" (55). At the end of Act 2, having failed at getting power over her linguistically, John is reduced to restraining her physically to try to get her to listen to him. This move becomes his undoing, as it is Carol's language that defines his action. She responds by shouting, "LET ME GO. LET ME GO. WOULD SOMEBODY *HELP* ME?" (57).

In Act 3, Carol clearly wields power over John. The tenure committee has accepted her charges, and he has asked her to his office so he can make one more plea to avoid being fired. Carol has her own agenda. She tells him, "I came here to instruct you" (67), asserting that what he really wants is power, and that what she wants is not revenge but understanding. When he admits that all he is really interested in is keeping his job, she says she will speak to the tenure committee if he supports her Group's demand to ban a list of books, including his own. He refuses. When another phone call informs him that Carol and her Group are in the process of pursuing criminal charges because, as she says, in restraining her physically at their last meeting, "you 'pressed' your body into me," and, "under the statute. I am told. It was battery . . . And attempted rape" (78). John tells Carol to get out of his office. But another turn is precipitated by Carol's eavesdropping. Listening to his phone conversation with his wife, Carol says, "don't call your wife 'baby'" (79). This unleashes John's ultimate fury, as he is reduced to exerting the advantage of brute strength he has over her. He grabs her and beats her, spewing misogynistic invective. The play ends with John lowering the chair he holds over Carol and sitting down at his desk. He looks at her and says, "well"[4] and she looks at him, saying "Yes. That's right" and then looks away and says to herself, "yes. That's right" (80).

During the 1990s, when he was writing, directing, and adapting *Oleanna*, Mamet published two books which have proven characteristically controversial and influential: *On Directing Film* (1991), based on a series of lectures he delivered at Columbia's film school in 1987, and *True and False: Heresy and Common Sense for the Actor* (1997). First produced as a play in 1992 and adapted as a film in 1994, *Oleanna* exemplifies many of the ideas and attitudes he expresses in these two books. In the face of American acting's devotion to the introspective Method, Mamet declares that "the actor does not need to 'become' the character. The phrase, in fact, has no meaning. There *is* no character. There are only lines upon a page."[5] Mamet was an actor before he was a playwright. The challenge of the actor, he says, is "to open the mouth, stand straight, and say the words bravely – adding nothing, denying nothing, and without the intent to manipulate anyone: himself, his fellows, the audience."[6] At bottom, his precepts on acting are all based on a respect for the text to communicate what needs to be communicated, without creating a backstory or ruminating on the character's emotions.

Oleanna's original production was under Mamet's tight control. It was produced by the Back Bay Theatre of Boston, a wing of the American Repertory Theatre that was founded partly by Mamet and William H. Macy, who has been Mamet's close friend and collaborator since Macy was his acting student at Goddard College in the 1960s. Macy played John opposite Rebecca Pidgeon, who was newly married to Mamet in 1992. The production remained intact when it moved to New York, opening at the off-Broadway Orpheum Theatre on October 25, 1992. It was a stark, minimalist production. The acting demonstrated fidelity to Mamet's ideas. Macy has an uncanny ability to make the broken, often interrupted, and overlapping staccato dialogue of what has come to be known as "Mamet-speak" sound natural and to create character from straightforward dialogue and action. In this production, Pidgeon took Mamet's instructions to "open the mouth, stand straight, and say the words bravely" to heart. Her Carol said the lines almost without emotion or inflection, often awkwardly blurting them, and showing no emotional affect. She created the impression of a character with a serious lack of social skills or human empathy.[7]

Most reviewers saw Mamet's original production as slanted in favor of John's position, but he has consistently resisted that interpretation. He has acknowledged his own identification with both characters. As a student, he said, he had "no interest, just bored to flinders. I was like the professor in *Oleanna* who all his life had been told he was an idiot, so he behaved like an idiot."[8] He told Charlie Rose that "a lot of the, the verbiage in the play in both characters ... is my working out of the idea of what, what constitutes worth":

> The student says, "I've been told all my life I'm stupid, I'm stupid, I can't learn, I'm stupid, I'm stupid." And the professor says, "No, you aren't. You're rather smart, as a matter of fact. You're just angry. I think if I can get you past that point, you'll see there's a lot of enjoyment in life that you've

heretofore missed." Now ... to a certain extent, I'm being the professor comforting myself as the student. And the other thing is, is true, too. I'm being the student saying to the professor, "You can be clearer. You have a responsibility to me. I'm lost. I need your help. Paternalism's not going to help. Charisma is not going to help. Telling me to go and do my homework is not going to help. I need someone to explain to me what's required of me." So, there, again, I'm casting myself, the writer, as the student demanding that of figures in authority.[9]

Mamet said that each of the characters "has a very firm point of view, both of which I believe in ... each person, the man and the woman, is saying something absolutely true at every moment and absolutely constructive at most moments in the play, and yet at the end of the play they're tearing each other's throats out."[10] He has expressed surprise at the controversy the play excited, saying, "People stood up and screamed, 'Oh, bullshit,' at the stage before they realized they'd done it. A couple of people got a little crazy and lost their composure."[11] Asked what the controversy was about, he responded that many people thought that the "balance of rectitude" was lopsided, but "they didn't always think that the same person was on top. A lot of people thought that the, the man was right and the woman was wrong and that I'd slanted it that way, and a lot of people thought the opposite. And that's why people were slapping each other around in the lobby because ... the members of the audience vehemently believed that their hero in the play was correct and that the [other] person's hero was wrong."[12]

Partly because the play premiered during the furor over the confirmation hearings of Clarence Thomas's appointment to the Supreme Court, during which Anita Hill's allegations of sexual harassment were broadcast on television, many audience members and reviewers saw *Oleanna* as a play about sexual harassment. The programs for the New York production, half of which had cover pictures of Macy and half of which had pictures of Pidgeon, with targets superimposed on them, invited the audience to take sides. But Mamet has insisted that he

> never really saw it as a play about sexual harassment. I think the issue was, to a large extent, a flag of convenience for a play that's structured as a tragedy ... This play — and the film – is a tragedy about power. These are two people with a lot to say to each other, with legitimate affection for each other. But protecting their positions becomes more important than pursuing their own best interests.[13]

Despite Mamet's protests, however, every production of *Oleanna* seems to bring out the same controversy, with most critics assuming that Mamet

Figure 13.1 Carol (Debra Eisenstadt) receives her grade from her professor, John (William H. Macy), saying she is failing the course. (frame enlargement)

has calculatedly given John the stronger position in the play and made Carol a less sympathetic character, fulfilling what is often assumed to be a misogynistic agenda in the play.

For the most part, the newspaper and magazine reviews of the play expressed this view. *Newsday* called the play

> far more scurrilous than anything the skeptics could conjure. With "Oleanna" ... Mamet reaffirms his niche as avenging knight of the fraternal order of American slobbery. Less a play than a registry of complains, "Oleanna" is one man's reactionary protest, a howling "Enough already!" leveled at a standard of political correctness that is perceived to be spiraling out of control.[14]

In a phrase that caught on with reviewers of the play, *Theater*'s Daniel Mufson declared that "*Oleanna*'s working title could have been *The Bitch Set Him Up*."[15] Few critics thought that Carol was the more sympathetic character, although Gerald Weales noted that in the lobby arguments he overheard, "John is either a well-meaning professor at first intent on helping a confused student or a sexist and elitist whose every casual word is an indication of his comfortable place in the power structure. Carol is either a victim of that structure or a radical feminist who wishes to replace the professor as power figure."[16] In Weales's judgment, "the overstated characters balance one another, making for a standoff of the ideas they represent. Although the battle is unresolved, the play remains a fascinating disquisition on power."[17] Less positively, another critic wrote that Mamet's "forte remains ambiguity: it may be hard to sanctify the student in *Oleanna*, but for some of us, anyway, it's impossible to tolerate the teacher."[18]

In writing and directing his film adaptation of *Oleanna*, Mamet had to address the controversy. But it had to be done his way. Although his ideas on acting and directing have evolved over a forty-year career as an acting teacher, playwright, screenwriter, and director, his positions have always been firmly stated. Mamet writes that "the perfect movie doesn't have any dialogue. So you should always be striving to make a silent movie."[19] This seems a strange statement for a writer to make, especially one whose films are notoriously full of dialogue. But he is mainly addressing the dialogue that is there "to pick up the slack in the shot list." For Mamet, dialogue has to be purposeful: "The only reason people speak is to get what they want."[20] And it is in this way that dialogue serves the film's narrative: "What does the protagonist want? It's this journey that is going to move the story forward. What does the protagonist want? What does he or she do to get it – that's what keeps the audience in their seats. If you don't have that, you have to trick the audience into paying attention."[21]

In speaking of film direction, Mamet has always expressed his firm belief in montage as the major principle of filmmaking, as opposed to "following the character around with the camera," which he abhors. "You always want to tell the story in cuts. Which is to say, through a juxtaposition of images that are basically uninflected. Mr. Eisenstein tells us that the best image is an uninflected image. A shot of a teacup. A shot of a spoon. A shot of a fork. A shot of a door. Let the cut tell the story. Because otherwise you have not got dramatic action, you have narration."[22] And "just as the shot doesn't have to be inflected, the acting doesn't have to be inflected, nor should it be. The acting should be a performance of the simple physical action. Period. Go to the door, try the door, sit down."[23] Similarly, Mamet learned from director Alfred Hitchcock that "the *less* the hero of the play is inflected, identified, and characterized, the more we will endow him with our own internal meaning – the more we will *identify* with him – which is to say the more we will be assured that *we* are that hero."[24]

Like the stage production, the film was under Mamet's tight control. Since his first film, *House of Games* (1987), he has made a point of working with a group of collaborators, collectively known as the "Mamet mafia," who understand his aesthetic and with whom he feels comfortable. Macy, of course, is a core member of the group, as is film editor Barbara Tulliver,

Figure 13.2 The conversation between student and professor becomes personal,
if not intimate. (frame enlargement)

who had worked on Mamet's three preceding films when she took on
Oleanna, and costume designer Jane Greenwood is another Mamet fixture.
As Yannis Tzioumakis has noted, Mamet's situation as adapter of his own
play was unusually favorable, since the film was developed and produced
by Bay Kinescope Productions, a Boston-based film and television production company that he had established with Patricia Wolff, who was also a
producer of the stage production.[25] For this reason, and also because of the
success of *Glengarry Glen Ross*, which he had adapted in 1992, he was able
to leave his script essentially intact, without substantially opening it up,
adding characters, breaking up the long scenes, or even inter-cutting them,
as he had done with *Glengarry*.

Rebecca Pidgeon, for whom the role of Carol was written, was originally
supposed to play opposite William H. Macy in the film. When Pidgeon
had to give up the role because of her pregnancy, Debra Eisenstadt, who
had understudied her in the New York production directed by Mamet
(and had played Carol in the touring company), was tapped for the role on
two weeks' notice. Pidgeon, however, remained close to the project,
composing the film score to Mamet's lyrics and singing some of it. William
H. Macy was quoted in the film's press kit as saying, "We haven't brought
'Oleanna' to film ... We brought film to 'Oleanna.'"[26] And indeed, some
reviewers thought that Mamet "hasn't really adapted anything. He just

turns on the cameras and photographs the play."[27] Several reviewers complained that instead of moving the camera into the action, Mamet pulled it back, giving the audience the same perspective they would get from a theatre seat. He was accused of filming the whole movie in wide and medium shots, making a talky script more flat and boring. Mamet, however, rejected the idea that the burden of the film's narration was placed on the dialogue: "You're telling a story with pictures. You know, the rhythm in which the actors speak on stage is the rhythm that the audience is going to understand the play in. On the other hand, in a movie, the rhythm of the cutting is what's going to help them to understand."[28]

The uninflected image and rhythmic cutting are as basic to Mamet's conception of montage as the lack of inflection, identification, and characterization are basic to his approach to acting. In judging his adaptation of *Oleanna*, it is important to consider the extent to which he succeeded in realizing these concepts on film. While Mamet leaves the three-act structure and a good deal of the dialogue intact in his screenplay, a closer look at his shot selection and cutting shows that the film is far from simply being a static, filmed play. In the beginning of the film, for example, wide shots prevail, but as the confrontation between John and Carol escalates, Mamet intensifies it by moving in more and more closely on the actors, finally cutting quickly back and forth between tight close-ups. He also uses cutting to emphasize the locus of power in a scene. For example, at the end of the first meeting, Mamet cuts between long shots of John sitting professorially behind his desk and close-ups of Carol, looking through the rungs of a ladder at him. In the next scene, when John is presenting his case to Carol, Mamet cuts between close-ups of him and mid shots of Carol writing in her notebook, presumably recording more evidence against him. At the end of the second confrontation, when John tries physically to restrain Carol from leaving, Mamet uses a long shot of her hurrying down the hall toward a group of faculty members in the hall, saying "will somebody help me, please." The tight close-up on Macy's terrified face says all that it needs to about what has happened. Like Sidney Lumet with the adaptation of *Long Day's Journey into Night* and Mike Nichols with *Who's Afraid of Virginia Woolf?*, Mamet also used the arc shot to create a sense of action and tension in the enclosed space of the essentially single set, with John circling Carol (seated in a chair) as he tries to browbeat her with language.

There is little opening out in the film, most of which takes place in John's large office and an adjoining seminar room. The scenes that Mamet adds are essentially a brief establishing sequence at the beginning and several scenes that segue between the confrontations. In keeping with Mamet's views, all of these scenes use montage to advance the story, almost exclusive of dialogue, although there is a bit of "following around with the camera." More significant, in view of Mamet's outspoken rejection of the inflected image and any form of characterization, is the amount of inflection many of the images carry, and the degree to which the images and the mise en scène inflect the characterization.

The film opens with a wide shot of what looks like a generic New England college building, red brick with a gold-domed cupola, a portico with white columns, and a slate roof, with a wide lawn in front, where groups of students sit in the sunshine. Mamet's nostalgic college song, "Long Ago and Far Away," is sung in the pure tenor voice of Steven Goldstein, backed up by the Mansfield Choral Society. Like the song lyrics, the opening image is a metaphor for the lost ideal of academia. This is followed by a narrative sequence: a cramped hallway in which a snaking and slow-moving line of students resignedly waits outside an office for grades; Carol coming out of the office looking at her grades; and Carol going down the staircase. This short sequence presents a jarring image of the reality of college life juxtaposed with the idealized nostalgia of the college song. The next shot pans Carol's bleak dorm room, a setting which suggests a military barracks rather than a young woman's bedroom. A single postcard of a landscape on the blank white wall is the only decoration; the camera reveals a single bed with a brown blanket, made up with military precision, a night table piled high but neatly with books, and a mug holding pencils. Then it pans to Carol seated at a small student desk, behind a stack of books, poring over her grades. She looks down and then to the left, makes a decision, gets up to go, and as an afterthought grabs a green notebook from her desk. The next shot is of Carol coming out of a brick building, pulling on a shapeless green sweater over her white tee shirt and jeans as she runs. Thus the contrast between the ideal and the reality of academic life, as well as some sense of Carol's character and her anxiety over her grades, are established before any dialogue is introduced.

The first lines of dialogue, part of John's phone conversation with his wife, are said over a shot of the doors of an academic building, with students and faculty going out, and Carol coming in quickly. There is a shot of the Edith Lank *Homebuyer's Kit* and a real-estate fact sheet with a picture of a nine-room Victorian house on the desk. A wide shot shows John on the phone, looking through the Lank book as he talks to his wife about a supposed problem with an easement; Carol is in the background, sitting in a chair and listening to his phone conversation. The set for the office in the film differs significantly from the play's stark, minimal set, its careful detail inflecting the image with important cultural, social, and economic implications as well as elements of characterization for the viewer. The room is unusually spacious and well appointed for a faculty office. Its dark wooden paneling, built-in cabinets, and floor-to-ceiling bookcases, complete with a moveable ladder, suggest an elite liberal arts college with a comfortable endowment. A number of framed diplomas and pictures appear on the white walls. A blackboard is used several times to frame both John and Carol after he writes the words "Fear" and "Anger" on it. There are a number of chairs in different seating arrangements, a couch, and a bench, all used to provide variety in the shots during the long scenes. A door opens into an adjoining room with a seminar table and glass cabinets lining the walls, around the cornice of which is painted: "we will be judged by that least involved of magistrates: history." In the third confrontation scene, the table is covered with old trophies that are in the process of being polished. An objective correlative of the nostalgic, anachronistic view of college life that is suggested by the college songs on the soundtrack, the room also provides extended space in which to film each of the three confrontations.

These rooms feature mullioned windows, through which a leafy environment is visible. In the first scene, cinematographer Andrzej Sekula provides a gradual transition from bright sunlight to darkness, symbolizing the deteriorating relationship between teacher and student at the same time that it depresses the mood of the scene. During the second confrontation, rain is seen streaming down throughout the scene. This detail is also used symbolically as the rain drips on an open dictionary, blurring the words. One reviewer noted that when John wipes the water from the sill and then dries his hands, "I couldn't help thinking of Lady Macbeth."[29] Mamet opens the first confrontation scene up slightly by having John go into another classroom when he first tries to get rid of Carol, telling her to make an appointment. She follows him there, and into the hall, where the conversation continues. When John is handed a thick stack of files, presumably his tenure dossier, and has to return to his office, Carol follows him there. The accumulated effect is of a series of circumscribed spaces, of frustrated attempts at pursuit and escape, and of motion which ultimately goes in circles.

A second interpolated scene occurs at the end of the first confrontation (Act 1 in the play). John is alone in the empty living room of the new house, the surprise party clearly over. He pours the last of the wine from a bottle and looks at his gifts, a new briefcase and a mug. He takes the wine out to the porch and sits on a step, the large house completely lit up behind him. Sekula creates a striking image here of the lighted windows of the house juxtaposed against the darkness. Behind the small, slumped figure of Macy on the porch, the house looks huge, at the same time an image of the home and status he is seeking and of the enormous burden he is assuming. One can almost see the mortgage settling on his shoulders. After the second confrontation, which ends disastrously for John, Mamet interpolates a scene in a hotel room, where John, disheveled and barefoot, is lying on the bed, drinking from a pint bottle of liquor, and going over some official document, making notes for his defense before the tenure committee. There is a knock on door, and the maid comes in; John sits in a chair, smokes a cigarette, and intently scribbles notes on the document. This sequence shows John as shaken and anxious, but still confident in his ability to fight Carol through his chosen weapon, language.

The hotel scene is followed by the film's most significant interpolated scene, in which Carol, in dark glasses, makes photocopies. As one critic commented, "the most visceral image in *Oleanna* ... is the close-up of a copy machine as we watch the light flash back and forth."[30] Carol comes to the counter and asks to have a large poster made, and then a cut-away shows her hand stamping a symbol on sheets of paper with words visible in the shot: "for sexual misconduct and for injustice to students and the student body. I have come to apologize, as I see that I have failed. In my responsibilities to the young."[31] This is followed by a shot of a seedy-looking John in a rumpled raincoat walking down the hall of his building past the poster that now hangs there. The poster reads: "IT IS THE RIGHT OF ALL STUDENTS TO BE TREATED WITH RESPECT AND DIGNITY. THIS RIGHT DOES NOT NEED TO BE 'EARNED' OR 'DESERVED.' IT IS THEIR INALIENABLE RIGHT AS CITIZENS AND HUMAN BEINGS. IT IS NOT INCUMBENT UPON THE STUDENT TO TREAT PROFESSORS, ADMINISTRATORS, AND COLLEGE PERSONNEL WITH DEFERENCE, THE SIMPLE CIVILITY OWED TO EVERY WOMAN AND MAN IS SUFFICIENT. THESE CONCEPTS DEVOLVE NOT OUT OF THE DESIRE TO COERCE, OR TO REVOLUTIONIZE, BUT MERELY TO REFORM THAT WHICH, FOR A LONG WHILE, HAS STOOD IN NEED OF REFORMATION." "Long Ago and Far

Away" is heard in the background. Far from Mamet's favored uninflected image, this scene is "loaded," as he would say. It is clear that Carol has universalized her grievance into a cause that involves the whole student body, and that, vague as her charges may be, they contain words that will resonate in dangerous ways for John. The scene literally visualizes the power of language.

Mamet is the first to say that he does not have a strong visual sense, but *Oleanna* relies on a number of visual metaphors to carry symbolic resonance. Like John's wiping his hands and the light flashing through the copier, several images of objects become significant in the context of the film. Another example is the ladder attached to John's bookshelves, which suggests the academic hierarchy when John casually leans on it and when Carol looks through it as though the rungs are prison bars. In the final scene, John physically bashes Carol with the ladder in his crudest exercise of power. Yet another example is the cup of tea in the first confrontation, which John offers to Carol when he suggests that they start over as teacher and student. When Carol jumps to her feet, shouting, "I believe that I'M SPEAKING," after his constant interruptions, she drops the cup, and it shatters into pieces. A cut-away shot shows John's hands picking up the pieces and throwing them away, an image of his failure at engaging with Carol in this polite, civilized way. Then the camera moves back to show him kneeling at Carol's feet, a foreshadowing of his fate.

Carol's ubiquitous battered green notebook also carries a good deal of freight. At first it seems a figure of her ignorance and failure, as she constantly consults it when she first talks to John, and dutifully takes notes on his monologues. At the same time, the notebook is a comfort to her, a source of "Facts" that she can rely on. When, toward the end of the first confrontation, her attempt to open up to John and admit that she is "Bad" is interrupted by the phone, she takes the notebook and hugs it to her chest. In the later scenes, however, it becomes a weapon, as she consults it for evidence against him, or writes ominously in it, at one point taking his book down from the shelf while he is on the phone in order to write notes for herself, presumably to use against him later.

A visual sequence centered on the paper airplane that John picks up while he is talking to Carol in the hall is also loaded. The paper airplane inspires the story John tells Carol about a pilot who allows his attention to wander while he is flying a plane. He hands the plane to Carol after

Figure 13.3 Accused by Carol of attempted rape after her complaint of sexual harassment has cost him his job, John loses control and only barely stops himself from killing her. (frame enlargement)

he finishes the story, which brings them a moment of understanding. She puts the plane on the table between them as they sit drinking their tea, but leaves it there after she breaks her cup. Near the end of the film, when John is learning about the rape charge during a phone call from his lawyer, he opens his desk drawer, revealing the airplane. In the context of the preceding narrative, this seemingly uninflected image shows an aspect of John's character that the viewer has not seen before. He must have saved the airplane and put it in his drawer after his first meeting with Carol, suggesting not only that he cared something about her and their encounter, but that he is a collector of sentimental mementos. At the same time, the airplane, appearing at this point in the film, is an image of his failure in attempting to teach this student. As the copier, the poster, and the notebook signify the chillingly legalistic expression of Carol's antipathy for John, the paper airplane signifies John's originally sentimental, perhaps idealistic feeling about Carol.

In looking at these elements, it becomes clear that the film is far from the uninflected montage that Mamet presents as an ideal. Overall, both the added scenes and the visual metaphors tend to make John more sympathetic to the viewer and Carol less so, as do the close-ups on Macy's expressive face. Not only are these elements a departure from Mamet's approach to filmmaking, they would seem to act against any intention he might have to address the critics' complaint that he made John the more sympathetic character in the play. Aesthetically, however, they may serve a purpose that was more important to him than demonstrating that he is not a misogynist. Drawing the audience's sympathy toward John makes his reversion to physical brutality at the end of the film all the more shocking. And Mamet does not shrink from the violence. Macy's beating of Eisenstadt is prolonged and ugly, an explosion of fury in contrast to the physical stasis of the rest of the film. The close-up on the look of utter horror that comes over Macy's face as he says, "Oh, my God" after the beating says all it needs to about his failure as a teacher and a human being.

Mamet also used the soundtrack overtly to emphasize academia's failed idealism. Eschewing the obvious choice of the actual folk song "Oleanna," he and Rebecca Pidgeon composed "college songs" that express the nostalgia for a romantically idealized academic life in a past that never existed. Besides "Long Ago and Far Away" and "Brief College Days," sung by Steven Goldstein over the opening credits and the initial image of the college building, and "Hail to the Men of Merit," Rebecca Pidgeon reprises "Brief College Days" over the closing credits, following a final shot of the college. The songs are sung to the accompaniment of a single piano, sometimes with the Mansfield Choral Society suggesting the college choir or glee club of days gone by. Juxtaposed against the events of the film, the effect is deeply ironic, emphasizing the contrast between academia's idealized self-conception and its reality.

Oleanna was a commercial failure after a very limited release by the Samuel Goldwyn Company, realizing only $123,089 in gross receipts. For the most part, it did not fare well with critics either. Besides complaining about the amount of dialogue and the lack of action, most thought the debate was lopsided and that John was victimized by Carol. There were some who understood and respected what Mamet was trying to do in the film, however. While David Sterritt thought that "some imperfectly tuned nuances of dialogue and camera work give John a slight edge in the movie that he didn't have onstage," he acknowledged that "other spectators may feel just the opposite," and he praised Mamet for making the "most truly Hitchcockian film of recent years, with an uncanny ability to orchestrate moment-by-moment identification between viewers and characters."[32] Unfortunately for Mamet and Oleanna, viewers like Sterritt were all too rare.

Endnotes

1 David Mamet, *Oleanna: A Play* (New York: Vintage, 1993), n.p. Subsequently referred to in the text.

2 The lyrics Mamet quotes are actually by Pete Seeger. The Kingston Trio sang a different version of the song.

3 "David Mamet's 'Oleanna' Provokes Strong Response," *Morning Edition*, National Public Radio, November 4, 1994, accessed December 31, 2010.

4 In the film, Mamet changed John's line to "Oh, my God."

5 David Mamet, *True and False: Heresy and Common Sense for the Actor* (New York: Random House, 1997), 9.

6 Ibid., 22.

7 A video tape of the New York production is available at the New York Public Library for the Performing Arts.

8 Quoted in John Lahr, "David Mamet: The Art of Theatre XI," *Paris Review* 39.142 (spring 1997), in *David Mamet in Conversation*, ed. Leslie Kane (Ann Arbor: University of Michigan Press, 2001), 112.

9 Quoted in Charlie Rose, "Theater, Politics, and Tragedy," from *Charlie Rose Show*, WNET-TV, New York, November 11, 1994, in *David Mamet in Conversation*, 169.

10 Ibid., 164.

11 Quoted in Geoffrey Norman and John Rezek, "Playboy Interview: David Mamet," *Playboy* (April 1995), in *David Mamet in Conversation*, 124–125.

12 Rose, "Theater, Politics, and Tragedy," 164–165.

13 Norman and Rezek, "Playboy Interview," 125.

14 Jan Stuart, "Mamet's Reactionary Howl on Sexual Harassment," *Newsday*, October 26, 1992, Part 11, 44.

15 Daniel Mufson, "Sexual Perversity in Viragos," *Theater* 24.1 (1993), 111.

16 Gerald Weales, "Gender Wars: 'Oleanna' and 'Desdemona,'" *Commonweal*, December 4, 1992, 15.

17 Ibid., 20.

18 Jeanne Silverthorne, "PC Playhouse," *Artforum International* 31.7 (March 1993), 10.

19 David Mamet, *On Directing Film* (New York: Viking Penguin, 1991), 72.

20 Ibid., 71.

21 Ibid., 10–11.

22 Ibid., 2.

23 Ibid., 68.

24 Ibid., 38.

25 Yannis Tzioumakis, "Adapting *Oleanna* for the Screen: Film Adaptation and the Institutional Apparatus of American Independent Cinema," *Crossings: David Mamet's Work in Different Genres and Media*, ed. Johan Callens (Newcastle upon Tyne: Cambridge Scholars Publishing, 2009), 155.

26 *Oleanna* Press Kit, Samuel Goldwyn Company, vi.

27 Ibid.

28 "David Mamet's 'Oleanna' Provokes Strong Response."

29 Ron Weiskind, "'Oleanna': Lost on Film, So to Speak," *Pittsburgh Post-Gazette*, December 7, 1994, B6.

30 Brent Kliewer, "Mamet's 'Oleanna' Still Polarizing the Audience," *Santa Fe New Mexican*, December 9, 1994, 29.

31 The original Boston production of the play ended with John making a public apology of this kind. This was also the script that Harold Pinter used, with Mamet's reluctant authorization, when he directed the play in London. The more ambiguous ending in the published play was used in the New York production.

32 David Sterritt, *Christian Science Monitor*, November 4, 1994: Arts, 12.

CHAPTER 14

To what end a cinematic Wit?

John D. Sykes, Jr.

Three carefully staged endings provide a visual framework for understanding intertextual interactions concerning religion in Margaret Edson's 1999 Pulitzer Prize–winning play *Wit*. The first scene is directed and acted by John Donne, the seventeenth-century English poet.[1] Nothing in Donne's life was more dramatic than his preparation for death. Acutely aware of his impending rendezvous with mortality, the Dean of St. Paul's summoned a painter, had his servants light charcoal braziers in his study, stripped off his clothes, had himself bound in his winding sheet, and somehow found the strength to stand on a specially made platform representing a funeral urn while the artist rendered a life-sized drawing of him on a wooden plank. Facing east in anticipation of Christ's return on Judgment Day, the emaciated Donne presented a tableau of paradoxical hope from the very portal of the tomb. As he so often does in his poetry, at this last stage of his life Donne finds in death the occasion for a grand gesture, a statement of surpassing gravity on the gravest of subjects. His contemporaries seem to have appreciated this act of self-fashioning. Donne's face (with winding sheet topknot) was reproduced for the title page of Donne's final sermon, published as "Death's Duel." And the entire effigy was the basis for Nicholas Stone's marble statue, executed soon after Donne's death and still on display in St. Paul's Cathedral, London.

Wit ends with a similarly spectacular gesture, and one that viewers have frequently puzzled over. Edson's formidable Donne scholar Vivian Bearing, having bravely endured the long ordeal of terminal ovarian cancer, dies. After a chaotic scene in which an overzealous research fellow attempts to revive her, Vivian is left alone with an attentive nurse. And in stark contrast to the noisy failure of the unjustified medical intervention, Vivian silently, yet triumphantly, rises from her bed, removes her hospital gowns, and stands "naked and beautiful, reaching for the light" (85).[2] Is this gesture an attempt on Edson's part to provide defiant symbolic affirmation in the face of clinical finality? If so, we might take the ending either as a tribute to the way Professor Bearing faced her death or as a means to encourage an emotionally exhausted audience. Reviewers' comments have gone in both these directions, and not all have been complimentary. *Washington Post* reviewer Lloyd Rose called the ending "gooey," and "unworthy of Edson's heroine."[3]

The Mike Nichols–Emma Thompson 2001 Home Box Office (HBO) film adaptation of *Wit* takes a different tack, however. In his single biggest departure from Edson's script, Nichols leaves us with a snapshot close-up of Vivian's younger, healthy face, which replaces the diseased visage of the deceased Vivian. The fact that this older photograph is in black-and-white hints that Vivian has died.[4] Except for a voiceover of Thompson reciting Donne's "Death be not proud" to the accompaniment of Arvo Pärt's elegiac "Spiegel im Spiegel," there is nothing in the film to suggest that Vivian has survived in any sense except as a memory, and in stark contrast to Donne's final portrait our last image of Bearing is of a younger self who had not faced death.

The film version of *Wit* provides the opportunity for viewers to consider a three-way intertextual interaction among Edson's play, the Donne poetry that has been her protagonist's vocational preoccupation, and the film co-written by director Mike Nichols and star Emma Thompson. Of special interest is the theological issue that Edson identified as central to her play: redemption. In both play and film, Vivian Bearing is presented as confronting the same obstacle to redemption that she identified in Donne, the fear her former student Jason Posner terms "salvation anxiety." Although the nature of redemption is construed differently in the late twentieth-century world of the play than it was in Donne's early modern England, in Edson's *Wit* it is still understood primarily in Christian terms that the filmmakers recognize but ultimately obscure. In addition to anxiety, which, as we will see, is an affliction stemming from new notions of knowledge, redemption in Donne and in the two versions of *Wit* turns on assumptions about the body. Both of these subjects – knowledge and the body – have special force in the setting of the play: a research hospital devoted to understanding disease and conquering death. Indeed, as was true for Donne, for Edson's character, and for the principal filmmakers, death proves an irresistible subject. It is the crucible that produces truths we would prefer to avoid.

No doubt the subject-matter of the play weighed heavily in producers' initial reluctance to stage it. *Wit* remains Margaret Edson's only play. It grew out of her experience as a clerk in the AIDS and cancer unit of a research hospital beginning in 1985.[5] Edson began writing the play in the summer of 1991, before beginning master's work in literature at George-town University. She recalls that she wished to follow the changes in a character who passed from a position of power and authority to one of dependence, and considered several possibilities until she hit on the idea of using a Donne scholar. Memories of her Smith College classmates groaning at the difficulties of Donne nudged her in the direction she eventually took; Donne's own verbal brilliance and fascination with death no doubt did the rest. Having written the play, Edson took up the daunting task of getting it produced.

Following repeated rejections and revisions, the play was finally staged by the South Coast Repertory Company in Costa Mesa, California, in 1995. From there it was picked up by the Long Wharf Theater in New Haven, Connecticut, largely through the tireless efforts of Edson's high-school friend, director Derek Anson Jones. Jones showed the script to actress Kathleen Chalfant, 1993 Tony Award Best Actress for her work in *Angels in America*, who championed the new play and accepted the part of Vivian Bearing. After a successful run in Connecticut, the play moved to New York, where it received numerous accolades, culminating in the 1999 Pulitzer Prize for Drama. At least as surprising as the first-time playwright's success has been her seemingly sincere indifference to fame. By the time *Wit* began to win accolades, Edson had become a devoted kindergarten teacher in Atlanta, Georgia, a vocation that she insists she finds utterly fulfilling. In a recent public speech, her 2008 commencement address at her alma mater, Smith College, she does not mention *Wit* or writing, but instead extols the joys of classroom teaching, a venture that she believes to be an act of love.[6] Indeed, Edson's attitude toward both productions of her play and the film adaptation seems almost diffident. In interviews she reports attending and enjoying performances, but only as an anonymous viewer. She seems content to trust directors and actors with her work and makes no effort to shape public reception of it; by choice she was not involved in the making of the film, although she has said that she likes it.[7]

Edson's preferred role in relation to her drama seems to be that of the observer; she watches reactions to her play in much the same way that she observed the workings of a research hospital: as an all but invisible presence. However, on one topic, that of the play's theme, she has on occasion been uncharacteristically emphatic. As Martha Greene Eads was the first to point out in print, since an early interview with journalist Adrienne Martini, Edson has consistently maintained that Vivian Bear-ing's struggle is essentially religious: "The play is about redemption, and I'm surprised no one mentions it." Continuing, Edson explains, "Grace is

Figure 14.1 Professor Vivian Bearing (Emma Thompson) receives the news of her stage-four ovarian cancer, coldly delivered by Dr. Kelekian (Christopher Lloyd). (frame enlargement)

the opportunity to experience God in spite of oneself, which is what Dr. Bearing ultimately achieves."[8] Although Edson has deflected questions concerning details of her own religious belief, it is clear that the theological elements in *Wit* are not mere props borrowed from Donne. She professes Christianity and lived for a time in a French Dominican convent in Rome. The subject of her only other (unproduced) play is country Gospel radio in Kentucky. She came to her calling as a kindergarten teacher after volunteering to tutor through St. Margaret's Episcopal Church in Washington, DC (Cohen). As she made clear in an interview with Betty Carter, Edson regards issues such as the state of medicine or interpretation of Donne's poetry as secondary to the drama of redemption in the play, despite most critical response.[9]

When HBO bought the film rights to *Wit*, Colin Callender, president of HBO Films, had Emma Thompson in mind for the part of Vivian Bearing. Thompson and Nichols became the major shaping forces of the project, co-writing the adapted script. The film debuted on March 24, 2001. In an interview with Sian Kirwan before the 2001 Edinburgh International Film Festival, Thompson notes that, in addition to the marvelous script, she was attracted to the challenge of bringing a film that deals so grippingly with illness and death to an American audience.[10] In explaining why she wanted Nichols to direct, she first notes that he is a witty director with a long history in comedy, stretching back to his deadpan improv collaborations with Elaine May in the late 1950s, which launched his career. Thompson felt that drawing out the subtle humor of the script was the crucial counter to its grim setting. But she also wanted Nichols because "he's terrified of dying and the whole subject of death – as is America. They seem to view it as an optional extra over there ..."[11] Indeed, Thompson and Nichols would soon work together on another HBO film adaptation project that deals straightforwardly with disease and death, Tony Kushner's *Angels in America* (2003).

In his own Edinburgh Film Festival interview (with James Mottram), Nichols likewise notes the difficulty of the subject-matter, but he seems to consider the film therapeutic: "I like to think there is something free[ing] about it, like really looking at death."[12] Considering the fact that Thompson has declared herself to be an atheist[13] and that Nichols, as a largely secularized Jew, has no investment in Christian theology, it is unsurprising that they see Vivian Bearing's plight in humanistic and psychotherapeutic terms. And yet, perhaps out of respect for the charac- ter's devotion to Donne, the film includes touches which call definite attention to the religious coloring of Vivian's suffering. The most signifi- cant of these is the visual motif of martyrdom. During the flashback to Vivian's collegiate encounter with Professor Ashford (Chapter 3, "Begin with the Text"), we see, for the first time, a reproduction of Perugino's *c.*1495 painting of St. Sebastian pierced with arrows hanging in the profes- sor's office. Vivian keeps a miniature of the painting by her hospital bedside, suggesting that what she has studied she must now live. In fact, the image might be said to replicate the moral lesson Ashford tries to impress upon the collegiate Vivian, who is not yet prepared to receive it: uncompromising scholarly standards and simple human truth are con- nected. Yet upon reflection, it is clear that the martyrdom analogy is incomplete. A martyr dies for her faith. Vivian's spiritual suffering might better be explained as springing from a lack of faith. She fears the loss of her power to control her circumstances; she fiercely clings to her autonomy even as she slips into dependence. And considering the treatment she receives at the hands of the physicians who take charge of her case, one can hardly blame her for resisting. If Vivian is a martyr to any cause, it is the cause of knowledge, and in *Wit*, knowledge proves to be an idol, as we  will see. Thus in the film religious imagery is secularized; in this instance, religious martyrdom is transposed into the suffering Vivian must endure as a willing victim of the quest for scientific knowledge.

A similar logic is at work in the film's handling of Bearing's lecture on the holy sonnet, "If poysonous mineralls." This scene, presented as a flashback to the scholar at the height of her powers, is one in which Bearing advances the thesis that in this poem, instead of asking God to remember him, the speaker asks God to forget him, hoping in this way to escape divine wrath. However, the film leaves out a key phrase from the play's version of the lecture: *forgiveness*. This may seem an insignificant omission, and indeed the notion of Vivian's resembling the speaker in Donne's poem in her inability to trust is retained. But what is lost is the implication that both the speaker and Vivian are at fault in some fundamental way. In the film version, the speaker has made a miscalculation; in the play, the speaker has committed a sin. By analogy, in the film Vivian is cast as the victim of an error in judgment who bears no blame for her mistake. Her self-examination takes the form of searching out her missteps in the way she might trace out the abrupt turns in a Donne poem. And indeed, in both play and film she pulls up short of accepting full culpability for her refusal to love others or to allow herself to be loved by them.

Two of the four flashbacks in the film deal with moments at which Vivian's quest for knowledge led her to turn her back on others. In the first, Vivian recalls her undergraduate conference with Ashford. The major lesson the established scholar tries to teach is one drawn from proper punctuation of "Death be not proud": death is not a noisy disruption, but a breath – a comma – separating life from life everlasting. It will take the remainder of the film (and play) to work out the meaning of this lesson for Vivian's own life. A second lesson, however, has a direct bearing on the process of Vivian's self-criticism. At the end of the conference Ashford recommends that Vivian put aside her books for the afternoon and enjoy herself with her friends. But Vivian recalls that after having stepped outside into the bright sunshine and noticing other students in conversation, she returned to the library. The manner of Thompson's recounting of this episode clearly indicates, in faithfulness to Edson's play, that this decision was a mistake – a choice of isolation over human connection. But Vivian cannot bring herself to admit fault.

The flashback in which Bearing dismisses the pleas of a student who asks for a deadline extension on a paper assignment follows a similar pattern. Having recalled her indifference to the student, Vivian reflects upon her actions: "I don't know . . . I feel so much . . . What is the word? I look back and I see these scenes and I . . ." (Chapter 14, "The Lesson"). These musings take Vivian to the verge of a confession she never quite makes. Clearly, she recognizes an error. And the word she nearly utters (before being interrupted by Nurse Susie) is certainly "regret." But she never quite says it. Even if she had done so, regret falls short of guilt, and is more accurately described as a failure of knowledge ("I don't know . . .") than as a moral fault. In the scene that cuts short these reflections, Vivian approaches another renunciation of her former ways – one that has more specifically to do with knowledge.

Vivian confides in Susie that she is frightened and uncertain in the face of her rapidly deteriorating condition. Over Popsicles, Susie tells Vivian plainly what the doctors have avoided saying – the treatments have not stopped the cancer, and Vivian will die. The question that remains is whether Vivian wants to be resuscitated when her heart stops, or if she wishes to be allowed to die. Susie suggests that the doctors will want to resuscitate her in order to learn as much from her case as possible. "[T]hey always want to know more things," Susie observes. Vivian replies that she, too, was a scholar – "When I had eyebrows. And shoes." As a scholar, "I always want to know more things," she says. And yet, when Susie concludes from these remarks that Vivian desires to be resuscitated, Vivian contradicts her. If her heart stops, she wants it simply to stop. "Don't complicate the matter," she insists (68).

The choice of simplicity over scholarly complication implies that Vivian has recognized the limits of scientific knowledge. She is rejecting a model of knowledge that eschews feeling and community in hopes of finding sympathy and human connection. And she acknowledges her own complicity in a system that turns patients into "research." As she commented earlier, "Now I know how poems feel" (16). Yet even at this point, Vivian cannot bring herself to take a step in a more positive direction that might lead toward a fuller, more existential sort of knowledge. Once again, she comes up short of a crucial word: "I'm scared. Oh God. I want . . . I want . . . No. I want to hide. I just want to curl up in a little ball" (70). It is more difficult to fill in this ellipsis. But the fact that she calls on God, however unthinkingly, at least hints at a religious answer. And if we recall the clearly intended parallel with the speaker in "If poysonous mineralls," the missing word might well be *forgiveness*, the divine gift the speaker refuses, according to the play version of Bearing's lecture. Of course, the word is entirely missing from the film version. However, forgiveness, and the closely related notion of grace, are exactly what is needed to make sense of both the death scene and the ending as written in the play script.

Near the beginning of play and film, Vivian announces that she is learning to suffer. She means not only that she is learning to deal with pain, but also that she is learning *from* suffering – her suffering has a purpose. But for her suffering to make sense, it must not only point out to her the fundamental error of her life, but also show her the telos toward which her life should have been directed. This double-sided process is at work in a similar way in perhaps the most famous modern literary examination of approaching death, Tolstoy's story "The Death of Ivan Ilych." It is a revealing coincidence that the word that begins to free Ivan Ilych from his suffering is the word I am proposing for Vivian's ellipsis. Ilych is attempting to ask his son's forgiveness, although he is too weak to make himself understood and says *forego* instead.[14]

Although Vivian falls short of even Ilych's incomplete declaration of culpability, her incipient recognition of the need for forgiveness is necessary to make full sense of what happens after she loses coherence. In order for her to make the leap out of the "salvation anxiety" that seizes Donne's persona in Vivian's lecture, she, like he, must acknowledge her guilty complicity in her own misery. Just as there can be no martyrdom without faith, so there can be no redemption without contrition. Vivian's earlier actions depict not one who has merely made a rational miscalculation but rather one whose entire moral compass is set to the wrong North. Vivian is the Everyman in a morality play of the type Donne's audience knew well; Death is not alone in suffering from pride. Vivian needs forgiveness because she has sinned, in the very basic sense of having turned her back on God and others for the sake of absolute autonomy. I have argued elsewhere that the powerful if metaphoric ending is thus confirmation of another famous Donnean line: "That he may raise the Lord throws down."[15] Vivian's illness, although not sought by her and not good in itself, has been the occasion for her salvation, an antidote to Pride. And she is thus presented to us as an exemplum.

The penultimate chapter of the DVD version of the HBO *Wit* is appropriately titled, "Permission to Die." Reviewers have rightly pointed to it as the most poignant episode in the film. Ashford, brilliantly played by Eileen Atkins, is now an old woman, and she comes to Vivian's bedside as the first visitor Vivian has had throughout her long hospitalization. Vivian is no longer capable of conversation, and she refuses her old teacher's offer to recite Donne, so Evelyn Ashford crawls into bed with Vivian and reads her the children's book she has bought for her grandson's birthday. The import of *The Runaway Bunny* is religious, as Ashford observes. The story, she says, is "a little allegory of the soul": no matter where it hides, God will find it. In Margaret Wise Brown's tale, the bunny-child finally accepts the love offered by the mother, and is last seen happily munching the carrot the mother bunny provides. Vivian falls asleep as the

Figure 14.2 Dying, Vivian is comforted by an unexpected visit from her academic
mentor Evelyn Ashford (Eileen Atkins), who reads to her from Margaret
Wise Brown's children's book *The Runaway Bunny*. (frame enlargement)

story concludes, and Ashford blesses her with a final benediction (from
Shakespeare): "And flights of angels attend thee to thy rest." A brief time
later, after Ashford has departed, Vivian is dead. By implication, Vivian has
finally stopped hiding and has accepted the gift offered to her. This
moment of grace in the film, when Vivian receives what she could not
bring herself to ask for and is embraced by mothering love, is indeed
moving. At a strictly naturalistic level, the bodily presence and sympathetic
wisdom of Ashford as she cradles her former student is a powerful image of
the human solidarity the once formidable Bearing has lacked. Yet if we
remain at this level, as the film seems to do, the "little allegory of the soul"
is incomplete. For as Ashford tells us, this moment of grace comes from
God: "No matter where it [the soul] hides, God will find it."

The emotional as well as philosophical difference this makes becomes
clear in the contrast between endings. The "naked and reaching for the
light" ending of the play has an overwhelming impact upon audiences,
even if a minority of viewers criticize it upon reflection. By contrast, the
film's final close-up of a young Vivian's healthy face seems almost an
afterword – a calming segue into the credits after the tension of the
previous two scenes. The words of "Death be not proud," intoned reassur-
ingly by Thompson's voiceover, affirm that death is not ultimate, but the
only counter to it seems to be memory, signified by the photo. The play

ending is more triumphant for the simple reason that it makes God the agent of grace, completing the logic of the allegory of the soul. Edson's ending gives us an image of resurrection, not one of a natural, reptilian re-emergence, as at least one critic has suggested.[16] In a move Donne would have recognized, Edson shows her protagonist rising in the body on the last day, at God's command, to meet her savior. In fact, what happens to Vivian in Edson's ending, is similar in important ways to Donne's funeral portrait. In the drawing and the sculpture fashioned after it, Donne stands on a funeral urn, facing east in anticipation of his Lord's return, as his friend Izaak Walton tells us. Symbolically, then, Donne is rising from the dead to meet Christ, covered only by his winding sheet, which has not yet fallen away. Vivian likewise rises from her death bed to newness of life, shedding the trappings of mortality as she goes, reaching for the light. This is indeed a scene to take away the audience's breath, not one to calm them to a resigned acceptance of the inevitable. And theologically the scene points emphatically to God. As Raymond-Jean Frontain has argued, with this ending, Edson has given us her own metaphysical conceit: "In the midst of the modern medical universe, Edson paradoxically demands the audience's acknowledgment of an animating deity whose presence is rendered on stage only in Prof. Ashford's allegory of the soul and in the light for which Vivian reaches" (12–13). And she does so most emphatically by forcing us to look at Vivian's body – and thus the human body in general – in an unaccustomed light.

Edson's ending is quite orthodox in insisting upon a bodily resurrection. Despite what Platonic influences within the church and Cartesian, positivist views outside it have led many contemporary people to believe, historic Christianity has for the most part been faithful to its Jewish roots in maintaining that our final restoration to God after death includes the body. Beginning with the New Testament writings of Paul, Christians have looked forward to a general resurrection, following the pattern of Christ's resurrection, in which the dead will be raised and the righteous will be gathered to the Father. The later notion that the soul of the redeemed leaves the body at death and goes immediately to heaven was a kind of stopgap measure – a way to provide a layover for the spirit until it was returned to the body to meet Christ upon his return. The fate and status of the soul between death and resurrection has been more at issue in the mainstream of Christian reflection than has the expectation of a general resurrection. According to Paul's teaching, although the summoned bodies will be changed and rendered incorruptible, bodies – not disembodied souls – they will be.[17] Donne probes, dissects, and dramatizes this mystery in poetry and prose, but his affirmation of it at the end of his life – particularly in his carefully prepared death portrait – is clear. And Edson follows him in this. When Betty Carter asked Edson to explain why Vivian removes her clothes at the end, Edson replied, "What else would you wear to a redemption?" (25).

Edson has made it clear that orthodoxy is not her goal, and that she has no interest in making a doctrinal statement in her play. Yet her use of her character's body to provide an instructive emblem for her audience has theological and philosophical implications. The resurrection scene implies God to be the agent of Vivian's redemption, and it also shows her as an embodied self. This second assertion may seem too obvious to be interesting, but it has very much to do with an important debate in the play concerning the nature of knowledge. During the research trial she endures, Vivian's body is rendered into an object separate from her self. The film explores this bifurcation brilliantly. From the initial scene in which Dr. Kelekian bluntly informs Dr. Bearing that she has ovarian cancer which has reached Stage IV, Vivian becomes a partner with her physicians in objectifying her body. A tightening around the eyes and a brief look of distraction from Thompson are the only hints that Vivian has received an emotional blow. The dialogue is that of two professionals coming to a common analytical conclusion; they might be two bankers discussing a financial matter concerning a third party. Likewise, Doctors Bearing and Kelekian are downright conspiratorial during Grand Rounds, the training sessions in which a team of interns and residents led by Kelekian as attending physician examine the patient and discuss her case. A chipper and amused Thompson exchanges winks with Kelekian (wryly played by Christopher Lloyd) as the young doctors struggle to hit on "hair loss" as the obvious symptom they have failed to note. When the doctors pull up her gown and prod her abdomen, Vivian looks down at herself as though she, too, is a scientist trying to make sense of a specimen. Vivian is perhaps most clearly presented as a specimen in an early scene with her former student, Jason Posner, Kelekian's research fellow. Jason administers a pelvic exam with a social clumsiness that borders on criminality. Having forgotten prescribed clinical protocol, he leaves Bearing alone, her feet in stirrups and her knees bent at a sharp angle while he goes in search of "a girl" – the female staffer whose presence is required when a male doctor performs a gynecological procedure. Nichols gives us the vivid image of Vivian stretched out like a frog on a dissecting tray, the camera peering down at her from above in imitation of the detached scientific observer. When Jason finally returns with Susie, he completes the exam, exclaiming, "Jesus!" at what he finds, but he refuses to discuss his discovery with Vivian, deflecting her question with chatter about the course he took from her.

The moral failings of the scholars in the play spring not merely from individual character flaws but from the paradigm of knowledge under which they work. Detachment, isolation, and objectification follow naturally from a Cartesian dualism which sharply distinguishes subject from object and alleges the true self to be the thinking self – the *cogito* that inhabits the body as a ghost in a machine. Bacon's conviction that the purpose of knowledge is power and that science gives humanity power over nature helps complete the picture. Medical historian Iago Galdston summarizes Bacon's program in this way: "A science that was not practically useful was, in Bacon's eyes, worth nothing. By means of science, Bacon argued, it would be possible to establish the 'dominion of man,' the *regnum hominis*, over all things, so that the wants of Man's life might be satisfied, his pleasure multiplied, and his power increased. The dominion of Man over things, Bacon urged, is the highest and indeed the sole end of science."[18]

Despite the seemingly humanitarian interests of Bacon's program, a view which sees nature as thing and knowledge as power does not bode well for the human spirit, especially when the body is one of the things to be dominated by the power-mad mind. In addition to the objectification of Vivian that we have already seen (at one point she wryly notes that one day she may be famous in the medical journals – or rather her ovaries will be), the detrimental effects of conceiving knowledge as power abound. During the Grand Rounds scene, Vivian confides to the audience that she enjoys the spectacle of the competitive maneuvering: "Full of subservience, hierarchies, gratuitous displays, sublimated rivalries – I feel right at home. It is just like a graduate seminar" (37). Here we see both knowledge as a struggle for individual power and Vivian's recognition that her profession's approach to poetry operates under a "scientific" model. Thus when Jason later observes that working through the intricacies of Donne was excellent training for peeling back the layers of cellular complexity encountered in cancer research, his claim is plausible. For Jason, cancer is "awesome" because its secrets are so ingeniously hidden. What drives his interest is solving the puzzle – a grand game that he believes he can win. His patients, on the other hand, are a nuisance, a distraction from pure research.

When Jason is forced to explain why he called the code team to revive Vivian, the best he can manage is, "She's research!" And of course, he has said more than he knows. In the course of her treatment, Vivian's body has been completely objectified – reduced to the quantifiable knowledge that can be wrung from it. And this is yet another reason why the resurrection image that follows is vitally necessary. When Vivian rises after Susie removes what has become in effect her winding sheet, her body becomes the bridge joining matter and spirit, subject and object, the earthly with the transcendent. Perhaps the best way to describe this identification theologically is to call it sacramental. Like baptism and Eucharist, Vivian's resurrection is an instance in which the material of the created order becomes the medium of divine grace. Bodily resurrection, like the sacraments and the Incarnation, affirms the living connection between God and the world, rejecting Gnosticisms both ancient and modern.

Although for the reasons I have advanced, I am convinced that Vivian's stage resurrection returns us to Donne's Christian faith and echoes the message of his death effigy, it is plain that Edson's conceit is far from self-interpreting. The filmmakers, who have expressed admiration of Edson's script and have generally been faithful to it, entirely eliminate this scene, supplying a naturalistic conclusion. And at least one philosophically sophisticated critic, Elizabeth Klaver, who is very perceptive in other ways, completely misreads Edson's ending by forcing it into the either/or of dualism or materialism. She argues that both play and film endings may be seen either as an affirmation of the continued existence of the soul after the death of the body (dualism) or as an illustration of the stages of death, when the brain briefly outlives the rest of the body, hallucinating as it expires (materialism).[19] For Klaver, as no doubt for much of *Wit*'s audience, the third, sacramental option I have outlined is no longer plausible, and thus does not even come into the conversation.

Besides the huge cultural shift begun in Donne's time, which now has four hundred years' momentum, *Wit*'s ultimately theological message is obscured by an internal factor: Edson's rejection of mere wit as a way to wisdom. By the seventeenth century, the term *wit*, which formerly referred to mental ability generally, had come to suggest dazzling intellectual brilliance and inventiveness. When Vivian pointedly refuses Ashford's offer to recite Donne during her visit, the action seems to complete what has been a running criticism of wit when it is used to complicate and confuse simple if profound matters. The play strongly implies that it is not only Donne's speaker in poems such as "If poisonous minerals," but Donne himself who suffers from "salvation anxiety." The children's book, in which a wayward bunny returns to its mother, serves as an antidote to the tortured paradoxes of metaphysical poetry. However, one must be careful not to take the wit Jason so admires to be the whole of Donne.

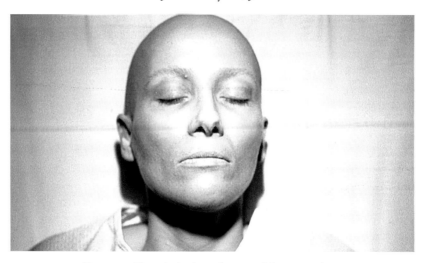

Figure 14.3 Vivian's death mask – peaceful, transcendent,
otherworldly – is the film's final image. (frame enlargement)

Donne shows us both the disease of modern notions of death and its
potential cure. The conflicted, doubtful, and conscience-stricken speaker
of many of the holy sonnets does indeed dramatize the dangers of the new
Baconian-Cartesian knower: isolation, scepticism, egotism. In turning
against such wit in her extremity, Vivian is rejecting the paradigm of the
new knowledge as too narrow and too infected with pride to guide her
through her "minute's last point." But another side of Donne is affirmed:
the side that manages to overcome anxiety through faith. Ashford's early
comments about death, which serve as a kind of thesis for the play, assert
that when properly understood, "Death be not proud" is not wit, but truth
(15). "Nothing but a breath – a comma – separates life from life everlasting" (14). The filmmakers rightly underscore the thematic significance of
this holy sonnet by having it sound as the final spoken words of the film.
And of course the play's resurrection ending – which could have been
inspired not only by Donne's effigy but also by poems such as "Hymn to
God my God, in my sicknesse" – even more emphatically duplicates
Donne's hope in God's graciousness.

Although several critics have called attention to the explicitly religious
aspects of *Wit*,[20] it has more often been taken as a humanistic brief for
treating patients with kindness. *Wit* has been extensively used in medical
education classes, beginning with stage productions on-site in hospitals
and medical schools. The Wit Film Project, supported by the Robert

Wood Johnson Foundation, offers training materials to medical schools and other medical training organizations who wish to incorporate it into their curricula. According to the project's website, the goal of the program is "to enhance trainee education in the humanistic elements of end-of-life care."[21] The project directors suggest that the program will be especially beneficial in "helping third- and fourth-year trainees think about how to successfully integrate humanistic behaviors into their professional persona." From using the film in undergraduate medical ethics courses, I know that it is an effective means for introducing inherent contradictions in the practice of modern scientific medicine. However, if the more directly theological issues of sin and grace are bracketed from our reception of play or film, the loss is greater than that of missing a few seventeenth-century allusions. One of the chief benefits of watching the work in either medium is the challenge it issues to the cultural bifurcation which has been passed on to us. And the terms of that challenge for Donne and for Edson are religious. One who sets out to "integrate humanistic behaviors" into her "professional persona" has not really learned Vivian's existential lesson.

Endnotes

1 Donne's death was first described in print by his contemporary Izaak Walton in *The Lives of John Donne, Sir Henry Wotton, Richard Hooker, & Robert Sanderson* (1670, repr. 1927).

2 Parenthetical page numbers for *Wit* refer to Margaret Edson, *Wit* (New York: Faber and Faber, 1999). When referring specifically to the film, I will use the chapter titles listed on the DVD version.

3 March 3, 2000.

4 Elizabeth Klaver makes this observation in "A Mind-Body-Flesh Problem: The Case of Margaret Edson's *Wit*," *Contemporary Literature* 45.4 (2004), 676. Future page references to her article will appear parenthetically in the text.

5 The audience guide for production of *Wit* staged at the University of Wisconsin-Madison in 2000, written by Carol Cohen, is valuable classroom resource. I cite it here for background on Edson. At this writing (January 7, 2011) it is available at http://faculty.smu.edu/tmayo/witguide.htm. In the text I will refer to this source as "Cohen."

6 Audio and text versions of Edson's 2008 commencement address are available at www.smith.edu/collegerelations/com2008.

7 Edson makes this remark in the HBO press release that accompanied the promotion of the film on February 12, 2001. It is available at www.timewarner.com/corp/newsroom.

8 Martha Greene Eads, "Unwitting Redemption in Margaret Edson's Wit," *Christianity and Literature* 51.2 (2002), 241–254. The quotation is from

Adrienne Martini, "The Playwright in Spite of Herself," *American Theater* 16.8 (October 1999), 22.

9 Betty Carter, "John Donne Meets *The Runaway Bunny*," *Books and Culture* (Sept/Oct 1999), 24–26. Future page references to this interview will appear parenthetically in the text.

10 Sian Kirwan, 2001 Edinburgh International Film Festival interview with Emma Thompson. Available at www.bbc.co.uk/films/2001/08/30/emma_thompson_ wit 2001_interview.shtml.

11 Ibid.

12 James Mottram, 2001 Edinburgh International Film Festival interview with Mike Nichols. Available at www.bbc.co.uk/films/2001/08/20/mike_nichols_ interview.shtml.

13 See her interview with Jane Cornwell in *The Australian*, October 15, 2008. Available at www.theaustralian.com.au/news/arts/acting-on-outspoken-beliefs/story.

14 These are the English words used in Louise and Aylmer Maude's translation of 1935.

15 John D. Sykes, Jr., "Wit, Pride, and the Resurrection: Margaret Edson's Play and John Donne's Poetry," *Renascence* 55.2 (2003), 163–174.

16 Klaver, "A Mind-Body-Flesh Problem," 676.

17 Among Pauline passages, 1 Thess. 4:13–18 and 1 Cor. 15:12–28 have been especially formative. Of the early Church Fathers, Clement of Rome, Justin Martyr, and Irenaeus all make forceful statements within the first two centuries of the Common Era, and acceptance of the doctrine has been widespread among Christians ever since.

18 Iago Galdston, *The Social and Historical Foundations of Modern Medicine* (New York: Brunner/Mazel, 1981), 32. I am indebted to Joel James Shuman for pointing me to Galdston in his excellent book, *The Body of Compassion: Ethics, Medicine, and the Church* (Eugene, OR: Wipf and Stock, 1999). See his chapter, "Before Bioethics: The Moral Paradox of Modern Medicine."

19 Klaver, "A Mind-Body-Flesh Problem," 675–677.

20 I have mentioned articles by Eads, Frontain, and Sykes. To differing degrees, the following articles also explore these themes: Shlomith Rimmon-Kenan, "Margaret Edson's Wit and the Art of Analogy," *Style* 40.4 (Winter 2006), 346–356, and Chad Wriglesworth, "Theological Humanism as Living Praxis: Reading Surfaces and Depth in Margaret Edson's Wit," *Literature and Theology* 22.2 (June 2008), 210–222.

21 The website for the Wit Film Project is available at www.growthhouse.org/ witfilmproject. The following quotations are from "Goals of the Project" and "Program Materials" sections of the site, respectively.

CHAPTER 15

Theatrical, cinematic, and domestic epic in Tony Kushner's Angels in America

Tison Pugh

Few cinematic adaptations of theatrical plays boast such an impressive pedigree as Mike Nichols's production of Tony Kushner's *Angels in America*.[1] Nichols's oeuvre stands as one of the most respected in Hollywood history, and many of his greatest successes have resulted from theatrical adaptations, foremost his translation of Edward Albee's *Who's Afraid of Virginia Woolf?* (1966), but also his re-creations of Neil Simon's *Biloxi Blues* (1988), Jean Poiret's *Le Cage aux folles* as *The Birdcage* (1996), and Margaret Edson's *Wit* (2001). Kushner himself wrote the screenplay for this adaptation of his play and closely adhered to his award-winning text.[2] The cast featured actors celebrated not merely for their celebrity but for their pitch-perfect dramatic skills, including Al Pacino as Roy Cohn, Meryl Streep as Hannah Pitt, Emma Thompson as the Angel, and Mary-Louise Parker as Harper Pitt. An impressive array of up-and-comers – including Justin Kirk as Prior Walter, Ben Shenkman as Louis Ironson, and Patrick Wilson as Joe Pitt – more than held their own when paired with these heavyweights. Jeffrey Wright reprised his Tony-winning role as Belize for the film version, again capturing critical acclaim – as well as a Golden Globe and an Emmy – for his performance. The ancillary components of the film, including its set design, costume design, and musical score, contribute effectively to the film's coherence, as they each capture respective components of the play's storyline.[3] The critical acclaim among the popular press for the film version of *Angels in America* was virtually unanimous: "a masterpiece," one that is "hauntingly, unshakably memorable, and ranks among television's finest recent achievements," extols David Bianculli;[4] "*Angels in America* calls for celebration," declares Nancy Franklin.[5]

No matter how faithfully a cinematic adaptation adheres to the words and spirit of its theatrical forebear, the material cannot help but be changed in its transition from live theatrical experience to filmed dramatic event. Change is unavoidable under such circumstances, especially due to the collaborative nature of film production, in which many hands, including those of the director, screenwriter, editor, cinematographer, actors, costume designers, set designers, and myriad others, influence the film's final incarnation. Whether such changes are to be celebrated or lamented, whether they improve on or detract from their source material, they inexorably alter the story facing this metamorphosis of medium. Appropriately enough, *Angels in America* addresses the meaning of change and a corresponding desire for stasis, which, for the purposes of this essay, metaphorically capture the challenges of adaptation. In Harper Pitt's dialogue with the Mormon Mother, she wonders how people change, and the Mormon Mother answers:

> God splits the skin with a jagged thumbnail from throat to belly and then plunges a huge filthy hand in, he grabs hold of your bloody tubes and they slip to evade his grasp but he squeezes hard, he *insists*, he pulls and pulls till all your innards are yanked out and the pain! We can't even talk about that. And then he stuffs them back, dirty, tangled and torn. It's up to you to do the stitching. (211; italics in original)

Change, dealing with and adapting to change, serves as one of the dominant themes throughout *Angels in America*, no matter the means of its production: as Steven Kruger notes, "*Angels in America* is in many ways a play about conversion ... Indeed, in the course of the play all its characters undergo startling shifts in identity."[6] Change and conversion run thematically throughout *Angels in America*, and the Mormon Mother's words could well apply to the process of adapting a theatrical drama into a film. Replace "God" with "the new director" or "the new screenplay," and the potential messiness and pain of change – no matter the outcome – emerge as an inescapable dynamic in the transition from one artistic medium to another.

　　In respect for the nature and challenge of adaptations, I do not attempt to "grade" the film version of *Angels in America* in relation to its theatrical incarnation in this essay, but to meditate on some of these changes, considering how they create a different but no less epic story of love and loss during the early years of the AIDS epidemic. Theatrical elements must be transformed into cinematic ones, but cinema cannot always resonate with the feel and experience of live theatre. Concomitantly, films are liberated from many of the physical restraints of theatre, and in the case of *Angels in America* the tension between these separate media results in two works that, united yet separate, tell the same story. Despite the play's theatrical roots, Kushner eschews privileging staged productions over the cinematic interpretation:

Figure 15.1 A gay Republican? The closeted Joe Pitt (Patrick Wilson) introduces himself to Louis Ironson (Ben Shenkman), the man he is going to love, in a men's room. (frame enlargement)

> There are some things about the way that the Angel [Emma Thompson] is treated in the film that have a kind of a wildness and a power that would be difficult to do on stage … But comparing the film and the play is something I don't like to do. I certainly would never say that one is better than the other. There'd be no profit for me in that, and honestly, I don't feel that way.[7]

To rely on a well-worn cliché, comparing film to theatre represents an aesthetic version of comparing apples to oranges: since both are fruits, such analyses can be offered, but the differences overwhelm the similarities and, in many ways, boil down to a matter of personal taste. Kushner also declares, "I think that because it's for television, it was an easier adaptation than it might have been for a cinematic release because television, for some reason, feels more like theater … It's a framed box so it felt like an easier move."[8] Kushner points to the closer relationship between theatre and television as facilitating the transition from page to stage and then to screen, yet in many ways, the film version of *Angels in America* transcends television and achieves a more cinematic aesthetic than a standard mini-series, thus negating his attempt to lessen the inherent difficulties of adaptation. Part of this effect is due to the high wattage of such film stars as Pacino, Streep, and Thompson, but it also involves the immense scope

Figure 15.2 Roy Cohn (Al Pacino) says he's dying of cancer, but AIDS is not
stopping him from pursuing legal intrigues, here attempting to seduce
the offscreen Joe Pitt (Patrick Wilson). (frame enlargement)

of the play itself. Adapting this play to a filmed medium – with big stars
and an epic story – metamorphoses the more personal experience of an
evening at the theatre into a cinematic event (even if this event was then
experienced in the comfort of one's home).

As a play turned into a film shown on television, *Angels in America*
hybridizes these distinct artistic media into an intriguing whole, and Justin
Kirk describes the chief accomplishment of the film version arising in its
hybridity as theatrical cinema. He recalls the amorphousness of the project
in its beginning stages, when no one was sure exactly how the transformation from theatre to film would be effected:

> We weren't sure how it would all work, and so we went about doing our
> business. When we started, Nichols said, "I don't know if this is going to
> work." *Angels in America* is unquestionably a play, a very theatrical play. For
> the most part we're shooting the play and adhering very closely to its script,
> yet the success of the movie depends upon it becoming a whole new animal,
> in that it must be cinematic and yet unquestionably theatrical. You essen-
> tially could imagine the wires behind the angels in the film, which made for
> a weird hybrid of theater and film that was a great way to go. It was a line
> that was deftly trod.[9]

In referring to the "wires behind the angels," Kirk alludes to Kushner's
stage instructions for *Angels in America*, a play conceived of as a meta-

theatrical experience that did not attempt to cloak its very theatricality. Rather, Kushner endorses the theatricality of his play as one of its defining features:

> The play benefits from a pared-down style of presentation, with minimal scenery and scene shifts done rapidly (no blackouts!), employing the cast as well as stagehands – which makes for an actor-driven event, as this must be. The moments of magic – the appearance and disappearance of Mr. Lies and the ghosts, the Book hallucination, and the ending – are to be fully realized, as bits of wonderful *theatrical* illusion – which means it's OK if the wires show, and maybe it's good that they do, but the magic should at the same time be thoroughly amazing. (xi, cf. 141; italics in original)

The tension between a "pared-down" theatrical presentation and the necessity of transforming the play into cinema – in which the "wires showing" would typically testify to poor craftsmanship rather than aesthetic success – is nicely modulated in Kirk's analysis of the film's accomplishment: one of technical mastery yet one which invites the audience to imagine the "wires" behind the illusion, in effect, to experience the film as intimately as theatre.

If some theatrical productions ask their audiences to acknowledge yet ignore the wires, to suspend disbelief and succumb willingly to the artificiality of the dramatic event, cinema's tendency is to mask its illusions through special effects designed to camouflage its fictionality. For example, when Prior climbs the "ladder of even brighter, purer light, reaching up into infinity" (251) in the theatre, infinity – no matter how extravagant the production – is circumscribed by the physical limits of the stage. This moment is transformed in the film, as Prior ascends a flaming ladder against a nighttime backdrop that suggests the vast expanse of space, heaven, and, indeed, eternity. In such moments, the film plays with the tension between Kushner's call for a "pared-down style of presentation" and effects of cinematic wonder. Its opening shots strike a decidedly expansive tone, as the camera soars from the Golden Gate Bridge in San Francisco to the Gateway Arch in St. Louis, finally alighting at the Bethesda Fountain in Central Park. In this respect, what is lost in terms of a pared-down presentation is gained in the addition of virtually a new character to the play: New York City, which hums with an urgent rhythm that painfully illuminates Prior's frantic quest for life in a city that seems only too capable of continuing without him. Nichols embraces and innovates upon the theatricality of the story in such moves, while nonetheless adorning it with cinematic motifs, such as Prior's dream sequence, in which the character enters a setting inspired by Jean Cocteau's *La Belle et la bête* (1946). Indeed, one can see elements of Nichols's other films in *Angels in America* as well, such as the opulent drag queen funeral featuring Barbra Streisand look-alikes, a nun on roller skates, and a New Orleans jazz processional, all of which appear directly inspired by *The Birdcage*. Also, scenes of intense personal dialogue between estranged lovers are a recurring motif in Nichols's films, most famously in *Who's Afraid of Virginia Woolf? Angels in America* features particularly poignant and searing encounters – such as the fraught moments between Prior and Louis, as well as between Joe and Harper – that are as vivid as the sparring between Albee's George and Martha.

In adapting a play into a film, actors face the additional challenge of transforming roles that have been played before, and in regard to *Angels in America*, Justin Kirk was confronted with a role that Stephen Spinella played on Broadway with iconic and Tony-winning success. Kirk describes the challenges of adapting the role of Prior Walter to a new medium:

> I saw *Millennium Approaches* with Stephen Spinella as Prior, and I worked with Stephen in *Love, Valor, Compassion*, and so I felt the weight of his indelible performance. As much I appreciated his wonderful performance, I pretty much needed to forget it so I could approach the role from scratch. The pressure of the legend of the play – that was the main burden to get out from under. On the other hand, plenty of people were not familiar with it, with what came before. And so I approached it as a regular job, proceeded normally, spent a substantial amount of time – not rehearsals per se – but a couple of months of hanging out with Nichols and the other actors. [Ben] Shenkman and I worked on the scenes, and, by the time we got going, we had been addressing things and developing a rapport with our roles and each other.

Kirk's Prior, especially hypnotic when he assumes his role as a prophet, strikes a stance of somber and incipient disaster but also of a passion for living, a strikingly effective incarnation of a character forced to live on the precipice of extinction. Although mightily praised for his performance, garnering a Golden Globe Nomination for Outstanding Supporting Actor in a Miniseries or Movie, some sniped at his portrayal of Prior: "in Kirk's hands [Prior is] classy, not sassy," carped Nancy Franklin.[10] Franklin's criticism, however, is predicated upon two assumptions: that "sassy" is truer to the character of Prior than "classy," despite the implausibility of sassiness for a character in death's throes, and that Prior, a fictional character, is once and forever sassy. Here the weight of previous perform-ances appears to have impinged upon the fictionality of the character, who is neither sassy nor classy in himself but must be incarnated as such by an actor making new and fresh decisions in order to protect a protean character from the weight of stasis.

In adapting his play into a screenplay, Kushner did not dramatically change the characters' dialogue. The film version adheres meticulously to the play in this regard, and most changes involve cutting lines, which accelerates the film while not detracting from the plot, themes, or characterizations. For example, in Louis's conversation with Rabbi Chemelwitz, in which he attempts to justify his decision to abandon Prior, much of the dialogue is deleted; rather than curtailing an audience's access to his thoughts, these excisions metamorphose Louis into a more appealing character:

LOUIS: Rabbi, what does the Holy Writ say about someone who abandons someone he loves at a time of great need?
RABBI CHEMELWITZ: Why would a person do such a thing?
LOUIS: Because he has to.

> [Maybe because this person's sense of the world, that it will change for the better with struggle, maybe a person who has this neo-Hegelian positivist sense of constant historical progress towards happiness or perfection or something, who feels very powerful because he feels connected to these forces, moving uphill all the time] ... maybe that person can't, um, incorporate sickness into his sense of how things are supposed to go. Maybe vomit ... and sores and disease ... really frighten him, maybe ... he isn't so good with death. (31)[11]

Film viewers receive less insight into Louis's thoughts than playgoers, but what is lost in the translation from play to film is, perhaps, deceptive. Louis's description of himself as basically an optimist, a "neo-Hegelian positivist," makes him sound a bit stuffy and pretentious, which conflicts with his decidedly anti-intellectual lifestyle – smart enough to pursue vocations more challenging than word processing yet uninterested in doing so. The paring down of Louis's musings – as also evident in his discourse on White Straight Male America (96–98), smells as sexually arousing (164), and his regret over leaving Prior (227) – in many ways renders the character less solipsistic and thus more sympathetic. Humanizing Louis presents an incredible challenge for an actor, in that the character must commit morally reprehensible acts in abandoning Prior and immediately seducing Joe, yet he must simultaneously remain somewhat appealing, even likeable, if the audience is to be heartened by the couple's ultimate reunion.

Although Prior's likeability is never much in jeopardy, especially with Kirk's mesmerizing performance, emendations to his cinematic dialogue make him more of an Everyman figure than in the play. In the play's dramatis personae, Prior is described as "liv[ing] very modestly but with great style off a small trust fund," and his esteemed ancestry is an essential part of his character, notably in regard to the appearance of the previous Prior Walter. In the film version, however, much of the aristophilia surrounding the character – for instance, the story about his ancestor, the sea captain who went down with his ship (47–48), and his comparison of himself to La Reine Mathilde, who patiently stitched the Bayeux Tapestry while awaiting William the Conqueror's return (57–58) – is jettisoned.[12] Some of Prior's more flamboyant traits, remnants of his drag-queen past, are dropped as well, including his tendency to sprinkle French phrases in his conversation: "Oh, not this drug, [ce n'est pas pour le joyeux noël et la bonne année,] this drug she is serious poisonous chemistry [ma pauvre bichette]" (66). Kirk's performance, teetering harrowingly between the lyric and the apocalyptic, provides ballast to the intertwining storylines, and these changes assist in infusing a resigned yet hearty gravitas to his character.

Somewhat surprisingly, for a play that tackles issues of gender, sexuality, disease, and dying, the film version is bowdlerized in some small yet telling ways. HBO's reputation for cutting-edge drama aside, financial concerns intrinsically affect decisions on how to avoid alienating audiences and thus win wider market share. Notably, Act 1 of *Perestroika* is entitled "Spooj," but the film's corresponding Chapter 4 is renamed "Stop Moving."[13] Furthermore, most of the following dialogue between Prior and Belize over Prior's ejaculation is cut from the film:

PRIOR: [I am drenched in spooj.]
BELIZE: [Spooj?]
PRIOR: [Cum. Jiz. Ejaculate.] I've had a wet dream.
BELIZE: [Well about time. Miss Thing has been abstemious. She has stored up beaucoup de spooj.] (153)

Kushner replaces Belize's response to Prior's announcement of his nocturnal emission with the titillating but less graphic question: "The Calvin Klein underwear man?" Such prudery is somewhat surprising, especially given the lines that remain in the film. Ejaculate is not sufficiently sentient to take umbrage by being referred to as "spooj," but Roy's nasty diatribes, such as referring to Belize as a "butterfingers spook faggot nurse" (160), remain uncensored. One can only surmise why "spooj" was excised from the film, but it seems likely that, in moving the play from the intellectual and artistic playground of Broadway in New York City to the homes of America's heartland, certain words and exchanges were deemed inappropriate.

In the play, the actors assume a variety of roles beyond their primary parts. For example, the actor playing Hannah doubles as Rabbi Isidor Chemelwitz, Henry (Roy's doctor), Ethel Rosenberg, Aleksii Antedilluvianovich Prelapsarianov, and the Angel Asiatica.[14] The film maintains much of the multiple role-playing, and with actors as accomplished as Streep and Thompson, one of its real pleasures arises in observing their seamless transitions from character to character, even though at times the transitions suffer from overzealous applications of makeup and prosthetics. Streep's transformation into the aged rabbi Chemelwitz relies too heavily on cinematic effect rather than simply utilizing her amazing ability to metamorphose herself, in that the camera allows viewers to see too clearly the fake skin. This flaw renders the illusion a bit off-putting, which lighting would obscure in a darkened theatre. Such a quibble, however, does not meaningfully detract from the emotional power generated by these multiple performances, especially regarding the ways in which they generate deeper thematic meanings in the story. Justin Kirk maintains the doubling inherent in his roles by also tackling the part of the Man in the Park, with whom Louis seeks risky sex. By playing both Louis's lover dying of AIDS and the man who might casually infect him, Kirk maintains the ironic balance of the doublings, as well as the overlapping storylines of the gay male characters.

In regard to Hannah Pitt and her doublings, she loses her son Joe to Roy Cohn, as the corrupt lawyer assumes the role of paternal mentor to his protégé, and Joe ignores her upon her relocation to New York City. Hannah thus represents a motherless son, but in the scene in which Ethel Rosenberg sings to Roy, as he tricks her into acting as if she were his mother, the familial dynamics revolving around Hannah/Ethel are ultimately uplifting: the combined characters' maternal tendencies triumph over their initial distaste for Joe's homosexuality (in regard to Hannah) and Roy's loathsome humanity (in regard to Ethel). This parallelism is key to the development of the themes of change, acceptance, forgiveness, and redemption, with Hannah overcoming her disgust with homosexuality by accepting Prior as a replacement for her lost son and Ethel moving beyond Roy. The ways in which vastly disparate storylines unite through doubling characters allow *Angels in America* to transcend the potential parochialism of discrete narratives that might otherwise fail to unite into a symbiotic whole. To achieve the play's epic potential, in which all events assume magnified and magnificent meaning, the doubling of roles by certain actors catalyzes its thematic progressions.

But some of the thematic power of doubling is lost in the film through decisions for certain actors not to perform roles allotted them in the play.

As Hannah, Streep should also play Roy's doctor Henry, thus interweaving the storylines of the alienated mother and the corrupt lawyer even more, but this part is played by James Cromwell. Cromwell's strong and sympathetic performance, which he plays to a fine wrinkle in his confrontations both with Roy (48–52) and Belize (154–156), gives surprising poignancy to a bit part, but Hannah/Ethel loses an additional orbital point around the ailing attorney. Roy is despised by so many of the characters, yet they mostly tend to him during his diseased distress, and this surprising mix of pathos and vitriol is escalated through Hannah/Ethel's joint relationship with him. Such a heady brew of conflicting desires to despise and to nurture, embodied as it is in one actor's adopting of complementary roles, benefits from the additional gendered overlapping of Henry with Hannah and Ethel.

In a similar instance of recasting, Brian Markinson takes the role of Martin Heller, a part that Kushner describes as "A Reagan Administration Justice Department flackman, played by the actor playing Harper" (x). Like Cromwell, Markinson makes the most of a small role, striking an intriguing mix of sycophantic toadying and Mephistophelean seduction in his performance, but, again, the thematic overlapping of storylines is lost. As Harper Pitt, Mary-Louise Parker should play this role, and her performance would thus inject another needed instance of gender reversal within the play. With Harper doubling Heller, the emotional core of the scene takes on surprising tensions: Heller attempts to lure Joe away from New York to Washington, DC, yet Harper, as Joe acknowledges, is not psychologically strong enough for such a transition. Again, though, it is men who seduce Joe as he struggles with his homosexuality, and thus Harper/Heller (with their thematic divide accentuated through the onomastic play between the heavenly Harper and the hellish Heller) should unite into one as they disorient Joe from his prior sense of masculinity.

As a last example of the lost doubling in the film version of *Angels in America*, Prior 1, who should be played by Patrick Wilson as Joe, is acted by Michael Gambon, and Prior 2, who should be played by Al Pacino as Roy, is acted by Simon Callow. Again, the thematic meaning of doubling is paramount in this scene: if anything, Joe and Roy are Prior's enemies in the play, since Joe pairs off with Prior's lover Louis; and Roy, ignoring Belize's pleas to share, hoards the AZT that might save Prior's life. Here, though, despite the muted homophobia of Prior 1 (with his comment, "Hah. Now I see why he's got no children. He's a sodomite," to which Prior 2 counters, "Oh be quiet, you medieval gnome, and let them dance" [120]), the sexual and amatory connections among these gay men are weakened. *Angels in America* continually asks readers to consider the meaning of lovers, families, and friends, and the doubling of characters imbues these issues with less certain answers due to the difficulty of pinning down the nebulous and shifting cores of these multiple and conflicting roles.

Beyond these lost doublings, the cinematic *Angels in America* cuts certain theatrical scenes altogether, but, for the most part, these excised scenes do not detract from its overall cohesion. Indeed, Kushner allows that "Act Five Scenes 6 and 9, as noted in the text, can be cut" from the play (143), and these scenes – the first depicting Prior's meeting with Rabbi Chemelwitz and Louis's grandmother Sarah Ironson, who play cards in heaven (267–269), the second depicting Roy in hell (274) – are duly removed from the film. In the scene with Prior, Sarah Ironson, and Rabbi Chemelwitz, the Rabbi describes the pleasures of the afterlife: "So from what comes the pleasures of Paradise? *Indeterminacy!*" (268, italics in original), a celebration of chance and change in a play dedicated to exploring their at times painful interrelationship. The scene depicting Roy in hell, in which he determines to represent God in the incipient lawsuit over His abandonment of creation, is amusing, but does not contribute much to a deeper understanding of the character. Where else would Roy go in the afterlife, but to hell?[15] Given Kushner's own sense of the marginal nature of these scenes to his project, their absence in the film strengthens rather than weakens it.

Other scenes, including those not marked by Kushner as suitable for excision, are deleted from the film as well. Scene 1 of *Perestroika*, featuring Aleksii Antedilluvianovich Prelapsarianov, the World's Oldest Living Bol-shevik, is cut entirely (147–149), but even in the play, this scene is somewhat anomalous and uninteresting. In Aleksii's questions – "Are we doomed? ... Will the Past release us? ... Can we Change? In Time?" (247), Kushner points to the dominant themes of his play, but in a somewhat heavy-handed manner. Indeed, Kushner acknowledges the threat of pretentiousness creeping into his work – "When I started to write these plays, I wanted to attempt something of ambition and size even if that meant I might be accused of straying too close to ambition's ugly twin, pretentiousness" (284). With the obvious allegorical qualities of Aleksii's surnames and the scene's tendentious links to the overarching story, the play could lose this scene, too, with no real detriment to its thematic core. Another segment removed in its entirety is Scene 10 of *Millennium Approaches*, in which Sister Ella Chapter encourages Hannah to stay in Salt Lake City:

This is the home of saints, the godliest place on earth, they say, and I think
they're right. That mean there's no evil here? No. Evil's everywhere. Sin's
everywhere. But this . . . is the spring of sweet water in the desert, the desert
flower. Every step a believer takes away from here is a step fraught with
peril. I fear for you, Hannah Pitt, because you are my friend. Stay put. This
is the right home of saints. (89)

In expressing her desire for stasis, Sister Chapter complements Prior's
fear of change, as evident in his desire to live and his subsequent journey
to heaven carrying "the Book of the Anti-Migratory Epistle" (252). These
characters could not be more dissimilar in background, but their shared
yearning for inertia to stop the world from changing highlights the
tremendous fears and apocalyptic times they both face. The removal of
this scene does not immeasurably scar the cinematic version of *Angels
in America*, yet much of the story's power arises in the shared values
of radically different characters, and thus the loss of Sister Ella Chapter
is somewhat regrettable, but certainly not fatal to the film's aesthetic
vision.[16]

Of the interpersonal relationships established throughout the interweaving storylines, Harper's friendship with Prior suffers most in its translation
from play to screen, as, for the most part, it is jettisoned. Their shared
dialogue in the Diorama Room of the Mormon Visitor's Center is cut,
with the scene being entirely recast between Harper and Hannah. Harper
and Prior's scene together in heaven (Scene 2 of Act 5, "Heaven, I'm in
Heaven") is removed as well. Both of these characters suffer the loss of
their partners, with Joe leaving her to explore his homosexuality and Louis
leaving him to escape the grimness of mortality, and these two forsaken
characters must interact for their stories to unite, as well as for Harper to
pronounce the link between loss and change: "I've finally found the secret
of all that Mormon energy. Devastation. That's what makes people
migrate, build things. Heartbroken people do it, people who have lost
love" (253). The cinematic *Angels in America* runs over six hours, and so it
is apparent that the complexities of some storylines needed to be stream-
lined, yet such poignant connections between Harper and Prior would
build a deeper emotional core to the narrative, in that, in their meeting,
the characters who suffer the most loss seek to understand that loss
through their interactions with each other. To reiterate an earlier point,
however, these changes and transitions that mark *Angels in America*'s
movement from theatre to film do not detract from its own aesthetic
accomplishments, and the many awards garnered by the film, including a
Golden Globe and an Emmy for Best Miniseries, are richly deserved.

Figure 15.3 Feverish and reacting to anti-immune suppressant drugs,
Prior Walter (Justin Kirk) experiences visions of an enraged
Angel America (Emma Thompson). (frame enlargement)

And so in *Angels in America* we see an epic theatrical experience transformed into an epic cinematic event, despite the vast dissimilarities between
these forms. In responding to the play and the film, critics casually note
their epic qualities. Nancy Franklin calls *Angels in America* a "fearless,
ambitious work," in that "it took in, and took on, the Reagan years ...
American history, the AIDS plague, sexuality, love, death, religion, and the
meaning of community. In its rigor, it made no distinction between the
personal and the political, but it was open-minded and open-hearted, epic
not just in its intent but in its effect on audiences."[17] John Coulbourn refers
to the play's epic qualities as well, suggesting that those who adapted "Tony
Kushner's epic play" were "clearly in the throes of divine inspiration,"[18] and
Robert Bianco concurs, "Beautiful and profane, intimate and epic, *Angels*
overflows with comedy, drama, violence, sex and death – just like life
itself."[19] One might, however, wonder exactly what these critics mean by
epic, as the term is bandied about with little contextualization. It appears to
denote primarily the impressive length of a play or film rather than one
attempting to accomplish certain artistic goals or to adhere to the framework of a particular genre. Obviously, *epic* refers to a wider range of
theatrical and cinematic traditions than the term's literary references to
such classics as the *Iliad*, *Aeneid*, and *Beowulf*, yet in many ways, it is unclear
to which epic elements of *Angels in America* these critics are responding.

More specifically, *Angels in America*, in its theatrical productions, is aligned with the epic theatre of Bertolt Brecht: as Art Borreca succinctly observes, "a Brechtian spirit resides at the center of the work."[20] Brecht believed that drama should not attempt to convince the audience of the "truth" of the theatrical illusion but rather to confront them with the alienating possibilities of viewership. Through his famed ideas regarding the *Verfremdungseffekt*, Brecht sought to engage his audience paradoxically through alienation, especially in regard to the episodic nature of the narratives on stage. As Janelle Reinelt argues,

> Epic theater needs to construct the experience of ideological contradiction as the mode of subjectivity it projects for spectators rather than the ideological totalization implied in *supporter, judgment, empathy*, or even *detachment* . . . It is an epic play *if* it does not let spectators off the hook by allowing too much psychological investment in particular characters or too much good feeling of resolution at the end.[21]

Sarah Bryant-Bertail agrees that epic theatre

> called for the relating of stage events to the material situation of the spectators and characters; the theater was to demystify the operation of social, economic, and political forces by showing how certain orders of reality had developed historically and were perpetuated. This demonstration meant arming actors and spectators with disillusionment, not as a helpless state of mind but as an active critical practice.[22]

Kushner discusses Brecht's influences on his writing, remembering that he "wanted to be a playwright and . . . wanted to be a playwright very much like Brecht"[23] and noting points of similarity and dissimilarity between *Angels in America* and Brecht's work: "The principal subject of [Brecht's *Lehrstücke*] plays was the painful dismantling, as a revolutionary necessity, of the individual ego. This dismantling is often figured, in the learning plays, as death" (285). Certainly, the many characters of *Angels in America* undergo a dismantling of their individual egos, but death's role in the process is ambiguous in Kushner's play: Roy dies, and his death metaphorically symbolizes thousands of other AIDS deaths, yet Prior lives. Kushner's relationship to Brecht's epic theatre resists easy categorization, as Martin Harries argues: "It would, however, be a mistake to see *Angels in America* as sheer demolition of the Brechtian tradition of demystification."[24] *Angels in America*, as theatre, invokes Brecht's epic theatre while nonetheless expanding its parameters by engaging the emotionality of viewership.

In regard to its cinematic denotations, *epic* seems to have mostly lost any meaning except in regard to a film's length and extravagance: an epic, in popular parlance, is "a picture that's real long and has lots of things going on."[25] Running over six hours, the film version of *Angels in America* certainly fits this simple definition, but beyond their reliance on length, cinematic epics often foreground an opulence of story, set design, and cinematography by gilding their historical or literary foundations, as Derek Elley points out: "Epic cinema is not necessarily reliant upon the artificiality of the studio, but the vast majority of works happily capitalise upon this quality, which provides the all-important distancing from reality that distinguishes epic from historical narrative."[26] Elley highlights the artificiality of many Hollywood epics, and for Vivian Sobchack, extravagance suffuses such films, such that epic "defines History as occurring to music – pervasive symphonic music underscoring every moment by overscoring it. And it evokes spectacular, fantastic costumes – particularly gold lamé ones with underwire bras."[27] Hollywood's epics exploit the possibilities of big productions to stun their audiences with extravagance, frequently resulting in films that impress visually yet disappoint emotionally.

From these conflicting views of theatrical and cinematic epics, it is apparent that the Marxist spirit inherent in Brecht's theatrical epic conflicts with the capitalist excess of Hollywood's epics. Consequently, to describe *Angels in America* as an epic blurs these distinct terminologies, especially since these separate varieties of epic intermingle in the film by maintaining the play's focus on the ideological construction of individuals in history while nonetheless imbuing the story with cinematically epic touches, including big stars and lavish effects. It is an ideologically confused combination, but nonetheless an aesthetically satisfying one, I would argue, through its elevation of domestic narrative to the status of epic. For *Angels in America*, despite its vastness of scope, is at heart the story of two couples on the edge of dissolution, and finding the epic potential inherent in domestic drama radically shifts the foundations of epic in its many incarnations. The success of *Angels in America*, in both its theatrical and cinematic incarnations, arises in its celebration of the domestic epic, one in which the small events of home life – lovers breaking up, a mother's emotionally fraught relationship with her son – are coupled with issues of vast historical and cosmic importance.

At the close of *Angels in America*, Prior declares, "The world only spins forward" (280), and this observation applies to narrative and narrative forms as well. Stories move, mutate, and evolve, and the transition from theatre to cinema allows an opportunity to view how stories spin forward into new incarnations. By allowing a space to consider the intermeshing of theatrical and cinematic epics, as well as by modulating the epic's focus on society to domesticity, the film version of *Angels in America* proves itself, in its own way, as innovative and as challenging as its theatrical forebear, which is no small accomplishment for a play that was frequently deemed unfilmable.

Endnotes

1 Citations of the film refer to *Angels in America*, dir. Mike Nichols, perf. Al Pacino, Meryl Streep, and Emma Thompson, 2003, DVD (HBO Video, 2004); citations of the play refer to Tony Kushner, *Angels in America: A Gay Fantasia on National Themes, Part One: Millennium Approaches and Part Two: Perestroika* (New York: Theater Communications Group, 1995). Labeling the filmed version of *Angels in America* a cinematic work involves a slight misidentification in terms of genre, as the production was not released in theaters but debuted as a television miniseries on Home Box Office (HBO).

2 The critical acclaim bestowed upon *Angels in America*, as measured in dramatic awards, ranks it as one of the most honored American plays of the twentieth century. Among many other prizes, it won Tony Awards for Best Play of 1993 and 1994 and the 1993 Pulitzer Prize for Drama. See Kushner, *Angels in America*, 291–292, for a more complete list of the play's honors.

3 For example, the musical score reaches lyric heights of originality while adhering to the thematics of the play. Thomas Newman's compositions primarily feature the oboe, an instrument that plaintively vocalizes the longings expressed by the characters, as described by Mr. Lies: "The oboe: official instrument of the International Order of Travel Agents. If the duck was a songbird it would sing like this. Nasal, desolate, the call of migratory things" (149).

4 David Bianculli, "Angels Looks Heavenly," *Daily News* (New York), Wednesday, December 3, 2003, Television: 85.

5 Nancy Franklin, "America, Lost and Found: Mike Nichols and an All-Star Cast Tackle Tony Kushner's Masterwork," *New Yorker*, December 8, 2003, 125.

6 Steven Kruger, "Identity and Conversion in *Angels in America*," in *Approaching the Millennium: Essays on* Angels in America, ed. Deborah Geis and Steven Kruger (Ann Arbor: University of Michigan Press, 1997), 155–156.

7 Tony Kushner, quoted in Gord McLaughlin, "Character-Based Politics: *Angels in America* Miniseries Exposes a New Generation to Kushner's Prize Play," *National Post* (Canada), Wednesday, December 31, 2003, Arts and Life: AL03.

8 Tony Kushner, quoted in Stuart Levine, "*Angels* Fly from Legit to HBO as Six-Hour Telepic," *Daily Variety*, Friday, September 12, 2003, Special Section: A 16.

9 Phone interview with Justin Kirk, February 19, 2008. Subsequent quotations from Kirk refer to this interview.

10 Franklin, "America, Lost and Found," 125.

11 In this and subsequent quotations of *Angels in America*, the bracketed passages indicate lines from the play omitted in the film.

12 Allen Frantzen suggests that the Bayeux Tapestry symbolizes "the Anglo-Saxons as a monolithic, triumphant culture that has reached a symbolic end point in Prior's blood" ("Prior to the Normans: The Anglo-Saxons in *Angels in America*," *Approaching the Millennium*, 140). Of course, Mathilde's weaving of the Bayeux Tapestry is a historical fiction. For a recent examination of the tapestry's historical roots, see George Beech, *Was the Bayeux Tapestry Made in France?: The Case for St. Florent of Saumur* (New York: Palgrave Macmillan, 2005). This moment of historical inaccuracy is similar to Louis's fallacious statement that the Kaddish is in Hebrew, a solecism to which Kushner appends the footnote, "I know, I know, it's not Hebrew, it's Aramaic, but for the sake of the joke . . ." (256). In these instances, historical accuracy was worthily sacrificed for artistic freedom and dramatic effect.

13 The five acts of the play *Perestroika* – "Spooj," "The Epistle," "Borborygmi (The Squirming Facts Exceed the Squamous Mind)," "John Brown's Body," and "Heaven, I'm in Heaven" – are reconfigured into three chapters in the film: "Stop Moving," "Beyond Nelly," and "Heaven, I'm in Heaven."

14 For an overview of the various roles adopted by the play's main characters, see "The Characters" and "Other Characters in Part One" for *Millennium Approaches* (ix–x) and "The Characters" and "Other Characters in Part Two" for *Perestroika* (137–139).

15 Roy's exact location in the afterlife is at least somewhat ambiguous in Kushner's text, as it is described thusly: "Roy, in Heaven, or Hell or Purgatory – standing waist-deep in a smoldering pit, facing a great flaming Aleph, which bathes him and the whole theater in a volcanic, pulsating red light. Underneath, a basso-profundo roar, like a thousand Bessemer furnaces going at once, deep underground" (274).

16 Justin Kirk reports that this scene was shot but cut from the film.

17 Franklin, "America, Lost and Found," 125.

18 John Coulbourn, "Winged Victory: Epic Broadway Play *Angels in America* Becomes Triumphant Television Event," *Toronto Sun*, Saturday, January 10, 2004: Entertainment, 31.

19 Robert Bianco, "Believe in HBO's *Angels*," *USA Today*, Friday, December 5, 2003: Life, 13E.

20 Art Borreca, "'Dramaturging' the Dialectic: Brecht, Benjamin, and Declan Donellan's Production of *Angels in America*," in *Approaching the Millennium*, 245.

21 Janelle Reinelt, "Notes on *Angels in America* as American Epic Theater," in *Approaching the Millennium*, 236; her italics.

22 Sarah Bryant-Bertail, *Space and Time in Epic Theater: The Brechtian Legacy* (Suffolk, UK: Camden House, 2000), 2–3.

23 Carol Weber, "I Want to Go Back to Brecht," in *Tony Kushner in Conversation*, ed. Robert Vorlicky (Ann Arbor: University of Michigan Press, 1998), 108.

24 Martin Harries, "Flying the Angel of History," in *Approaching the Millennium*, 186.

25 Dixon to Mildred in *In a Lonely Place* (1950), quoted in Derek Elley, *The Epic Film: Myth and History* (London: Routledge & Kegan Paul, 1984), 13.

26 Ibid., 16.

27 Vivian Sobchack, "'Surge and Splendor': A Phenomenology of the Hollywood Historical Epic," in *Film Genre Reader II*, ed. Barry Keith Grant (Austin: University of Texas Press, 1995), 281.

Filmography

A RAISIN IN THE SUN (1961)

Director	Daniel Petrie
Producer	David Susskind and others for Columbia Pictures
Script	Lorraine Hansberry from her play
Cinematography	Charles Lawton, Jr.
Principal Actors	Sidney Poitier (Walter Lee), Ruby Dee (Ruth), Claudia McNeil (Mrs. Younger), Diana Sands (Beneatha), John Fiedler (Mr. Lindner), Ivan Dixon (Asagai), Stephen Perry (Travis)

A STREETCAR NAMED DESIRE (1951)

Director	Elia Kazan
Producer	Charles K. Feldman for Warner Brothers
Script	Tennessee Williams and Oscar Saul
Cinematography	Harry Stradling
Principal Actors	Vivien Leigh (Blanche), Marlon Brando (Stanley), Kim Hunter (Stella), Karl Malden (Mitch)

ANGELS IN AMERICA (2003)

Director	Mike Nichols
Producer	Cary Brokaw and others for Home Box Office
Script	Tony Kushner
Cinematography	Stephen Goldblatt
Principal Actors	Al Pacino (Roy Cohn), Justin Kirk (Prior Walter), Ben Shenkman (Louis Ironson), Emma Thompson (Nurse Emily/the Angel America), Meryl Streep (Ethel Rosenberg/the Angel Australia)

THE BIG KNIFE (1955)

Director	Robert Aldrich
Producer	Robert Aldrich for MGM
Script	James Poe from the play by Clifford Odets
Cinematography	Ernest Laszlo
Principal Actors	Jack Palance (Charles), Ida Lupino (Marion), Wendell Corey (Smiley), Rod Steiger (Stanley), Everett Sloane (Nat)

THE CHILDREN'S HOUR (1961)

Director	William Wyler
Producer	William Wyler for United Artists
Script	John Michael Hayes from the play by Lillian Hellman
Cinematography	Franz Planer
Principal Actors	Shirley MacLaine (Martha), Audrey Hepburn (Karen), James Garner (Joe), Fay Bainter (Mrs. Tilford), Miriam Hopkins (Lily), Karen Balkin (Mary), Veronica Cartwright (Rosalie)

COME BACK, LITTLE SHEBA (1952)

Director	Daniel Mann
Producer	Hal B. Wallis for Paramount Pictures
Script	Ketti Frings from the play by William Inge
Cinematography	James Wong Howe
Principal Actors	Burt Lancaster (Doc), Shirley Booth (Lola), Terry Moore (Marie), Richard Jaeckel (Turk)

DEAD END (1937)

Director	William Wyler
Producer	Samuel Goldwyn
Script	Lilian Hellman from the play by Sidney Kingsley
Cinematography	Gregg Tolland
Principal Actors	Joel McCrea (Dave), Silvia Sidney (Drina), Humphrey Bogart (Baby Face Martin), Wendy Barrie (Kay), Claire Trevor (Francie)

DEATH OF A SALESMAN (1951)

Director	László Benedek
Producer	Stanley Kramer for Columbia Pictures

Script	Stanley Roberts from the play by Arthur Miller
Cinematography	Franz Planer
Principal Actors	Fredric March (Willy), Mildred Dunnock (Linda), Kevin McCarthy (Biff), Cameron Mitchell (Happy), Royal Beal (Ben)

FOOL FOR LOVE (1985)

Director	Robert Altman
Producer	Yoran Globus and Menahem Golan for the Cannon Group
Script	Sam Shepard from his play
Cinematography	Pierre Mignot
Principal Actors	Sam Shepard (Eddie), Kim Basinger (May), Harry Dean Stanton (Old Man), Randy Quaid (Martin)

HURLYBURLY (1998)

Director	Anthony Drazan
Producer	Anthony Drazan for Fine Line Pictures
Script	David Rabe from his play
Cinematography	Changwei Gu
Principal Actors	Sean Penn (Eddie), Kevin Spacey (Mickey), Robin Wright Penn (Darlene), Chazz Palminteri (Phil), Gary Shandling (Artie)

LONG DAY'S JOURNEY INTO NIGHT (1962)

Director	Sidney Lumet
Producer	Ely Landau and Joseph E. Levine for Embassy Pictures
Script	Eugene O'Neill
Cinematography	Boris Kaufman
Principal Actors	Jason Robards, Jr. (James, Jr.), Katharine Hepburn (Mary), Ralph Richardson (James, Sr.), Dean Stockwell (Edmund)

OLEANNA (1994)

Director	David Mamet
Producer	Sarah Green and Patricia Wolff for Samuel Goldwyn Company
Script	David Mamet from his play
Cinematography	Andrzej Sekula

Principal Actors   William H. Macy (John), Debra Eisenstadt (Debra)

OUR TOWN (1940)

Director	Sam Wood
Producer	Saul Lesser for United Artists
Script	Harry Chandler, Frank Craven, and Thornton Wilder from his play
Cinematography	Bert Glennon
Principal Actors	William Holden (George), Martha Scott (Emily), Fay Bainter (Mrs. Gibbs), Beulah Bondi (Mrs. Webb), Thomas Mitchell (Dr. Gibbs)

THESE THREE (1936)

Director	William Wyler
Producer	Samuel Goldwyn for Samuel Goldwyn Productions
Script	Lillian Hellman from her play *The Children's Hour*
Cinematography	Gregg Toland
Principal Actors	Joel McCrea (Joe), Merle Oberon (Karen), Miriam Hopkins (Martha), Alma Kruger (Mrs. Tilford), Catherine Doucet (Lily), Bonita Granville (Mary), Marcia Mae Jones (Rosalie)

WHO'S AFRAID OF VIRGINIA WOOLF? (1966)

Director	Mike Nichols
Producer	Ernest Lehman for Warner Brothers
Script	Ernest Lehman from the play by Edward Albee
Cinematography	Haskell Wexler
Principal Actors	Richard Burton (George), Elizabeth Taylor (Martha), Sandy Dennis (Honey), George Segal (Nick)

WIT (2001)

Director	Mike Nichols
Producer	Simon Bosanquet for Home Box Office
Script	Emma Thompson and Mike Nichols from the play by Margaret Edson
Cinematography	Seamus McGarvey
Principal Actors	Emma Thompson (Vivian), Christopher Lloyd (Dr. Kelekian), Jonathan M. Woodward (Dr. Posner), Eileen Atkins (Evelyn Ashford)

Index